WORLD BOOK
ELECTION 2000

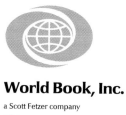

World Book, Inc.
a Scott Fetzer company
Chicago

Staff

**Executive Vice President
and Publisher**
Michael Ross

Editorial

Editor in Chief
Dale W. Jacobs

Managing Editors
Sara Dreyfuss
Warren Silver

Assistant Managing Editors
Timothy Falk
Michael B. Schuldt

Subject Editors
Brad Finger
Nicholas Kilzer
Barbara Lanctot
Jay Myers
Mike Noren
Jay Powers
Thomas J. Wrobel
Daniel O. Zeff

Associate Production Editor
Megan Caras

Production Editors
Jeff De La Rosa
Dawn Krajcik
Daniel J. Marotta
Katie McClure
Scott Richardson

Contributing Editor
David Dreier

Head, Indexing Services
David Pofelski

Staff Indexer
Tina Trettin

Head, Statistical Services
Kenneth J. Shenkman

Head, Cartographic Services
H. George Stoll

**Manager, Cartographic
Database**
Wayne K. Pichler

Staff Cartographer
Don Minnick

Staff Services Coordinator
Rose M. Barberio

Support Staff
Teresa Dunne
Carmen Jusino

Intern
Alana Papernik

Art

Executive Director
Roberta Dimmer

Art Director
Wilma Stevens

Senior Designers
Don Di Sante
Isaiah W. Sheppard, Jr.

Photography Manager
Sandra M. Dyrlund

Photographs Editor
Sylvia Ohlrich

Production Assistant
John Whitney

Research

**Director of Research and
Product Development**
Paul Kobasa

Researchers
Loranne K. Shields, *Coordinator*
Madolynn Cronk
Lynn Durbin
Cheryl Graham
Karen McCormack
Andrew W. Roberts
Thomas Ryan Sullivan

Head, Library Services
Jon M. Fjortoft

Permissions
Janet T. Peterson

Production

Manufacturing/Pre-Press
Carma Fazio, *Senior Manager*
Audrey Casey
Debra Gill
Janice Rossing

Proofreaders
Anne Dillon
Chad Rubel

World Book, Inc.
233 North Michigan
Chicago, IL 60601

Printed in the United States
of America

1 2 3 4 5 6 7 8 9 0 1

Library of Congress Cataloging-in-Publication Data

World Book election 2000.--Special ed.
    p. cm.
    Includes index.
    ISBN 0-7166-1292-5
    1. Presidents--United States--Election--2000. I. World Book, Inc.

JK526 2000b
324.973'0929--dc21   00-054543

About this book

In 2000, Republican George W. Bush was elected president of the United States in one of the closest and most disputed races in U.S. history. For weeks after Election Day, the contest between Bush and his Democratic opponent, Vice President Al Gore, was too close to name a winner. Florida became the chief political battleground because its voting results were disputed. Eventually, the Supreme Court of the United States, in effect, settled the contest in favor of Bush. Gore won the *popular vote* (most total votes in the election). However, Bush won the required majority of votes in the Electoral College, the group of representatives chosen by the voters of each state to elect the president and vice president.

The popular vote victory by Gore and the numerous court challenges over disputed vote counts raised a number of questions about the American democratic system: Are the country's election procedures fair? Is the Electoral College still necessary? How did the election of 2000 compare with other historic U.S. presidential elections? *World Book Election 2000* explores these questions, examines the complex events surrounding the election, and records the results.

The book opens with a review of the election's main events and follows with an in-depth examination of the Electoral College adapted from *The 2001 World Book Year Book*. Much of *World Book Election 2000* is based on a framework of 63 articles adapted from *The World Book Encyclopedia*. These articles represent the heart of *World Book*'s authoritative coverage of United States government, elections, and political history. Sprinkled throughout the book are nuggets of information in distinctive boxes labeled *It's a fact*. These features provide intriguing insights into American government and history, and add to the fun of browsing through the volume. In addition, five distinguished scholars who serve as *World Book* contributors or consultants give their unique views on the election. The book closes with a review of notable elections held outside the United States in 2000.

World Book Election 2000 includes several features that help students develop their thinking and research skills. For example, new maps, graphs, and tables offer different ways of learning about the election. Primary sources include excerpts from the opinion of the Supreme Court, the concession speech of Al Gore, and the victory speech of George W. Bush. Topics for study suggest ideas for school assignments that require students to develop, analyze, and evaluate information. Seventy-five Web sites provide additional direction for research.

The election of 2000 produced a national civics lesson, testing the nation's political, electoral, and legal systems in new and unpredictable ways. *World Book Election 2000* traces the events of this amazing election and offers a treasury of articles and skill-building features. The result is a comprehensive, authoritative, and richly detailed reference work that is up to date and easy to read. As such, *World Book Election 2000* is equally suited for the general reader or student, and for home or school.

The editors

Table of contents

Introduction

The 2000 Election: What Happened?

The 2000 presidential election in the United States had it all—a close vote, an uncertain outcome, voting machine recounts, hand recounts, and dramatic legal battles. Finally, a ruling by a divided Supreme Court of the United States decided the winner.

This introduction reviews the main events in the extraordinary election of 2000. It includes a new article on *Bush v. Gore,* the case decided by the Supreme Court. In addition, it presents excerpts from the court's decisive ruling and from the four justices who disagreed with the 5-4 majority opinion.

AP/Wide World

George W. Bush, winner of the presidential election of 2000, addresses the nation from the chambers of the Texas House of Representatives on December 13. Seated are Bush's wife, Laura *(left),* and Nelda Laney, wife of Texas Speaker of the House Pete Laney.

The 2000 Election: What Happened?

The election of 2000 was one of the closest and most unusual presidential elections in United States history. The outcome—that Republican candidate George W. Bush defeated his Democratic opponent Al Gore—remained in doubt for five weeks after the election. The winner received more electoral votes but fewer popular votes than his opponent. A decision by the Supreme Court of the United States led to the final resolution of the contest.

Election Day

The presidential candidates. George W. Bush, the son of former President George H. W. Bush, was serving his second term as governor of Texas when he won the Republican nomination for the presidency in 2000. Al Gore was in his second term as U.S. vice president under President Bill Clinton when he became the Democratic nominee.

In addition to these representatives of the country's major political parties, several third-party candidates ran in the 2000 election. Ralph Nader, a consumer advocate, represented the Green Party. Former presidential adviser Pat Buchanan was a Reform Party candidate. Physicist John Hagelin represented a faction of the Reform Party as well as the Natural Law Party. In the election, Nader received about 3 percent of the vote, and Buchanan and Hagelin each got less than 1 percent.

Barbara Lanctot, the contributor of this article, is Senior Area Studies Editor, The World Book Encyclopedia.

The vote. The country's official Election Day, the first Tuesday in November, fell on November 7 in 2000. On that day, more than 100 million U.S. citizens went to the polls to vote.

The race between Bush and Gore was close. Gore led in the popular vote, but the popular vote does not directly decide the winner of the election. Instead, it determines the delegates who will represent each state in the Electoral College and officially elect the president. Whoever wins the most votes in a particular state usually receives all the state's electoral votes.

By the time reports were in from most states, Gore had a narrow lead over Bush in electoral votes. In Florida, however, where the results had not yet been finalized, the race was particularly close. It became obvious that the election depended upon who received Florida's 25 electoral votes.

Confusion in Florida. Early in the evening of November 7, television newscasters predicted that Gore would win Florida. Their statement was based not on official counts but on what voters said in *exit polls,* surveys taken as voters left their polling place.

As the evening wore on, official tallies from the state showed an increasing number of votes for Bush. As a result, the television networks retracted their original prediction and declared Bush the winner in Florida.

Gore called Bush to concede the election. Shortly after the call, however, Bush's lead in Florida began to shrink. The networks announced that the vote in Florida was too close to predict, and Gore called Bush to retract his concession.

Recounts

Machine recount. On the morning of November 8, many people were startled to learn that the presidential election remained in doubt. At that point, Gore led Bush by at least 200,000 popular votes, but the winner of the electoral votes was unknown.

The count in Florida showed Bush ahead of Gore by nearly 1,800 votes out of about 6 million cast. A Florida state law requires that the votes be recounted if the margin is less than one-half of 1 percent. The law specifies that the final results must be reported by one week from Election Day. Thus, the deadline was November 14. Most of that recount was done by machine.

Manual recounts. Before the required recount was completed, Gore requested a recount by hand as well in four Florida counties, where results were in dispute.

In Palm Beach County, for example, voters said the layout of their punch-card ballots was so confusing they may have mistakenly voted for Pat Buchanan instead of Gore. The two names appeared across from each other on facing pages of the ballot with punch holes in the middle. Palm Beach County is predominantly Democratic, but tallies showed Reform Party candidate Buchanan had received about 3,400 votes there, more than three times what he received in any other county. Also, Palm Beach voting officials reported they had thrown out thousands of ballots that were marked for more than one presidential candidate or for none at all.

Palm Beach officials argued that the candidates had a chance to review the ballot design. They said that they had explained the ballot to the public before the election. They pointed out that confused voters could have asked for help at the polls. When a number of Palm Beach residents later brought the matter to court, a state judge ruled that the *canvassing board* (panel of election officials) had complied sufficiently with state law in designing the ballot.

The Palm Beach County canvassing board agreed to conduct a hand recount. Volusia County also began a hand recount. Miami-Dade County and Broward County decided initially to do only a partial recount. The deadline for the ballot counters was Tuesday, November 14.

Resolving the crisis

During the next four weeks, the election drama played out in a number of courtrooms. The focus was on the recounts—whether the manual recounts would continue and, if they did, whether the totals would be officially accepted as part of the final tally of Florida's votes.

Court challenges. Gore sought support in the courts for the manual recounts. He argued that a recount by hand was the only way to make sure every person's vote was included in the final tally. He pointed out that machines did not count partially punched ballots. On such ballots, the *chad, a* small piece of paper that covered the punch hole, was not completely removed.

Bush fought through the courts to halt the recounts. He insisted that the process was less fair and less precise than a machine count because of the human judgment involved.

Some early court rulings allowed the recounts to continue. On November 13, for example, a federal judge in

Miami rejected Bush's request to stop the recounts. Also, on November 15, the Florida Supreme Court denied motions brought by Florida Secretary of State Katherine Harris, the official responsible for certifying the state's vote. Harris opposed an extension of the November 14 deadline for the recounts. Gore argued that the deadline gave too little time for workers to complete the manual recounts. The court set a new deadline of November 26.

Miami-Dade County voting officials halted their recount, saying that even with the extended deadline, there would not be time to manually recount all the votes. Broward and Volusia counties met the deadline. Palm Beach County continued its recount but did not finish in time. Secretary of State Harris refused to accept the tally because it was submitted about two hours after the deadline. On November 26, she certified a Florida win for Bush with a margin of 537 votes. Gore contested the certified vote. The legal battle continued.

Bush v. Gore. When Gore's contest of the vote came before the Florida Supreme Court, the court ordered a manual recount of all ballots in the state where no vote for president had been registered by machine. Bush appealed the ruling to the Supreme Court of the United States, the nation's highest court.

On December 9, the U.S. Supreme Court justices voted 5 to 4 to halt the recounts until they heard further arguments. On December 11, lawyers for the presidential candidates argued the case of *Bush v. Gore.* The Supreme Court announced its decision the next day. The justices, again voting 5 to 4, ruled that the Florida recounts should not continue.

The justices halted the recounts, they said, because the various vote-counting standards being used from county to county violated the Constitution's guarantee that all citizens are entitled to "equal protection of the laws." The justices also ruled that there was not enough time to develop a consistent statewide standard and perform a manual recount.

Conclusion

In a televised address to the nation on December 13, Gore conceded the election to Bush. Gore began by saying that he had called Bush to offer his congratulations and promised that he would not call Bush back this time to withdraw them.

In his speech, Gore said, "Let there be no doubt: While I strongly disagree with the court's decision, I accept it....And tonight, for the sake of our unity as a people and the strength of our democracy, I offer my concession." He urged all Americans to put country before political party and stand behind the new president.

In a speech that followed Gore's, Bush expressed his wish to unite the country. He said, "The president of the United States is president of every single American, of every race and every background. Whether you voted for me or not, I will do my best to serve your interests and I will work to earn your respect."

Thus, the winner was finally known 36 days after the election. Official figures for the popular vote showed that Gore defeated Bush by 539,947 votes. However, Bush defeated Gore 271 to 266 in electoral votes. On Jan. 20, 2001, George Walker Bush was inaugurated as the 43rd president of the United States.

Bush v. Gore was a landmark ruling by the Supreme Court of the United States that played a major role in the 2000 presidential election. In its decision, the court ruled that a state could not order a vote recount without applying a consistent statewide standard.

The race between Texas Governor George W. Bush and Vice President Al Gore was one of the tightest presidential elections in U.S. history. The outcome depended on which candidate won the state of Florida, where the vote was extremely close. With Bush ahead by fewer than 1,000 votes, the Supreme Court of Florida ordered a manual recount that would include any ballot where there was "clear indication of the intent of the voter." Bush appealed the decision to the U.S. Supreme Court.

In its majority opinion, the U.S. Supreme Court stated that the Florida court failed to establish a specific, uniform standard by which to determine the voter's intent. As a result, the existing vote-counting guidelines failed to meet "minimal constitutional standards" involving equal protection and due process of law. In addition, because there was not enough time to develop and apply a uniform standard before the Electoral College deadline, the court ruled that no further recounts could take place. Gore then conceded the election to Bush.

The court passed *Bush v. Gore* by a 5-4 vote. The majority consisted of Chief Justice William H. Rehnquist and Justices Anthony M. Kennedy, Sandra Day O'Connor, Antonin Scalia, and Clarence Thomas.

Excerpts from the Supreme Court ruling in *Bush v. Gore* on Dec. 12, 2000

No. 00–949
GEORGE W. BUSH, ET AL., PETITIONERS *v.*
ALBERT GORE, JR., ET AL.
ON WRIT OF CERTIORARI TO THE FLORIDA SUPREME COURT
PER CURIAM.

The petition presents the following questions: whether the Florida Supreme Court established new standards for resolving Presidential election contests, thereby violating Article II, Section 1, clause 2, of the United States Constitution and failing to comply with 3 U.S. Code, Section 5, and whether the use of standardless manual recounts violates the Equal Protection and Due Process Clauses. With respect to the equal protection question, we find a violation of the Equal Protection Clause. …

This case has shown that punch card balloting machines can produce an unfortunate number of ballots which are not punched in a clean, complete way by the voter.

…The question before us … is whether the recount procedures the Florida Supreme Court has adopted are consistent with its obligation to avoid arbitrary and disparate treatment of the members of its electorate.

Much of the controversy seems to revolve around ballot cards designed to be perforated by a stylus but which, either through error or deliberate omission, have not been perforated with sufficient precision for a machine to count them. In some cases a piece of the card—a chad—is hanging, say by two corners. In other cases there is no separation at all, just an indentation.

The Florida Supreme Court has ordered that the intent of the voter be discerned from such ballots. …This is unobjectionable as an abstract proposition and a starting principle.

The problem inheres in the absence of specific standards to ensure its equal application. …

…we are presented with a situation where a state court with the power to assure uniformity has ordered a statewide recount with minimal procedural safeguards. When a court orders a statewide remedy, there must be at least some assurance that the rudimentary requirements of equal treatment and fundamental fairness are satisfied. …

Upon due consideration of the difficulties identified to this point, it is obvious that the recount cannot be conducted in compliance with the requirements of equal protection and due process without substantial additional work. …

That statute *[3 U.S. Code, Section 5]*, in turn, requires that any controversy or contest that is designed to lead to a conclusive selection of electors be completed by December 12. That date is upon us, and there is no recount procedure in place under the State Supreme Court's order that comports with minimal constitutional standards. Because it is evident that any recount seeking to meet the December 12 date will be unconstitutional for the reasons we have discussed, we reverse the judgment of the Supreme Court of Florida ordering a recount to proceed.

None are more conscious of the vital limits on judicial authority than are the members of this Court, and none stand more in admiration of the Constitution's design to leave the selection of the President to the people, through their legislatures, and to the political sphere. When contending parties invoke the process of the courts, however, it becomes our unsought responsibility to resolve the federal and constitutional issues the judicial system has been forced to confront.

The judgment of the Supreme Court of Florida is reversed, and the case is remanded for further proceedings not inconsistent with this opinion. It is so ordered.

Excerpts from the dissenting opinions in *Bush v. Gore* on Dec. 12, 2000

Justice John Paul Stevens: In the interest of finality, … the majority effectively orders the disenfranchisement of an unknown number of voters whose ballots reveal their intent—and are therefore legal votes under state law—but were for some reason rejected by ballot-counting machines.…

…Although we may never know with complete certainty the identity of the winner of this year's Presidential election, the identity of the loser is perfectly clear. It is the Nation's confidence in the judge as an impartial guardian of the rule of law.

Justice David H. Souter: In deciding what to do about this, we should take account of the fact that electoral votes are due to be cast in six days. I would therefore remand the case to the courts of Florida with instructions to establish uniform standards for evaluating the several types of ballots that have prompted differing treatments, to be applied within and among counties when passing on such identical ballots in any further recounting (or successive recounting) that the courts

might order.

Justice Ruth Bader Ginsburg: There is no cause here to believe that the members of Florida's high court have done less than "their mortal best to discharge their oath of office," … and no cause to upset their reasoned interpretation of Florida law.…

…the Court's conclusion that a constitutionally adequate recount is impractical is a prophecy the Court's own judgment will not allow to be tested. Such an untested prophecy should not decide the Presidency of the United States.

Justice Stephen G. Breyer: The Court was wrong to take this case. It was wrong to grant a stay. It should now vacate that stay and permit the Florida Supreme Court to decide whether the recount should resume.…

By halting the manual recount, and thus ensuring that the uncounted legal votes will not be counted under any standard, this Court crafts a remedy out of proportion to the asserted harm. And that remedy harms the very fairness interests the Court is attempting to protect.

Section One

Special Report:

War for the White House: A Legacy of the U.S. Constitution

The debate over whether the Electoral College is still needed reemerged during the presidential election of 2000. This section features a special report from *The 2001 World Book Year Book* that traces the history of the Electoral College and reviews modern arguments for and against keeping an institution established by the Founding Fathers.

War for the White House:
A Legacy of the U.S. Constitution

"Too close to call." That was the virtually unanimous conclusion of American pollsters and political analysts as the 2000 presidential campaign entered its final hours on the eve of Election Day, November 7. Polls showed the two main contenders—Republican Governor George W. Bush of Texas and Democratic Vice President Al Gore—locked in a statistical dead heat. One thing seemed certain, however: By the morning of November 8, the nation would know who its next president was. No one expected that they were about to witness election history in the making.

The election, in fact, remained too close to call even after all the votes were in. For the first time in almost 125 years, the outcome of a United States presidential election remained unknown in the days and weeks following the balloting. Though Gore defeated Bush by a narrow margin in the nationwide popular vote, he had not amassed enough of the votes that matter most—electoral votes.

In the 2000 election, a presidential candidate needed at least 270 electoral votes to win the presidency. The popular vote in each state determines who gets the state's electoral votes. In the states of Florida, New Mexico, and Oregon, the popular tally was so close that the states' electoral votes remained in limbo well after Election Day.

Of those three states, Florida, with 25 electoral votes, was the key to the election. Both Bush, with 246 electoral votes, and Gore, with 255, needed Florida's 25 votes to reach the magic number of 270. Despite an Election Day turnout in Florida of over 6 million voters, only several hundred votes separated the two candidates, with Bush in the lead. Weeks of ballot recounts, angry disputes, and legal challenges, including appeals to the Florida Supreme Court and the Supreme Court of the United States, followed as the two camps strove to win that vital state. In the end, Bush prevailed, and on December 13 Gore conceded the election.

The battle for Florida's electoral votes highlighted the central role of a little-understood institution, the Electoral College, in U.S. presidential elections. Gore's situation brought home to Americans a peculiarity of the Electoral College system that most had learned in high-school civics class but had not given much thought to since: It is possible for a presidential candidate to win the popular vote but lose the election. That fact struck many people as unfair, and in the aftermath of the 2000 election a growing number of Americans felt that the time had come to abolish the Electoral College.

The Founding Fathers debate a difficult question

The Electoral College was a creation of the 1787 Constitutional Convention in Philadelphia, at which representatives of the 13 original states labored to establish a stronger national government for the United States of America. Of the many issues that the representatives grappled with, none proved more troublesome than the question of how to elect the president.

Some delegates favored direct election by popular vote. Delegate James Wilson of Pennsylvania, who put forth the first proposal for direct election, argued that the office of the presidency would be weak unless its power "flowed from the people at large." However, popular election was strongly opposed by many others at the convention. One objection they put forth was that the people of a particular state would not know enough about presidential candidates from other states to make an informed decision. Furthermore, they argued, voters would naturally tend to prefer candidates from their own states, so candidates from the largest, most populous states would always win. Beyond those arguments, there was a general mistrust among many of the delegates of pure democracy, which the nervous gentry of the new nation equated with mob rule.

Another proposal called for letting Congress choose the president. The delegates rejected that system as well, largely because it would make the executive branch of the government subordinate to the legislative branch and would invite intrigue and corruption. Some representatives even suggested that the state legislatures elect the president. However, because the whole purpose of the new Constitution was to strengthen the national government, this idea had few takers.

Finally, exasperated with their inability to settle the matter, the delegates referred the election issue to a special committee. The solution the committee arrived at, which the convention accepted with almost no argument, was the elector system, later known as the Electoral College.

David Dreier, the author of this special report, is a contributing editor of The World Book Year Book.

Under the elector system, each state was allotted a number of electoral votes equal to the combined total of the state's representatives and senators. The votes were to be cast by designated electors. A state was free to choose its slate of electors in any way it preferred. The electors were to meet in their respective state capitals at a specified time and cast two votes for president, one of which had to be for a candidate from outside the state. The votes were then to be sent to the U.S. capital, where they would be counted in the presence of both houses of Congress. The candidate receiving the most votes would be elected president, and the candidate with the second most votes would become vice president.

In the event of a tie, or of any one candidate failing to receive a majority of the electoral votes, the election would be decided by the House of Representatives. The members of the House from each state would vote among themselves for the president. Then each state's representatives, acting as a group, would cast one vote for the candidate who had received the most ballots. The delegates actually saw election by the House as the likely outcome of most elections, because they thought that few presidential candidates would have enough support to win a majority of electoral votes.

The rise of political parties brings changes

The elector system was awkward, but it worked for a while. In the first two presidential elections, in 1789 and 1792, George Washington won votes from all the electors. John Adams received a smaller majority of electoral votes in these elections and became vice president. However, a weakness in the system became clear in the election of 1796, when Adams and Thomas Jefferson were elected president and vice president, respectively, even though they belonged to opposing political parties. Adams, a Federalist, favored a strong central government. Jefferson, a Democratic-Republican, was wary of governmental power, placing his faith in the people.

The elector system broke down completely in 1800. By that time, political parties had become more important in elections than the candidates' home states. In the election of 1800, Jefferson was the presidential choice of the Democratic-Republican Party, and Aaron Burr was the party's choice for vice president. They ran against Adams and Charles C. Pinckney, the Federalist candidates for president and vice president.

Although Jefferson was confident of a Democratic-Republican victory, he worried that the party's electors would inadvertently cast equal numbers of votes for him and Burr, which would throw the election into the House. Jefferson got assurances that two or three Democratic-Republican electors planned to cast their second votes for candidates other than Burr to ensure that Jefferson would be elected president. But that did not happen, perhaps because of secret maneuvering by Burr and his allies. When the electoral votes were counted, Jefferson and Burr had ended Adams's hope for a second term, but they were tied with 73 votes each. Burr refused to defer to Jefferson, so the election moved to the House, where it took 36 ballots before Jefferson was finally elected president.

To prevent that kind of deadlock from ever recurring, Congress in 1803 passed the 12th Amendment, changing the Electoral College procedures. The amendment, ratified by the states in 1804, stipulated that electors would cast a vote for president and a separate vote for vice president.

By that time, the states themselves had begun to alter the way they determined their electoral votes. One major change involved procedures for choosing electors. Originally, most states left the selection of electors up to their legislatures, but after 1800 an increasing number of states chose electors through popular elections. By the mid-1830's, that system was being used in all but one state, South Carolina, which finally adopted it in the 1860's.

But even with the popular selection of electors, there was a big problem in the first decades of the 1800's, because groups within a political party might support different candidates for president. In 1824, the presidential election again wound up in the House when four Democratic-Republican candidates—John Quincy Adams, Henry Clay, William H. Crawford, and Andrew Jackson—split the electoral vote, with none receiving a majority. Jackson, who received the most electoral votes and the most popular votes, considered himself the rightful president. But in the political maneuvering that followed, Clay threw his support to Adams, who was then chosen president by the House.

Elections became more orderly later in the 1800's when parties began to run a single presidential ticket in all the states. In each state, the party put forth a slate of electors pledged to cast ballots for that party's candidates in the Electoral College vote. With this change, the individual electors became less important, and eventually their names disappeared from most ballots, giving voters the mistaken impression that they were voting directly for the candidates.

Another important change was a move to the "winner-take-all" method of allocating electoral votes. In that system, which is used today by every state except Maine and Nebraska, all of a state's electoral votes go to the presidential and vice presidential candidates who capture the most popular votes within that state.

Electoral controversies of the past

The 2000 election was hardly the first one in which the Electoral College system caused problems. In the 1800's, four elections either wound up being decided by Congress or resulted in the election of a president who had not received the most popular votes.

Rutherford B. Hayes

John Quincy Adams

Thomas Jefferson

Other troubled elections

Despite the changes made to Electoral College procedures over the years, it remained a problematic way of choosing a president. The system's flaws were on display once again in the presidential election of 1876, one of the most chaotic elections in United States history. The Democratic presidential candidate, Samuel J. Tilden, defeated Republican Rutherford B. Hayes by about 250,000 popular votes out of some 8.3 million cast. But Tilden's apparent victory was thrown into doubt when Oregon and three deeply divided Southern states—Florida, Louisiana, and South Carolina—submitted two sets of electoral votes, one from the Democrats and one from the Republicans. Twenty electoral votes from those states were disputed in Congress, and until those votes could be sorted out, both candidates were short of an electoral majority. Tilden, with 184 votes, was just one vote short of the 185 electoral votes required for election. Hayes, with 165 votes, needed all 20 votes to win.

In January 1877, Congress appointed a special 15-member commission to settle the issue. The commission, however, was dominated by Republicans, so it ruled in favor of Hayes on every disputed electoral vote. As the commission deliberated, members of the two parties argued bitterly, and some hot-heads threatened to seize the government by force.

Hayes was finally awarded all 20 of the contested votes, but even then the crisis was not over. The commission's report had to be accepted by both houses of Congress, and the House of Representatives had a Democratic majority. A group of Southern Democrats in Congress then made a private deal with the Republicans. They agreed not to oppose the decision of the commission in return for a Republican vow to end *Reconstruction* (Northern control of the South after the Civil War [1861-1865]). On March 2, 1877—just 56 hours before Inauguration Day—the Southern Democrats voted with the Republicans to accept the commission's report. Hayes was declared the winner of the election, but he was so tainted by the whole process that he was openly derided as His Fraudulency.

Another controversial election occurred just 12 years later, in 1888. In that contest, incumbent President Grover Cleveland, a Democrat, defeated Republican Benjamin Harrison in the popular ballot by more than 90,000 votes out of about 11 million cast and won the electoral votes of 19 states. Harrison also won 19 states, but those states had enough electoral votes to give Harrison an Electoral College majority of 233 votes to 168. Thus, even though Cleveland won the popular vote, he lost the election.

In 1800, it took 36 ballots in the House of Representatives to elect Thomas Jefferson. The election of 1824 was also decided by the House, which chose John Quincy Adams, even though Andrew Jackson had received more popular votes. After a disputed election in 1876, a congressional commission awarded 20 contested electoral votes to Rutherford B. Hayes, giving him the presidency. Despite losing the popular vote in the 1888 election, Benjamin Harrison was the victor, winning a majority in the Electoral College.

Library of Congress

Benjamin Harrison

A flawed system, but perhaps a needed one

Clearly, the Electoral College system has its faults. Besides its potential for denying the presidency to the winner of the popular vote, it skews presidential campaigns. Because of the winner-take-all arrangement in all but two states, candidates conduct intensive campaigns in so-called battleground states in which either ticket has a reasonably good chance of winning the popular vote. Conversely, candidates mostly ignore states in which preference polls have revealed that voters favor one ticket over the other by a large margin. It makes no sense for candidates to campaign in a state where they have no chance of winning enough popular votes to claim the state's electoral votes. The popular ballots in a state do not count for anything outside the state. That fact also makes it pointless for the likely winner in a state to seek to increase the margin of victory in the state's popular vote.

The biggest problem with the Electoral College system, however, is that it can result in political train wrecks such as the ones that occurred in 1876 and 2000. After the 2000 election, there were renewed calls for the Electoral College to be abolished in favor of direct popular election of the president. But would that really be a good idea? Political experts have differing opinions.

Arguments against and for the Electoral College

Against

★ In a tight presidential race, a close popular vote in one or more key states can lead to a fierce post-election battle—recounts and legal challenges—resulting in a possible constitutional crisis if no clear winner emerges.

★ A candidate who receives a majority of the nationwide popular vote can lose the election.

★ Candidates campaign heavily in states where either candidate stands a good chance of winning the popular vote and mostly ignore other states.

★ Voter turnout may be depressed in states where preference polls have indicated that one candidate is strongly ahead of the other.

★ The growth of third parties is discouraged because it is very difficult for their candidates to earn electoral votes.

★ The system is unfair, because an electoral vote in smaller or less populous states represents fewer people than an electoral vote in a large, heavily populated state.

★ An election that results in a close electoral victory could be overturned by "faithless electors" who do not vote for their party's candidate.

For

★ The system strengthens national unity by forcing candidates to campaign in smaller and less populous states rather than just seeking masses of popular votes in large urban centers.

★ Third parties are encouraged to moderate their views and join with one of the two major parties, which contributes to the political stability of the nation.

★ Candidates must address the interests of minority groups because minority ballots may be needed to win a state's popular vote and thus its electoral votes.

★ The system preserves the federal power-sharing arrangement established by the Founding Fathers between the states and the federal government.

Those in favor of abolishing the Electoral College argue that, in addition to affecting presidential campaigns and sometimes denying the presidency to the winner of the popular vote, the system depresses voter turnout. They claim that if a candidate is an almost sure winner in a state, many voters there will feel that there is little point in going to the polls, since their votes will mean nothing beyond the state.

Opponents of the Electoral College system also point out that it tends to overrepresent the interests of small states. That occurs because of the way electoral votes are apportioned, with every state getting an electoral vote for each of its representatives in the House as well as a vote for each of its two senators. A senator in a small or sparsely populated state represents far fewer people than a senator in a populous state. Thus, an electoral vote in New York represents 550,000 people, while an electoral vote in South Dakota represents 232,000.

Another argument against the Electoral College is that it discourages third parties. Because of the winner-take-all system, a third-party presidential ticket can attract a reasonably large number of popular votes throughout the nation but collect not a single electoral vote.

There is also the issue of so-called faithless electors, electors who vote for candidates other than the ones they are pledged to. A few electors have jumped ship over the years, but they have never influenced the outcome of an election. Nonetheless, electors who cast surprise votes could conceivably be a factor in a very close election.

Supporters of the Electoral College system see most of its supposed weaknesses as strengths. They argue that while it is unfortunate for the winner of the popular vote to lose an election, the system protects the interests of smaller states by making it necessary for candidates to campaign nationwide. A candidate in a close race cannot afford to ignore small or less populous states that could go either way. If the presidency were determined by the popular vote alone, candidates would tend to concentrate their efforts in a handful of metropolitan areas with huge populations. In addition, candidates must pay attention to the interests of minority groups, because the ballots of minorities can make the difference between winning or losing a key state. Therefore, the Electoral College's proponents contend, the system strengthens the cohesiveness and stability of the nation.

Furthermore, supporters contend that our present method of electing presidents, by making it difficult for third parties to succeed, persuades splinter groups to moderate their stands and join with one of the two major parties. In this view, a two-party system, whatever its faults, is better than a proliferation of parties representing ever-smaller segments of the population.

Finally, advocates of the Electoral College argue, the system preserves the federal power-sharing arrangement established by the Founding Fathers between the states and the central government. They caution that we should be wary of tampering with that delicate balance.

Supporters of the Electoral College add that the problem of faithless electors could be overcome by eliminating actual electors. Each state's electoral votes would then be just a numerical total that is automatically assigned to the winner of the state's popular vote. But this change, as with eliminating the Electoral College altogether, would require a constitutional amendment.

The Electoral College issue is undeniably a thorny one. As the election of 2000 played itself out, many people thought that the obvious solution for preventing similar electoral crises in the future was to simply junk this aging institution and rely on the will of the people. Some political experts agreed, but others cautioned against a rush to judgment. The Founding Fathers, they pointed out, did not think that a system for electing the president was a simple matter in 1787, and it may not be so simple today either.

For further information:

Books

Best, Judith A. *The Choice of the People?: Debating the Electoral College.* Rowman & Littlefield, 1996.

Longley, Lawrence D. *The Electoral College Primer.* Yale University Press, 1996.

Web sites

U.S. Electoral College
www.nara.gov/fedreg/elctcoll
The official home page of the Electoral College.

Federal Election Commission
www.fec.gov
Extensive information about U.S. elections and the Electoral College.

Section Two

Understanding United States Government

The presidential election of 2000 focused worldwide attention on the values and procedures of American democracy. This section features 16 *World Book* articles that cover the major institutions of the United States government, the ways the different branches work together, and political leaders of Congress. In this section's articles, you will learn:

❏ *in what ways the power of the Congress of the United States is limited.*

❏ *what compromises were made in forming the Constitution of the United States.*

❏ *how each branch of the U.S. government exercises its powers of checks and balances.*

❏ *what are some of the current issues in U.S. government.*

Congress, the lawmaking branch of the United States government, consists of the Senate and the House of Representatives. During a joint session, *shown here,* all members meet in the House chamber.

Congress of the United States

Congress of the United States makes the nation's laws. Congress consists of two bodies, the *Senate* and the *House of Representatives.* Both bodies have about equal power. The people elect the members of Congress.

Although Congress's most important task is making laws, it also has other major duties. For example, the Senate approves or rejects the U.S. president's choices for the heads of government departments, Supreme Court justices, and certain other high-ranking jobs. The Senate also approves or rejects treaties that the president makes.

Each member of Congress represents many citizens. Therefore, members must know the views of the voters and be guided by those views when considering proposed laws. Being a member of Congress also means answering citizens' letters, appearing at local events, and having local offices to handle people's problems with the government.

This article provides a broad description of Congress. For more information, see the separate articles **House of Representatives; Senate** in this volume.

How Congress is organized

Congress is a *bicameral* (two-chamber) legislature. The 100-member Senate consists of 2 senators from each of the 50 states. The House of Representatives, usually called simply the *House,* has 435 members. House members, or *representatives,* are elected from *congres-*

Roger H. Davidson, the contributor of this article, is Professor of Government and Politics Emeritus at the University of Maryland and coauthor of Congress and Its Members.

sional districts of about equal population into which the states are divided. Every state must have at least one House seat. Representatives are often called *congressmen* or *congresswomen,* though technically the titles also apply to senators.

The Democratic and Republican parties have long been the only major political parties in Congress. In each house of Congress, the party with more members is the *majority party.* The other one is the *minority party.* Before every new session of Congress, Republicans and Democrats in each house meet in what is called a *caucus* or *conference* to choose party leaders and to consider legislative issues and plans.

Committees form an important feature of each chamber's organization. They prepare the bills to be voted on. The committee system divides the work of processing legislation and enables members to specialize in particular types of issues. The majority party in each chamber elects the head of each committee and holds a majority of the seats on most committees.

The Senate. According to Article I, Section 3 of the Constitution, the vice president of the United States serves as head of the Senate with the title *president of the Senate.* However, the vice president is not considered a member of that body and rarely appears there, except on ceremonial occasions or to break a tie vote. The Senate elects a *president pro tempore* (temporary president) to serve in the vice president's absence. The Senate usually elects the majority party senator with the longest continuous service. The president pro tempore signs official papers for the Senate but presides infrequently. Most of the time, the president pro tempore appoints a junior senator as temporary president.

Democrats and Republicans each elect a chief officer

called a *floor leader.* A floor leader is also known as the *majority leader* or the *minority leader,* depending on the senator's party. Each party elects an officer called a *whip* to assist the floor leaders. Floor leaders or whips are typically at their desks at the front of the chamber. They arrange the Senate's schedule, work for passage of their party's legislative program, and look after the interests of absent senators.

All senators treasure their right to be consulted on bills, to offer amendments, and to speak at length in debate. Just one senator can slow down or halt the work of the Senate. Thus, Senate leaders spend much time considering fellow senators' needs and arranging compromises that will enable the work of the chamber to go on.

Sixteen permanent *standing committees* and several temporary *special* or *select committees* help the Senate make laws. Most committees have *subcommittees* to handle particular topics. Typically, a senator sits on about four committees and six subcommittees.

The House of Representatives. The *speaker of the House,* mentioned in Article I, Section 2 of the Constitution, serves as presiding officer and party leader. The majority party nominates the speaker, who is then elected by a party-line vote of the entire House. The speaker is the most important member of Congress because of the office's broad powers. The speaker refers bills to committees, names members of special committees, and nominates the majority party's members of the powerful Rules Committee. The speaker votes in case of ties and grants representatives the right to speak during debates. With the help of assistants, the speaker also influences committee assignments, arranges committee handling of bills, and schedules bills for House debate. As in the Senate, the House majority and minority parties each choose a floor leader and a whip.

The House has 19 standing committees and several special or select committees. Except under certain circumstances, a representative is limited to serving on 2 standing committees and 4 subcommittees.

When Congress meets. A new Congress is organized every two years, after congressional elections in November of even-numbered years. Voters elect all the representatives, resulting in a new House of Representatives. About a third of the senators come up for election every two years. The Senate is a *continuing body* because it is never completely new. Beginning with the First Congress (1789-1791), each Congress has been numbered in order. The lawmakers elected in 2000 made up the 107th Congress.

Congress holds one regular session a year. The session begins on January 3 unless Congress sets a different date. During the year, Congress recesses often so members can visit their home states or districts. Congress adjourns in early fall in election years and in late fall in other years. After Congress adjourns, the president may call a *special session.* The president may adjourn Congress only if the two houses disagree on an adjournment date.

The Senate and the House meet in separate chambers in the Capitol in Washington, D.C. The building stands on Capitol Hill, often called simply *the Hill.* Senators and representatives occasionally meet in a *joint session* in the larger House of Representatives chamber, mainly to hear an address by the president or a foreign official.

The Constitution requires Congress to meet jointly to count the electoral votes after a presidential election. Legislation is never acted on in a joint session.

Congress's power to make laws

Origin of power. The Constitution gives Congress "all legislative powers" of the federal government. At the heart of Congress's lawmaking powers is its "power of the purse"—its control over government taxing and spending. Article I, Section 8 of the Constitution lists a wide range of powers granted to Congress. These *delegated,* or *expressed, powers* include the authority to coin money, regulate trade, declare war, and raise and equip military forces.

Article I, Section 8 also contains an *elastic clause* that gives Congress authority to "make all laws which shall be necessary and proper" to carry out the delegated powers. The elastic clause grants Congress *implied powers* to deal with many matters not specifically mentioned in the Constitution. For example, Congress has the expressed power to coin money. It has the implied power to create a treasury department to print money.

Limitations of power. Congress is limited in the use of its powers. The Constitution prohibits some types of laws outright. For example, Congress may not pass trade laws that favor one state of the United States over another. The Bill of Rights, the first 10 amendments to the Constitution, forbids certain other laws. For instance, the First Amendment bars Congress from establishing a national religion; preventing religious freedom; or limiting freedom of speech, press, assembly, or petition.

The executive and judicial branches of government also limit Congress's powers. The president may veto any bill Congress passes. Congress can *override* (reverse) a veto only by a two-thirds vote in each chamber, which is usually difficult to obtain. The president's power to propose legislation acts as another check on Congress. By its implied power of *judicial review,* the Supreme Court may declare a law passed by Congress to be unconstitutional. The courts also shape laws

Facts in brief about members of Congress

Number: The Senate has 100 members, and the House of Representatives has 435.

Qualifications: Senate: (1) at least 30 years old, (2) a U.S. citizen for at least 9 years, and (3) a resident of the state from which the candidate seeks election. House: (1) at least 25 years old, (2) a U.S. citizen for at least 7 years, and (3) a resident of the state from which the candidate seeks election.

Nomination: Nearly all candidates for Congress are nominated in primary elections. A few are chosen by party conventions.

Election: A senator is elected by the voters from all parts of the state. A representative is elected by the voters of one congressional district of the state. If the state has only one House seat, voters from the whole state elect the state's representative.

Term: Senators are elected to six-year terms, and representatives to two-year terms. There is no legal limit to the amount of time a member of Congress can serve.

Income: The speaker of the House receives $181,400 a year. Majority and minority leaders of the House earn $157,000 a year. All other members of the House receive $141,300. In the Senate, the president pro tempore and the majority and minority leaders earn $157,000 a year. All other senators receive $141,300. All members of Congress receive allowances for office expenses, staff salaries, travel, and similar expenses.

Removal from office: Members of Congress may be expelled by a two-thirds vote of their particular chamber.

through their interpretations of them.

Finally, the power of public opinion limits what Congress can do. Lawmakers know that their actions must, in general, reflect the will of the people.

How Congress makes laws

Congress passes and the president signs about 600 laws during every two-year Congress. During that period, senators and representatives introduce up to 10,000 bills. The legislative process sifts the proposals at every stage in the development of a bill to a law. To be enacted, a bill must survive committee and floor debates in both houses. It often must win the support of *special-interest groups,* or *lobbies.* A lobby represents a particular group, such as farmers or labor unions, and tries to influence legislators to pass laws favorable to that group. A bill must also gain a majority of votes in Congress and the president's signature. If the president vetoes the bill, it needs overwhelming support in Congress to override the veto.

Proposing new laws. Laws can be proposed by anyone, including lawmakers or their staffs, executive officials, or special-interest groups. The president can propose laws in speeches or public appearances. At a national convention, a political party may suggest laws to reflect the party's position on major issues. But to become a law, a bill must be sponsored and formally introduced in Congress by a member. Any number of senators or representatives may co-sponsor a bill.

A bill may be *public* or *private.* A public bill deals with matters of concern to people in general. Such matters include taxation, national defense, and foreign affairs. A private bill applies only to specific individuals, as in an immigration case or a claim against the government. To become a law, either kind of bill must be passed in exactly the same form by both houses of Congress and then signed by the president. Each proposed bill is printed and assigned a number, such as S. 1 in the Senate and H.R. 1 in the House of Representatives. Bills are also often known by popular names or by the names of their sponsors or authors.

Working in committees. After being introduced, a bill goes to a committee that deals with the matters the bill covers. Some bills involve various subjects and may be handled by several committees. For example, a trade bill may include sections on taxes, commerce, and banking. The bill may thus interest congressional tax, commerce, and banking committees.

The chief congressional committees are the 16 Senate and the 19 House standing committees. They handle most major fields of legislation, such as agriculture, banking, foreign policy, and transportation. Most standing committees have subcommittees, which hold hearings and work on bills on specialized matters.

The select and special committees of Congress propose laws on particular subjects or conduct investigations. In 1987, for example, each house appointed a select committee to examine the Iran-contra affair. The affair involved the sale of U.S. weapons to Iran in exchange for hostages, and the use of profits from the weapons sale to help the contra rebel forces in Nicaragua. *Joint committees* have members from both the House and the Senate. Such committees handle mainly research and administrative matters.

A proposed law reaches a critical stage after being referred to a committee. Committees *report* (return) only about 15 percent of all bills they receive to the full Senate or House for consideration. Most bills are *tabled,* or *pigeonholed*—that is, never acted on. A committee's failure to act on a bill almost always spells death for the measure.

If committee leaders decide to proceed with a bill, they usually hold public hearings to receive testimony for and against the proposal. Testimony may be heard from a range of people, such as members of the president's Cabinet, scholars, representatives of special-interest groups, or lawmakers themselves.

Some bills go from committee to the full House or Senate without change. But most bills must be revised in committee *markup* sessions. In a markup session, members debate the sections of a measure and write amendments, thereby "marking up" the bill. When a majority of the committee's members vote for the revised bill, they report it to the full chamber with the recommendation that it be passed.

Legislative bargaining. To gain passage of a congressional bill, its sponsors must bargain for their fellow lawmakers' support. They need to give other legislators good reason to vote for the measure. To win a majority vote, the bill must be attractive to members with widely differing interests. Skillful legislators know how to draft a bill with broad appeal.

In a bargaining technique called *compromise,* legislators agree to take a position between two viewpoints. For example, lawmakers who want a major new government program and those who oppose any program at all might agree on a small trial project to test the idea.

In another form of legislative bargaining, called *pork barrel,* a bill is written so that many lawmakers benefit. For instance, a 1987 highway bill in the House included projects in so many members' districts that few representatives dared vote against it.

Some congressional bargaining involves an exchange

Standing committees of Congress

Senate	House of Representatives
Agriculture, Nutrition, and Forestry	Agriculture
Appropriations	Appropriations
Armed Services	Armed Services
Banking, Housing, and Urban Affairs	Banking and Financial Services
Budget	Budget
Commerce, Science, and Transportation	Commerce
Energy and Natural Resources	Education and the Workforce
Environment and Public Works	Government Reform
Finance	House Administration
Foreign Relations	International Relations
Governmental Affairs	Judiciary
Health, Education, Labor, and Pensions	Resources
Judiciary	Rules
Rules and Administration	Science
Small Business	Small Business
Veterans' Affairs	Standards of Official Conduct
	Transportation and Infrastructure
	Veterans' Affairs
	Ways and Means

The buildings where Congress works include the United States Capitol (1), the House office buildings (2), and the Senate office buildings (3).

Shostal

of support over time. Lawmakers may vote for a fellow member's bill expecting that they will need that person's support later on another measure. This mutual help in passing bills is called *logrolling.*

In other instances, a member who is ill-informed on a bill may follow the lead of a lawmaker who is an expert on the subject. Some other time, the influence may flow the other way. This technique is called *cue giving* and *cue taking.* Lawmakers cannot be experts on every bill. They rely on associates who have worked on the bill.

Passing a bill. After a committee reports a bill, it is placed on a *calendar* (list of business) of whichever house of Congress is considering it. The Senate assigns all public and private bills to one calendar. It has a separate calendar for matters originating in the executive branch, such as treaties and presidential appointments. The House has four regularly used calendars. They involve (1) bills that raise or spend money, (2) all other major public bills, (3) private bills, and (4) noncontroversial bills.

Committees screen out bills that lack broad support. Therefore, most measures that reach the House or Senate floor for debate and voting eventually pass. The Senate usually considers a bill by a simple motion or by *unanimous consent*—that is, without anyone's objection. The objection of one senator can block unanimous consent, and so Senate leaders work to make sure the bill is acceptable to their associates. Senators, however, cherish their tradition of free and sometimes lengthy debate. Senators opposed to a bill may make *filibusters*—long speeches designed to kill the bill or force its sponsors to compromise. To halt a filibuster, the Senate can vote *cloture*—that is, to limit the debate.

The House considers most bills by unanimous consent, like the Senate, or by the *suspension-of-rules procedure.* Both methods speed up legislation on largely noncontroversial bills. Representatives consider controversial bills under rules made by the Rules Committee. The rules control debate on a bill by setting time limits, restricting amendments, and, occasionally, barring objections to sections of the bill. Debate time is divided between the bill's supporters and opponents.

Legislators use various methods to vote on a bill. In a *voice vote,* all in favor say aye together, and those opposed say no. In *division,* the members stand as a group to indicate if they are for or against a bill. In a *roll-call vote,* the lawmakers each vote yes or no after their name

is called. The House usually records and counts votes electronically. Members vote by pushing a button.

Senators and representatives tend to vote according to their party's position on a bill. If legislators know the views of their *constituents* (the people who elected them), they may vote accordingly. The president and powerful lobbies also influence how members vote.

From bill to law. After a bill passes one house of Congress, it goes to the other. The second house approves many bills without change. Some bills go back to the first house for further action. At times, the second house asks for a meeting with the first house to settle differences. Such a *conference committee* brings together committee leaders from both chambers to decide on the final bill. The two chambers then approve the bill, and it is sent to the president.

The president has 10 days—not including Sundays—to sign or veto a bill. The veto is most powerful when used as a threat—lawmakers working on a bill want to know if the president is likely to approve it. If the president fails to sign or return the bill within 10 days and Congress is in session, the bill becomes law. But if Congress adjourns during that time, the bill does not become law. Such action is called a *pocket veto.* See **Veto.**

Other duties of Congress

Passing laws lies at the heart of Congress's duties. But Congress also has nonlegislative tasks that influence national government and shape public policies.

Approving federal appointments. The Constitution requires the president to submit nominations of Cabinet members, federal judges, ambassadors, and certain other officials to the Senate for approval. A majority vote of the senators present confirms a presidential appointment. Senators approve almost all nominations to the executive branch because they believe that the president deserves loyal people in top jobs. The Senate examines judicial appointments more critically. About a fourth of all Supreme Court nominees have failed to win Senate confirmation. Some were rejected by a vote, but more commonly the Senate delayed acting on the nomination, often leading the president to withdraw it.

Approving treaties. According to Article II, Section 2 of the Constitution, the president has the power to make treaties "by and with the advice and consent of the Senate." A treaty requires the approval of two-thirds of the senators voting on it. The Senate has rejected very few treaties since the First Congress met in 1789.

The most famous treaty rejection was the Senate's refusal to approve the Treaty of Versailles, which established peace with Germany at the end of World War I (1914-1918). The treaty included President Woodrow Wilson's proposal for the League of Nations, an international association to maintain peace. Senators proposed reservations to the treaty—particularly the League—but Wilson rejected them, leading to the treaty's downfall.

In recent years, presidents have tried to keep the Senate informed as they arrange treaties. For example, President Ronald Reagan invited senators to follow negotiations for the Intermediate-Range Nuclear Forces (INF) Treaty, which called for the elimination of certain U.S. and Soviet nuclear weapons. Objections from the senators sent U.S. diplomats back to the bargaining table to revise the treaty. Signed in December 1987, the treaty won Senate approval by the following May.

Conducting investigations. Congress has the implied power to investigate executive actions and public and private wrongdoing because such inquiries may lead to new laws. Congressional committees conduct the investigations. Congress has launched investigations to uncover scandals, spotlight certain issues, embarrass the president, or advance the reputations of the lawmakers themselves. Televised congressional investigations have aroused great public interest and highlighted Congress's role in keeping the people informed. In an early televised investigation in 1954, millions of TV viewers watched Senator Joseph R. McCarthy charge the U.S. Army with "coddling Communists."

Proposing constitutional amendments. Congress can propose amendments to the U.S. Constitution by a two-thirds vote in both houses. Congress can also call a constitutional convention to propose amendments if at least two-thirds of the states formally request it. In addition, Congress determines whether the states vote on an amendment by means of state legislatures or special state conventions. Congress also decides how long the states have to consider an amendment. It allows seven years in most cases.

Handling presidential election results. Congress counts and checks the votes cast by the Electoral College, the group of electors that chooses the U.S. president and vice president. Congress then announces the results of the election. In most cases, the public knows the winners from the outcome of the popular election. If no candidate has a majority of Electoral College votes, Congress selects the winners. The House chooses the president, and the Senate elects the vice president.

Impeaching and trying federal officials. An impeachment is a charge of serious misconduct in office. The House of Representatives has the power to draw up charges of impeachment against officials of the national government. If a majority of representatives vote for impeachment, the Senate then sits as a court to hear the charges against the official. Impeachments rarely occur. The House voted to impeach President Andrew Johnson in 1868, but the Senate narrowly acquitted him. President Richard M. Nixon resigned in 1974 before representatives voted on impeachment charges recommended by the House Judiciary Committee. In 1998, Bill Clinton became the second president to be impeached. But the Senate acquitted him the following year.

Reviewing its own members. Congress can review the election and judge the qualifications of its own members. It can also *censure* (officially condemn) or expel members for improper conduct as well as apply a milder form of discipline, such as a fine or reprimand. Congress has censured members for such reasons as the conviction of crimes, *unethical* (morally wrong) conduct, or disgracing Congress.

Members of Congress at work

A typical day. The daily schedule of members of Congress reflects their jobs both as lawmakers and as representatives for their districts and states. Most members work at least 11 hours a day. Mornings involve office work and committee meetings, often with two or three meetings scheduled at the same time. Members choose which meeting to attend. They make brief appearances at other meetings or send aides. During the afternoon, and during many mornings and evenings, the Senate and House are in session. Most legislators, busy with other work, do not stay in their particular chamber for debates. Instead, they follow them on closed-circuit TV. Members must be ready to go to their chamber for a vote or a *quorum call*—that is, a count taken to determine if the minimum number of lawmakers needed to hold a vote is present.

Telephone calls, letters, and visits from constituents take up much of a legislator's time. Many people contact members of Congress to give their views on bills. Other people seek help with jobs, immigration problems, Social Security payments, or appointments to military academies.

Senators and representatives have assistants in their Washington, D.C., offices and in their state or district offices. The size of a senator's staff depends on the population of the senator's state—the larger the population, the larger the staff. The average staff consists of about 40 to 50 people. By law, representatives may employ up to 18 aides. Party and committee leaders in Congress have additional aides. Most members also accept students who work without pay to gain political experience. The students work either in Washington or in local offices on legislation and relations with constituents.

Congressional travel. Members of Congress travel often to their home states or districts to appear at public events, study area problems, and talk with voters or local officials. In fact, about a third of all representatives return to their districts nearly every weekend. Sessions of the Senate and House are scheduled to accommodate the members' need to appear frequently before their constituents, and legislators receive allowances to cover their expenses. If members fail to visit their home states or districts fairly often, they are apt to be criticized for forgetting their constituents.

Fact-finding missions at home or abroad—sometimes called *junkets*—also crowd the schedules of senators and representatives. Critics charge that legislators enjoy foreign travel at public expense. Legislators argue that experience gained by travel abroad helps them understand world developments and legislate wisely.

Social responsibilities. Membership in Congress carries many social obligations. Both at home and in Washington, individuals and groups interview legislators and expect them to attend social events.

Representation in Congress

In the Senate, each state has equal representation—two senators per state. In the House of Representatives, population determines the number of representatives sent from each state. This table shows the number of representatives per state based on the 1990 U.S. Census.

State	Senate	House	State	Senate	House	State	Senate	House
Alabama	2	7	Louisiana	2	7	Ohio	2	19
Alaska	2	1	Maine	2	2	Oklahoma	2	6
Arizona	2	6	Maryland	2	8	Oregon	2	5
Arkansas	2	4	Massachusetts	2	10	Pennsylvania	2	21
California	2	52	Michigan	2	16	Rhode Island	2	2
Colorado	2	6	Minnesota	2	8	South Carolina	2	6
Connecticut	2	6	Mississippi	2	5	South Dakota	2	1
Delaware	2	1	Missouri	2	9	Tennessee	2	9
Florida	2	23	Montana	2	1	Texas	2	30
Georgia	2	11	Nebraska	2	3	Utah	2	3
Hawaii	2	2	Nevada	2	2	Vermont	2	1
Idaho	2	2	New Hampshire	2	2	Virginia	2	11
Illinois	2	20	New Jersey	2	13	Washington	2	9
Indiana	2	10	New Mexico	2	3	West Virginia	2	3
Iowa	2	5	New York	2	31	Wisconsin	2	9
Kansas	2	4	North Carolina	2	12	Wyoming	2	1
Kentucky	2	6	North Dakota	2	1			

History of Congress

The founding of Congress grew out of a tradition of representative assemblies that was brought from England and took root in the American Colonies in the early 1600's. Colonial assemblies had a wide range of powers, including authority to collect taxes, issue money, and provide for defense. In time, the assemblies increasingly voiced the colonists' interests against those of the British-appointed colonial governors.

As tensions worsened between United Kingdom and the American Colonies in the 1760's, the colonial assemblies took up the colonists' cause. The First Continental Congress met in Philadelphia in 1774. It drew lawmakers from every colony but Georgia and could be considered the colonists' first "national" assembly. In 1776, the Second Continental Congress declared the colonies' independence from United Kingdom. It served as a temporary national government until 1781, when the states adopted the Articles of Confederation and set up a national legislature called the Congress of the Confederation. This body functioned without an independent executive or judicial branch and soon showed its weakness.

In 1787, the Constitutional Convention met to strengthen the Articles of Confederation. But the delegates drew up a new plan of government instead—the Constitution of the United States. The power of the legislature remained important, but it was balanced by executive and judicial branches. The Constitution called for two chambers for the new Congress—earlier Congresses had one house—with equal representation in one chamber and representation by population in the other. The establishment of a two-house legislature became known as the *Great Compromise*. It solved a bitter dispute between delegates from small states, who favored equal representation for every state, and those from large states, who wanted representation based on state population.

Growth and conflict. When the new Congress met for the first time in New York City in 1789, the two chambers were small and informal. At the end of the First Congress, the Senate had only 26 members, and the House of Representatives 65. As new states joined the Union, the House grew faster than the Senate and developed strong leaders. Such House speakers as Henry Clay in the early 1800's and Thomas B. Reed in the late 1800's brought power and high honor to their office. They also increased the power of the House of Representatives. The Senate enjoyed a golden age from about the 1830's to the 1860's, when it had such great speechmakers as Clay, Daniel Webster, and John C. Calhoun. Those men and their fellow senators debated the existence of slavery in the United States and other burning issues of the day.

Relations between Congress and the president shifted wildly throughout the 1800's. Most presidents yielded to Congress and initiated few policies. During the early and middle 1800's, however, several strong presidents sought to deal with Congress as an equal. Thomas Jefferson worked with congressional supporters to enact legislation drafted by the executive branch. Andrew Jackson promoted his policies through *patronage*—that is, his authority to make federal job appointments—and through his use of the veto. Abraham Lincoln used emergency authority to force Congress to accept his policies during the American Civil War (1861-1865).

Congress recaptured power after each of the strong presidents. Following the Civil War, the House ruled supreme, and the speaker became almost as important as the president. The speaker became so strong that House members revolted in 1910 to limit the office's power.

Continued struggle for power. During the early to middle 1900's, voters elected several strong-willed individuals who established the president as a leader in the legislative process. These men included Presidents Theodore Roosevelt, Woodrow Wilson, and especially Franklin D. Roosevelt. Each proposed a package of new laws and worked to persuade or pressure Congress to enact that package. Congress began to rely increasingly on its committees to process legislation.

Relations between Congress and the presidency changed markedly in the late 1960's and early 1970's. Such events as the Vietnam War (1957-1975) and the Watergate scandal led Congress to limit the president's authority. The Vietnam War had never been officially declared by Congress. But Presidents Lyndon B. Johnson and Nixon, as commanders in chief of the nation's armed forces, had sent hundreds of thousands of U.S. troops into the conflict. Public opposition to the war spurred Congress to pass the War Powers Resolution in 1973 over Nixon's veto. The resolution restricts the president's authority to keep U.S. troops in a hostile area without Congress's consent. The law reasserted Congress's role in foreign affairs but has had mixed success in curbing the president's warmaking authority.

In 1973, a Senate select committee began hearings on the Watergate scandal, which involved illegal campaign activities during the 1972 presidential race. The investigation led the House to begin impeachment proceedings against President Nixon. In July 1974, the House Judiciary Committee voted to recommend three articles of impeachment against Nixon—for obstructing justice, abusing presidential powers, and illegally withholding evidence. Nixon resigned in August 1974, before the full House voted on the three charges. Congress further declared its authority in 1974, when it passed an act that restricts the president's freedom to *impound* (refuse to spend) funds for projects approved by Congress.

In 1996, Congress took the unusual step of trying to increase presidential power. It did so by passing a law to enable the president to veto some items in spending bills. The new power, known as the *line-item veto,* went into effect in 1997. Many members of Congress voted for the bill because they thought presidents might use it to block unneeded spending that Congress, under pressure from local groups, often included in federal legislation. In 1998, however, the Supreme Court ruled the line-item veto unconstitutional.

Later that year, the Republican-controlled House impeached President Bill Clinton, a Democrat. The House charged him with perjury and obstruction of justice. The charges stemmed from Clinton's efforts to deal with a federal investigation of an extramarital affair he had while in office. The Senate, also controlled by Republicans, acquitted Clinton of both charges in 1999. See **Clinton, Bill.**

Congressional ethics has been a main area of concern in recent years. In 1989, for example, House Speaker James C. Wright, Jr., resigned his seat after being accused of accepting improper gifts and of earning more income from outside sources than House rules permitted. In 1994, Representative Dan Rostenkowski was indicted on corruption charges and was forced to resign as chairman of the House Ways and Means Committee. In 1996, he pleaded guilty to some of the charges and was sentenced to 17 months in prison.

In 1997, Newt Gingrich became the first House speaker ever to be reprimanded by the House of Representatives. The House reprimanded Gingrich, and fined him $300,000, for using tax-exempt donations for political purposes and for giving the House Ethics Committee false information about the contributions.

Many people have objected to Congress's ability to vote itself pay raises. In 1992, to limit this ability, the last of the required number of states ratified the 27th Amendment to the Constitution of the United States. This amendment requires that whenever a raise is authorized, it may not take effect until after the next congressional election.

The soaring cost of congressional campaigns has led to growing public concern that members of Congress spend too much time raising money and that large donors have too much influence on policy decisions. Big donors include *political action committees* (PAC's). A political action committee obtains voluntary contributions from members or employees of a special-interest group and gives the funds to candidates it favors.

Roger H. Davidson

Related articles. See the articles **House of Representatives** and **Senate** and their *Related articles.* See also:

Questions

Why are there two houses of Congress?
In what ways is the power of Congress limited?
What powers does the Speaker of the House have?
What are *delegated powers* of Congress? *Implied powers*?
How does Congress influence the president's treaty-making power?
What techniques are used in legislative bargaining?
How did relations between Congress and the presidency change markedly in the late 1960's and early 1970's?
Why does Congress conduct investigations?
What is a *standing committee*? A *conference committee*?
Why do members of Congress travel often to their home states or districts?

Additional resources

Level I
Gourse, Leslie. *The Congress.* Watts, 1995.
Stein, R. Conrad. *The Powers of Congress.* Childrens Pr., 1995.
Weber, Michael. *Our Congress.* Millbrook, 1994.

Level II
Bacon, Donald C., Davidson, Roger H., and Keller, Morton, eds. *Encyclopedia of the United States Congress.* 4 vols. Simon & Schuster, 1995.
Congress A to Z. 2nd ed. Congressional Quarterly, 1993.

It's a fact

The average staff of a United States senator consists of 40 to 50 people. By law, U.S. representatives may employ up to 18 aides.

Daschle, *DASH uhl,* **Tom** (1947-   ), a South Dakota Democrat, became minority leader in the United States Senate in 1995. He is regarded as a political moderate.

Daschle was born in Aberdeen, South Dakota. His full name is Thomas Andrew Daschle. He received a bachelor's degree from South Dakota State University in 1969. In 1978, Daschle won election to the U. S. House of Representatives. He served in the House from 1979 to 1987, when he took his Senate seat. He had been elected to the Senate in 1986.

In Congress, Daschle became known for defending the interests of American farmers. In 1990, for example, he and other senators from rural areas, called the "prairie populists," led an unsuccessful effort to raise federal price supports for farm products. Daschle also sought money for Vietnam War veterans for illnesses believed to be caused by exposure to a weedkiller known as Agent Orange. The U.S. military had used the chemical in the war.   Carroll Doherty

Web site

Daschle, Thomas Andrew (1947-   ) Biographical Information
http://bioguide.congress.gov/scripts/
    biodisplay.pl?index=D000064
The Biographical Directory of the United States Congress site on Tom Daschle.

Gephardt, Richard Andrew (1941-   ), a Democrat from Missouri, became minority leader of the United States House of Representatives in 1995. He served as majority leader of the House from 1989 to 1995. Gephardt was an unsuccessful candidate for the 1988 Democratic presidential nomination.

Gephardt was born in St. Louis, Missouri. He received a B.S. degree from Northwestern University in 1962 and a law degree from the University of Michigan in 1965. Gephardt was first elected to the U.S. House of Representatives in 1976. He has served on two important House committees, the Budget Committee and the Ways and Means Committee. He was elected chairman of the House Democratic Caucus in 1984 and again in 1986. As a congressman, Gephardt has promoted tax re-

form, expansion of national health care, and arms control. He has also supported legislation to penalize nations that restricted the importation of goods from the United States.   Guy Halverson

Web site

ABCNews.com Bio: Richard A. Gephardt
http://www.abcnews.go.com/reference/bios/gephardt.html
This profile from ABC News features a link to recent news stories about Richard A. Gephardt.

Hastert, J. Dennis (1942-   ), an Illinois Republican, became speaker of the United States House of Representatives in 1999. Newt Gingrich had resigned from the office in 1998. Bob Livingston was supposed to succeed Gingrich, but he decided not to take the office. Hastert was then chosen speaker.

John Dennis Hastert, who is usually known by his middle name, was born in Aurora, Illinois. He earned a bachelor's degree from Wheaton College in 1964 and a master's degree from Northern Illinois University in 1967.

Hastert served as a member of the Illinois House of Representatives from 1980 to 1986. He was elected to the U.S. House of Representatives in 1986 and took office in 1987. Hastert held the post of chief deputy majority whip of the U.S. House before he became speaker.

Web site

Hastert, John Dennis (1942-   ) Biographical Information
http://bioguide.congress.gov/scripts/
    biodisplay.pl?index=H000323
The Biographical Directory of the United States Congress site on Dennis Hastert.

Lott, Trent (1941-   ), a Mississippi Republican, became majority leader of the United States Senate in June 1996. He gained the office when the Republican senators chose him as their leader to replace Robert J. Dole, who had resigned to run for president. Lott had been Republican Senate *whip* (assistant leader) since January 1995.

Lott served in the U.S. House of Representatives from 1973 to 1989. He was Republican House whip from 1981 to 1989. He was first elected to the Senate in 1988, and took office in 1989. In Congress, Lott became known for his aggressive leadership style and his conservatism. He opposed increases in federal taxes and worked to limit federal spending. He supported a strong military.

Lott, whose full name is Chester Trent Lott, was born in Grenada, Mississippi. He attended the University of Mississippi, where he earned a bachelor's degree in 1963 and a law degree in 1967. Lott switched from the Democratic Party to the Republican Party in 1972.

Jackie Koszczuk

Web site

United States Senator Trent Lott (R-MS)
http://www.senate.gov/~lott/
The official United States Senate Web site of Trent Lott.

Topic for study

Look at the Index to the Constitution *given in the article* **Constitution of the United States.** *Notice the subjects that have been amended a number of times. Select one of these subjects and study how constitutional amendments have affected that subject.*

Constitution of the United States

Constitution of the United States sets forth the nation's fundamental laws. It establishes the form of the national government and defines the rights and liberties of the American people. It also lists the aims of the government and the methods of achieving them.

The Constitution was written to organize a strong national government for the American states. Previously,

Bruce Allen Murphy, the contributor of this article, is Professor of History and Politics, and Fellow, Institute for the Arts and Humanistic Studies, at Pennsylvania State University.

the nation's leaders had established a national government under the Articles of Confederation. But the Articles granted independence to each state. They lacked the authority to make the states work together to solve national problems.

After the states won independence in the Revolutionary War (1775-1783), they faced the problems of peacetime government. The states had to enforce law and order, collect taxes, pay a large public debt, and regulate trade among themselves. They also had to deal with Indian tribes and negotiate with other governments. Leading statesmen, such as George Washington and Alexan-

The signing of the Constitution took place on Sept. 17, 1787, at the Pennsylvania State House (now called Independence Hall) in Philadelphia. American artist Howard Chandler Christy painted this picture in 1940. The painting hangs in the United States Capitol in Washington, D.C.

Scene at the Signing of the Constitution of the United States, an oil painting on canvas; U.S. Capitol Historical Society (National Geographic Society)

Signers of the Constitution included William Jackson, who was the secretary of the convention but not a delegate. John Dickinson of Delaware was absent but had another delegate sign for him.

1. George Washington
2. Benjamin Franklin
3. James Madison, Jr.
4. Alexander Hamilton
5. Gouverneur Morris
6. Robert Morris
7. James Wilson
8. Charles C. Pinckney
9. Charles Pinckney
10. John Rutledge
11. Pierce Butler
12. Roger Sherman
13. William S. Johnson
14. James McHenry

15. George Read
16. Richard Bassett
17. Richard D. Spaight
18. William Blount
19. Hugh Williamson
20. Daniel of St. Thomas Jenifer
21. Rufus King
22. Nathaniel Gorham

23. Jonathan Dayton
24. Daniel Carroll
25. William Few
26. Abraham Baldwin
27. John Langdon
28. Nicholas Gilman
29. William Livingston
30. William Paterson
31. Thomas Mifflin

32. George Clymer
33. Thomas FitzSimons
34. Jared Ingersoll
35. Gunning Bedford, Jr.
36. Jacob Broom
37. John Dickinson
38. John Blair
39. David Brearley
40. William Jackson

Ratification of the Constitution

Article VII of the U.S. Constitution required the approval of 9 states to put the Constitution into effect. This table gives the dates on which each of the 13 states ratified the Constitution.

Delaware	Dec. 7, 1787
Pennsylvania	Dec. 12, 1787
New Jersey	Dec. 18, 1787
Georgia	Jan. 2, 1788
Connecticut	Jan. 9, 1788
Massachusetts	Feb. 6, 1788
Maryland	April 28, 1788
South Carolina	May 23, 1788
New Hampshire	June 21, 1788
Virginia	June 25, 1788
New York	July 26, 1788
North Carolina	Nov. 21, 1789
Rhode Island	May 29, 1790

der Hamilton, began to discuss the creation of a strong national government under a new constitution.

Hamilton helped bring about a national convention that met in Philadelphia in 1787 to revise the Articles of Confederation. But a majority of the delegates at the convention decided instead to write a new plan of government—the Constitution of the United States. The Constitution established not merely a league of states but a government that exercised its authority directly over all citizens. The Constitution also defined clearly the powers of the national government. In addition, it established protection for the rights of the states and of every individual.

The supreme law of the land

The Constitution consists of a preamble, 7 articles, and 27 amendments. It sets up a *federal system* by dividing powers between the national and state governments. It also establishes a balanced national government by dividing authority among three independent branches—the executive, the legislative, and the judicial. The executive branch enforces the law, the legislative branch makes the law, and the judicial branch interprets the law. The executive branch of the national government is usually represented by the president, the legislative branch by Congress, and the judicial branch by the Supreme Court. This division of the government into three branches is known as the *separation of powers*. Each branch can use its powers to *check and balance* (exercise control over) the other two. See **United States, Government of the** (Separation of powers).

Federal powers listed in the Constitution include the right to collect taxes, declare war, and regulate trade. In addition to these *delegated,* or *expressed, powers* (those listed in the Constitution), the national government has *implied powers* (those reasonably suggested by the Constitution). The implied powers enable the government to respond to the changing needs of the nation. For example, Congress had no delegated power to print paper money. But such a power is implied in the delegated powers of borrowing and coining money.

There are some powers that the Constitution does not give to the national government or forbid to the states. These *reserved powers* belong to the people or to the states. State powers include the right to legislate on divorce, marriage, and public schools. Powers reserved for the people include the right to own property and to be tried by a jury. In some cases, the national and state governments have *concurrent powers*—that is, both levels of government may act. The national government has supreme authority in case of a conflict.

The Supreme Court has the final authority to explain the Constitution. The court can set aside any law—federal, state, or local—that conflicts with any part of the Constitution.

The need for the Constitution

The government established by the Articles of Confederation was not strong enough to govern the new nation. For example, it lacked an executive branch and a system of national courts. It could not regulate trade between the states or tax the states or their citizens. In ad-

From *The National Archives of the United States* by Herman J. Viola, Publisher Harry N. Abrams, Inc., photographed by Jonathan Wallen

The United States Constitution is on display at the National Archives Building in Washington, D.C. A bronze and glass storage case filled with helium helps preserve the document. The case is lowered into a vault in the floor each night for safekeeping. More than 1 million people view the Constitution each year.

dition, it could not maintain its own army. The government was little more than an assembly of the representatives of 13 independent states. Before almost any measure could be adopted, it had to be approved by at least 9 of the states.

In 1783, after the Revolutionary War, the nation entered a period of unstable commercial and political conditions. Alexander Hamilton and his supporters would have had little success in their campaign for a new constitution if conditions had been better. Some historians have painted the troubles of the new republic in much too gloomy colors. But little doubt remains that the situation became steadily worse after 1783. Each state acted almost like an independent country. Each ran its own affairs exactly as it saw fit, with little concern for the needs of the republic. The states circulated a dozen different currencies, most of which had little value. Neighboring states taxed each other's goods. Britain refused to reopen the channels of trade that the colonies had depended on for their economic well-being. The state legislatures refused to pay the debts they had assumed during the Revolutionary War. Many states passed laws that enabled debtors to escape paying their obligations.

Worst of all, some people began to think once again of taking up arms to solve their problems. In western Massachusetts in 1786, hundreds of farmers under Captain Daniel Shays rebelled against the state government in Boston. State troops finally put down Shays's Rebellion. George Washington and other leaders wondered whether the colonies had rebelled against Britain in vain. They felt it was time to end these troubles and bring peace and order by forming a new national government. This new government would have to be strong enough to gain obedience at home and respect abroad.

Representatives from five states met in Annapolis, Maryland, in 1786. They proposed that the states appoint commissioners to meet in Philadelphia and consider revising the Articles of Confederation. Congress agreed to the proposal and suggested that each state select delegates to a constitutional convention.

The Constitutional Convention

The convention was supposed to open on May 14, 1787. But few of the 55 delegates had arrived in Philadelphia by that date. Finally, on May 25, the convention formally opened in Independence Hall. Twelve states had responded to the call for the convention. Rhode Island refused to send delegates because it did not want the national government to interfere with its affairs.

Of the 55 delegates, 39 signed the United States Constitution on Sept. 17, 1787. One of the signers was John Dickinson of Delaware, who left the convention but asked another delegate, George Read, to sign for him. William Jackson of Philadelphia, a former major in the

Photri

The Assembly Room of the Pennsylvania State House, where regular sessions of the Constitutional Convention of 1787 were held, is shown as it looks today. The Declaration of Independence was adopted in this room in 1776, and the Articles of Confederation were ratified there in 1781.

Revolutionary War who was chosen to serve as the convention secretary, witnessed the signatures. The delegates included some of the most experienced and patriotic men in the new republic. George Washington served as president of the convention. Benjamin Franklin, at the age of 81, attended as a representative of Pennsylvania. The brilliant Alexander Hamilton represented New York. James Madison of Virginia received the title of "Father of the Constitution" with his speeches, negotiations, and attempts at compromise. Madison told the delegates they were considering a plan that "would decide forever the fate of republican government." He kept a record of the delegates' debates and decisions.

Other men who had much to do with writing the new Constitution included John Dickinson, Gouverneur Morris, Edmund Randolph, Roger Sherman, James Wilson, and George Wythe. Morris was given the task of putting all the convention's resolutions and decisions into polished form. Morris actually "wrote" the Constitution. The original copy of the document is preserved in the National Archives Building in Washington, D.C.

Several important figures of the time did not attend the convention. John Adams and Thomas Jefferson were absent on other government duties. Samuel Adams and John Jay failed to be appointed delegates from their states. Patrick Henry refused to serve after his appointment because he opposed granting any more power to the national government. Three leading members of the convention—Elbridge Gerry, George Mason, and Edmund Randolph—refused to sign the Constitution because they disagreed with parts of it.

The background of the Constitution. The delegates to the Constitutional Convention relied greatly on past experience as they worked to create a new government. They recalled many important events in the development of constitutional government. These included the granting of Magna Carta, an English constitutional document, in 1215 and the meeting of the Jamestown representative assembly in 1619. Some of the American Colonies also served as examples of constitutional forms of government. While colonial governments had weaknesses, they had progressed beyond other governments of their time in achieving liberty under law.

All American states established constitutional governments after they declared their independence from Britain in 1776. In 1777, John Jay of New York had helped write a constitution for his state. John Adams of Massachusetts had helped write the Massachusetts Constitution of 1780. Delegates to the convention in Philadelphia used many ideas and words from the constitutions of these and other states.

The delegates also drew on their own experiences. Franklin had proposed a plan at the Albany Congress of 1754 to unify the colonies under a central government. Washington remembered his own problems during the war when, as commander in chief, he had to work with the frequently divided Continental Congress. Almost every delegate to the convention had served as a soldier or administrator of the government. They often disagreed on details but were united in wanting the new government to be strong enough to rule the nation. They also wanted it to respect the liberties of the states and of the people.

The compromises. The task of creating a new government was not easily accomplished. Disputes among the delegates nearly ended the convention on several occasions. For example, delegates from the large states disagreed with those from the small states about representation in the national legislature. The larger states favored the *Virginia Plan,* under which population would determine the number of representatives a state could send to the legislature. The small states supported the *New Jersey Plan,* which proposed that all the states would have an equal number of representatives. The Connecticut delegates suggested a compromise that settled the problem. Their plan provided for equal representation in the Senate, along with representation in proportion to population in the House of Representatives. This proposal became known as the *Connecticut Compromise* or the *Great Compromise.*

Compromises also settled conflicts over the issue of slavery. The delegates from the Northern states wanted Congress to have the power to forbid the foreign slave trade. Most Southern delegates did not wish Congress to have this power. A compromise decided that Congress would not be allowed to regulate the foreign slave trade until 1808. Another compromise involved the question of how to count slaves in determining how many members of Congress a state could have. Slaves were not considered citizens, and so the convention agreed that only three-fifths of a state's slaves could be counted.

The delegates agreed that each state should hold a special convention to discuss and vote on the Constitution. They also decided that as soon as nine states had *ratified* (approved) the Constitution, the Constitution would take effect and they could begin to organize the new government.

Ratifying the Constitution

Less than three months after the Constitution was signed, Delaware became the first state to ratify it, on Dec. 7, 1787. New Hampshire was the ninth state, putting the Constitution into effect on June 21, 1788. But the Founding Fathers could not be sure that the Constitution would be generally accepted until the important states of New York and Virginia had ratified it. Powerful organized opposition to the Constitution had developed in these two states and in others. Such people as Elbridge Gerry, Patrick Henry, Richard Henry Lee, and George Mason spoke out against ratification.

Critics objected that a bill of rights had not been included, that the president had too much independence, and that the Senate was too aristocratic. They also thought Congress had too many powers and the national government had too much authority. Friends of the Constitution rallied support for ratification. They became known as *Federalists.* Their opponents were called *Anti-Federalists.* The two groups promoted their causes in newspapers, in pamphlets, and in debates in the ratifying conventions. The groups developed into the first American political parties.

Virginia ratified the Constitution on June 25, 1788, and New York did so on July 26. Early in January 1789, all the ratifying states except New York selected presidential electors in their legislatures or by a direct vote of the people. On February 4, the electors named George Washington as the first president of the United States.

The first Congress under the Constitution met in New York City on March 4. Washington was inaugurated as president on April 30. North Carolina and Rhode Island refused to approve the Constitution and take part in the new government until Congress agreed to add a bill of rights.

The Bill of Rights

The Federalists might never have obtained ratification of the Constitution in several important states if they had not promised to support amendments to the document. These amendments were written to protect individual liberties against possible unjust rule by the national government.

Most state constitutions that were adopted during the Revolution had included a clear declaration of the rights of all people. Most Americans believed that no constitution could be considered complete without such a declaration.

George Mason of Virginia was responsible for the first and most famous American bill of rights, the Virginia Declaration of Rights of 1776. He and Patrick Henry might have prevented ratification of the Constitution in Virginia if the Federalists had not agreed to their demands for amendments.

James Madison led the new Congress in proposing amendments. He suggested 15 amendments, and the Congress accepted 12 of them to be submitted for approval by the states under the amending process outlined in the Fifth Article of the Constitution. By Dec. 15, 1791, enough states had approved 10 of the 12 amendments to make them a permanent addition to the Constitution. These amendments are known as the *Bill of Rights*.

One of the two unapproved amendments dealt with the size of the House of Representatives. It would have changed representation from no more than one representative for every 30,000 people to one for every 50,000 people. The other unapproved amendment provided that whenever Congress changed the salaries of its members, the change could not take effect until after the next election of representatives had been held. This amendment was ratified in 1992.

The development of the Constitution

Through the years, the Constitution has developed to address changing needs in the country. James Madison declared, "In framing a system which we wish to last for ages, we should not lose sight of the changes which ages will produce." The Constitution was designed to serve the interests of the people—rich and poor, Northerners and Southerners, farmers, workers, and business people.

The Anti-Federalists accepted defeat when the Constitution was adopted and set about to win power under its rules. Their action set a style for American politics that has never changed. Americans sometimes feel dissatisfied with the policies of those who govern. However, few Americans have condemned the constitutional system or demanded a second constitutional convention.

Delegates to the Constitutional Convention believed strongly in the rule of the majority, but they wanted to protect minorities against any unjustness by the majori-

Interesting facts about the Constitution

Which two signers of the Constitution later became U.S. presidents? George Washington and James Madison.

Which signers of the Declaration of Independence also signed the Constitution? George Clymer, Benjamin Franklin, Robert Morris, George Read, Roger Sherman, and James Wilson.

Who were the youngest and oldest signers of the Constitution? Youngest: Jonathan Dayton, 26 years old. Oldest: Benjamin Franklin, 81 years old.

Who was the first delegate to sign the Constitution? George Washington.

Who was called the "Father of the Constitution"? James Madison earned this title because he was a leading member of the convention and wrote a record of the delegates' debates.

Who actually "wrote" the Constitution? Gouverneur Morris.

When was the Constitution signed? Sept. 17, 1787.

What state did not send representatives to the Constitutional Convention? Rhode Island refused to send representatives because it did not want the federal government to interfere with Rhode Island's affairs.

In what order did the delegates sign the Constitution? In geographical order from north to south: New Hampshire, Massachusetts, Connecticut, New York, New Jersey, Pennsylvania, Delaware, Maryland, Virginia, North Carolina, South Carolina, and Georgia.

Which three leading delegates refused to sign the Constitution? Elbridge Gerry, George Mason, and Edmund Randolph refused because they objected to the powers that the Constitution gave the federal government.

How many delegates signed the Constitution? 39.

Where is the original Constitution displayed? In the National Archives Building in Washington, D.C.

ty. They achieved this goal by separating and balancing the powers of government. Other basic constitutional aims included respect for the rights of individuals and states, rule by the people, separation of church and state, and supremacy of the national government.

Amendments are additions to the Constitution. Today, there are 27 amendments.

An amendment may be proposed by two-thirds of each house of Congress, or by a national convention called by Congress in response to requests by two-thirds of the state legislatures. It becomes part of the Constitution after being ratified either by the legislatures of three-fourths of the states or by conventions in three-fourths of the states. Congress decides which form of ratification should be used and how much time the states have to consider each amendment. In many cases, Congress has chosen a seven-year period for such consideration. The process of amending the Constitution was designed to be difficult, so that the nation would have to think carefully about any proposed changes before adopting them.

Laws have added to the meaning of the Constitution. The delegates to the Constitutional Convention knew they could not write laws for every possible situation. Therefore, they gave Congress the right to pass all laws that were "necessary and proper" to carry out powers granted by the Constitution to the president, Congress, and federal courts. Congress has passed laws to establish such administrative organizations as the Federal Aviation Administration and the United States Postal Service. Congress has also passed laws to regulate interstate commerce, thereby controlling many aspects of the economy.

Court decisions. Federal and state judges apply the Constitution in many court cases. The Supreme Court has the final authority in interpreting the meaning of the Constitution in any specific case. The court has the power of *judicial review*—that is, it can declare a law unconstitutional. The court has this power largely because of the decision of Chief Justice John Marshall in the case of *Marbury v. Madison* in 1803. Since that time, the court has ruled that all or parts of more than 125 federal laws and over 1,000 state laws were unconstitutional. The court can also overrule itself, and it has done so about 200 times.

Presidential actions. Strong presidents have used their authority to expand the simple words of the Second Article of the Constitution into a source of great presidential power. Such presidents include George Washington, Thomas Jefferson, Andrew Jackson, Abraham Lincoln, Theodore Roosevelt, Woodrow Wilson, and Franklin D. Roosevelt. Washington, for example, made the president the leading figure in foreign affairs. Lincoln used the powers set forth in the article to free slaves during the American Civil War (1861-1865).

Customs have made the Constitution flexible and have added to the powers of the national government. For example, the president's Cabinet developed from the words in the Second Article that permit the chief executive to "require the opinion, in writing, of the principal officer in each of the executive departments, upon any subject relating to the duties of their respective offices.…"

State and party actions. The Constitution provides

Index to the Constitution

This index lists some important subjects discussed in the Constitution and the specific article or amendment that deals with each one. The index also gives the page in this article on which the information appears.

for a general method of electing a president. It does not mention political parties. But state laws and political-party practices have changed the constitutional system of voting into the exciting campaigns and elections that take place today. The Constitution has continued to develop in response to the demands of an ever-growing society through all these methods. Yet the spirit and wording of the Constitution have remained constant. People of each generation have applied its provisions to their own problems in ways that seem reasonable to them.

The British statesman William E. Gladstone described the Constitution as "the most wonderful work ever struck off at a given time by the brain and purpose of man." In a world of change and struggle, the American people have no more precious possession than this great document. The complete text of the Constitution of the United States, with explanatory notes, begins on the next page.　　　Bruce Allen Murphy

Related articles include:
Congress of the United States
Court
Jefferson, Thomas
Political party
President of the United States
Supreme Court of the United States
United States, Government of the
Vice president of the United States
Voting

Outline

I. **The supreme law of the land**
II. **The need for the Constitution**
III. **The Constitutional Convention**
　A. The background of the Constitution
　B. The compromises
IV. **Ratifying the Constitution**
V. **The Bill of Rights**
VI. **The development of the Constitution**

Questions

Why were the Articles of Confederation of 1781 inadequate for governing the United States?
What compromises were made at the Constitutional Convention in forming the Constitution?
What were some major objections against the newly formed Constitution?
How did controversy over the Constitution result in creating the first American political parties?
In what two states was there especially powerful organized opposition to ratifying the Constitution?
What government body has the final authority in interpreting the Constitution?
What were some of the reasons for including a bill of rights in the Constitution?
What are *delegated powers*? *Implied powers*? *Reserved powers*? *Concurrent powers*?
Why did North Carolina and Rhode Island refuse to approve the Constitution at first?

Additional resources

Bernstein, Richard B., and Agel, Jerome. *Amending America: If We Love the Constitution So Much, Why Do We Keep Trying to Change It?* Times Bks., 1993.
Johnson, Linda C. *Our Constitution.* Millbrook, 1992. Younger readers.
Leinwand, Gerald. *Do We Need a New Constitution?* Watts, 1994.
Levy, Leonard W., and others, eds. *Encyclopedia of the American Constitution.* 4 vols. Macmillan, 1986. *Supplement I.* 1992.
Renstrom, Peter G. *Constitutional Law and Young Adults.* ABC-Clio, 1992.
Vile, John R. *A Companion to the United States Constitution and Its Amendments.* Praeger, 1993.

Web sites

National Constitution Center
http://www.constitutioncenter.org/
This site provides extensive information about the Constitution of the United States and other historical documents, such as the Magna Carta, the Emancipation Proclamation, and the Gettysburg Address. Includes special sections geared to students and teachers.

The American Constitution - A Documentary Record
http://www.yale.edu/lawweb/avalon/constpap.htm
The Avalon Project at the Yale Law School presents an extensive archive of documents about the Constitution divided into the following categories: The Roots of the Constitution; Revolution and Independence; Credentials of the Members of the Federal Convention; The Constitutional Convention; and Ratification and Formation of the Government.

United States Constitution
http://www.house.gov/Constitution/Constitution.html
Text of the Constitution of the United States.

(Text of the U.S. Constitution begins on the next page.)

It's a fact

Senator Strom Thurmond of South Carolina, the president *pro tempore* of the Senate, stood third in the line of succession to the presidency in 2000. Thurmond ranked as the oldest and longest-serving senator in United States history. He reached the age of 98 years in 2000 and had served in the Senate since 1955.

Before the 22nd Amendment to the Constitution was approved in 1951, a president could serve an unlimited number of terms.

The Constitution of the United States, drafted in 1787, is the world's oldest written constitution.

Senators and representatives receive exactly the same salary—$141,300 as of Jan. 1, 2000.

The Constitution of the United States went into effect on June 21, 1788, when New Hampshire became the ninth state to ratify it.

This copy of the Constitution shows the Preamble and part of the first article.

The Constitution of the United States

The text of the Constitution is printed here in boldface type. All words are given their modern spelling and capitalization. Brackets [ ] indicate parts that have been changed or set aside by amendments. The paragraphs printed in lightface type are not part of the Constitution. They explain the meaning of certain passages or describe how certain passages have worked in practice.

Preamble

We the people of the United States, in order to form a more perfect Union, establish justice, insure domestic tranquility, provide for the common defense, promote the general welfare, and secure the blessings of liberty to ourselves and our posterity, do ordain and establish this Constitution for the United States of America.

Article I

The legislative branch

Section 1. **All legislative powers herein granted shall be vested in a Congress of the United States, which shall consist of a Senate and House of Representatives.**

The first three articles of the Constitution divide the powers of the United States government among three separate branches: (1) the legislative branch, represented by Congress; (2) the executive branch, represented by the president; and (3) the judicial branch, represented by the Supreme Court. This division, called the *separation of powers,* is designed to prevent any branch of the government from becoming too powerful.

Article I says that only Congress has the power to make laws. Congress cannot give these powers to any other body. Through the years, however, Congress has created various federal agencies to make regulations and put its policies into practice. Such agencies include the Federal Trade Commission, the Federal Power Commission, and the Commission on Civil Rights.

The two-house Congress was one of the most important compromises of the Constitutional Convention. The small states at the convention supported the *New Jersey plan,* under which each state would have had the same number of representatives. The large states at the convention wanted the *Virginia plan,* which provided representation based on population. As a compromise, one house was chosen according to each plan.

The House of Representatives

Section 2. **(1) The House of Representatives shall be composed of members chosen every second year by the people of the several states, and the electors in each state shall have the qualifications requisite for electors of the most numerous branch of the state legislature.**

Members of the House of Representatives are elected to two-year terms. If a person is eligible to vote for the "most numerous branch" of his or her state legislature, he or she is also eligible to vote for members of Congress. The "most numerous branch" is the house that has the most members. All states except Nebraska have a two-house state legislature. The question of who can vote for state legislators is entirely up to the state, subject to the restrictions of the Constitution and federal law. The 15th, 19th, 24th, and 26th amendments forbid the states to deny or restrict a citizen's right to vote because of race, sex, or failure to pay a tax; or age if the person is at least 18 years old.

(2) No person shall be a representative who shall not have attained to the age of twenty-five years, and been seven years a citizen of the United States, and who shall not, when elected, be an inhabitant of that state in which he shall be chosen.

Each state decides for itself the requirements for legal residence, subject to constitutional limits. Most representatives live not only in the state but also in the district from which they are chosen.

(3) Representatives and direct taxes shall be apportioned among the several states which may be included within this Union, according to their respective numbers, [which shall be determined by adding to the whole number of free persons, including those bound to service for a term of years, and excluding Indians not taxed, three-fifths of all other persons].The actual enumeration shall be made within three years after the

first meeting of the Congress of the United States, and within every subsequent term of ten years, in such manner as they shall by law direct. The number of representatives shall not exceed one for every thirty thousand, but each state shall have at least one representative; [and until such enumeration shall be made, the state of New Hampshire shall be entitled to choose 3, Massachusetts 8, Rhode Island and Providence Plantations 1, Connecticut 5, New York 6, New Jersey 4, Pennsylvania 8, Delaware 1, Maryland 6, Virginia 10, North Carolina 5, South Carolina 5, and Georgia 3].

The effect of this paragraph has been greatly changed, both by amendments and by new conditions. It now provides only three things: (1) the number of representatives given to each state shall be based on its population; (2) Congress must see that the people of the United States are counted every 10 years; and (3) each state gets at least one representative.

The Founding Fathers probably considered the words "and direct taxes" to apply to poll and property taxes. The 16th Amendment gives Congress the right to tax a person according to the size of his or her income, rather than to tax a person according to the population of the state in which the person happens to live.

In the reference to "three-fifths of all other persons," the "other persons" meant black slaves. Since there are no longer any slaves in the United States, this part of the paragraph no longer has any meaning.

The average House district has well over half a million people, so the requirement that there shall be no more than one representative for every 30,000 people no longer has any practical force. In 1929, Congress fixed the total number of representatives at 435.

(4) When vacancies happen in the representation from any state, the executive authority thereof shall issue writs of election to fill such vacancies.

If a vacancy occurs in a House seat, the state governor must call a special election to fill it. However, if the next regularly scheduled election is to be held soon, the governor may allow the seat to remain empty rather than call a special election.

(5) The House of Representatives shall choose their speaker and other officers; and shall have the sole power of impeachment.

The House chooses an officer called the speaker to lead meetings. The House alone has the power to bring impeachment charges against an official. The Senate tries impeachment cases.

The Senate

Section 3. (1) The Senate of the United States shall be composed of two senators from each state, [chosen by the legislature thereof,] for six years; and each senator shall have one vote.

The Constitution at first provided that each state legislature should pick two senators. The 17th Amendment changed this rule by allowing the voters of each state to choose their senators.

(2) Immediately after they shall be assembled in consequence of the first election, they shall be divided as equally as may be into three classes. The seats of the senators of the first class shall be vacated at the expiration of the second year, of the second class at the expiration of the fourth year, and of the third class at the expiration of the sixth year, so that one-third may be chosen every second year; [and if vacancies happen by resignation, or otherwise, during the recess of the legislature of any state, the executive thereof may make temporary appointments until the next meeting of the legislature, which shall then fill such vacancies].

Senators are elected to six-year terms. Every two years, one-third of the senators are elected and two-thirds are holdovers. This arrangement makes the Senate a continuing body, unlike the House, whose entire membership is elected every two years. The 17th Amendment changed the method of filling vacancies in the Senate. The governor chooses a senator until the people elect one.

(3) No person shall be a senator who shall not have attained to the age of thirty years, and been nine years a citizen of the United States, and who shall not, when elected, be an inhabitant of that state for which he shall be chosen.

In 1806, Henry Clay of Kentucky was appointed to fill an unexpired term in the Senate. He was only 29, a few months younger than the minimum age, but no one challenged the appointment. In 1793, Albert Gallatin was elected to the Senate from Pennsylvania. He was removed from office when the Senate ruled that he had not yet been a citizen for nine years.

(4) The vice president of the United States shall be president of the Senate, but shall have no vote, unless they be equally divided.

The vice president serves as president of the Senate, but votes only when a tie vote occurs. The vice president's power to break ties can be important. In 1789, for example, Vice President John Adams cast the vote that decided the president could remove Cabinet members without Senate approval.

(5) The Senate shall choose their other officers, and also a president pro tempore, in the absence of the vice president, or when he shall exercise the office of president of the United States.

The Senate elects an officer called the president pro tempore to lead meetings when the vice president is absent.

(6) The Senate shall have the sole power to try all impeachments. When sitting for that purpose, they shall be on oath or affirmation. When the president of the United States is tried, the Chief Justice shall preside: and no person shall be convicted without the concurrence of two-thirds of the members present.

The provision that the chief justice of the United States, rather than the vice president, shall preside over the Senate when a president is on trial probably grows out of the fact that a conviction would make the vice president the president. The phrase "on oath or affirmation" means that senators are placed under oath when trying impeachment cases, just as jurors are in a regular court trial.

(7) Judgment in cases of impeachment shall not extend further than to removal from office, and disqualification to hold and enjoy any office of honor, trust or profit under the United States: but the party convicted shall nevertheless be liable and subject to indictment, trial, judgment and punishment, according to law.

If an impeached person is found guilty, he or she can be removed from office and forbidden to hold federal office again. The Senate cannot impose any other punishment, but the person may also be tried in regular courts. The Senate has convicted only seven people, all of them judges. These men were removed from office.

Organization of Congress

Section 4. (1) The times, places and manner of holding elections for senators and representatives, shall be prescribed in each state by the legislature thereof; but the Congress may at any time by law make or alter such regulations, [except as to the places of choosing senators].

As long as state legislatures chose the senators, it would not do to let Congress fix the place of choosing. This would have amounted to giving Congress the power to tell each state where to locate its capital. The words of the Constitution "except as to the places of choosing senators" were set aside by the 17th Amendment.

(2) The Congress shall assemble at least once in every year, [and such meeting shall be on the first Monday in December,] unless they shall by law appoint a different day.

In Europe, monarchs could keep parliaments from meeting, sometimes for many years, simply by not calling them together. This is the reason for the requirement that the Congress of the United States must meet at least once a year. The 20th Amend-

ment changed the date of the opening day of the session to January 3, unless Congress sets another date by law.

Section 5. (1) **Each house shall be the judge of the elections, returns and qualifications of its own members, and a majority of each shall constitute a quorum to do business; but a smaller number may adjourn from day to day, and may be authorized to compel the attendance of absent members, in such manner, and under such penalties as each house may provide.**

Each house determines if its members are legally qualified and have been elected fairly. In judging the qualifications of its members, each house may consider the age, citizenship, and residence requirements set forth in the Constitution. In acting on motions to expel a member, however, either house of Congress may consider other matters bearing on that member's fitness for office. A *quorum* is a group large enough to carry on business. Discussion and debate can go on whether a quorum is present or not, as long as a quorum comes in to vote.

(2) **Each house may determine the rules of its proceedings, punish its members for disorderly behavior, and, with the concurrence of two-thirds, expel a member.**

Either house can expel one of its members by a two-thirds vote. Each house makes its own rules. For example, the House of Representatives puts strict time limits on debate to speed up business. It is much more difficult to end debate in the Senate. A senator may speak as long as he or she wishes. Senators use this privilege to make long speeches called *filibusters* to delay Senate action. The Senate, however, may vote for *cloture,* a motion to end debate. On most matters, cloture requires a vote of 60 senators, or three-fifths of the total Senate membership.

(3) **Each house shall keep a journal of its proceedings, and from time to time publish the same, excepting such parts as may in their judgment require secrecy; and the yeas and nays of the members of either house on any question shall, at the desire of one-fifth of those present, be entered on the journal.**

The House *Journal* and the Senate *Journal* are published at the end of each session of Congress. They list all the bills and resolutions considered during the session, as well as every vote. All messages from the president to Congress also are included. The journals are considered the official documents for the proceedings of Congress.

(4) **Neither house, during the session of Congress, shall, without the consent of the other, adjourn for more than three days, nor to any other place than that in which the two houses shall be sitting.**

Section 6. (1) **The senators and representatives shall receive a compensation for their services, to be ascertained by law, and paid out of the treasury of the United States. They shall in all cases, except treason, felony and breach of the peace, be privileged from arrest during their attendance at the session of their respective houses, and in going to and returning from the same; and for any speech or debate in either house, they shall not be questioned in any other place.**

The privilege of *immunity* (freedom from arrest) while going to and from congressional business has little importance today. Members of Congress, like anyone else, may be arrested, tried, convicted, and sent to prison.

Congressional immunity from charges of *libel* and *slander* remains important. Libel is an untrue written statement that damages a person's reputation. Slander is a spoken statement that does so. Immunity under the speech and debate clause means that members of Congress may say whatever they wish in connection with congressional business without fear of being sued. This immunity extends to anything said by members during debate, in an official report, or while voting.

(2) **No senator or representative shall, during the time for which he was elected, be appointed to any civil office under the authority of the United States, which shall have been created, or the emoluments whereof shall have been increased**

during such time; and no person holding any office under the United States, shall be a member of either house during his continuance in office.

These provisions keep members of Congress from creating jobs to which they can later be appointed, from raising salaries of jobs they hope to hold in the future, or from holding office in the other branches of government while they are serving in Congress.

Section 7. (1) **All bills for raising revenue shall originate in the House of Representatives; but the Senate may propose or concur with amendments as on other bills.**

Tax bills must originate in the House. The tradition that tax laws should originate in the lower house of the legislature came from England. There, the lower house—the House of Commons—is more likely to reflect the people's wishes because the people elect its members. They do not elect the upper house, the House of Lords. In the United States, this rule has little importance because the people elect both the Senate and the House. In addition, the Senate can amend a tax bill to such an extent that it rewrites the whole measure.

(2) **Every bill which shall have passed the House of Representatives and the Senate, shall, before it become a law, be presented to the president of the United States; if he approve he shall sign it, but if not he shall return it, with his objections to that house in which it shall have originated, who shall enter the objections at large on their journal, and proceed to reconsider it. If after such reconsideration two-thirds of that house shall agree to pass the bill, it shall be sent, together with the objections, to the other house, by which it shall likewise be reconsidered, and if approved by two-thirds of that house, it shall become a law. But in all such cases the votes of both houses shall be determined by yeas and nays, and the names of the persons voting for and against the bill shall be entered on the journal of each house respectively. If any bill shall not be returned by the president within ten days (Sundays excepted) after it shall have been presented to him, the same shall be a law, in like manner as if he had signed it, unless the Congress by their adjournment prevent its return, in which case it shall not be a law.**

A bill passed by Congress goes to the president for the president's signature. If the president disapproves the bill, it must be returned to Congress with a statement of the objections within 10 days, not including Sundays. This action is called a *veto.* Congress can pass a law over the president's veto by a two-thirds vote of each house of those members present. The president can also let a bill become law without signing it merely by letting 10 days pass. But a bill sent to the president during the last 10 days of a session of Congress cannot become law unless it is signed. If a bill the president dislikes reaches the president near the end of a session, the bill may simply be held unsigned. This practice is known as a *pocket veto.*

In 1996, Congress enacted a law designed to add to the veto powers established by the Constitution. This law, which went into effect in 1997, gave the president the power to veto certain parts of bills passed by Congress. These parts included some spending items and tax breaks. The power to veto individual items in bills is often called a *line-item veto.* In 1998, however, the Supreme Court ruled that the power created by the 1996 law was unconstitutional. See **Veto.**

(3) **Every order, resolution, or vote to which the concurrence of the Senate and House of Representatives may be necessary (except on a question of adjournment) shall be presented to the president of the United States; and before the same shall take effect, shall be approved by him, or being disapproved by him, shall be repassed by two-thirds of the Senate and House of Representatives, according to the rules and limitations prescribed in the case of a bill.**

Powers granted to Congress

Section 8. **The Congress shall have power:**
(1) **To lay and collect taxes, duties, imposts and excises, to**

pay the debts and provide for the common defense and general welfare of the United States; but all duties, imposts and excises shall be uniform throughout the United States;

Duties are taxes on goods coming into the United States. *Excises* are taxes on sales, use, or production, and sometimes on business procedures or privileges. For example, corporation taxes, cigarette taxes, and amusement taxes are excises. *Imposts* is a general tax term that includes both duties and excises.

(2) To borrow money on the credit of the United States;

(3) To regulate commerce with foreign nations, and among the several states, and with the Indian tribes;

This section, called the *commerce clause,* gives Congress some of its most important powers. The Supreme Court has interpreted *commerce* to mean not only trade but also all kinds of commercial activity. Commerce "among the several states" is usually called *interstate commerce.* The Supreme Court has ruled that interstate commerce includes not only transactions across state boundaries but also any activity that affects commerce in more than one state. The court has interpreted the word *regulate* to mean *encourage, promote, protect, prohibit,* or *restrain.* As a result, Congress can pass laws and provide funds to improve waterways, to enforce air safety measures, and to forbid interstate shipment of certain goods. It can regulate the movement of people, of trains, of stocks and bonds, and even of television signals. Congress has made it a federal crime to flee across state lines from state or local police. It also has forbidden people who operate interstate facilities or who serve interstate passengers to treat customers unfairly because of race.

(4) To establish an uniform rule of naturalization, and uniform laws on the subject of bankruptcies throughout the United States;

(5) To coin money, regulate the value thereof, and of foreign coin, and fix the standard of weights and measures;

From this section, along with the section that allows the Congress to regulate commerce and to borrow money, Congress gets its right to charter national banks and to establish the Federal Reserve System.

(6) To provide for the punishment of counterfeiting the securities and current coin of the United States;

Securities are government bonds.

(7) To establish post offices and post roads;

(8) To promote the progress of science and useful arts, by securing for limited times to authors and inventors the exclusive right to their respective writings and discoveries;

Photographs and films may also be copyrighted under this rule.

(9) To constitute tribunals inferior to the Supreme Court;

Examples of federal courts "inferior to the Supreme Court" include the U.S. district courts and the U.S. courts of appeals.

(10) To define and punish piracies and felonies committed on the high seas, and offenses against the law of nations;

Congress, rather than the states, has jurisdiction over crimes committed at sea.

(11) To declare war, grant letters of marque and reprisal, and make rules concerning captures on land and water;

Only Congress can declare war. However, the president, as commander in chief, has engaged the United States in wars without a declaration by Congress. Undeclared wars include the Korean War (1950-1953), the Vietnam War (1957-1975), and the Persian Gulf War (1991). *Letters of marque and reprisal* are documents that authorize private vessels to attack enemy shipping.

(12) To raise and support armies, but no appropriation of

money to that use shall be for a longer term than two years;

(13) To provide and maintain a navy;

(14) To make rules for the government and regulation of the land and naval forces;

(15) To provide for calling forth the militia to execute the laws of the Union, suppress insurrections and repel invasions;

Congress has given the president power to decide when a state of invasion or *insurrection* (uprising) exists. At such times, the president can call out the National Guard.

(16) To provide for organizing, arming, and disciplining, the militia, and for governing such part of them as may be employed in the service of the United States, reserving to the states respectively, the appointment of the officers, and the authority of training the militia according to the discipline prescribed by Congress;

The federal government helps the states maintain the militia, also known as the National Guard. Until 1916, the states controlled the militia entirely. That year, the National Defense Act provided for federal funding of the guard and for drafting the guard into national service under certain circumstances.

(17) To exercise exclusive legislation in all cases whatsoever, over such district (not exceeding ten miles square) as may, by cession of particular states, and the acceptance of Congress, become the seat of the government of the United States, and to exercise like authority over all places purchased by the consent of the legislature of the state in which the same shall be for the erection of forts, magazines, arsenals, dockyards, and other needful buildings;—And

This section makes Congress the legislative body not only for the District of Columbia, but also for federal property on which forts and other federal works or buildings are located.

(18) To make all laws which shall be necessary and proper for carrying into execution the foregoing powers, and all other powers vested by this Constitution in the government of the United States, or in any department or officer thereof.

This section is known as the "necessary and proper" clause or the *elastic clause.* It allows Congress to deal with many matters that are not specifically mentioned in the Constitution but are suggested by powers granted to Congress in Article I. As times have changed, Congress has been able to pass needed laws with few amendments to the Constitution. This flexibility helps explain why the Constitution is one of the oldest written constitutions.

Powers forbidden to Congress

Section 9. (1) The migration or importation of such persons as any of the states now existing shall think proper to admit, shall not be prohibited by the Congress prior to the year one thousand eight hundred and eight, but a tax or duty may be imposed on such importation, not exceeding ten dollars for each person.

This paragraph refers to the slave trade. Dealers in slaves, as well as some slaveholders, wanted to make sure that Congress could not stop anyone from bringing African slaves into the country before the year 1808. That year, Congress did ban the importing of slaves into the United States.

(2) The privilege of the writ of *habeas corpus* shall not be suspended, unless when in cases of rebellion or invasion the public safety may require it.

A *writ of habeas corpus* is a legal order that commands people who have a person in custody to bring the person into court. They must explain in court why the person is being restrained. If their explanation is unsatisfactory, the judge can order the prisoner released.

(3) No bill of attainder or ex post facto law shall be passed.

A *bill of attainder* is an act passed by a legislature to punish a person without trial. An *ex post facto law* is one that provides punishment for an act that was not illegal when the act was committed.

(4) No capitation, [or other direct] tax shall be laid, unless in proportion to the census or enumeration herein before directed to be taken.

A *capitation* is a tax that is collected equally from everyone. A capitation is also called a *head tax* or a *poll tax.* The Supreme Court held that this section of the Constitution prohibits an income tax. The 16th Amendment set aside the court's decision.

(5) No tax or duty shall be laid on articles exported from any state.

In this sentence, *exported* means sent to other states or to foreign countries. The Southern States feared that the new government would tax their exports and that their economies would suffer as a result. This sentence forbids such a tax. However, Congress can prohibit shipment of certain items or regulate the conditions of their shipment.

(6) No preference shall be given by any regulation of commerce or revenue to the ports of one state over those of another: nor shall vessels bound to, or from, one state, be obliged to enter, clear, or pay duties in another.

Congress cannot make laws concerning trade that favor one state over another. Ships going from one state to another need not pay taxes to do so.

(7) No money shall be drawn from the treasury, but in consequence of appropriations made by law; and a regular statement and account of the receipts and expenditures of all public money shall be published from time to time.

Government money cannot be spent without the consent of Congress. Congress must issue a financial statement from time to time. Congress authorizes money for most government programs in lump sums because too much time would be needed to authorize each item separately.

(8) No title of nobility shall be granted by the United States: And no person holding any office of profit or trust under them, shall, without the consent of the Congress, accept of any present, emolument, office, or title, of any kind whatsoever, from any king, prince, or foreign state.

Congress cannot give anyone a title of nobility, such as countess or duke. Federal officials may not accept a gift, office, payment, or title from a foreign country without the consent of Congress.

Powers forbidden to the states

Section 10. (1) No state shall enter into any treaty, alliance, or confederation; grant letters of marque and reprisal; coin money; emit bills of credit; make anything but gold and silver coin a tender in payment of debts; pass any bill of attainder, ex post facto law, or law impairing the obligation of contracts, or grant any title of nobility.

(2) No state shall, without the consent of the Congress, lay any imposts or duties on imports or exports, except what may be absolutely necessary for executing its inspection laws: and the net produce of all duties and imposts, laid by any state on imports or exports, shall be for the use of the treasury of the United States, and all such laws shall be subject to the revision and control of the Congress.

Without the consent of Congress, a state cannot tax goods entering or leaving the state except for small fees to cover the cost of inspection. Profits from a tax on interstate commerce go to the federal government.

(3) No state shall, without the consent of Congress, lay any duty of tonnage, keep troops, or ships of war in time of peace, enter into any agreement or compact with another state, or with a foreign power, or engage in war, unless actually invaded, or in such imminent danger as will not admit of delay.

Only the federal government has the power to make treaties and to carry out measures for national defense.

Article II

The executive branch

Section 1. (1) The executive power shall be vested in a president of the United States of America. He shall hold his office during the term of four years, and, together with the vice president, chosen for the same term, be elected, as follows:

(2) Each state shall appoint, in such manner as the legislature thereof may direct, a number of electors, equal to the whole number of senators and representatives to which the state may be entitled in the Congress: but no senator or representative, or person holding an office of trust or profit under the United States, shall be appointed an elector.

This section establishes the Electoral College, a group of people chosen by the voters of each state to elect the president and vice president (see Electoral College).

(3) [The electors shall meet in their respective states, and vote by ballot for two persons, of whom one at least shall not be an inhabitant of the same state with themselves. And they shall make a list of all the persons voted for, and of the number of votes for each; which list they shall sign and certify, and transmit sealed to the seat of the government of the United States, directed to the president of the Senate. The president of the Senate shall, in the presence of the Senate and House of Representatives, open all the certificates, and the votes shall then be counted. The person having the greatest number of votes shall be the president, if such number be a majority of the whole number of electors appointed; and if there be more than one who have such majority, and have an equal number of votes, then the House of Representatives shall immediately choose by ballot one of them for president; and if no person have a majority, then from the five highest on the list the said House shall in like manner choose the president. But in choosing the president, the votes shall be taken by states, the representation from each state having one vote; a quorum for this purpose shall consist of a member or members from two-thirds of the states, and a majority of all the states shall be necessary to a choice. In every case, after the choice of the president, the person having the greatest number of votes of the electors shall be the vice president. But if there should remain two or more who have equal votes, the Senate shall choose from them by ballot the vice president.]

The 12th Amendment changed this procedure for electing the president and vice president.

(4) The Congress may determine the time of choosing the electors, and the day on which they shall give their votes; which day shall be the same throughout the United States.

(5) No person except a natural-born citizen, or a citizen of the United States at the time of the adoption of this Constitution, shall be eligible to the office of president; neither shall any person be eligible to that office who shall not have attained to the age of thirty-five years, and been fourteen years a resident within the United States.

(6) In case of the removal of the president from office, or of his death, resignation, or inability to discharge the powers and duties of the said office, the same shall devolve on the vice president, and the Congress may by law provide for the case of removal, death, resignation or inability, both of the president and vice president, declaring what officer shall then act as president, and such officer shall act accordingly, until the disability be removed, or a president shall be elected.

On Aug. 9, 1974, President Richard M. Nixon resigned as chief executive and was succeeded by Vice President Gerald R. Ford. Until then, only death had ever cut short the term of a president of the United States. The 25th Amendment provides that the vice president succeed to the presidency if the president becomes disabled, and specifies the conditions applying to that succession. See **Presidential succession.**

(7) The president shall, at stated times, receive for his services, a compensation, which shall neither be increased nor diminished during the period for which he shall have been elected, and he shall not receive within that period any other emolument from the United States, or any of them.

The Constitution made it possible for a poor person to become president by providing a salary for that office. The president's salary cannot be raised or lowered during his or her term of office. The chief executive may not receive any other pay from the federal government or the states.

(8) Before he enter on the execution of his office, he shall take the following oath or affirmation:—"I do solemnly swear (or affirm) that I will faithfully execute the office of president of the United States, and will to the best of my ability, preserve, protect and defend the Constitution of the United States."

The Constitution does not say who shall administer the oath to the newly elected president. President George Washington was sworn in by Robert R. Livingston, then a state official in New York. After that, it became customary for the chief justice of the United States to administer the oath. Calvin Coolidge was sworn in by his father, a justice of the peace, at his home in Vermont. Coolidge took the oath again before Justice Adolph A. Hoehling of the Supreme Court of the District of Columbia.

Section 2. **(1) The president shall be commander in chief of the Army and Navy of the United States, and of the militia of the several states, when called into the actual service of the United States; he may require the opinion, in writing, of the principal officer in each of the executive departments, upon any subject relating to the duties of their respective offices, and he shall have power to grant reprieves and pardons for offenses against the United States, except in cases of impeachment.**

The president's powers as commander in chief are farreaching. But even in wartime, the president must obey the law.

(2) He shall have power, by and with the advice and consent of the Senate, to make treaties, provided two-thirds of the senators present concur; and he shall nominate, and by and with the advice and consent of the Senate, shall appoint ambassadors, other public ministers and consuls, judges of the Supreme Court, and all other officers of the United States, whose appointments are not herein otherwise provided for, and which shall be established by law: but the Congress may by law vest the appointment of such inferior officers, as they think proper, in the president alone, in the courts of law, or in the heads of departments.

The framers of the Constitution intended that in some matters the Senate should serve as an advisory body for the president.

The president can make treaties and appoint various government officials. However, two-thirds of the senators present must approve a treaty before it is confirmed. In addition, high appointments require approval of more than half the senators present.

(3) The president shall have power to fill up all vacancies that may happen during the recess of the Senate, by granting commissions which shall expire at the end of their next session.

This means that when the Senate is not in session, the president can make temporary appointments to offices which require Senate confirmation.

Section 3. **He shall from time to time give to the Congress**

information of the state of the Union, and recommend to their consideration such measures as he shall judge necessary and expedient; he may, on extraordinary occasions, convene both houses, or either of them, and in case of disagreement between them, with respect to the time of adjournment, he may adjourn them to such time as he shall think proper; he shall receive ambassadors and other public ministers; he shall take care that the laws be faithfully executed, and shall commission all the officers of the United States.

The president gives a State of the Union message to Congress each year. Presidents George Washington and John Adams delivered their messages in person. For more than 100 years after that, most presidents sent a written message, which was read in Congress. President Woodrow Wilson delivered his State of the Union messages in person, as did President Franklin D. Roosevelt and all presidents after Roosevelt. The president's messages often have great influence on public opinion, and thus on Congress. Famous messages to Congress include the Monroe Doctrine and President Wilson's "Fourteen Points."

During the 1800's, presidents often called Congress into session. Today, Congress is in session most of the time. No president has ever had to adjourn a session of Congress.

The responsibility to "take care that the laws be faithfully executed" puts the president at the head of law enforcement for the national government. Every federal official, civilian or military, gets his or her authority from the president.

Section 4. **The president, vice president and all civil officers of the United States, shall be removed from office on impeachment for, and conviction of, treason, bribery, or other high crimes and misdemeanors.**

Article III

The judicial branch

Section 1. **The judicial power of the United States, shall be vested in one Supreme Court, and in such inferior courts as the Congress may from time to time ordain and establish. The judges, both of the Supreme and inferior courts, shall hold their offices during good behavior, and shall, at stated times, receive for their services, a compensation, which shall not be diminished during their continuance in office.**

The Constitution makes every effort to keep the courts independent of both the legislature and the president. The guarantee that judges shall hold office during "good behavior" means that, unless they are impeached and convicted, they can hold office for life. This protects judges from any threat of dismissal by the president. The rule that a judge's salary may not be reduced protects the judge against pressure from Congress, which could otherwise threaten to fix the salary so low that the judge could be forced to resign. See **Court; Supreme Court of the United States.**

Section 2. **(1) The judicial power shall extend to all cases, in law and equity, arising under this Constitution, the laws of the United States, and treaties made, or which shall be made, under their authority;—to all cases affecting ambassadors, other public ministers and consuls;—to all cases of admiralty and maritime jurisdiction;—to controversies to which the United States shall be a party;—to controversies between two or more states; [between a state and citizens of another state;] between citizens of different states;—between citizens of the same state claiming lands under grants of different states, and between a state, or the citizens thereof, and foreign states, [citizens or subjects].**

The right of the federal courts to handle "cases arising under this Constitution" is the basis of the Supreme Court's right to declare laws of Congress unconstitutional. This right of "judicial review" was established by Chief Justice John Marshall's historic decision in the case of *Marbury v. Madison* (1803).

The 11th Amendment to the Constitution set aside the phrase *between a state and citizens of another state.* A citizen of one state cannot sue another state in a federal court.

(2) In all cases affecting ambassadors, other public ministers and consuls, and those in which a state shall be party, the Supreme Court shall have original jurisdiction. In all the other cases before mentioned, the Supreme Court shall have appellate jurisdiction, both as to law and fact, with such exceptions, and under such regulations as the Congress shall make.

The statement that the Supreme Court has *original jurisdiction* in cases affecting the representatives of foreign countries and in cases to which a state is one of the parties means that cases of this kind go directly to the Supreme Court. In other kinds of cases, the Supreme Court has *appellate jurisdiction*. This means that the cases are tried first in a lower court and may come up to the Supreme Court for review if Congress authorizes an appeal. Congress cannot take away or modify the original jurisdiction of the Supreme Court. However, it can take away the right to appeal to the Supreme Court, or it can fix the conditions one must meet to present an appeal.

(3) The trial of all crimes, except in cases of impeachment, shall be by jury; and such trial shall be held in the state where the said crimes shall have been committed; but when not committed within any state, the trial shall be at such place or places as the Congress may by law have directed.

Section 3. (1) Treason against the United States, shall consist only in levying war against them, or in adhering to their enemies, giving them aid and comfort. No person shall be convicted of treason unless on the testimony of two witnesses to the same overt act, or on confession in open court.

No person can be convicted of treason against the United States unless he or she confesses in open court, or unless two witnesses testify that he or she has committed a treasonable act. Talking or thinking about committing a treasonable act is not treason.

(2) The Congress shall have power to declare the punishment of treason, but no attainder of treason shall work corruption of blood, or forfeiture except during the life of the person attainted.

The phrase *no attainder of treason shall work corruption of blood* means that the family of a traitor does not share the guilt. Formerly, an offender's family could also be punished.

Article IV

Relation of the states to each other

Much of this article was taken word for word from the old Articles of Confederation.

Section 1. Full faith and credit shall be given in each state to the public acts, records, and judicial proceedings of every other state. And the Congress may by general laws prescribe the manner in which such acts, records and proceedings shall be proved, and the effect thereof.

This section requires the states to honor one another's laws, records, and court rulings. The rule prevents a person from avoiding justice by leaving a state.

Section 2. (1) The citizens of each state shall be entitled to all privileges and immunities of citizens in the several states.

This means that citizens traveling from state to state are entitled to all the privileges and immunities that automatically go to citizens of those states. Some privileges, such as the right to vote, do not automatically go with citizenship, but require a period of residence and perhaps other qualifications. The word *citizen* in this provision does not include corporations.

(2) A person charged in any state with treason, felony, or other crime, who shall flee from justice, and be found in another state, shall on demand of the executive authority of the state from which he fled, be delivered up, to be removed to the state having jurisdiction of the crime.

If a person commits a crime in one state and flees to another,

the governor of the state in which the crime was committed can demand that the fugitive be handed over. Returning an accused person is called *extradition*. A few governors have refused to extradite, perhaps because the crime was committed many years ago, or because they believed the accused would not get a fair trial. It is not clear how the federal government could enforce this section.

(3) [No person held to service or labor in one state, under the laws thereof, escaping into another, shall, in consequence of any law or regulation therein, be discharged from such service or labor, but shall be delivered up on claim of the party to whom such service or labor may be due.]

A "person held to service or labor" was a slave or an *indentured servant* (a person bound by contract to serve someone for several years). No one is now bound to servitude in the United States, so this part of the Constitution no longer has any force, being overruled by the 13th Amendment.

Federal-state relations

Section 3. (1) New states may be admitted by the Congress into this Union; but no new state shall be formed or erected within the jurisdiction of any other state; nor any state be formed by the junction of two or more states, or parts of states, without the consent of the legislatures of the states concerned as well as of the Congress.

New states cannot be formed by dividing or joining existing states without the consent of the state legislatures and Congress. During the Civil War (1861-1865), Virginia fought for the Confederacy, but people in the western part of the state supported the Union. After West Virginia split from Virginia, Congress accepted the new state on the ground that Virginia had rebelled.

(2) The Congress shall have power to dispose of and make all needful rules and regulations respecting the territory or other property belonging to the United States; and nothing in this Constitution shall be so construed as to prejudice any claims of the United States, or of any particular state.

Section 4. The United States shall guarantee to every state in this Union a republican form of government, and shall protect each of them against invasion; and on application of the legislature, or of the executive (when the legislature cannot be convened) against domestic violence.

This section requires the federal government to make sure that every state has a "republican form of government." A republican government is one in which the people elect representatives to govern. The Supreme Court ruled that Congress, not the courts, must decide whether a state government is republican. According to the court, if Congress admits a state's senators and representatives, that action indicates that Congress considers the state's government republican.

The legislature or governor of a state can request federal aid in dealing with riots or other violence. During the Pullman strike of 1894, federal troops were sent to Illinois even though the governor said he did not want them.

Article V

Amending the Constitution

The Congress, whenever two-thirds of both houses shall deem it necessary, shall propose amendments to this Constitution, or, on the application of the legislatures of two-thirds of the several states, shall call a convention for proposing amendments, which, in either case, shall be valid to all intents and purposes, as part of this Constitution, when ratified by the legislatures of three-fourths of the several states, or by conventions in three-fourths thereof, as the one or the other mode of ratification may be proposed by the Congress; provided [that no amendment which may be made prior to the year one thousand eight hundred and eight shall in any manner affect the first and fourth clauses in the ninth section of the first article; and] that no state, without its consent, shall be deprived of its equal suffrage in the Senate.

Amendments may be proposed by a two-thirds vote of each house of Congress or by a national convention called by Congress at the request of two-thirds of the states. A national convention has never been called, in part because there are no established procedures for operating such a meeting and because of fear that such a convention could result in vast and possibly dangerous changes. To become part of the Constitution, amendments must be *ratified* (approved) by the legislatures of three-fourths of the states or by conventions in three-fourths of the states.

The framers of the Constitution purposely made it hard to put through an amendment. Congress has considered more than 9,000 amendments, but it has passed only 33 and submitted them to the states. Of these, 27 have been ratified. Only one amendment, the 21st, was ratified by state conventions. All the others were ratified by state legislatures.

The Constitution sets no time limit during which the states must ratify a proposed amendment. Ratification of the 27th Amendment took 203 years, longer by far than that of any other amendment. The amendment was first proposed in 1789 and did not become part of the Constitution until 1992. Nevertheless, the courts have held that amendments must be ratified within a "reasonable time" and that Congress decides what is reasonable. Since the early 1900's, most amendments have included a requirement that ratification be obtained within seven years.

Article VI

National debts

(1) All debts contracted and engagements entered into, before the adoption of this Constitution, shall be as valid against the United States under this Constitution, as under the Confederation.

This section promises that all debts and obligations made by the United States before the adoption of the Constitution will be honored.

Supremacy of the national government

(2) This Constitution, and the laws of the United States which shall be made in pursuance thereof; and all treaties made, or which shall be made, under the authority of the United States, shall be the supreme law of the land; and the judges in every state shall be bound thereby, anything in the constitution or laws of any state to the contrary notwithstanding.

This section, known as the *supremacy clause,* has been called *the linchpin of the Constitution*—that is, the part that keeps the entire structure from falling apart. It means simply that when state laws conflict with national laws, the national laws are superior. It also means that, to be valid, a national law must follow the Constitution.

(3) The senators and representatives before mentioned, and the members of the several state legislatures, and all executive and judicial officers, both of the United States and of the several states, shall be bound by oath or affirmation, to support this Constitution; but no religious test shall ever be required as a qualification to any office or public trust under the United States.

This section requires both federal and state officials to give supreme allegiance to the Constitution of the United States rather than to any state constitution. The section also forbids any religious test for holding federal office. The 14th Amendment applies the same rule to state and local governments.

Article VII

Ratifying the Constitution

The ratification of the conventions of nine states, shall be sufficient for the establishment of this Constitution between the states so ratifying the same.

Done in convention by the unanimous consent of the states present the seventeenth day of September in the year of our Lord one thousand seven hundred and eighty-seven and of the independence of the United States of America the twelfth. In witness whereof we have hereunto subscribed our names,

George Washington—president and deputy from Virginia

Delaware
George Read
Gunning Bedford, Jr.
John Dickinson
Richard Bassett
Jacob Broom

Maryland
James McHenry
Daniel of St. Thomas Jenifer
Daniel Carroll

Virginia
John Blair
James Madison, Jr.

North Carolina
William Blount
Richard Dobbs Spaight
Hugh Williamson

South Carolina
John Rutledge
Charles Cotesworth Pinckney
Charles Pinckney
Pierce Butler

Georgia
William Few
Abraham Baldwin

New Hampshire
John Langdon
Nicholas Gilman

Massachusetts
Nathaniel Gorham
Rufus King

Connecticut
William Samuel Johnson
Roger Sherman

New York
Alexander Hamilton

New Jersey
William Livingston
David Brearley
William Paterson
Jonathan Dayton

Pennsylvania
Benjamin Franklin
Thomas Mifflin
Robert Morris
George Clymer
Thomas FitzSimons
Jared Ingersoll
James Wilson
Gouverneur Morris

Amendments to the Constitution
The Bill of Rights

The first 10 amendments, known as the Bill of Rights, *were proposed on Sept. 25, 1789. They were ratified on Dec. 15, 1791. They were adopted because some states refused to approve the Constitution unless a bill of rights was added.*

The amendments protect individuals from various unjust acts of government. Originally, the amendments applied only to the federal government. But the 14th Amendment declares that no state can deprive any person of life, liberty, or property without "due process of law." The Supreme Court has interpreted those words to mean that most of the Bill of Rights applies to the states as well.

Amendment 1

Freedom of religion, speech, and the press; rights of assembly and petition

Congress shall make no law respecting an establishment of religion, or prohibiting the free exercise thereof; or abridging the freedom of speech, or of the press; or the right of the people peaceably to assemble, and to petition the government for a redress of grievances.

Many countries have made one religion the *established* (official) church and supported it with government funds. This amendment forbids Congress to set up or in any way provide for an established church. It has been interpreted to forbid government endorsement of, or aid to, religious doctrines. In addition, Congress may not pass laws limiting worship, speech, or the press, or preventing people from meeting peacefully. Congress also may not keep people from asking the government for relief from unfair treatment.

All the rights protected by this amendment have limits. For example, the guarantee of freedom of religion does not mean that the government must allow all religious practices. In the 1800's, some Mormons believed it was a man's religious duty to have more than one wife. The Supreme Court ruled that Mormons had to obey the laws forbidding that practice.

Amendment 2

Right to bear arms

A well-regulated militia, being necessary to the security of a free state, the right of the people to keep and bear arms shall not be infringed.

This amendment has been interpreted in two ways. Some people believe it gives ordinary citizens the right to possess firearms. Others believe it only gives each state the right to maintain its own militia.

Amendment 3

Housing of soldiers

No soldier shall, in time of peace be quartered in any house, without the consent of the owner, nor in time of war, but in a manner to be prescribed by law.

This amendment grew out of an old complaint against the British, who had forced people to take soldiers into their homes.

Amendment 4

Search and arrest warrants

The right of the people to be secure in their persons, houses, papers, and effects, against unreasonable searches and seizures, shall not be violated, and no warrants shall issue, but upon probable cause, supported by oath or affirmation, and particularly describing the place to be searched, and the persons or things to be seized.

This measure does not forbid legal authorities to search, to seize goods, or to arrest people. It simply requires that in most cases the authorities obtain a search or arrest warrant from a judge by showing the need for it. If a warrant cannot be obtained, the search or arrest is permitted only if the state's need for evidence outweighs the individual's right to privacy. In addition, the search or arrest may not be carried out in an unreasonable manner.

Amendment 5

Rights in criminal cases

No person shall be held to answer for a capital, or otherwise infamous crime, unless on a presentment or indictment of a grand jury, except in cases arising in the land or naval forces, or in the militia, when in actual service in time of war or public danger; nor shall any person be subject for the same offense to be twice put in jeopardy of life or limb; nor shall be compelled in any criminal case to be a witness against himself, nor be deprived of life, liberty, or property, without due process of law; nor shall private property be taken for public use, without just compensation.

A *capital crime* is one punishable by death. An *infamous crime* is one punishable by death or imprisonment. This amendment guarantees that no one has to stand trial for such a federal crime unless he or she has been *indicted* (accused) by a *grand jury*. A grand jury is a special group of people selected to decide whether there is enough evidence against a person to hold a trial. A person cannot be *put in double jeopardy* (tried twice) for the same offense by the same government. But a person may be tried a second time if a jury cannot agree on a verdict, if a mistrial is declared for some other reason, or if the person re-

quests a new trial. The amendment also guarantees that people cannot be forced to testify against themselves.

The statement that no person shall be deprived of life, liberty, or property "without due process of law" expresses one of the most important rules of the Constitution. The same words are in the 14th Amendment as restrictions on the power of the states. The phrase expresses the idea that a person's life, liberty, and property are not subject to the uncontrolled power of the government. This idea can be traced to Magna Carta, which provided that the king could not imprison or harm a person "except by the lawful judgment of his peers or by the law of the land." Due process is a vague rule, and the Supreme Court has applied it to widely different cases. At one time, the court used the due-process rule to strike down laws that prevented people from using their property as they wished. In 1857, for example, the court overturned the Missouri Compromise, which prohibited slavery in certain U.S. territories. The court said the compromise unjustly prevented slave owners from taking slaves—their property—into the territories. Today, the courts use the rule to strike down laws that interfere with personal liberty.

The amendment also forbids the government to take a person's property for public use without fair payment. The government's right to take property for public use is called *eminent domain.* Governments use it to acquire land for highways, schools, and other public facilities.

Amendment 6

Rights to a fair trial

In all criminal prosecutions, the accused shall enjoy the right to a speedy and public trial, by an impartial jury of the state and district wherein the crime shall have been committed, which district shall have been previously ascertained by law, and to be informed of the nature and cause of the accusation; to be confronted with the witnesses against him; to have compulsory process for obtaining witnesses in his favor, and to have the assistance of counsel for his defense.

A person accused of crime must have a prompt, public trial by an open-minded jury. The requirement for a speedy and public trial grew out of the fact that some political trials in England had been delayed for years and then were held in secret. Accused persons must be informed of the charges against them and must be allowed to meet the witnesses against them face to face. Otherwise, innocent individuals may be punished if a court allows the testimony of unknown witnesses to be used as evidence. This amendment guarantees that persons on trial can face and cross-examine those who have accused them. They may be able to show that their accusers lied or made a mistake. Finally, accused individuals must have a lawyer to defend them if they want one.

Amendment 7

Rights in civil cases

In suits at common law, where the value in controversy shall exceed twenty dollars, the right of a trial by jury shall be preserved, and no fact tried by a jury, shall be otherwise re-examined in any court of the United States, than according to the rules of the common law.

The framers of the Constitution considered the right to jury trial extremely important. In the Sixth Amendment, they provided for jury trials in criminal cases. In the Seventh Amendment, they provided for such trials in civil suits where the amount contested exceeds $20. The amendment applies only to civil cases in federal courts. But because of a great decline in the value of the dollar over the years, it now applies to almost all such cases. Most states also call for jury trials in civil cases.

Amendment 8

Bails, fines, and punishments

Excessive bail shall not be required, nor excessive fines imposed, nor cruel and unusual punishments inflicted.

Bails, fines, and punishments must be fair and humane. In the case of *Furman v. Georgia,* the Supreme Court ruled in 1972 that capital punishment, as it was then imposed, violated this amendment. The court held that the death penalty was cruel and unusual punishment because it was not applied fairly and uniformly. Many states then adopted new laws designed to meet the court's objections. The court has ruled that the death penalty may be imposed if certain standards are applied to guard against its arbitrary use.

Amendment 9

Rights retained by the people

The enumeration in the Constitution, of certain rights, shall not be construed to deny or disparage others retained by the people.

Some people feared that the listing of some rights in the Bill of Rights would be interpreted to mean that other rights not listed were not protected. This amendment was adopted to prevent such an interpretation.

Amendment 10

Powers retained by the states and the people

The powers not delegated to the United States by the Constitution, nor prohibited by it to the states, are reserved to the states respectively, or to the people.

This amendment was adopted to reassure people that the national government would not swallow up the states. It confirms that the states or the people retain all powers not given to the national government. For example, the states have authority over such matters as marriage and divorce. But the Constitution says the federal government can make any laws "necessary and proper" to carry out its specific powers. This rule makes it hard to determine the exact rights of states.

Amendment 11

Lawsuits against states

This amendment was proposed on March 4, 1794, and ratified on Feb. 7, 1795. However, the amendment was not proclaimed until 1798 because of delays that occurred in certifying the ratification.

The judicial power of the United States shall not be construed to extend to any suit in law or equity, commenced or prosecuted against one of the United States by citizens of another state, or by citizens or subjects of any foreign state.

This amendment makes it impossible for a citizen of one state to sue another state in federal court. The amendment resulted from the 1793 case of *Chisholm v. Georgia,* in which a man from South Carolina sued the state of Georgia over an inheritance. Georgia argued that it could not be sued in federal court, but the Supreme Court ruled that the state could be. Georgia then led a movement to adopt this amendment. However, individuals can still sue state authorities in federal court for depriving them of their constitutional rights.

Amendment 12

Election of the president and vice president

This amendment was proposed on Dec. 9, 1803, and ratified on July 27, 1804.

The electors shall meet in their respective states and vote by ballot for president and vice president, one of whom, at least, shall not be an inhabitant of the same state with themselves; they shall name in their ballots the person voted for as president, and in distinct ballots the person voted for as vice president, and they shall make distinct lists of all persons voted for as president, and of all persons voted for as vice president, and of the number of votes for each, which lists they

shall sign and certify, and transmit sealed to the seat of the government of the United States, directed to the president of the Senate;——the president of the Senate shall, in the presence of the Senate and House of Representatives, open all the certificates and the votes shall then be counted;——the person having the greatest number of votes for president, shall be the president, if such number be a majority of the whole number of electors appointed; and if no person have such majority, then from the persons having the highest numbers not exceeding three on the list of those voted for as president, the House of Representatives shall choose immediately, by ballot, the president. But in choosing the president, the votes shall be taken by states, the representation from each state having one vote; a quorum for this purpose shall consist of a member or members from two-thirds of the states, and a majority of all the states shall be necessary to a choice. And if the House of Representatives shall not choose a president whenever the right of choice shall devolve upon them, [before the fourth day of March next following,] then the vice president shall act as president, as in the case of the death or other constitutional disability of the president.——The person having the greatest number of votes as vice president, shall be the vice president, if such number be a majority of the whole number of electors appointed, and if no person have a majority, then from the two highest numbers on the list, the Senate shall choose the vice president; a quorum for the purpose shall consist of two-thirds of the whole number of senators, and a majority of the whole number shall be necessary to a choice. But no person constitutionally ineligible to the office of president shall be eligible to that of vice president of the United States.

This amendment provides that members of the Electoral College, called *electors,* vote for one person as president and for another as vice president. The amendment resulted from the election of 1800. At that time, each elector voted for two men, not saying which he wanted for president. The man who received the most votes became president, and the runner-up became vice president. Thomas Jefferson, the presidential candidate, and Aaron Burr, the vice presidential candidate, received the same number of votes. The tie threw the election into the House of Representatives. The House chose Jefferson but took so long that people feared it would fail to choose before Inauguration Day. The House has chosen one other president—John Quincy Adams in 1825.

Amendment 13

Abolition of slavery

This amendment was proposed on Jan. 31, 1865, and ratified on Dec. 6, 1865.

Section 1. Neither slavery nor involuntary servitude, except as a punishment for crime whereof the party shall have been duly convicted, shall exist within the United States, or any place subject to their jurisdiction.

President Abraham Lincoln's Emancipation Proclamation of 1863 had declared slaves free in the Confederate States still in rebellion. This amendment completed the abolition of slavery in the United States.

Section 2. Congress shall have power to enforce this article by appropriate legislation.

Amendment 14

Civil rights

This amendment was proposed on June 13, 1866, and ratified on July 9, 1868.

Section 1. All persons born or naturalized in the United States, and subject to the jurisdiction thereof, are citizens of the United States and of the state wherein they reside. No state shall make or enforce any law which shall abridge the privileges or immunities of citizens of the United States; nor shall any state deprive any person of life, liberty, or property, without due process of law; nor deny to any person within its jurisdiction the equal protection of the laws.

The principal purpose of this amendment was to make former slaves citizens of both the United States and the state in which they lived. The amendment also forbids the states to deny equal rights to any person. The terms of the amendment clarify how citizenship is acquired. State citizenship is a by-product of national citizenship. By living in a state, every U.S. citizen automatically becomes a citizen of that state as well. All persons *naturalized* (granted citizenship) according to law are U.S. citizens. People born in the United States are also citizens regardless of the nationality of their parents, unless they are diplomatic representatives of another country or enemies during a wartime occupation. Such cases are exceptions because the parents are not "subject to the jurisdiction" of the United States. The amendment does not grant citizenship to Indians on reservations, but Congress passed a law that did so.

The phrase "due process of law" has been ruled to forbid the states to violate most rights protected by the Bill of Rights. It has also been interpreted as protecting other rights by its own force. The statement that a state cannot deny anyone "equal protection of the laws" has provided the basis for many Supreme Court rulings on civil rights. For example, the court has outlawed segregation in public schools. The judges declared that "equal protection" means a state must make sure all children, regardless of race, have an equal opportunity for education.

Section 2. Representatives shall be apportioned among the several states according to their respective numbers, counting the whole number of persons in each state, [excluding Indians not taxed]. But when the right to vote at any election for the choice of electors for president and vice president of the United States, representatives in Congress, the executive and judicial officers of a state, or the members of the legislature thereof, is denied to any of the male inhabitants of such state, being twenty-one years of age, and citizens of the United States, or in any way abridged, except for participation in rebellion, or other crime, the basis of representation therein shall be reduced in the proportion which the number of such male citizens shall bear to the whole number of male citizens twenty-one years of age in such state.

This section proposes a penalty for states which refuse to give the vote in federal elections to all adult male citizens. States which restrict voting can have their representation in Congress cut down. This penalty has never been used. The section has been set aside by the 19th and 26th amendments.

Section 3. No person shall be a senator or representative in Congress, or elector of president and vice president, or hold any office, civil or military, under the United States, or under any state, who, having previously taken an oath, as a member of Congress, or as an officer of the United States, or as a member of any state legislature, or as an executive or judicial officer of any state, to support the Constitution of the United States, shall have engaged in insurrection or rebellion against the same, or given aid or comfort to the enemies thereof. But Congress may by a vote of two-thirds of each House, remove such disability.

This section's purpose was to keep federal officers who joined the Confederacy from becoming federal officers again. Congress could vote to overlook such a record.

Section 4. The validity of the public debt of the United States, authorized by law, including debts incurred for payment of pensions and bounties for services in suppressing insurrection or rebellion, shall not be questioned. But neither the United States nor any state shall assume or pay any debt or obligation incurred in aid of insurrection or rebellion against the United States, or any claim for the loss of emancipation of any slave; but all such debts, obligations and claims shall be held illegal and void.

This section ensured that the Union's Civil War debt would be paid, but voided all war debts run up by the Confederacy.

The section also said that former slaveowners would not be paid for slaves who were freed.

Section 5. The Congress shall have power to enforce, by appropriate legislation, the provisions of this article.

Amendment 15

Black suffrage

This amendment was proposed on Feb. 26, 1869, and ratified on Feb. 3, 1870.

Section 1. The right of citizens of the United States to vote shall not be denied or abridged by the United States or by any state on account of race, color, or previous condition of servitude.

African Americans who had been slaves became citizens under the terms of the 14th Amendment. The 15th Amendment does not specifically say that all blacks must be allowed to vote. The states are free to set qualifications for voters. But a voter cannot be denied the ballot because of race. Attempts by some states to do this indirectly have been struck down by Supreme Court decisions, federal and state laws, and the 24th Amendment. See **Voting.**

Section 2. The Congress shall have power to enforce this article by appropriate legislation.

Amendment 16

Income taxes

This amendment was proposed on July 12, 1909, and ratified on Feb. 3, 1913.

The Congress shall have power to lay and collect taxes on incomes, from whatever source derived, without apportionment among the several states, and without regard to any census or enumeration.

In 1894, Congress passed an income tax law, but the Supreme Court declared it unconstitutional. This amendment authorized Congress to levy such a tax.

Amendment 17

Direct election of senators

This amendment was proposed on May 13, 1912, and ratified on April 8, 1913.

(1) The Senate of the United States shall be composed of two senators from each state, elected by the people thereof for six years; and each senator shall have one vote. The electors in each state shall have the qualifications requisite for electors of the most numerous branch of the state legislatures.

(2) When vacancies happen in the representation of any state in the Senate, the executive authority of such state shall issue writs of election to fill such vacancies: Provided, That the legislature of any state may empower the executive thereof to make temporary appointments until the people fill the vacancies by election as the legislature may direct.

(3) This amendment shall not be so construed as to affect the election or term of any senator chosen before it becomes valid as part of the Constitution.

This amendment takes the power of electing senators from the state legislatures and gives it to the people of the states.

Amendment 18

Prohibition of liquor

This amendment was proposed on Dec. 18, 1917, and ratified on Jan. 16, 1919.

Section 1. After one year from the ratification of this article the manufacture, sale, or transportation of intoxicating liquors within, the importation thereof into, or the exportation thereof from the United States and all territory subject to the jurisdiction thereof for beverage purposes is hereby prohibited.

Section 2. The Congress and the several states shall have concurrent power to enforce this article by appropriate legislation.

Section 3. This article shall be inoperative unless it shall have been ratified as an amendment to the Constitution by the legislatures of the several states, as provided in the Constitution, within seven years from the date of the submission hereof to the states by the Congress.

This is the prohibition amendment, which forbade people to make, sell, or transport liquor. The amendment was widely ignored by the people and was repealed by the 21st Amendment in 1933.

Amendment 19

Woman suffrage

This amendment was proposed on June 4, 1919, and ratified on Aug. 18, 1920.

Section 1. The right of citizens of the United States to vote shall not be denied or abridged by the United States or by any state on account of sex.

Section 2. Congress shall have power to enforce this article by appropriate legislation.

Amendments giving women the right to vote were introduced in Congress one after another for more than 40 years before this one was finally passed.

Amendment 20

Terms of the president and Congress

This amendment was proposed on March 2, 1932, and ratified on Jan. 23, 1933.

Section 1. The terms of the president and vice president shall end at noon on the 20th day of January, and the terms of senators and representatives at noon on the third day of January, of the year in which such terms would have ended if this article had not been ratified; and the terms of their successors shall then begin.

Section 2. The Congress shall assemble at least once in every year, and such meeting shall begin at noon on the third day of January, unless they shall by law appoint a different day.

Section 3. If, at the time fixed for the beginning of the term of the president, the president elect shall have died, the vice president elect shall become president. If a president shall not have been chosen before the time fixed for the beginning of his term, or if the president elect shall have failed to qualify, then the vice president elect shall act as president until a president shall have qualified; and the Congress may by law provide for the case wherein neither a president elect nor a vice president elect shall have qualified, declaring who shall then act as president, or the manner in which one who is to act shall be selected, and such person shall act accordingly until a president or vice president shall have qualified.

Section 4. The Congress may by law provide for the case of the death of any of the persons from whom the House of Representatives may choose a president whenever the right of choice shall have devolved upon them, and for the case of the death of any of the persons from whom the Senate may choose a vice president whenever the right of choice shall have devolved upon them.

Section 5. Sections 1 and 2 shall take effect on the 15th day of October following the ratification of this article.

Section 6. This article shall be inoperative unless it shall have been ratified as an amendment to the Constitution by the legislatures of three-fourths of the several states within seven years from the date of its submission.

This *lame duck amendment* moves the date that newly elected presidents and members of Congress take office closer to election time. A *lame duck* is an official who continues to serve though not reelected. Before the amendment came into force, defeated members of Congress continued to hold office for four months.

Amendment 21

Repeal of prohibition

This amendment was proposed on Feb. 20, 1933, and ratified on Dec. 5, 1933.

Section 1. The eighteenth article of amendment to the Constitution of the United States is hereby repealed.

Section 2. The transportation or importation into any state, territory, or possession of the United States for delivery or use therein of intoxicating liquors, in violation of the laws thereof, is hereby prohibited.

Section 3. This article shall be inoperative unless it shall have been ratified as an amendment to the Constitution by conventions in the several states, as provided in the Constitution, within seven years from the date of the submission hereof to the states by the Congress.

This amendment repeals the 18th Amendment. Section 2 promises federal help to "dry" states in enforcing their own laws.

Amendment 22

Limitation of presidents to two terms

This amendment was proposed on March 24, 1947, and ratified on Feb. 27, 1951.

Section 1. No person shall be elected to the office of the president more than twice, and no person who has held the office of president, or acted as president, for more than two years of a term to which some other person was elected president shall be elected to the office of the president more than once. But this article shall not apply to any person holding the office of president when this article was proposed by the Congress, and shall not prevent any person who may be holding the office of president, or acting as president, during the term within which this article becomes operative from holding the office of president or acting as president during the remainder of such term.

Section 2. This article shall be inoperative unless it shall have been ratified as an amendment to the Constitution by the legislatures of three-fourths of the several states within seven years from the day of its submission to the states by the Congress.

This amendment provides that no person can be elected president more than twice. Nobody who has served for more than two years of someone else's term can be elected more than once. A president can hold office for no more than 10 years. The amendment was supported by those who thought Franklin D. Roosevelt should not serve four terms. No other president had run for election to more than two consecutive terms.

Amendment 23

Suffrage in the District of Columbia

This amendment was proposed on June 16, 1960, and ratified on March 29, 1961.

Section 1. The district constituting the seat of government of the United States shall appoint in such manner as the Congress may direct: A number of electors of president and vice president equal to the whole number of senators and representatives in Congress to which the district would be entitled if it were a state, but in no event more than the least populous state; they shall be in addition to those appointed by the states, but they shall be considered, for the purposes of the election of president and vice president, to be electors appointed by a state; and they shall meet in the district and perform such duties as provided by the twelfth article of amendment.

Section 2. The Congress shall have power to enforce this article by appropriate legislation.

This amendment allows citizens of the District of Columbia to vote in presidential elections. However, they cannot vote for members of Congress.

Amendment 24

Poll taxes

This amendment was proposed on Aug. 27, 1962, and ratified on Jan. 23, 1964.

Section 1. The right of citizens of the United States to vote in any primary or other election for president or vice president, for electors for president or vice president, or for senator or representative in Congress, shall not be denied or abridged by the United States or any state by reason of failure to pay any poll tax or other tax.

Section 2. The Congress shall have power to enforce this article by appropriate legislation.

This amendment forbids making voters pay a *poll tax* before they can vote in a national election. A poll tax, which is also called a *head tax,* is a tax collected equally from everyone. Some states once used such taxes to keep poor people and African Americans from voting. The term *poll tax* does not mean a tax on voting. It comes from the old English word *poll,* meaning *head.*

Amendment 25

Presidential disability and succession

This amendment was proposed on July 6, 1965, and ratified on Feb. 10, 1967.

Section 1. In case of the removal of the president from office or of his death or resignation, the vice president shall become president.

Section 2. Whenever there is a vacancy in the office of the vice president, the president shall nominate a vice president who shall take office upon confirmation by a majority vote of both houses of Congress.

This section provides for filling a vacancy in the vice presidency. In 1973, Gerald R. Ford became the first person chosen vice president under this provision. He was nominated by President Richard M. Nixon after Vice President Spiro T. Agnew resigned.

In 1974, Nixon resigned and Ford became president. Nelson A. Rockefeller then became vice president under the new procedure. For the first time, the United States had both a president and a vice president who had not been elected to their office. Before this amendment came into force, vacancies in the vice presidency remained unfilled until the next presidential election.

Section 3. Whenever the president transmits to the president pro tempore of the Senate and the speaker of the House of Representatives his written declaration that he is unable to discharge the powers and duties of his office, and until he transmits to them a written declaration to the contrary, such powers and duties shall be discharged by the vice president as acting president.

This section provides that the vice president succeeds to the presidency if the president becomes disabled. Vice President George Bush became the first acting president. He officially held the position eight hours on July 13, 1985, when President Ronald Reagan had cancer surgery.

Section 4. Whenever the vice president and majority of either the principal officers of the executive departments or of such other body as Congress may by law provide, transmit to the president pro tempore of the Senate and the speaker of the House of Representatives their written declaration that the president is unable to discharge the powers and duties of his office, the vice president shall immediately assume the powers and duties of the office as acting president.

Thereafter, when the president transmits to the president pro tempore of the Senate and the speaker of the House of Representatives his written declaration that no inability exists, he shall resume the powers and duties of his office unless the vice president and a majority of either the principal officers of the executive department or of such other body as Congress may by law provide, transmit within four days to the president pro tempore of the Senate and the speaker of the House of Representatives their written declaration that the president is unable to discharge the powers and duties of his office. Thereupon Congress shall decide the issue, assembling within forty-eight hours for that purpose if not in session. If the Congress, within twenty-one days after receipt of the latter written declaration, or, if Congress is not in session, within twenty-one days after Congress is required to assemble, determines by two-thirds vote of both houses that the president is unable to discharge the powers and duties of his office, the vice president shall continue to discharge the same as acting president; otherwise, the president shall resume the powers and duties of his office.

Amendment 26

Suffrage for 18-year-olds

This amendment was proposed on March 23, 1971, and ratified on July 1, 1971.

Section 1. The right of citizens of the United States, who are eighteen years of age or older, to vote shall not be denied or abridged by the United States or by any state on account of age.

Section 2. The Congress shall have power to enforce this article by appropriate legislation.

This amendment grants the vote to citizens 18 years of age or older. Passed during the Vietnam War, it reflected the opinion of many people of the time that young men who are old enough to be drafted into the armed forces should be able to vote for or against officials who lead the nation into war.

Amendment 27

Congressional salaries

This amendment was proposed on Sept. 25, 1789, and ratified on May 7, 1992.

No law varying the compensation for the services of the senators and representatives shall take effect, until an election of representatives shall have intervened.

This amendment prevents Congress from passing immediate salary increases for itself. It requires that salary changes passed by Congress cannot take effect until after the next congressional election. The amendment had been passed in 1789 and sent to the states for ratification. It had no time limit for ratification. The amendment became part of the Constitution in 1992, after Michigan became the 38th state to ratify it.

Annotations by Bruce Allen Murphy

Court is a government institution that settles legal disputes and administers justice. Courts resolve conflicts involving individuals, organizations, and governments. Courts also decide the legal guilt or innocence of individuals accused of crimes and sentence the guilty.

All courts are presided over by judges. These officials decide all questions of law, including what evidence is fair to use. In many cases, the judge also decides the truth or falsity of each side's claims. In other cases, a jury decides any questions of fact. The word *court* may refer to a judge alone or to a judge and jury acting together. It also may refer to the place where legal disputes are settled.

Some court rulings affect only the people involved in a case. Other decisions deal with broad public issues, such as freedom of the press, racial discrimination, and the rights of individuals accused of a crime. In this way, courts serve as a powerful means of social and political change.

Types of courts

Courts differ in their *jurisdiction* (authority to decide a case). Generally, courts are classified as *trial courts* or *appellate courts,* and as *criminal courts* or *civil courts.*

Trial and appellate courts. Nearly all legal cases begin in trial courts, also called *courts of original jurisdiction.* These courts may have general jurisdiction or limited, also called *special,* jurisdiction. Courts of general jurisdiction hear many types of cases. The major trial court of any county, state, or other political unit is a court of general jurisdiction. Courts of limited or special jurisdiction specialize in certain types of cases, such as those involving juvenile offenders or traffic violations.

The losing side often has the right to *appeal*—that is, to ask that aspects of the case be reconsidered by a higher court called an appellate or *appeals court.* Appellate courts review cases decided by trial courts if the losing side questions the ruling of the lower court on a matter of law. Appellate courts cannot review a trial court's decision on the facts.

Criminal and civil courts. Criminal courts deal with actions considered harmful to society, such as murder and robbery. In criminal cases, the government takes legal action against an individual. The sentences handed down by criminal courts range from probation and fines to imprisonment and, in some states, death.

Civil courts settle disputes involving people's private relations with one another. Civil suits involve such non-criminal matters as contracts, family relationships, and accidental injuries. In most civil cases, an individual or organization sues another individual or organization. Most civil decisions do not involve a prison sentence, though the party at fault may be ordered to pay damages.

How courts work

How criminal courts work. Most individuals arrested on suspicion of a crime appear before a judge called a *magistrate* within 24 hours after the arrest. In cases involving minor offenses, the magistrate conducts a trial and sentences the guilty. In more serious cases, the magistrate decides whether to keep the *defendant* (accused person) in jail or to release him or her on bail. The magistrate also may appoint a state-paid defense attorney, called a *public defender,* to represent a defendant who cannot afford a lawyer.

Pretrial proceedings. In a case involving a serious crime, the police give their evidence of the suspect's guilt to a government attorney called a *prosecutor.* In some states, the prosecutor formally charges the defendant in a document called an *information.* The prosecutor presents the information and other evidence to a magistrate at a *preliminary hearing.* If the magistrate decides that there is *probable cause* (good reason for assuming) that the defendant committed the crime, the magistrate orders the defendant held for trial. In other states and in federal courts, the prosecutor presents the evidence to a *grand jury,* a group of citizens who decide whether the evidence justifies bringing the case to trial. If the grand jury finds sufficient evidence for a trial, it issues a formal accusation called an *indictment* against the suspect.

The defendant then appears in a court of general jurisdiction to answer the charges. This hearing is called an *arraignment.* If the defendant pleads guilty, the judge pronounces sentence. Many defendants plead guilty, rather than go to trial, in return for a reduced charge or a shorter sentence. This practice is called *plea bargaining.* Most criminal cases in the United States are settled in this way. But if the accused pleads not guilty, the case goes to trial.

Trial. The defendant may request a jury trial or a *bench trial,* which is a trial before a judge. The jury or judge must decide if the evidence presented by the prosecutor proves the defendant guilty "beyond a reasonable doubt." If not, the defendant must be *acquitted* (found not guilty).

If the defendant is found guilty, the judge pronounces sentence. Convicted defendants may take their case to an appellate court. However, prosecutors may not appeal an acquittal because the United States Constitution forbids the government to *put a person in double jeopardy* (try a person twice) for the same crime.

How civil courts work. A civil lawsuit begins when an individual or organization, called the *plaintiff,* files a complaint against another individual or organization, called the *defendant.* The complaint formally states the injuries or losses the plaintiff believes were caused by the defendant's actions. The complaint also asks for a certain amount of money in damages.

The defendant receives a *summons,* a notice that a complaint has been filed. It directs the defendant to appear in court on a certain date. The defendant then files a document called an *answer.* The answer contains the defendant's version of the facts of the case and asks the court to dismiss the suit. The defendant also may file a *counterclaim* against the plaintiff.

In most cases, the complaint and the answer are the first of a series of documents called the *pleadings.* In the pleadings, the plaintiff and defendant state their own claims and challenge the claims of their opponents. Most civil cases are settled out of court on the basis of the pleadings. However, if serious questions of fact remain, a formal *discovery* takes place. This procedure forces each *litigant* (party involved in the case) to reveal the testimony or records that would be introduced as evidence in court. If the case still remains in dispute after the discovery, it goes to trial.

Civil cases may be decided by a judge or by a jury. The judge or jury determines who is at fault and how much must be paid in damages. Both sides may appeal.

Courts in the United States

The United States has a dual system of federal and state courts. Federal courts receive their authority from the U.S. Constitution and federal laws. State courts receive their powers from state constitutions and laws.

Federal courts handle both criminal and civil cases involving the Constitution or federal laws, and cases in which the U.S. government is one of the sides. They also try cases between individuals or groups from different states, and cases involving other countries or their citizens. They handle *maritime* (sea) cases, bankruptcy actions, and cases of patent and copyright violation.

The federal court system includes district courts, courts of appeals, and the Supreme Court of the United States. District courts are federal courts of *original jurisdiction*—that is, they are the first courts to hear most cases involving a violation of federal law. The United States and its possessions have about 95 district courts. Each state has at least one such court.

Courts of appeals try federal cases on appeal from district courts. They also review the decisions made by such federal agencies as the Securities and Exchange Commission and the National Labor Relations Board. The United States is divided into 12 *circuits* (districts), each of which has a court of appeals. An additional federal court of appeals, the United States Court of Appeals for the Federal Circuit, has nationwide jurisdiction.

The Supreme Court of the United States is the highest court in the nation. A person who loses a case either in a federal court of appeals or in the highest state court may appeal to the Supreme Court, but it may refuse to review many cases. In addition to its appellate jurisdiction, the court has original jurisdiction over cases involving two states or representatives of other countries.

The federal court system also includes several specialized courts. The United States Court of Federal Claims hears cases involving claims against the federal government. The Court of International Trade settles disputes over import duties. Taxpayers ordered to pay additional federal income taxes may appeal to the Tax Court of the United States. Military courts, called *courts-martial,* have jurisdiction over offenses committed by members of the armed forces. The Court of Military Appeals reviews court-martial rulings.

State courts. The lowest state courts are courts of limited or special jurisdiction. Some of these courts handle a variety of minor criminal and civil cases. Such courts include *police courts, magistrate's courts,* or *county courts,* and *justices of the peace.* Other lower courts specialize in only one type of case. For example, *small-claims courts* try cases that involve small amounts of money. *Probate* or *surrogate courts* handle wills and disputes over inheritances. Other specialized courts include *courts of domestic relations, juvenile courts,* and *traffic courts.*

Courts of general jurisdiction rank above courts of limited jurisdiction. These higher courts are known as *circuit courts, superior courts,* or *courts of common pleas.* About half the states have intermediate appeals courts, which hear appeals from courts of general juris-

diction. In some states, courts of general jurisdiction and appellate courts handle both criminal and civil cases. Other states have separate divisions on both levels. The highest court in most states is its supreme court.

Courts around the world

Courts in other countries. The judicial systems of most countries are based on either *common law* or *civil law.* Some combine the features of both systems. This use of the term *civil law* refers to a legal system. It should not be confused with the branch of law dealing with people's private relations with one another.

In common-law systems, judges base their decisions primarily on *precedents,* earlier court decisions in similar cases. Most English-speaking countries, including the United States, the United Kingdom, Canada, and Australia, have common-law systems.

Civil-law systems rely more strictly on written *statutes* (legislative acts). Judges may refer to precedents, but they must base every ruling on a particular statute and not on precedent alone. Most European, Latin-American, and Asian countries, and some African nations, have civil-law systems.

International courts deal only with disputes between nations. The International Court of Justice, the highest judicial body of the United Nations (UN), meets at The Hague in the Netherlands. Its decisions are not binding unless the nations involved in the dispute agree to accept its rulings.

History

Early courts. Tribal councils or groups of elders served as the first courts. They settled disputes on the basis of local custom. Later civilizations developed written legal codes. The need to interpret these codes and to apply them to specific situations resulted in the development of formal courts. For example, the ancient Hebrews had a supreme council, called the *Sanhedrin,* which interpreted Hebrew law.

The ancient Romans developed the first complete legal code as well as an advanced court system. After the collapse of the West Roman Empire in the A.D. 400's, the Roman judicial system gradually died out in western Europe. It was replaced by *feudal* courts, which were conducted by local lords. These courts had limited jurisdiction and decided cases on the basis of local customs.

Development of civil-law and common-law courts. During the early 1100's, universities in Italy began to train lawyers according to the principles of ancient Roman law. Roman law, which relied strictly on written codes, gradually replaced much of the feudal court system throughout mainland Europe. In the early 1800's, the French ruler Napoleon I used Roman law as the foundation of the *Code Napoléon.* This code, a type of civil law, became the basis of the court system in most European and Latin-American countries.

By the 1200's, England had established a nationwide system of courts. These courts developed a body of law called *common law* that applied uniformly to people everywhere in the country. Common-law courts followed traditional legal principles and based their decisions on precedents. English common law became the basis of the court system for most countries colonized by England, including the United States and Canada.

United States court system

The U.S. court system has two levels—state and federal. State courts handle cases that affect state constitutions and laws. Federal courts hear cases that involve the U.S. Constitution and federal laws, plus cases in which the U.S. government is one of the sides.

WORLD BOOK illustrations by Bill and Judie Anderson

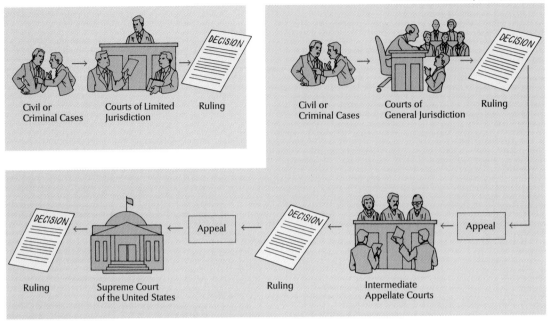

State courts vary according to their authority. Courts of limited jurisdiction decide minor cases. Courts of general jurisdiction hear more serious cases. These cases may be appealed to intermediate appellate courts, if the state has them, or go directly to the supreme court of the state.

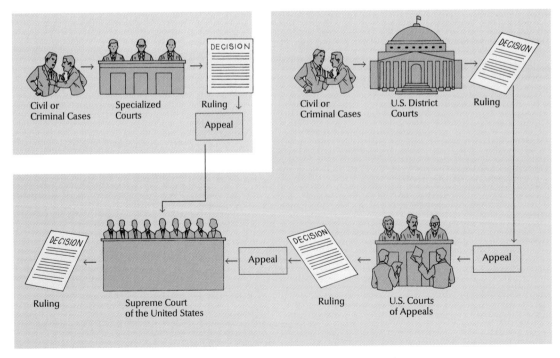

Federal courts include district courts, courts of appeals, and the Supreme Court of the United States. The federal system also has several specialized courts. The Supreme Court of the United States may review cases from state supreme courts if a question of federal law is involved.

Development of U.S. courts. The American Colonies based their courts on the English common-law system. These colonial courts became state courts after the United States became an independent nation in 1776. Only Louisiana modeled its court system on civil law. In 1789, Congress passed the Judiciary Act, which created the federal court system.   Jack M. Kress

See also **Supreme Court of the United States.**

Additional resources

Coffin, Frank M. *On Appeal: Courts, Lawyering, and Judging.* Norton, 1994.
Surrency, Erwin C. *History of the Federal Courts.* Oceana, 1987.
Warner, Ralph. *Everybody's Guide to Small Claims Court.* 6th ed. Nolo, 1996.

Web sites

Supreme Court of the United States
http://www.supremecourtus.gov/
The official site of the U.S. Supreme Court.

The Courthouse
http://www.ljx.com/courthouse/index.html
The full text of decisions of the U.S. Circuit Courts of Appeals.

Understanding the Federal Courts
http://www.uscourts.gov/understanding_courts/899_toc.htm
An overview of the entire U.S. federal court system.

Democracy is a form of government, a way of life, a goal or ideal, and a political philosophy. The term also refers to a country that has a democratic form of government. The word *democracy* means *rule by the people.* United States President Abraham Lincoln described such self-government as "government of the people, by the people, for the people."

The citizens of a democracy take part in government either directly or indirectly. In a *direct democracy,* also called a *pure democracy,* the people meet in one place to make the laws for their community. Such democracy was practiced in the ancient Greek city-state of Athens, and exists today in the New England town meeting.

Most modern democracy is *indirect democracy,* which is also known as *representative democracy.* In

©David R. Frazier

Free elections are held regularly in a democracy. The people use a secret ballot to elect officials to represent them and to run the government on all levels.

large communities—cities, states, provinces, or countries—it is impossible for all the people to meet as a group. Instead, they elect a certain number of their fellow citizens to represent them in making decisions about laws and other matters. An assembly of representatives may be called a council, a legislature, a parliament, or a congress. Government by the people through their freely elected representatives is sometimes called a *republican government* or a *democratic republic.*

Most voting decisions in democracies are based on majority rule—that is, more than half the votes cast. A decision by *plurality* may be used when three or more candidates stand for election. A candidate with a plurality receives more votes than any other candidate, but does not necessarily have a majority of the votes. In some countries, elections to legislative bodies are conducted according to *proportional representation.* Such representation awards a political party a percentage of seats in the legislature in proportion to its share of the total vote cast.

Throughout history, the most important aspects of the democratic way of life have been the principles of individual equality and freedom. Accordingly, citizens in a democracy should be entitled to equal protection of their persons, possessions, and rights; have equal opportunity to pursue their lives and careers; and have equal rights of political participation. In addition, the people should enjoy freedom from undue interference and domination by government. They should be free, within the framework of the law, to believe, behave, and express themselves as they wish.

Democratic societies seek to guarantee their citizens certain freedoms, including freedom of religion, freedom of the press, and freedom of speech. Ideally, citizens also should be guaranteed freedom of association and of assembly, freedom from arbitrary arrest and imprisonment, and the freedom to work and live where and how they choose.

Some people in democratic states have been eager to increase the role of government in society in order to make material conditions more equal for everyone. But other people have been concerned that the extension of government's role in such areas as welfare, education, employment, and housing may decrease the freedom of the people and subject them to too much government regulation. The supporters of more government involvement are known as *liberals.* The critics of more government involvement are known as *conservatives.* The division between these groups has helped furnish one of the main themes of controversy and discussion in modern democratic societies.

Applying democratic principles in everyday life can be challenging. In the United States, for example, freedom of speech, press, religion, and assembly are protected by the First Amendment to the Constitution. In guarding these freedoms, the U.S. judiciary has tried to balance the interests of individuals against possible injury and damage to other people and the community. Thus, the right of free speech does not allow people to falsely damage reputations of others. It also does not allow someone to shout "Fire!" in a crowd when there is no fire.

This article presents a broad survey of democracy—what it is, how it works, and how it has developed.

48

Features of democracy

The characteristics of democracy vary from one country to another. But certain basic features are more or less the same in all democratic nations.

Free elections give the people a chance to choose their leaders and express their opinions. Elections are held periodically to ensure that elected officials truly represent the people. The possibility of being voted out of office helps assure that these officials pay attention to public opinion. In most democracies, the only legal requirements for voting or for holding public office have to do with age, residence, and citizenship. The democratic process permits citizens to vote by secret ballot, free from force or bribes. It also requires that election results be protected against dishonesty. See **Election**.

Majority rule and minority rights. In a democracy, a decision often must be approved by a majority of voters before it may take effect. This principle, called majority rule, may be used to elect officials or decide a policy. Democracies sometimes decide votes by plurality. Most democracies go beyond a simple majority to make fundamental or constitutional changes. In the United States, constitutional amendments must be ratified by the legislatures of three-fourths of the states or by special conventions called in three-fourths of the states.

Majority rule is based on the idea that if all citizens are equal, the judgment of the many will be better than the judgment of the few. Democracy values freely given consent as the basis of legitimate and effective political power. But democracies are also concerned with protecting individual liberty and preventing government from infringing on the freedoms of individuals. Democratic countries guarantee that certain rights can never be taken from the people, even by extremely large majorities. These rights include the basic freedoms of speech, press, assembly, and religious worship. The majority also must recognize the right of the minority to try to become the majority by legal means.

Political parties are a necessary part of democratic government. Rival parties make elections meaningful by giving voters a choice among candidates who represent different interests and points of view.

The United States and the United Kingdom have chiefly two-party systems. Many democratic countries have multi-party systems, which have more than two major parties. Often in these countries, no single party gains a majority in the legislature. As a result, two or more parties must join to make up such a majority.

It's a fact

The first political parties in the United States, the Federalists and the Democratic-Republicans, developed during the late 1700's. The Federalists, led by Alexander Hamilton, called for a strong central government. The Democratic-Republicans, headed by Thomas Jefferson, favored a weaker central government.

These parties form a *coalition government*. In democratic countries, the party or parties that are out of power serve as the "loyal opposition." That is, they criticize the policies and actions of the party in power. In various dictatorships, criticism of the party in power may be labeled as treason. Often, only the "government party" is allowed to exist. The people have no real choice among candidates, and no opportunity to express dissatisfaction with the government. See **Political party**.

Controls on power. Democracies have various arrangements to prevent any person or branch of government from becoming too powerful. For example, the U.S. Constitution divides political power between the states and the federal government. Some powers belong only to the states, some only to the federal government, and some are shared by both.

The Constitution further divides the powers of the U.S. government among the president, Congress, and the federal courts. The power of each branch is designed to check or balance the power of the others.

In all democratic countries, government officials are subject to the law and are accountable to the people. Officials may be removed from office for lawless conduct or for other serious reasons. The communications media help keep elected officials sensitive to public opinion.

Constitutional government. Democratic government is based on law and, in most cases, a written constitution. Constitutions state the powers and duties of government and limit what the government may do. Constitutions also say how laws shall be made and enforced. Most constitutions have a detailed bill of rights that describes the basic liberties of the people and forbids the government to violate those rights.

Constitutions that have been in effect for a long time may include certain unwritten procedures that have become important parts of the operation of government. Such procedures are a matter of custom rather than written law. Britain has no single written document called "the constitution." In that country, however, certain customs and conventions, as well as certain major documents and many laws, are widely accepted as the "basic rules of the system."

An essential characteristic of democratic government is an independent judiciary. It is the duty of the justice system to protect the integrity of the "rules" and the rights of individuals under these rules, especially against the government itself.

Occasionally, dictatorships establish very elaborate constitutions and extensive lists of basic rights of citizens. For example, the 1977 constitution of the Soviet Union contained more detailed rights supposedly guaranteed to citizens than does the U.S. Bill of Rights. In practice, however, Soviet courts were not known to defend individuals' rights against the government.

Private organizations. In a democracy, individuals and private organizations carry on many social and economic activities that are, for the most part, free of government control. For example, newspapers and magazines are privately owned and managed. Labor unions are run by and for the benefit of workers, not the state. Democratic governments generally do not interfere with religious worship. Private schools operate along with public schools. The people may form groups to influence opinion on public issues and policies. Most businesses in democratic societies are privately owned and managed. Britain, Sweden, and other democracies have government ownership and control of certain basic industries and services.

In dictatorial societies, the government alone may organize and control most associations. The people are not permitted to establish or join most groups without the permission of the state. In some countries, the government almost completely owns and manages the economy.

Why democracy?

The Declaration of Independence adopted by the American patriots in 1776 expressed the belief that "all men are created equal, that they are endowed by their Creator with certain unalienable rights, that among these are Life, Liberty, and the pursuit of Happiness." The Declaration said that the people may change or abolish the government if it interferes with those rights.

People once thought that the greatest obstacles to individual freedom and equality were political. They believed they could preserve freedom simply by changing the form of government from a monarchy to a republic. They claimed that the government that governs least governs best. But in time, many people became convinced that some government regulation of society and the economy was necessary to make personal freedom more meaningful and to promote equality, as well as to improve the welfare of the nation.

In today's democracies, there are extensive programs to provide economic security, to ease suffering, and to develop human potential. Such programs include unemployment insurance, minimum wage laws, old-age pensions, health insurance, civil rights laws, and aid to education. Many democracies aim to provide a minimum standard of living and adequate medical care for all.

Making democracy work

Citizen participation. Democracy calls for widespread participation in politics by the people. It is believed to be the duty of all adult citizens to vote in local, state or provincial, and national elections. Qualified individuals should be willing to run for public office, to serve on juries, and to contribute to the welfare of their country. Citizens should help shape public opinion by speaking out on important issues and by supporting the political party of their choice. An active citizenry is thought to be one of the best guarantees against corrupt and inefficient government.

Education and democracy. Faith in the power of education is a characteristic of democracy. According to democratic ideals, widespread participation in politics does not necessarily ensure good government. The quality of government depends on the quality of participation. Well-informed and well-educated citizens are able to participate more intelligently.

A democracy needs educated citizens who can think for themselves. Citizens have a duty to take part in public affairs, to keep informed on public issues, and to vote intelligently. Democratic institutions must produce leaders worthy of public trust and responsibility. For this reason, democratic governments support education for their citizens.

Voluntary action. An important quality of democratic government is its emphasis on trying to get people to act on the basis of understanding and agreement instead of force. Although all governments use force sometimes, democracies usually emphasize dialogue, negotiation, bargaining, and ultimately, voluntary citizen cooperation. This approach is closely linked to the widely held democratic belief that people are generally rational and well disposed toward the common welfare.

Economic development and agreement on fundamentals. Most successful democracies have existed in developed societies. In such societies, literacy rates are high, *per capita* (per person) incomes are moderate to high, and there are few extremes of wealth and poverty. Some scholars believe democracy works best in countries with a large middle class.

Many democratic governments have collapsed during economic crises. The basic problem involved in the failures of such democracies has been the inability to maintain sufficient agreement among either the people or their political leaders on the purposes of government. Crises have often aggravated and sharpened divisions and suspicions among various classes, groups, parties, and leaders. Excessive divisions have helped block action by freely elected governments, often resulting in widespread public frustration and disorder.

Democratic governments are likely to be unstable whenever people become deeply divided and suspicious of one another. Sometimes racial, ethnic, or religious differences make democracies difficult to operate. In such instances, the people may not see one another as legitimate and trustworthy partners in the enterprise of government.

The development of democracy

Origins of democracy. Democracy began to develop in ancient Greece as early as the 500's B.C. The word *democracy* comes from the Greek words *demos,* meaning *people,* and *kratos,* which means *rule* or *authority.* Greek political thinkers stressed the idea of rule by law. They criticized dictatorship as the worst form of government. Athens and some other Greek city-states had democratic governments.

Democracy in ancient Athens differed in important ways from democracy today. Athenian democracy was a direct democracy rather than a representative one. Each male citizen had the duty to serve permanently in the assembly, which passed the laws and decided all important government policies. There was no division between legislative and executive branches of the government. Slaves made up a large part of the Athenian population, and did most of the work. Neither the slaves nor women could vote.

The ancient Romans experimented with democracy, but they never practiced it so fully as did the Athenians. Roman political thinkers taught that political power comes from the consent of the people. The Roman statesman Cicero contributed the idea of a universal law of reason that is binding on all people and governments everywhere. He suggested that people have natural rights which every state must respect.

The Middle Ages. Christianity taught that everyone is equal before God. This teaching promoted the democratic ideal of brotherhood among people. Christianity also introduced the idea that Christians are citizens of two kingdoms—the Kingdom of God and the kingdom of the world. It held that no state can demand absolute loyalty from its citizens because they must also obey God and His commandments. During the Middle Ages (A.D. 400's to the 1500's), the conflict between these two loyalties helped lay the foundation for constitutional government.

The Middle Ages produced a social system known as *feudalism.* Under feudalism, persons pledged their loyalty and services to one another. Individuals had certain rights which other persons were required to recognize. A feudal court system was established to protect these rights. Such courts later led to kings' councils, representative assemblies, and modern parliaments.

The Renaissance and the Reformation. The great cultural reawakening called the Renaissance spread throughout Europe during the 1300's, 1400's, and 1500's. A new spirit of individual thought and independence developed. It influenced political thinking and hastened the growth of democracy. People began to demand greater freedom in all areas of life.

The new independence of the individual found religious expression in the Protestant Reformation. The Reformation emphasized the importance of individual conscience. During the early 1500's, Martin Luther, a leader of the Reformation, opposed the Roman Catholic Church as an intermediary between God and people. A number of Protestant churches were established during the period. Some of these churches practiced the congregational form of government, which had a democratic structure. During the 1500's, both Catholics and Protestants defended the right to oppose absolute monarchy. They argued that the political power of earthly rulers comes from the consent of the people.

Democracy in England. In 1215, English nobles forced King John to approve Magna Carta. This historic document became a symbol of human liberty. It was used to support later demands for trial by jury, protection against unlawful arrest, and no taxation without representation.

English democracy developed slowly during the next several hundred years. In 1628, Parliament passed the Petition of Right. The petition called on King Charles I to stop collecting taxes without the consent of Parliament. It also provided that Parliament should meet at regular intervals. Charles refused to agree to limits on the royal power, and civil war broke out in 1642. The Puritans, led by Oliver Cromwell, fought the followers of the king. Charles was beheaded in 1649, and the Puritans established a short-lived *commonwealth* (republic).

The English revolution of 1688 finally established the supremacy of Parliament. John Locke, the philosopher of the revolution, declared that final authority in political matters belonged to the people. The government's main purpose, he said, was to protect the lives, liberties, and property of the people. Parliament passed the Bill of Rights in 1689, assuring the people basic civil rights.

Modern democracy was still far off. The larger factory towns were not represented in Parliament until after the adoption of the Reform Act of 1832. Property qualifications for voting disappeared only gradually. In 1918, for the first time, all men were permitted to vote. Not until 1928 could all women vote.

French contributions to democracy were made in the 1700's by such political thinkers as Montesquieu, Voltaire, and Jean-Jacques Rousseau. Their writings helped bring about the French Revolution, which began in 1789. Montesquieu argued that political freedom requires the separation of the executive, legislative, and judicial powers of government. Voltaire spoke out against government invasion of individual rights and freedoms. Rousseau declared in his book *The Social Contract* (1762) that people "have a duty to obey only legitimate powers." The only rightful rulers, he added, were, ultimately, the people.

The French Revolution, an important event in the history of democracy, promoted the ideas of liberty and equality. It did not make France a democracy, but it did limit the king's powers.

American democracy took root in traditions brought to North America by the first English colonists. The Pilgrims, who settled in Massachusetts in 1620, joined in signing the Mayflower Compact to obey "just and equal laws." The Revolutionary War began more than 150 years later, in 1775. The colonists wanted self-government and no taxation without representation. The Declaration of Independence, adopted by the Continental Congress in 1776, is a classic document of democracy. It established human rights as an ideal by which government must be guided.

Most of the Founding Fathers distrusted the Athenian version of direct democracy. They wanted to establish a republic because they feared that giving the people too much power would lead to mob rule. For this reason, the men who wrote the Constitution of the United States adopted a system of dividing power between the federal government and the states. They also provided that the federal powers be divided among the legislative, executive, and judicial branches. In addition, they provided that the president be elected by an electoral college rather than by the direct vote of the people (see **Electoral college**).

Thomas Jefferson favored a government that would pay more attention to the common citizen. After he became president in 1801, he spoke of his election as a "revolution." In 1828, the election of Andrew Jackson to the presidency further advanced American democracy. The pioneer spirit of the settlers in the West encouraged self-reliance, promoted individual liberty, and gave meaning to the promise of equal opportunity.

The long-term trend in the United States has been to give almost all adult citizens the right to vote. By 1850, white males could vote in all the states. The 15th Amendment to the Constitution, adopted in 1870, gave black men the right to vote. In 1920, the 19th Amendment gave women the vote. In 1964, the 24th Amendment prohibited poll taxes as voting requirements in national elections.

The spread of democracy. During the 1800's, democracy developed steadily. Many countries followed the American and British examples. Such democratic institutions as elections and legislatures became common. Where kings still ruled, they lost much of their power and performed mainly ceremonial duties.

The Industrial Revolution brought political changes of great importance. During the second half of the 1800's, the working classes demanded and received greater po-

Topic for study

Ask 10 people what democracy means to them. Summarize their answers and compare them with your own definition.

---

litical rights. New laws gave more citizens the right to vote. The freedoms of speech, the press, assembly, and religion were extended and enlarged.

Democracy did not take root everywhere. Some countries that adopted constitutions modeled after that of the United States later became dictatorships. These nations found that a constitution alone did not guarantee democracy. In Russia, a group of revolutionists set up a Communist dictatorship in 1917 and halted Russia's progress toward democracy. Germany adopted a democratic government in 1919, but Adolf Hitler's rise to power brought a fascist dictatorship in 1933.

Democracy today. Most governments today claim to be democratic, but many lack some essential freedoms usually associated with democracy. In some countries, for example, the people are not allowed certain basic freedoms, such as those of speech and of the press, or competitive elections.

Many modern nations have a long history of democratic government. These countries include Australia, Belgium, Canada, Denmark, the Netherlands, New Zealand, Norway, Sweden, Switzerland, the United Kingdom, and the United States. Other nations—including India, Israel, Italy, and Japan—have been democracies since the mid-1900's. The structure of French government has changed many times since the French Revolution. The present government is a democracy. Several newly independent nations in Africa and Asia are trying to develop democratic institutions. But inexperience with self-rule, and other problems, have made democratic government difficult to achieve. In the late 1980's and early 1990's, democracy increased in northern and central Asia and Eastern Europe as Communists lost control of the governments of the Soviet Union and many Eastern European countries. In 1991, the Soviet Union broke up into a number of independent nations.

Alexander J. Groth

Related articles include:

Ballot	Initiative and referendum	Recall
Constitution of the United States	Political party	Voting
Election		Voting machine

Additional resources

Hill, Kim Q. *Democracy in the Fifty States.* Univ. of Neb. Pr., 1994.
Klingemann, Hans-Dieter, and others. *Parties, Policies, and Democracy.* Westview, 1994.
Kronenwetter, Michael. *How Democratic Is the United States?* Watts, 1994.
Lipset, Seymour M., ed. *The Encyclopedia of Democracy.* 4 vols. Congressional Quarterly, 1995.
Meltzer, Milton. *American Politics: How It Really Works.* Morrow, 1989. Younger readers.

Web sites

Approaching Democracy Online
http://democracy.ucdavis.edu/
A companion Web site to the college text *Approaching Democracy,* offering reference information and links.

Welcome to Democracy 2000
http://www.democracy2000.org/
Information from an educational and research organization devoted to revitalizing representative democracy.

House of Representatives is one of the two lawmaking bodies of many legislatures. In many of these legislatures, the other chamber is called a *senate,* and the house of representatives is the larger of the two.

The national legislatures of the United States, Australia, Colombia, and Japan have a house of representatives. Most of the 49 two-chamber state legislatures in the United States also have a house of representatives. Nebraska has a one-house legislature. Several states and nations use a different name for a lower chamber. This article focuses on the U.S. House of Representatives.

The U.S. House of Representatives, usually called simply the *House,* is one of the two chambers of Congress. The other chamber is the Senate. The two houses of Congress have about the same amount of power. However, the Senate is frequently called the *upper house,* and the House is known as the *lower house.* Members of the House are generally called *representatives.* The House and Senate must approve identical versions of any legislation before it can become law.

The Constitutional Convention established the form of national government in 1787. But it reached a standstill on the problem of representation in Congress. Delegates from states with large populations favored representation according to population. Those from states that had small populations argued for equal representation for every state. Under a compromise, representation in the House was based on population. Each state was given two senators, regardless of population.

Membership of the U.S. House of Representatives

Size. The Constitution gives Congress the power to determine the size of the House and to distribute representatives among the states. According to the Constitution, each member of the House must represent at least 30,000 persons, but every state must have at least one representative. The Constitution also requires a census of the nation every 10 years to determine how many representatives each state should have.

The first House, which was formed before the initial census had been taken, had 59 members when it originally met and 65 members by the end of the first Congress. The House grew as new states joined the Union and as the nation's population increased. In 1929, Congress passed legislation that limited the House to 435 members. In 1959, when Alaska and Hawaii became states, the House gained two additional members. However, reapportionment took place after the 1960 census, and the House was again limited to 435 members in 1962. Today, the House has one member per about 572,000 people. In addition, the House has one delegate each from the District of Columbia, American Samoa, Guam, and the Virgin Islands and a resident commissioner from Puerto Rico. These five officials can vote in committees and on some questions in the full House.

Originally, Congress let each state decide how to choose its own representatives. Some of these states established congressional districts for this purpose. Each of the districts elected one representative. Other states chose all their representatives *at large,* with an entire

House of Representatives

The House of Representatives of the first session of the 107th Congress consisted of 212 Democrats, 221 Republicans, and 2 independents (not including representatives from American Samoa, the District of Columbia, Guam, Puerto Rico, and the Virgin Islands) when it convened on Jan. 3, 2001. There were 212 Democrats, 222 Republicans, and 1 independent when the second session of the 106th Congress convened. This table shows congressional district, legislator, and party affiliation. Asterisk (*) denotes those who served in the 106th Congress; dagger (†) denotes "at large."

Alabama
1. Sonny Callahan, R.*
2. Terry Everett, R.*
3. Bob Riley, R.*
4. Robert Aderholt, R.*
5. Bud Cramer, D.*
6. Spencer Bachus, R.*
7. Earl Hilliard, D.*

Alaska
†Donald E. Young, R.*

Arizona
1. Jeff Flake, R.
2. Ed Pastor, D.*
3. Bob Stump, R.*
4. John Shadegg, R.*
5. Jim Kolbe, R.*
6. J. D. Hayworth, R.*

Arkansas
1. Marion Berry, D.*
2. Vic Snyder, D.*
3. Asa Hutchinson, R.*
4. Mike Ross, D.

California
1. Mike Thompson, D.*
2. Wally Herger, R.*
3. Douglas Ose, R.*
4. John Doolittle, R.*
5. Robert T. Matsui, D.*
6. Lynn Woolsey, D.*
7. George E. Miller, D.*
8. Nancy Pelosi, D.*
9. Barbara Lee, D.*
10. Ellen Tauscher, D.*
11. Richard Pombo, R.*
12. Tom Lantos, D.*
13. Fortney H. (Peter) Stark, D.*
14. Anna Eshoo, D.*
15. Mike Honda, D.
16. Zoe Lofgren, D.*
17. Sam Farr, D.*
18. Gary Condit, D.*
19. George Radanovich, R.*
20. Calvin Dooley, D.*
21. William M. Thomas, R.*
22. Lois Capps, D.*
23. Elton Gallegly, R.*
24. Brad Sherman, D.*
25. Howard McKeon, R.*
26. Howard L. Berman, D.*
27. Adam Schiff, D.
28. David Dreier, R.*
29. Henry A. Waxman, D.*
30. Xavier Becerra, D.*
31. Hilda Solis, D.
32. Julian C. Dixon, D.*
33. Lucille Roybal-Allard, D.*
34. Grace Napolitano, D.*
35. Maxine Waters, D.*
36. Jane Harman, D.
37. Juanita Millender-
    McDonald, D.*
38. Steve Horn, R.*
39. Edward Royce, R.*
40. Jerry Lewis, R.*
41. Gary Miller, R.*
42. Joe Baca, D.*
43. Kenneth Calvert, R.*
44. Mary Bono, R.*
45. Dana Rohrabacher, R.*
46. Loretta Sanchez, D.*
47. C. Christopher Cox, R.*
48. Darrell Issa, R.*
49. Susan Davis, D.
50. Bob Filner, D.*
51. Randy (Duke) Cunningham, R.*
52. Duncan L. Hunter, R.*

Colorado
1. Diana DeGette, D.*
2. Mark Udall, D.*
3. Scott McInnis, R.*
4. Bob Schaffer, R.*
5. Joel Hefley, R.*
6. Tom Tancredo, R.*

Connecticut
1. John Larson, D.*
2. Rob Simmons, R.
3. Rosa DeLauro, D.*
4. Christopher Shays, R.*
5. James H. Maloney, D.*
6. Nancy L. Johnson, R.*

Delaware
†Michael Castle, R.*

Florida
1. Joe Scarborough, R.*
2. Allen Boyd, D.*
3. Corrine Brown, D.*
4. Ander Crenshaw, R.
5. Karen Thurman, D.*
6. Clifford B. Stearns, R.*
7. John Mica, R.*
8. Ric Keller, R.
9. Michael Bilirakis, R.*
10. C. W. Bill Young, R.*
11. Jim Davis, D.*
12. Adam Putnam, R.
13. Dan Miller, R.*
14. Porter J. Goss, R.*
15. Dave Weldon, R.*
16. Mark Foley, R.*
17. Carrie Meek, D.*
18. Ileana Ros-Lehtinen, R.*
19. Robert Wexler, D.*
20. Peter Deutsch, D.*
21. Lincoln Diaz-Balart, R.*
22. E. Clay Shaw, Jr., R.*
23. Alcee Hastings, D.*

Georgia
1. Jack Kingston, R.*
2. Sanford Bishop, Jr., D.*
3. Mac Collins, R.*
4. Cynthia A. McKinney, D.*
5. John Lewis, D.*
6. Johnny Isakson, R.*
7. Bob Barr, R.*
8. Saxby Chambliss, R.*
9. Nathan Deal, R.*

10. Charlie Norwood, R.*
11. John Linder, R.*

Hawaii
1. Neil Abercrombie, D.*
2. Patsy T. Mink, D.*

Idaho
1. Butch Otter, R.
2. Mike Simpson, R.*

Illinois
1. Bobby Rush, D.*
2. Jesse L. Jackson, Jr., D.*
3. William O. Lipinski, D.*
4. Luis Gutierrez, D.*
5. Rod R. Blagojevich, D.*
6. Henry J. Hyde, R.*
7. Danny Davis, D.*
8. Philip M. Crane, R.*
9. Janice Schakowsky, D.*
10. Mark Kirk, R.
11. Gerald Weller, R.*
12. Jerry F. Costello, D.*
13. Judy Biggert, R.*
14. J. Dennis Hastert, R.*
15. Timothy Johnson, R.
16. Donald Manzullo, R.*
17. Lane A. Evans, D.*
18. Ray LaHood, R.*
19. David Phelps, D.*
20. John Shimkus, R.*

Indiana
1. Peter J. Visclosky, D.*
2. Mike Pence, R.
3. Tim Roemer, D.*
4. Mark Souder, R.*
5. Steve Buyer, R.*
6. Danny L. Burton, R.*
7. Brian Kerns, R.
8. John Hostettler, R.*
9. Baron Hill, D.*
10. Julia M. Carson, D.*

Iowa
1. Jim Leach, R.*
2. Jim Nussle, R.*
3. Leonard Boswell, D.*
4. Greg Ganske, R.*
5. Tom Latham, R.*

Kansas
1. Jerry Moran, R.*
2. Jim Ryun, R.*
3. Dennis Moore, D.*
4. Todd Tiahrt, R.*

Kentucky
1. Edward Whitfield, R.*
2. Ron Lewis, R.*
3. Anne Northup, R.*
4. Kenneth Lucas, D.*
5. Harold (Hal) Rogers, R.*
6. Ernie Fletcher, R.*

Louisiana
1. David Vitter, R.*

2. William J. Jefferson, D.*
3. W. J. (Billy) Tauzin, R.*
4. Jim McCrery, R.*
5. John Cooksey, R.*
6. Richard Hugh Baker, R.*
7. Chris John, D.*

Maine
1. Thomas Allen, D.*
2. John Baldacci, D.*

Maryland
1. Wayne T. Gilchrest, R.*
2. Robert Ehrlich, Jr., R.*
3. Benjamin L. Cardin, D.*
4. Albert Wynn, D.*
5. Steny H. Hoyer, D.*
6. Roscoe Bartlett, R.*
7. Elijah Cummings, D.*
8. Constance A. Morella, R.*

Massachusetts
1. John W. Olver, D.*
2. Richard E. Neal, D.*
3. James McGovern, D.*
4. Barney Frank, D.*
5. Martin Meehan, D.*
6. John Tierney, D.*
7. Edward J. Markey, D.*
8. Michael Capuano, D.*
9. John Joseph Moakley, D.*
10. William Delahunt, D.*

Michigan
1. Bart Stupak, D.*
2. Peter Hoekstra, R.*
3. Vernon Ehlers, R.*
4. Dave Camp, R.*
5. James Barcia, D.*
6. Frederick S. Upton, R.*
7. Nick Smith, R.*
8. Mike Rogers, R.
9. Dale E. Kildee, D.*
10. David E. Bonior, D.*
11. Joseph Knollenberg, R.*
12. Sander M. Levin, D.*
13. Lynn Rivers, D.*
14. John Conyers, Jr., D.*
15. Carolyn Kilpatrick, D.*
16. John D. Dingell, D.*

Minnesota
1. Gil Gutknecht, R.*
2. Mark Kennedy, R.
3. Jim Ramstad, R.*
4. Betty McCollum, D.
5. Martin O. Sabo, D.*
6. William P. Luther, D.*
7. Collin C. Peterson, D.*
8. James L. Oberstar, D.*

Mississippi
1. Roger Wicker, R.*
2. Bennie Thompson, D.*
3. Charles Pickering, R.*
4. Ronnie Shows, D.*
5. Gene Taylor, D.*

Missouri
1. William Clay, D.*
2. Todd Akin, R.
3. Richard A. Gephardt, D.*
4. Ike Skelton, D.*
5. Karen McCarthy, D.*
6. Samuel Graves, R.
7. Roy Blunt, R.*
8. Jo Ann Emerson, R.*
9. Kenny Hulshof, R.*

Montana
†Dennis Rehberg, R.

Nebraska
1. Doug Bereuter, R.*
2. Lee Terry, R.*
3. Tom Osborne, R.

Nevada
1. Shelley Berkley, D.*
2. Jim Gibbons, R.*

New Hampshire
1. John E. Sununu, R.*
2. Charles Bass, R.*

New Jersey
1. Robert E. Andrews, D.*
2. Frank LoBiondo, R.*
3. H. James Saxton, R.*
4. Christopher H. Smith, R.*
5. Marge Roukema, R.*
6. Frank Pallone, Jr., D.*
7. Mike Ferguson, R.
8. William Pascrell, Jr., D.*
9. Steven Rothman, D.*
10. Donald M. Payne, D.*
11. Rodney Frelinghuysen, R.*
12. Rush Holt, D.*
13. Robert Menendez, D.*

New Mexico
1. Heather Wilson, R.*
2. Joe Skeen, R.*
3. Thomas Udall, D.*

New York
1. Felix Grucci, R.
2. Steve Israel, D.
3. Peter King, R.*
4. Carolyn McCarthy, D.*
5. Gary L. Ackerman, D.*
6. Gregory Meeks, D.*
7. Joseph Crowley, D.*
8. Jerrold Nadler, D.*
9. Anthony Weiner, D.*
10. Edolphus Towns, D.*
11. Major R. Owens, D.*
12. Nydia Velazquez, D.*
13. Vito J. Fossella, R.*
14. Carolyn Maloney, D.*
15. Charles B. Rangel, D.*
16. Jose E. Serrano, D.*
17. Eliot L. Engel, D.*
18. Nita M. Lowey, D.*
19. Sue Kelly, R.*
20. Benjamin A. Gilman, R.*
21. Michael R. McNulty, D.*
22. John Sweeney, R.*

23. Sherwood L. Boehlert, R.*
24. John McHugh, R.*
25. James Walsh, R.*
26. Maurice Hinchey, D.*
27. Thomas Reynolds, R.*
28. Louise M. Slaughter, D.*
29. John J. LaFalce, D.*
30. Jack Quinn, R.*
31. Amo Houghton, R.*

North Carolina
1. Eva Clayton, D.*
2. Bob Etheridge, D.*
3. Walter Jones, Jr., R.*
4. David Price, D.*
5. Richard Burr, R.*
6. Howard Coble, R.*
7. Mike McIntyre, D.*
8. Robin Hayes, R.*
9. Sue Myrick, R.*
10. Cass Ballenger, R.*
11. Charles H. Taylor, R.*
12. Melvin Watt, D.*

North Dakota
†Earl Pomeroy, D.*

Ohio
1. Steve Chabot, R.*
2. Rob Portman, R.*
3. Tony P. Hall, D.*
4. Michael G. Oxley, R.*
5. Paul E. Gillmor, R.*
6. Ted Strickland, D.*
7. David L. Hobson, R.*
8. John A. Boehner, R.*
9. Marcy Kaptur, D.*
10. Dennis Kucinich, D.*
11. Stephanie Jones, D.*
12. Pat Tiberi, R.
13. Sherrod Brown, D.*
14. Thomas C. Sawyer, D.*
15. Deborah Pryce, R.*
16. Ralph Regula, R.*
17. James A. Traficant, Jr., D.*
18. Bob Ney, R.*
19. Steven LaTourette, R.*

Oklahoma
1. Steve Largent, R.*
2. Brad Carson, D.
3. Wes Watkins, R.*
4. J. C. Watts, Jr., R.*
5. Ernest Jim Istook, R.*
6. Frank Lucas, R.*

Oregon
1. David Wu, D.*
2. Greg Walden, R.*
3. Earl Blumenauer, D.*
4. Peter A. DeFazio, D.*
5. Darlene Hooley, D.*

Pennsylvania
1. Robert Brady, D.*
2. Chaka Fattah, D.*
3. Robert A. Borski, Jr., D.*
4. Melissa Hart, R.
5. John Peterson, R.*
6. Tim Holden, D.*

7. W. Curtis Weldon, R.*
8. Jim Greenwood, R.*
9. E. G. (Bud) Shuster, R.*
10. Donald Sherwood, R.
11. Paul E. Kanjorski, D.*
12. John P. Murtha, D.*
13. Joseph Hoeffel, D.
14. William J. Coyne, D.*
15. Patrick Toomey, R.
16. Joseph Pitts, R.*
17. George W. Gekas, R.*
18. Michael Doyle, D.*
19. Todd Platts, R.
20. Frank Mascara, D.*
21. Philip English, R.*

Rhode Island
1. Patrick Kennedy, D.*
2. James Langevin, D.

South Carolina
1. Henry Brown, R.
2. Floyd Spence, R.*
3. Lindsey Graham, R.*
4. James DeMint, R.*
5. John M. Spratt, Jr., D.*
6. James Clyburn, D.*

South Dakota
†John Thune, R.*

Tennessee
1. William Jenkins, R.*
2. John J. Duncan, Jr., R.*
3. Zach Wamp, R.*
4. Van Hilleary, R.*
5. Bob Clement, D.*
6. Bart Gordon, D.*
7. Ed Bryant, R.*
8. John S. Tanner, D.*
9. Harold E. Ford, Jr., D.*

Texas
1. Max Sandlin, D.*
2. Jim Turner, D.*
3. Sam Johnson, R.*
4. Ralph M. Hall, D.*
5. Pete Sessions, R.*
6. Joe Barton, R.*
7. John Culberson, R.
8. Kevin Brady, R.*
9. Nick Lampson, D.*
10. Lloyd Doggett, D.*
11. Chet Edwards, D.*
12. Kay Granger, R.*
13. Mac Thornberry, R.*
14. Ron Paul, R.*
15. Ruben Hinojosa, D.*
16. Silvestre Reyes, D.*
17. Charles W. Stenholm, D.*
18. Sheila Jackson Lee, D.*
19. Larry Combest, R.*
20. Charlie Gonzalez, D.*
21. Lamar S. Smith, R.*
22. Tom DeLay, R.*
23. Henry Bonilla, R.*
24. Martin Frost, D.*
25. Ken Bentsen, D.*
26. Richard K. Armey, R.*
27. Solomon P. Ortiz, D.*

28. Ciro Rodriguez, D.*
29. Gene Green, D.*
30. Eddie Bernice Johnson, D.*

Utah
1. James V. Hansen, R.*
2. Jim Matheson, D.
3. Christopher Cannon, R.*

Vermont
†Bernard Sanders, Ind.*

Virginia
1. Jo Ann Davis, R.
2. Edward Schrock, R.
3. Robert Scott, D.*
4. Norman Sisisky, D.*
5. Virgil Goode, Jr., Ind.*
6. Robert Goodlatte, R.*
7. Eric Cantor, R.
8. James P. Moran, Jr., D.*
9. Rick C. Boucher, D.*
10. Frank R. Wolf, R.*
11. Thomas Davis III, R.*

Washington
1. Jay Inslee, D.*
2. Rick Larsen, D.
3. Brian Baird, D.*
4. Doc Hastings, R.*
5. George Nethercutt, Jr., R.*
6. Norman D. Dicks, D.*
7. Jim McDermott, D.*
8. Jennifer Dunn, R.*
9. Adam Smith, D.*

West Virginia
1. Alan B. Mollohan, D.*
2. Shelley Moore Capito, R.
3. Nick J. Rahall II, D.*

Wisconsin
1. Paul Ryan, R.*
2. Tammy Baldwin, D.*
3. Ron Kind, D.*
4. Gerald D. Kleczka, D.*
5. Thomas Barrett, D.*
6. Thomas E. Petri, R.*
7. David R. Obey, D.*
8. Mark Green, R.*
9. F. James Sensenbrenner, Jr., R.*

Wyoming
†Barbara Cubin, R.*

Nonvoting representatives
American Samoa
Eni F. H. Faleomavaega, D.*
District of Columbia
Eleanor Holmes Norton, D.*
Guam
Robert Underwood, D.*
Puerto Rico
Anibal Acevedo Vila, D.
Virgin Islands
Donna Christian-Christensen, D.

state serving as one congressional district. In 1842, Congress passed legislation that required every state to create a congressional district for each of its House seats. Under certain conditions, however, one or more of a state's representatives may be chosen at large.

At first, Congress required the congressional districts of each state to have a compact shape and nearly equal populations. However, these rules were largely ignored, and Congress omitted them from the 1929 law that limited the size of the House. In many cases, the most powerful party in a state legislature created oddly shaped districts that differed greatly in population. This practice, called *gerrymandering,* concentrated the supporters of other parties into only a few districts. The dominant party then gained an unfair share of seats in the House of Representatives by winning in all the other districts.

The growth of cities widened the differences in population among congressional districts. For example, a state might have had an urban district of 900,000 persons and a rural district of 150,000. Since each district elected one representative, many urban voters were underrepresented in the House.

During the 1960's, the Supreme Court of the United States largely ended unfair apportionment of House seats. In 1962, it ruled that citizens could ask federal courts to decide cases involving charges of unfair apportionment. In 1964, the court ruled that a state's congressional districts must be as equal in population as possible. As a result, gerrymandering declined as a tool to aid a dominant party.

Qualifications and election. The Constitution requires a representative to be at least 25 years old and to have been a United States citizen for at least seven years. House members must be legal residents of the state from which they are elected. They are not required to live in the district they represent, but nearly all voters insist that they do. Representatives serve two-year terms and are elected in the even-numbered years. There is no limit to the number of terms a representative may serve.

Salary and privileges. The basic salary of House members is $141,300. The speaker, who is the leader of the House, receives $181,400. Members are entitled to annual salary increases based on rises in the cost of living, but they may vote not to accept the increases. Each representative also gets a special allowance that covers such expenses as staff salaries, official mail, travel costs, and office expenses, including rental of office space in the representative's home district. Such factors as distance from the home district and local rent rates determine the exact sum of this allowance. Members of the House of Representatives are also provided with office space in Washington, D.C.

Representatives are given legal *immunity* (protection) for anything they write or say when conducting official business in the House chamber or in committee meetings. With this immunity, a representative can criticize policies or people without fear of being sued.

Organization of the U.S. House

In January after a congressional election, House members meet to choose their party leaders for the next two years. The meeting of the House Democrats is called the Democratic *caucus,* and that of the Republicans is the Republican *conference.* The representatives deal mainly with organizational matters at these meetings, but they also may adopt party positions on bills.

The speaker and other leaders. The speaker of the House presides over House sessions and gives representatives permission to debate. The speaker also appoints most House members of *joint committees,* which consist of members of both houses of Congress. The speaker is officially elected by the full House but actually has already been chosen at the meeting of the majority party. The House election simply confirms the majority party's choice because representatives support their party's candidates for leadership positions. A representative may hold the job of speaker for no more than four consecutive two-year terms.

The members of the majority party also select the *majority leader* of the House at their meeting. The candidate for speaker chosen by the minority party becomes the *minority leader.* Each party also elects an assistant leader called a *whip.* The whips work to persuade representatives of their party to support party policies.

Committees do most of the House's work. Each party has members on these committees. Representatives may serve on four types of committees: (1) *standing* (permanent), (2) select, (3) conference, and (4) joint.

Standing committees are the most important type. They consider bills that have been introduced in the House. The House has 19 standing committees, each of which handles a particular field of legislation. The most powerful of these committees include Appropriations; Judiciary; Rules; and Ways and Means, which deals with tax bills. Each standing committee may be divided into several subcommittees. The heads of committees and subcommittees are members of the majority party. They are elected at the party conference or caucus by secret ballot. In many cases, the person elected is the majority party representative who has the longest continuous service with the committee or subcommittee. Committee and subcommittee heads may hold their positions for no more than three consecutive two-year terms.

The proportion of Democrats and Republicans on the standing committees reflects that of each party's membership in the House. The Democratic caucus and the Republican conference make the committee assignments, which are then confirmed by the entire House. The speaker nominates the majority party's members of the Rules Committee. Any bill opposed by the Rules Committee has little chance of reaching the entire House for consideration.

Select committees, also called *special committees,* are temporary groups formed for investigations or other special purposes. Conference and joint committees have senators and representatives. Conference committees resolve differences between versions of certain bills that have passed in both chambers. A joint committee deals with topics that concern both chambers, such as energy problems or economic matters.

The work of the House

Considering legislation is the principal activity of the House. Representatives introduce thousands of bills during each session of Congress, and the House passes hundreds of them. All legislation that deals with taxes or spending must originate in the House.

After a bill has been introduced in the House, the

Speakers of the House of Representatives

Speaker	Party	Years served	Speaker	Party	Years served
Frederick A. C. Muhlenberg	Federalist	1789-1791	James G. Blaine	Republican	1869-1875
Jonathan Trumbull	Federalist	1791-1793	Michael C. Kerr	Democratic	1875-1876
Frederick A. C. Muhlenberg	Federalist	1793-1795	Samuel J. Randall	Democratic	1876-1881
Jonathan Dayton	Federalist	1795-1799	J. Warren Keifer	Republican	1881-1883
Theodore Sedgwick	Federalist	1799-1801	John G. Carlisle	Democratic	1883-1889
Nathaniel Macon	Dem.-Rep.*	1801-1807	Thomas B. Reed	Republican	1889-1891
Joseph B. Varnum	Dem.-Rep.*	1807-1811	Charles F. Crisp	Democratic	1891-1895
Henry Clay	Nat. Rep.†	1811-1814	Thomas B. Reed	Republican	1895-1899
Langdon Cheves	Dem.-Rep.*	1814-1815	David B. Henderson	Republican	1899-1903
Henry Clay	Nat. Rep.†	1815-1820	Joseph G. Cannon	Republican	1903-1911
John W. Taylor	Dem.-Rep.*	1820-1821	James B. Clark	Democratic	1911-1919
Philip P. Barbour	Dem.-Rep.*	1821-1823	Frederick H. Gillett	Republican	1919-1925
Henry Clay	Nat. Rep.†	1823-1825	Nicholas Longworth	Republican	1925-1931
John W. Taylor	Dem.-Rep.*	1825-1827	John N. Garner	Democratic	1931-1933
Andrew Stevenson	Dem.-Rep.*	1827-1834	Henry T. Rainey	Democratic	1933-1935
John Bell	Whig	1834-1835	Joseph W. Byrns	Democratic	1935-1936
James K. Polk	Democratic	1835-1839	William B. Bankhead	Democratic	1936-1940
Robert M. T. Hunter	Democratic	1839-1841	Sam Rayburn	Democratic	1940-1947
John White	Whig	1841-1843	Joseph W. Martin, Jr.	Republican	1947-1949
John W. Jones	Democratic	1843-1845	Sam Rayburn	Democratic	1949-1953
John W. Davis	Democratic	1845-1847	Joseph W. Martin, Jr.	Republican	1953-1955
Robert C. Winthrop	Whig	1847-1849	Sam Rayburn	Democratic	1955-1961
Howell Cobb	Democratic	1849-1851	John W. McCormack	Democratic	1962-1971
Linn Boyd	Democratic	1851-1855	Carl B. Albert	Democratic	1971-1977
Nathaniel P. Banks	American	1855-1857	Thomas P. O'Neill	Democratic	1977-1987
James L. Orr	Democratic	1857-1859	James C. Wright, Jr.	Democratic	1987-1989
William Pennington	Whig	1859-1861	Thomas S. Foley	Democratic	1989-1995
Galusha A. Grow	Republican	1861-1863	Newt Gingrich	Republican	1995-1999
Schuyler Colfax	Republican	1863-1869	J. Dennis Hastert	Republican	1999-
Theodore M. Pomeroy	Republican	1869			

*Democratic-Republican.   †National Republican.

speaker assigns it to a standing committee. Most bills die because the committee *tables* them—that is, lays them aside. Other bills are studied, released by the committee, and placed on a *legislative calendar* for consideration by the entire House. House leaders and the Rules Committee bring some bills out of calendar order to give them immediate consideration. A bill dies if Congress does not pass it before adjourning.

Most bills approved by the House are passed without debate. The House approves them under a *unanimous consent agreement,* a method of speeding legislative action. A bill that arouses disagreement among many representatives is likely to be debated. Under House rules, a representative may speak about a bill for one hour. However, representatives seldom get that much time. In most cases, the Rules Committee sets the amount of time for debate and divides it between the supporters and opponents of the legislation. Most bills require the support of only a simple majority—that is, more than half the representatives present—to pass.

Both houses of Congress must pass a bill in identical form for it to become law. A conference committee works out any differences between the House and Senate versions of many major bills. This committee then submits its version to each house for approval.

Bills passed by Congress are sent to the president. The president may sign a bill—and thus make it law—or veto it. If the president fails to act on a bill for 10 days— not including Sundays—while Congress is in session, it becomes law. A bill that reaches the president fewer

K. Jewell, U.S. House of Representatives

The House chamber, where the entire House of Representatives meets, has galleries for the public. Visitors may watch the legislators debate important bills. But most of the actual work of the House is done by committees.

than 10 days—not including Sundays—before Congress adjourns must be signed to become law. A vetoed bill is returned to Congress. If at least two-thirds of the members present in each house vote to *override* (reverse) the veto, the bill becomes law.

Other powers and duties of the House of Representatives include *impeaching* United States government officials and, under extraordinary conditions, electing the president of the United States. Impeachment is a charge of misconduct in office. The Senate conducts a trial to decide if the impeached official is guilty. The House elects the president if no candidate receives a majority of the votes in the *Electoral College.* The Electoral College is a group of officials chosen by the voters to elect the president and vice president.

Lower houses in other countries

About half of all nations have a two-house legislature. The names of the lower houses include *Chamber of Deputies, House of Commons,* and *National Assembly.* The lower houses in most countries with two-house legislatures have representation according to population. Some countries with such lower houses, including France, Britain, and Italy, have fewer people than the United States but have larger lower chambers. The lower chamber of most legislatures has more power than the upper chamber.

Members of lower chambers serve terms that range from two to six years. The members of the U.S. House receive a higher salary and more benefits than those of any other lower chamber.   Kenneth Janda

See also **Congress of the United States; Constitution of the United States; Impeachment; Senate; United States, Government of the.**

Additional resources

Bentley, Judith. *Speakers of the House.* Watts, 1994.
Cox, Gary W., and McCubbins, M. D. *Legislative Leviathan: Party Government in the House.* Univ. of Calif. Pr., 1993.

Web sites

U.S. House of Representatives
http://www.house.gov/
The official site of the House of Representatives.

The Office of the Clerk On-line Information Center
http://www.clerkweb.house.gov/
This Web site features legislation under consideration in the U.S. House of Representatives, other documents, biographies of former speakers, and a virtual tour of the House chamber.

Impeachment occurs when an authorized legislative body votes to bring a charge of serious misconduct in office against a government official. The impeached person may continue to perform the duties of office until he or she has been tried and found guilty of the charges. The term *impeachment* may also refer to the entire process by which a government official is removed from office. In this article, the term is used in the more restricted sense.

In the United States

Procedure. The House of Representatives has the sole power to bring charges of impeachment against the president, vice president, or other civilian officials of the United States government except members of Congress. A majority vote of the House is required for impeachment. The Senate then sits as a court to hear the charges against the impeached official. A two-thirds vote of the Senate is required for conviction. The vice president generally presides over the Senate. But when the Senate hears charges against the president, the Chief Justice of the United States presides. The Constitution makes this provision because the vice president would succeed to the presidency if the president were found guilty.

The Constitution specifies that officials shall be removed from office after impeachment for, and conviction of, "treason, bribery, or other high crimes and misdemeanors." Some people argue that these words mean an official may be discharged only for criminal conduct. Others claim that an official may be dismissed if he or she has displeased most of the Congress or most of the people. Congress has rejected both views. It has refused to limit the grounds for impeachment to criminal acts. However, it has refused to discharge officeholders merely because they have lost the confidence of Congress or of the people. Instead, it considers impeachable offenses to include criminal actions, serious abuse of power, and grave misconduct in office. Some scholars believe that Congress requires more serious grounds to remove a president than to dismiss a judge. The president is elected for a limited term, but judges are appointed for as long as they maintain "good behavior."

Officials found guilty by the Senate may be punished by more than being removed from office. The Senate may also prohibit them from ever again holding office in the U.S. government. Conviction of impeachment charges does not involve imprisonment or a fine. However, the official may be tried in a regular court of law.

Federal judges can be tried in court for a crime while still in office. But legal scholars do not know if a president or vice president can be. One vice president, Spiro T. Agnew, was charged with a federal crime. But he resigned in 1973 after refusing to contest the charges. In 1974, in the case of *United States v. Richard M. Nixon,* the Supreme Court ruled that the president could not withhold evidence demanded by a federal court. This decision meant that federal courts have jurisdiction over the president. But scholars remain undecided as to whether a president or vice president can be tried for a a crime while in office.

In general, the state governments follow the same rules for impeachment as the federal government does. The lower house of the legislature votes the impeachment charges, and the upper house tries the individuals. Few states have used their impeachment power.

History. The House of Representatives has voted articles of impeachment only 16 times in the history of the United States. The Senate has convicted only seven people. Only two presidents, Andrew Johnson and Bill Clinton, have been impeached. Another president, Richard M. Nixon, resigned before the full House voted on articles of impeachment recommended against him by the House Judiciary Committee. A few other officials have resigned to avoid impeachment. However, the House can impeach a former officeholder even after he or she has resigned.

Twelve of the 16 people who have been impeached were judges, and all of the 7 convictions involved judges. The 16 cases in which the House of Representatives voted articles of impeachment were the following:

(1) Senator William Blount of Tennessee was impeached in 1797 and charged with conspiring to help British and Indian forces attack the Spanish territories of Florida and Louisiana. However, the Senate ruled that it lacked jurisdiction and dismissed the charges. This ruling established that Congress would discipline its own members rather than use impeachment. Either house of Congress can expel one of its members by a two-thirds vote, and the Senate had expelled Blount the day after his impeachment.

(2) John Pickering of New Hampshire, judge of the United States District Court, was impeached in 1803 for drunkenness and profanity on the bench, and for unlawful decisions. It was generally agreed that the cause of his misconduct was insanity. He was found guilty and removed from office.

(3) Samuel Chase, associate justice of the Supreme Court of the United States, was impeached in 1804 for criticizing Thomas Jefferson, who was president at the time. Some of the congressional followers of Jefferson felt that impeachment was a proper means of keeping the courts in harmony with Congress and the executive branch of government. Chase was acquitted in March 1805. His acquittal provided a significant rejection of the theory that the tenure of judges should depend on the political climate of the times.

(4) James Peck of Missouri, judge of the U.S. District Court, was impeached in 1830. A Missouri lawyer named Luke Lawless had published a newspaper article criticizing one of Peck's decisions. Peck summoned Lawless to court, committed him to prison for 24 hours, and suspended him from law practice for 18 months.

Peck was acquitted in January 1831, but the case aroused concern for the freedom of the press. Congress promptly passed a statute limiting the power of judges to punish for contempt of court except when it consists of misbehavior in the presence of the court, or so near it as to obstruct the administration of justice.

(5) West H. Humphreys of Tennessee, a judge of the U.S. District Court, was impeached in 1862 for supporting the secession movement and unlawfully acting as judge of the Confederate District Court. He was found guilty and removed from office.

(6) Andrew Johnson, 17th president of the United States, was impeached in 1868 for violation of the Tenure of Office Act, corrupt use of the veto power, interference at elections, and other high crimes and misdemeanors. The Senate acquitted him later that year. In the background of the impeachment lay a bitter difference of opinion concerning the proper treatment of the defeated Confederate states. Johnson favored a much milder policy toward the South than the one proposed by a strong group in Congress.

(7) William W. Belknap, U.S. secretary of war, was impeached in 1876 for accepting bribes. Belknap resigned. The Senate later acquitted him.

(8) Charles Swayne of Florida, judge of the U.S. District Court, was impeached in 1904 for misconduct in office. He was acquitted.

(9) Robert W. Archbald, associate judge of the United States Commerce Court, was impeached in 1912 for entering into corrupt alliances with coal-mine owners and railroad officials while in office. Archbald was found guilty in January 1913 and discharged.

(10) George W. English of Illinois, judge of the U.S. District Court, was impeached for misdemeanors in 1926. He resigned before the trial.

(11) Harold Louderback of California, judge of the U.S. District Court, was impeached, but was acquitted in 1933.

(12) Halsted L. Ritter of Florida, judge of the U.S. District Court, was impeached and, in 1936, was removed from office.

(13) Harry E. Claiborne of Nevada, judge of the U.S. District Court, was impeached for filing false income tax returns. He was found guilty and removed from office in 1986.

(14) Alcee L. Hastings of Florida, judge of the U.S. District Court, was impeached in 1988. In 1989, the Senate convicted him of perjury and of trying to obtain a bribe, and he was removed from office. In 1992, a federal court ruled that Hastings may have been improperly tried by the Senate. Later that year, Hastings won a seat in the U.S. House of Representatives. In 1993, a higher federal court upheld Hastings' conviction.

(15) Walter L. Nixon, Jr., of Mississippi, judge of the U.S. District Court, was impeached in May 1989. Nixon had been convicted of perjury by a regular court of law and was serving a five-year sentence for the crime at the time of his impeachment. In 1989, the Senate convicted Nixon and removed him from office.

(16) Bill Clinton, 42nd president of the United States, was impeached in 1998 for perjury and obstruction of justice. The House charged Clinton with lying to a grand jury that was investigating an extramarital affair he had while in office. Other charges included hindering the investigation by lying to his aides and by encouraging others to lie and conceal evidence. The Senate acquitted Clinton in 1999. See **Clinton, Bill.**

In other countries

Canada and Australia provide that judges are to be removed by the governor-general on an *address,* or resolution of both houses of the federal legislature. The Canadian constitution gives parliament the right to impeach federally appointed judges. Judges who are found guilty are removed from office.

Other nations use impeachment in various forms. The tendency in Europe and South America is to confine impeachment to officers of ministerial rank, but to extend it to all offenses against the constitution or laws. In most nations, impeachment proceedings begin in the lower house of the legislature, and the upper house handles the trial and sentence.   Roger H. Davidson

Web site

Impeachment: The Process and History
http://www.nytimes.com/learning/general/specials/impeachment/
A New York Times report on the history of impeachment in the United States.

Initiative and referendum are actions that allow the voters of a city, state, or country a certain amount of direct control over lawmaking. Through the *initiative,* the voters can introduce a law. Through the *referendum,* a proposed law is submitted to the people for approval. When the expression *initiative and referendum* is used, it refers to a process in which the voters both introduce a law and vote on it.

Both initiative and referendum enable the people to take direct political action if their representatives refuse to pass some legislation that the people want. Only a tiny fraction of state and local laws have been passed by initiative and referendum, which are too costly and difficult to take the place of a lawmaking body.

The initiative. In cities, states, or countries that use the initiative, anyone may draw up a proposed law. If a specified number of voters sign a petition favoring it, the proposed law goes either to the voters or to the lawmaking body, which must vote on it.

The initiative is useful in cases where lawmakers refuse to enact, or even to consider, a law that the people want. However, the initiative has been criticized as a means of allowing a minority group to promote its special interests.

Laws providing for the initiative vary greatly. In some states, the whole question is ended if the legislature votes the bill down. In other states, the bill is then submitted to the people. If they vote for it, the bill becomes law. This procedure is called the *indirect initiative.* The governor cannot veto a bill passed in this way. Some states submit the proposed law directly to the people without bringing it before the legislature. This method is called the *direct initiative.* The initiative works in much the same way in a city as it does in a state. The city council, the city commissioners, or the people must pass on the proposed law, and the mayor cannot veto it.

The referendum puts a proposed law on the ballot at the next general election or at a special election. Most city charters and state constitutions provide for the referendum. For example, nearly all states hold a *constitutional referendum* on proposed amendments to their constitution. A constitutional referendum gives voters an opportunity to approve or reject the amendment. A large number of cities and states also hold a *statutory referendum,* which allows citizens to vote on laws passed by the legislature or proposed by an initiative. There are three kinds of statutory referendums: (1) *compulsory referendum,* (2) *optional referendum,* and (3) *referendum by petition.*

A compulsory referendum requires that the city or state submit certain kinds of measures to a vote by the people. Such kinds of measures may include proposals to issue municipal bonds, to raise property taxes for local schools, or to change the boundaries of a city.

An optional referendum permits the legislature to submit controversial measures to a direct vote of the people. The results of the referendum may be binding, or the legislature may use the referendum only to learn the people's opinion on an issue.

A referendum by petition takes place when a required number of citizens demand that a bill be submitted to a vote. For such a referendum to be held, the law must specify a waiting period, in most cases 90 days, before a bill takes effect. The required number of voters must sign a petition objecting to the bill during that period. Most states hold a referendum if 5 or 10 percent of the voters request it.

History. The initiative has been known only recently, but the referendum has been used for hundreds of years. Two cantons, or states, of Switzerland have had the referendum since the 1500's. Australia and New Zealand adopted the initiative and referendum in 1901.

The movement for initiative and referendum in the United States grew in the late 1800's and early 1900's. In 1898, South Dakota became the first state to adopt initiative and referendum laws. The initiative and referendum were included in the Oregon Constitution in 1902.

The combined power of initiative and referendum is provided by laws in many cities and in about half the states. Most other states provide for use of the referendum. The laws often include an additional provision called the *recall.* This is a method of removing officials from office by vote of the people (see **Recall**). The use of referendums in the United States increased in the late 1900's. Subjects covered included attempts to limit tax increases, the death penalty, nuclear power, handgun use, and the growth of cities.

The United Kingdom has no provision for the initiative and referendum as such, but the principle of the referendum is a regular part of the British election system. In Canada, the initiative and referendum have been discussed, but no steps have been taken to provide for them by law.   Robert Agranoff

Web site

Initiative and Referendum Institute
http://www.iandrinstitute.org/
Information on election issues and laws from a research group.

Presidential succession is provided for by Article II and Amendments 20 and 25 of the United States Constitution. Article II states that the vice president shall assume the duties and powers of the president if the president is removed from office, dies, resigns, or is unable to carry out the duties of the office.

Amendment 20, adopted in 1933, provides that the vice president-elect becomes president if the president-elect dies before the term begins but after the Electoral College has met. The Electoral College is a group of representatives chosen by the voters to officially elect the president. If the president-elect dies before the Electoral College meets, the national committee of the victorious political party would select a new candidate. Normally, this candidate would be the vice president-elect, though it need not be. After such a selection, however, the college would vote on that candidate.

If both the president and vice president should die or become disqualified, succession is determined by the Presidential Succession Act of 1947. This law states that the speaker of the House, and then the president *pro tempore* of the Senate, are next in succession. The Cabinet follows in this order:

1. Secretary of state
2. Secretary of the treasury

It's a fact

In 1898, South Dakota became the first state in the United States to adopt initiative and referendum legislation, which permits voters to introduce a law and vote on it.

3. Secretary of defense
4. Attorney general
5. Secretary of the interior
6. Secretary of agriculture
7. Secretary of commerce
8. Secretary of labor
9. Secretary of health and human services
10. Secretary of housing and urban development
11. Secretary of transportation
12. Secretary of energy
13. Secretary of education
14. Secretary of veterans affairs

Under the 1947 law, the secretaries of agriculture, commerce, and labor were added, and the secretary of defense replaced the secretary of war. In 1965, Congress added the secretaries of health, education, and welfare (now health and human services); and housing and urban development to presidential succession. The secretary of transportation was added in 1966, secretary of energy in 1977, secretary of education in 1979, and secretary of veterans affairs in 1989. No Cabinet member may become acting president unless the member is a citizen and at least 35 years old. If the member who would logically succeed to the presidency is less than 35, the presidency passes to the next eligible member.

Amendment 25, ratified in 1967, permits the president to nominate a vice president whenever a vacancy exists in that office. The nominee would take office when confirmed by a majority vote of both houses of Congress. Therefore, the office of vice president would almost always be filled. The amendment also establishes procedures for temporarily relieving a president who is unable to perform official duties because of an illness or for any other reason. The vice president would become acting president at such times. In 1973, Gerald R. Ford became the first person chosen vice president under Amendment 25. He was nominated by President Richard M. Nixon after Vice President Spiro T. Agnew resigned. Ford became president in 1974, after Nixon resigned. Vice President George Bush served as acting president for eight hours on July 13, 1985, when President Ronald Reagan had surgery. Thomas E. Cronin

See also **Constitution of the United States** (Amendments 20 and 25).

Recall enables voters to remove a person from office before a term is completed, and to elect a new public official. A special election is held for this purpose.

Before a recall election can be held, a petition must be filed that has been signed by a certain number of voters. Usually the number must equal from 10 to 25 percent of the votes cast for this particular office during the previous election. The individual in question may give up the office voluntarily. If the individual does not do this, candidates for the office may file petitions in the usual way. The special election then becomes a contest between the new candidates and the officer whose recall is sought. The person receiving the largest vote in the election serves the rest of the term.

The movement to provide for recall of state and local officials came with efforts to provide for more direct popular control over government generally. The modern use of recall in the United States began with the charter of Los Angeles in 1903. Several hundred cities and 15 states have since adopted it. The states include Oregon (1908), California (1911), Colorado, Washington, Idaho, Nevada, and Arizona (1912), Michigan (1913), Louisiana and Kansas (1914), North Dakota (1920), Wisconsin (1926), Alaska (1960), Montana (1976), and Georgia (1979). Some states that use the recall do not apply it to judges. Mayors have often been recalled. The recall of a state officer is unusual, but North Dakota removed a governor by recall in 1921.

People who favor the recall argue that voters should have a direct way of removing an officer whom they consider dishonest, incompetent, or heedless of public opinion. Most state constitutions provide for the removal of an officer by impeachment. But people sometimes wish to remove from office someone who is not guilty of an impeachable offense.

Opponents of recall point out that the practice may be abused. They say that able men and women may be unwilling to risk taking an office from which the voters may later remove them for no fault except the failure to go along with the public sentiment of the moment.
Robert Agranoff

It's a fact

The 1903 city charter of Los Angeles was the first in the United States to provide for recall, the procedure of removing a public official from office by a vote of the people. North Dakota removed a governor by recall in 1921.

Senate is one of the two lawmaking bodies of many legislatures. In many of these legislatures, the other chamber is called a *house of representatives*. In most cases, the senate is smaller. Many countries have a national legislature with a senate, including the United States, Canada, Australia, France, and Italy. In the United States, a senate is one of two chambers in 49 state legislatures. Nebraska has a one-chamber legislature. This article deals chiefly with the United States Senate.

The U.S. Senate is one of the two houses of Congress. The other one is the House of Representatives, usually simply referred to as the *House*. The Senate is often referred to as the *upper house* and the House of Representatives as the *lower house*. Both houses have about the same amount of power, but the office of senator is considered a higher distinction than that of representative.

The House and Senate must pass identical versions of a bill before it can become law. The Senate can originate all types of legislation except tax laws. Only the Senate can approve treaties and the president's nominations to certain government offices.

Membership of the U.S. Senate

Size. The Constitutional Convention, which established the form of the national government in 1787, disagreed on the question of congressional representation. Delegates from the states that had small populations wanted equal representation for every state. But delegates from states with large populations called for representation according to population. A compromise provided for equal representation in the Senate—two

The United States Senate, which has 100 members, meets in the Senate chamber of the United States Capitol, *shown here.* A gallery in the chamber allows visitors to watch the senators at work.

U.S. Capitol Historical Society (National Geographic)

senators from each state, regardless of population. The agreement set up representation in the House based on population. The first Senate had 22 members when it met in 1789 and 26 by the end of the first Congress. The Senate now has 100 members. Its membership reached 100 in 1959, when Hawaii became the 50th state.

Qualifications and election. The Constitution requires a U.S. senator to be at least 30 years old and to have been a citizen of the United States for at least nine years. Senators must maintain legal residence in the state they represent.

Today, voters elect all members of Congress. But the Constitution originally provided that the people elect only the House members, usually called *representatives.* State legislatures chose the senators and were expected to select wealthy, distinguished men who would promote conservative policies. But Senate elections distracted the legislatures from other duties. In 1913, the 17th Amendment to the Constitution gave voters the right to choose senators.

Senators serve six-year terms. About a third of all United States senators are chosen in the same year. There is no limit on the number of times a senator may be reelected.

Salary and privileges. The basic salary of senators is $141,300. Senators are entitled to annual salary increases based on rises in the cost of living, but they may vote not to accept the increases. Each senator also gets an allowance to pay the salaries of his or her staff. The size of the staff allowance depends on the number of people in the senator's state.

Senators also have the use of Senate office buildings in Washington, D.C., and get an allowance for an office in their home state. They also receive extra allowances to hire legislative assistants and to pay for office and travel expenses. Senators and representatives have legal *immunity* (protection) for anything they write or say as members of Congress. This immunity enables them to make critical statements about people without fear of being sued.

Organization of the U.S. Senate

The leaders of the Senate hold special positions established by the Constitution or by the political parties.

The Constitution provides that the vice president serve as *president of the Senate.* The vice president can preside over Senate debate but can vote only to break a tie. As a result, the vice president presides on ceremonial occasions or only when a close vote is expected on an important issue. The Constitution provides that the Senate choose a *president pro tempore* (temporary president) to preside when the vice president is absent. But the Senate usually gives this position to the senator of the *majority party* who has the longest continuous service. The majority party is the one with the most members in the Senate. Actually, the president pro tempore rarely presides, and different temporary presidents guide debate in most sessions.

Party leaders in the Senate have much more power than the leaders specified by the Constitution. Party leaders are chosen at a meeting called a *caucus* or *conference,* which is held before each new session of Congress begins. Democratic and Republican members hold separate caucuses. The majority party selects the *majority leader* of the Senate. The other party elects the *minority leader.* Each party also chooses an assistant leader called a *whip.* The whip estimates forthcoming votes and tries to persuade party members to support the party's position. In addition, each party chooses a *policy committee,* which helps schedule bills for consideration and largely plans the legislative strategy of the party.

Senate committees, which consist of members of both parties, do most of the actual work of the Senate. Senators serve on four types of committees. These types are (1) *standing* (permanent), (2) select, (3) conference, and (4) joint.

Standing committees, the most important type, deal with bills concerning specific legislative subjects. The Senate has 16 standing committees, the most powerful of which include Appropriations, Armed Services, Foreign Relations, and Judiciary. Select committees, also called *special* committees, are temporary groups formed for investigations or other special purposes. Conference committees and joint committees consist of members of each house of Congress. Conference committees resolve differences in bills that have passed in both houses. Joint committees deal with topics that con-

United States Senate

The Senate of the first session of the 107th Congress consisted of 50 Democrats and 50 Republicans when it convened on Jan. 3, 2001. The first date in each listing shows when the senator's term began. The second date in each listing shows when the senator's term expires.

State	Term	State	Term	State	Term
Alabama		**Louisiana**		**Ohio**	
Richard C. Shelby, R.	1987-2005	John B. Breaux, D.	1987-2005	Mike DeWine, R.	1995-2007
Jeff Sessions, R.	1997-2003	Mary L. Landrieu, D.	1997-2003	George V. Voinovich, R.	1999-2005
Alaska		**Maine**			
Theodore F. Stevens, R.	1968-2003	Olympia Snowe, R.	1995-2007	**Oklahoma**	
Frank H. Murkowski, R.	1981-2005	Susan M. Collins, R.	1997-2003	Don Nickles, R.	1981-2005
				James M. Inhofe, R.	1994-2003
Arizona		**Maryland**			
John McCain III, R.	1987-2005	Paul S. Sarbanes, D.	1977-2007	**Oregon**	
Jon Kyl, R.	1995-2007	Barbara A. Mikulski, D.	1987-2005	Ron Wyden, D.	1996-2005
				Gordon Smith, R.	1997-2003
Arkansas		**Massachusetts**			
Tim Hutchinson, R.	1997-2003	Edward M. Kennedy, D.	1962-2007	**Pennsylvania**	
Blanche Lambert Lincoln, D.	1999-2005	John F. Kerry, D.	1985-2003	Arlen Specter, R.	1981-2005
				Rick Santorum, R.	1995-2007
California		**Michigan**			
Dianne Feinstein, D.	1992-2007	Carl Levin, D.	1979-2003	**Rhode Island**	
Barbara Boxer, D.	1993-2005	Debbie Stabenow, D.	2001-2007	Jack Reed, D.	1997-2003
				Lincoln D. Chafee, R.	1999-2007
Colorado		**Minnesota**			
Ben N. Campbell, R.	1993-2005	Paul D. Wellstone, D.	1991-2003	**South Carolina**	
Wayne Allard, R.	1997-2003	Mark Dayton, D.	2001-2007	Strom Thurmond, R.	1955-2003
				Ernest F. Hollings, D.	1966-2005
Connecticut		**Mississippi**			
Christopher J. Dodd, D.	1981-2005	Thad Cochran, R.	1978-2003	**South Dakota**	
Joseph I. Lieberman, D.	1989-2007	Trent Lott, R.	1989-2007	Thomas A. Daschle, D.	1987-2005
				Tim Johnson, D.	1997-2003
Delaware		**Missouri**			
Joseph R. Biden, Jr., D.	1973-2003	Christopher S. (Kit) Bond, R.	1987-2005	**Tennessee**	
Thomas Carper, D.	2001-2007	Jean Carnahan, D.	2001-2002	Fred Thompson, R.	1994-2003
				Bill Frist, R.	1995-2007
Florida		**Montana**			
Bob Graham, D.	1987-2005	Max Baucus, D.	1978-2003	**Texas**	
Bill Nelson, D.	2001-2007	Conrad Burns, R.	1989-2007	Phil Gramm, R.	1985-2003
				Kay Bailey Hutchison, R.	1993-2007
Georgia		**Nebraska**			
Max Cleland, D.	1997-2003	Chuck Hagel, R.	1997-2003	**Utah**	
Zell Miller, D.	2000-2007	Ben Nelson, D.	2001-2007	Orrin G. Hatch, R.	1977-2007
				Robert F. Bennett, R.	1993-2005
Hawaii		**Nevada**			
Daniel K. Inouye, D.	1963-2005	Harry M. Reid, D.	1987-2005	**Vermont**	
Daniel K. Akaka, D.	1990-2007	John Ensign, R.	2001-2007	Patrick J. Leahy, D.	1975-2005
				James M. Jeffords, R.	1989-2007
Idaho		**New Hampshire**			
Larry E. Craig, R.	1991-2003	Robert C. Smith, R.	1990-2003	**Virginia**	
Mike Crapo, R.	1999-2005	Judd Gregg, R.	1993-2005	John W. Warner, R.	1979-2003
				George F. Allen, R.	2001-2007
Illinois		**New Jersey**			
Richard J. Durbin, D.	1997-2003	Robert G. Torricelli, D.	1997-2003	**Washington**	
Peter Fitzgerald, R.	1999-2005	Jon S. Corzine, D.	2001-2007	Patty Murray, D.	1993-2005
				Maria Cantwell, D.	2001-2007
Indiana		**New Mexico**			
Richard G. Lugar, R.	1977-2007	Pete V. Domenici, R.	1973-2003	**West Virginia**	
Evan Bayh, D.	1999-2005	Jeff Bingaman, D.	1983-2007	Robert C. Byrd, D.	1959-2007
				John D. Rockefeller IV, D.	1985-2003
Iowa		**New York**			
Charles E. Grassley, R.	1981-2005	Charles E. Schumer, D.	1999-2005	**Wisconsin**	
Tom Harkin, D.	1985-2003	Hillary Rodham Clinton, D.	2001-2007	Herbert Kohl, D.	1989-2007
				Russell D. Feingold, D.	1993-2005
Kansas					
Sam Brownback, R.	1996-2005	**North Carolina**		**Wyoming**	
Pat Roberts, R.	1997-2003	Jesse A. Helms, R.	1973-2003	Craig Thomas, R.	1995-2007
		John Edwards, D.	1999-2005	Mike Enzi, R.	1997-2003
Kentucky					
Mitch McConnell, R.	1985-2003	**North Dakota**			
Jim Bunning, R.	1999-2005	Kent Conrad, D.	1987-2007		
		Byron L. Dorgan, D.	1992-2005		

cern both houses, such as energy problems and economic matters.

Most Senate committees are divided into subcommittees, which handle much of the committee work. Members of the majority party head most of the committees and subcommittees. Members of both parties vote for committee heads. Often, however, the *seniority principle* determines who serves as the head of a committee. Under this principle, the majority party senator with the longest continuous service on a committee becomes the head.

Other members of committees are elected by the Senate. However, each party's caucus makes the committee assignments before the formal election. Every Senate committee has more members from the majority party than from the minority party.

The work of the U.S. Senate

Considering legislation is the Senate's chief task. After a senator introduces a bill, it is sent to a committee for study. The committee may lay the bill aside, keeping the Senate from voting on it, or release it with a recommendation to pass it. If a bill is released, it goes on a list for consideration by the Senate. The majority leader largely determines if and when such bills are considered.

The Senate considers most bills under a *unanimous consent agreement.* Such an agreement allows more flexible procedures than would otherwise be allowed. An objection from even one senator blocks a unanimous consent agreement. Most of these agreements include a limit on debate. Under the normal rules of the Senate, members may speak for as long as they wish on any topic whatsoever. Some senators occasionally use this freedom so they can make long speeches called *filibusters,* which prevent the Senate from voting. Small groups of senators sometimes use filibusters to force the withdrawal or changing of legislation that is favored by most members. To end a filibuster, the Senate can vote *cloture*—that is, to limit the debate. Cloture requires the support of at least three-fifths of the Senate.

Most bills require the support of only a simple majority—that is, more than half the senators present—to pass. A bill that the Senate has originated and passed is sent to the House, where it goes through a similar process. If both houses pass a bill, a conference committee may resolve any differences between the two versions of the legislation. After both houses pass identical versions of the bill, it goes to the White House for approval by the president. The bill becomes law if the president signs it or fails to act on it for 10 days—not including Sundays—while Congress is in session. A bill requires the president's signature to become law if it reaches the chief executive fewer than 10 days—not including Sundays—before Congress adjourns. If the president vetoes the bill, it is sent back to Congress. A vetoed bill becomes law if at least two-thirds of the members present in each House vote to *override* (reverse) the veto.

Other powers and duties of the Senate include four important nonlegislative functions. The Senate approves or rejects certain presidential appointments. It also approves or rejects treaties. The Senate elects the vice president if the Electoral College, the group of representatives chosen by the voters in presidential elections, fails to give any candidate a majority. In addition, the Senate judges *impeachment* cases brought against U.S. government officials by the House. Impeachment is a charge of misconduct in office.

Presidential appointments of ambassadors, federal judges, Cabinet members, and certain other officials are subject to approval by the Senate. The Senate votes on thousands of appointments yearly and usually gives close attention only to the most important ones. Under a custom called *senatorial courtesy,* the president confers with the senator or senators of his or her party from a state before nominating anyone for an office in that state. If the senator or senators do not approve of the appointment, the Senate almost always rejects it.

Any treaty made by the United States is subject to the approval of at least two-thirds of the senators present. This requirement limits the president's powers in foreign relations. A two-thirds vote of the Senate is also required for conviction in an impeachment case.

Senates in other countries

Almost half of all nations have a two-house legislature. However, not all upper houses are called senates. Many nations have representation by population in the lower house and equal representation for each state or province in the upper house.

Most upper houses not directly chosen by the voters have limits on their power. For example, the Canadian Senate, whose members are appointed by the governor general on the prime minister's recommendation, cannot introduce bills involving the spending of money, and cannot stop the passage of a constitutional amendment approved by the House of Commons. Ireland's senate, which is partly appointed and partly elected by other officials, is an advisory body.   Kenneth Janda

Related articles include:
Congress of the United States
Constitution of the United States
House of Representatives
Impeachment
United States, Government of the
Vice president of the United States

Web sites

C-SPAN
http://www.c-span.org/
C-SPAN's Web site serves as an online guide to politics in Washington, D.C. It Includes news and such special features as presidential biographies and teacher guides. C-SPAN was created as a public service by United States cable television companies to broadcast information about the political process.

The United States Senate
http://www.senate.gov/
Official Web site of the United States Senate.

Supreme Court of the United States is the highest court in the nation. Its basic duty is to determine whether federal, state, and local governments are acting according to the Constitution of the United States. The Supreme Court does its job by deciding specific legal cases on the basis of established legal rules. Much of the court's work involves rules that are laid down in the Constitution. These rules are stated in general terms, and the Supreme Court must determine their meaning and apply them to the cases presented for decision.

A Supreme Court decision has great importance.

Once it decides a constitutional question, all other courts throughout the United States are required to follow the decision in similar cases. In this way, the Supreme Court helps guarantee equal legal justice to all Americans. The court is not required to consider every case that is presented to it. It mainly accepts cases involving problems of special importance.

The Supreme Court heads the judicial branch of the federal government. It is the only court specifically created by the Constitution. The judicial system of each state is also headed by a supreme court. For the most part, state courts hear cases concerning state laws. However, the United States Supreme Court may review the decisions of the highest state courts that involve the U.S. Constitution or acts of Congress. This article deals only with the Supreme Court of the United States. For information on the entire federal court system and on the state courts, see Court.

The role of the Supreme Court and its interpretation of the law change occasionally. These changes depend partly on the political, social, and economic beliefs of its members, and partly on the national conditions of the time. In the early days of the nation, for example, the court concerned itself chiefly with the proper division of authority between the federal and state governments. A major concern today is the protection of the rights and liberties of individuals.

How the Supreme Court is organized

Article III of the Constitution provides for the creation of the Supreme Court and states the limits of its jurisdiction. But details of its organization and the work it can do are left largely to Congress. Congress set up the federal court system in the Judiciary Act of 1789.

Membership. The Supreme Court has nine members —a chief justice and eight associate justices. The number is set by the U.S. Congress and has changed through the years. The first Supreme Court had six members. Since 1869, the court has had nine members.

The Constitution sets no qualifications for justices but states that they shall be appointed by the president, with the advice and consent of the Senate. But all justices have had some legal training and experience, and most have been prominent judges, lawyers, law teachers, or government officials. The Senate has rejected outright only 12 Supreme Court nominees. Fourteen other nominations have been not acted upon or been withdrawn.

Once appointed, justices may remain in office for life, and Congress cannot reduce their salary. These provisions protect the justices from political control and help ensure their independence. A justice can be removed through impeachment for corruption or other abuses of office, but that has never occurred.

Salary and terms. The court meets regularly in the Supreme Court Building in Washington, D.C. The annual term of the court begins the first Monday in October and usually ends in June.

The chief justice receives $181,400 a year, and each associate justice receives $173,600. A justice 70 years of age, who has served as a justice or judge of the United States 10 or more years, may retire and continue to receive this salary. A justice who has served at least 15 years as a justice or judge may retire at 65 and receive the salary.

Authority of the Supreme Court

The Supreme Court declares what the law is only when an actual case comes before it. The case must involve a real dispute between opposing parties. The court does not give legal advice or advisory opinions, even if requested by the president or Congress.

The Constitution permits the court to decide cases arising under the Constitution, federal laws, and treaties. The Supreme Court also decides disputes involving the United States or two or more states. The most important of these cases are those that require the court to interpret the Constitution or the laws enacted by Congress.

The Supreme Court has the power to decide whether a federal or state law or executive action is constitutional. This power, known as *judicial review,* is not expressly granted in the Constitution. However, the Constitution by its own terms is the "supreme law of the land." The court has ruled that it must review conflicts between the Constitution and a federal or state law.

The Constitution gives the Supreme Court two types of authority: (1) *original jurisdiction* and (2) *appellate jurisdiction.* The court has original jurisdiction in cases affecting ambassadors or other representatives of foreign countries and in cases in which a state is one of the parties. These cases go directly to the Supreme Court but make up only a small part of the court's workload.

Most of the work of the Supreme Court comes from its appellate jurisdiction, which is its authority to confirm or reverse lower court decisions. Most Supreme Court cases come from the federal courts of appeals and the highest state courts. Federal district court decisions are normally reviewed first by the courts of appeals. However, in a few cases, the Supreme Court reviews the decisions of federal district courts. The court also reviews the decisions of the Court of Appeals for the Federal Circuit and the Supreme Court of Puerto Rico.

The Supreme Court may decide which of the cases under its appellate jurisdiction it will review. Because it cannot possibly review all the cases, it selects the ones it considers the most important. The court agrees to hear a case by granting a *writ of certiorari* (pronounced SUR

Photri

The courtroom of the Supreme Court Building in Washington, D.C., is shown here from the back of the room, where spectators can sit and watch court proceedings. At the front of the room is the bench, where the nine justices sit.

64

Stephen G. Breyer   **Ruth Bader Ginsburg**   **Anthony M. Kennedy**   **Sandra O'Connor**

All photos from the Collection, Supreme Court Historical Society

Chief Justice William H. Rehnquist   **Antonin Scalia**   **David H. Souter**   **John Paul Stevens**   **Clarence Thomas**

shee uh RAIR ee), a written order calling the case up from a lower court for review. The attorney for the side requesting a review submits a written petition for certiorari. It explains why the lower court judge is in error and why the case is of special importance. Most appeals are made on grounds that the judge has made an error in declaring the law that applies to the facts of the case. The opposing attorney is given copies of the documents and has a short time to file a written statement in opposition. If four justices vote to grant the petition, the court agrees to hear the case. The court controls its workload by granting only a small percentage of requests for a writ of certiorari.

The court in action

Pleading cases before the Supreme Court is normally done by attorneys who have been admitted to the bar of the court. However, a *litigant* (person engaged in a lawsuit) may argue his or her own case with the court's permission. Most litigants hire and pay their own attorneys. If a litigant has no money, free legal service may be provided. When the U.S. government has an interest in a case before the Supreme Court, it is usually represented by the solicitor general or members of the solicitor general's staff. The attorney general of the United States will sometimes argue an important case before the court.

Deciding cases. The justices decide a case after they have considered written and oral arguments from each side. The written argument is called a *brief.* During oral arguments, the justices are free to interrupt and to ask questions. After the attorneys' oral arguments, the justices discuss the case *in conference* (in private). The chief justice begins the discussion. Then, in order of seniority, the associate justices give their opinions. After discussion ends, the justices vote in reverse order of

seniority. Cases are decided by majority vote. If a tie occurs, the lower court decision is left standing. The parties have no further appeal.

If the chief justice has voted with the majority, he or she selects a justice to write the *opinion of the court.* This opinion is also called the *majority opinion.* If the chief justice has not voted with the majority, the senior justice of the majority assigns the opinion. A justice who disagrees with this opinion may write a *dissenting opinion.* Justices may write *concurring opinions* if they agree with the conclusion of the majority but not with the reasons for reaching it, or if they wish to express similar reasons in their own words.

All opinions are published in the *United States Reports.* The publishing of opinions also enables the public to study the decisions of the court. This is an important tradition in a free society, and is a safeguard against unreasonable use of power.

Effects of decisions. Supreme Court decisions have far-reaching effects. Once the court decides a case, lower courts must follow the decision in similar cases. The Supreme Court itself usually follows its earlier decisions. The policy of following previous decisions is known as *stare decisis.* It lends stability and predictability to the law. But the court is not bound by an earlier decision if it is convinced an error has been made or changed circumstances require a different approach. This provides for the court's recognition of a previous error or of social, political, and economic change.

Landmark decisions

The Supreme Court has decided cases that touch almost every aspect of American life. On some issues, the court's position has remained constant. But on others, it has shifted due to changes in members of the court, the law, and political and social factors. One of the most his-

Supreme Court justices

Name	Term	Appointed by	Name	Term	Appointed by
Chief justices			Stanley Matthews	1881-1889	Garfield
John Jay	1789-1795	Washington	Horace Gray	1882-1902	Arthur
* John Rutledge	1795	Washington	Samuel Blatchford	1882-1893	Arthur
Oliver Ellsworth	1796-1800	Washington	Lucius Q. C. Lamar	1888-1893	Cleveland
John Marshall	1801-1835	J. Adams	David J. Brewer	1890-1910	Harrison
Roger B. Taney	1836-1864	Jackson	Henry B. Brown	1891-1906	Harrison
Salmon P. Chase	1864-1873	Lincoln	George Shiras, Jr.	1892-1903	Harrison
Morrison R. Waite	1874-1888	Grant	Howell E. Jackson	1893-1895	Harrison
Melville W. Fuller	1888-1910	Cleveland	Edward D. White	1894-1910	Cleveland
Edward D. White	1910-1921	Taft	Rufus W. Peckham	1896-1909	Cleveland
William H. Taft	1921-1930	Harding	Joseph McKenna	1898-1925	McKinley
Charles E. Hughes	1930-1941	Hoover	Oliver W. Holmes, Jr.	1902-1932	T. Roosevelt
Harlan F. Stone	1941-1946	F. D. Roosevelt	William R. Day	1903-1922	T. Roosevelt
Frederick M. Vinson	1946-1953	Truman	William H. Moody	1906-1910	T. Roosevelt
Earl Warren	1953-1969	Eisenhower	Horace H. Lurton	1910-1914	Taft
Warren E. Burger	1969-1986	Nixon	Charles E. Hughes	1910-1916	Taft
William H. Rehnquist	1986-	Reagan	Willis Van Devanter	1911-1937	Taft
			Joseph R. Lamar	1911-1916	Taft
Associate justices			Mahlon Pitney	1912-1922	Taft
James Wilson	1789-1798	Washington	James C. McReynolds	1914-1941	Wilson
John Rutledge	1789-1791	Washington	Louis D. Brandeis	1916-1939	Wilson
William Cushing	1790-1810	Washington	John H. Clarke	1916-1922	Wilson
John Blair	1790-1796	Washington	George Sutherland	1922-1938	Harding
James Iredell	1790-1799	Washington	Pierce Butler	1923-1939	Harding
Thomas Johnson	1792-1793	Washington	Edward T. Sanford	1923-1930	Harding
William Paterson	1793-1806	Washington	Harlan F. Stone	1925-1941	Coolidge
Samuel Chase	1796-1811	Washington	Owen J. Roberts	1930-1945	Hoover
Bushrod Washington	1799-1829	J. Adams	Benjamin N. Cardozo	1932-1938	Hoover
Alfred Moore	1800-1804	J. Adams	Hugo L. Black	1937-1971	F. D. Roosevelt
William Johnson	1804-1834	Jefferson	Stanley F. Reed	1938-1957	F. D. Roosevelt
H. Brockholst Livingston	1807-1823	Jefferson	Felix Frankfurter	1939-1962	F. D. Roosevelt
Thomas Todd	1807-1826	Jefferson	William O. Douglas	1939-1975	F. D. Roosevelt
Gabriel Duvall	1811-1835	Madison	Frank Murphy	1940-1949	F. D. Roosevelt
Joseph Story	1812-1845	Madison	James F. Byrnes	1941-1942	F. D. Roosevelt
Smith Thompson	1823-1843	Monroe	Robert H. Jackson	1941-1954	F. D. Roosevelt
Robert Trimble	1826-1828	J. Q. Adams	Wiley B. Rutledge	1943-1949	F. D. Roosevelt
John McLean	1830-1861	Jackson	Harold H. Burton	1945-1958	Truman
Henry Baldwin	1830-1844	Jackson	Tom C. Clark	1949-1967	Truman
James M. Wayne	1835-1867	Jackson	Sherman Minton	1949-1956	Truman
Philip P. Barbour	1836-1841	Jackson	John M. Harlan	1955-1971	Eisenhower
John Catron	1837-1865	Van Buren	William J. Brennan, Jr.	1956-1990	Eisenhower
John McKinley	1838-1852	Van Buren	Charles E. Whittaker	1957-1962	Eisenhower
Peter V. Daniel	1842-1860	Van Buren	Potter Stewart	1958-1981	Eisenhower
Samuel Nelson	1845-1872	Tyler	Byron R. White	1962-1993	Kennedy
Levi Woodbury	1845-1851	Polk	Arthur J. Goldberg	1962-1965	Kennedy
Robert C. Grier	1846-1870	Polk	Abe Fortas	1965-1969	Johnson
Benjamin R. Curtis	1851-1857	Fillmore	Thurgood Marshall	1967-1991	Johnson
John A. Campbell	1853-1861	Pierce	Harry A. Blackmun	1970-1994	Nixon
Nathan Clifford	1858-1881	Buchanan	Lewis F. Powell, Jr.	1972-1987	Nixon
Noah H. Swayne	1862-1881	Lincoln	William H. Rehnquist	1972-1986	Nixon
Samuel F. Miller	1862-1890	Lincoln	John P. Stevens	1975-	Ford
David Davis	1862-1877	Lincoln	Sandra Day O'Connor	1981-	Reagan
Stephen J. Field	1863-1897	Lincoln	Antonin Scalia	1986-	Reagan
William Strong	1870-1880	Grant	Anthony M. Kennedy	1988-	Reagan
Joseph P. Bradley	1870-1892	Grant	David H. Souter	1990-	G. H. W. Bush
Ward Hunt	1873-1882	Grant	Clarence Thomas	1991-	G. H. W. Bush
John M. Harlan	1877-1911	Hayes	Ruth Bader Ginsburg	1993-	Clinton
William B. Woods	1881-1887	Hayes	Stephen G. Breyer	1994-	Clinton

*Served during U.S. Senate recess and later rejected by the Senate.

toric Supreme Court decisions was reflected in an opinion written by Chief Justice John Marshall in 1803, in the case of *Marbury v. Madison*. Marshall stated that the court may rule an act of Congress unenforceable if the act violates the Constitution. This power of *judicial review* is *implied* (expressed indirectly) but not clearly stated in the Constitution. Some people have protested the exercise of judicial review. But this power has become a basic part of the U.S. constitutional system.

Federalism. The court has interpreted the Constitu-

tion as granting broad powers to the national government. These powers are designed to bar certain exercises of state power. For example, the court's ruling in the case of *Gibbons v. Ogden* in 1824 has given Congress exclusive power to regulate all business activity that affects *interstate commerce* (trade among states). The trend toward strengthening the power of the federal government was greatly aided by the Union victory in the American Civil War and the adoption of the 14th Amendment in 1868. This amendment forbids the states to deny any person due process, equal protection, or the rights and privileges of citizens of the United States.

Regulation of business. During the late 1800's and early 1900's, federal and state legislatures became active in regulating business practices, including the hours and conditions of work. In the case of *Lochner v. New York* in 1905, the court struck down a state law limiting employees in bakeries from working over 60 hours a week. Other Supreme Court rulings further limited such exercises of the legislative power. Since the late 1930's, however, the court has allowed legislatures great freedom in regulating business.

Civil rights. In 1857, in *Dred Scott v. Sandford,* the court held that blacks, even those freed from slavery, were not and could not become U.S. citizens. Then, in 1868, the 14th Amendment made blacks citizens and guaranteed to all people "equal protection of the laws." In 1896, in *Plessy v. Ferguson,* the court interpreted that provision to allow "separate but equal" facilities for whites and blacks. But in 1954, in *Brown v. Board of Education of Topeka,* the court ruled that racially separate schools are unequal and thus unconstitutional. Later, the court decided that it is sometimes permissible to give preference to blacks in jobs and other matters as a way to correct the effects of past discrimination.

In 1873, in *Bradwell v. State,* the Supreme Court decided that Illinois could exclude women from the practice of law. The 19th Amendment, adopted in 1920, gave women the right to vote. Women's rights generally remained restricted until the 1960's, when many laws limiting the employment and educational opportunities of women were changed. A landmark decision in the area of women's rights occurred in the 1973 decision of *Roe v. Wade.* In this ruling, the court declared that a state may not prohibit abortion during the first three months of pregnancy, and may do so only under certain conditions in the second three months.

Election issues. For most of its history, the Supreme Court has been reluctant to hear challenges to election districting. But in 1962, in *Baker v. Carr,* the court changed its position and said that unfair distribution of seats in state legislatures could be challenged in federal courts. Then in 1964, in *Reynolds v. Sims,* it announced a one-person, one-vote standard. It ruled that election district lines must be redrawn to guarantee that all districts are roughly equal in population.

The Supreme Court played a major role in deciding the presidential election of 2000. The race between Texas Governor George W. Bush and Vice President Al Gore was one of the tightest presidential elections in U.S. history. The outcome depended on which candidate carried the state of Florida, where the vote was extremely close. Five weeks after the election, the court ruled in *Bush v. Gore* that Florida could not continue vote recounts without applying a consistent statewide standard. And because there was not enough time to develop such a standard before the vote in the Electoral College, the court ruled that no further recounts should take place. Gore then conceded the election to Bush.

Freedom of speech. Starting in years around World War I (1914-1918), the Supreme Court heard many cases based on the guarantee of free speech in the First Amendment. From the 1930's to the 1960's, the legal protection of free speech grew. In 1964, in *New York Times v. Sullivan,* the court ruled a newspaper could not be punished for publishing false statements about a public official unless it knew the statements were false or had good reason to know. In 1969, in *Brandenburg v. Ohio,* the court held that the general *advocacy* (support) of ideas could not be punished, no matter how distasteful those ideas might be.

Criminal law. In the 1960's, the Supreme Court strengthened the protections given a person accused of a crime. In *Mapp v. Ohio* in 1961, the court ruled that evidence obtained without a search warrant could not be admitted into a trial, though later court rulings provided for certain exceptions. In 1963, in *Gideon v. Wainwright,* the court required that states provide free legal counsel to any person charged with a felony who could not afford a lawyer. In *Miranda v. Arizona* in 1966, the court ruled that an accused person must be informed of his or her right to remain silent and obtain legal counsel before being questioned.

The Supreme Court has also placed limits on a state's power to impose the death penalty. In 1972, in *Furman v. Georgia,* the court held that some state laws authorizing the death penalty were not consistent with the 8th and 14th amendments. The court based its ruling on its opinion that the death penalty, as it was administered under the laws, was cruel and unusual punishment. In response to this decision, more than 35 states enacted new laws authorizing the death penalty. The Supreme Court approved these laws in *Gregg v. Georgia* in 1976.

Church and state. The Bill of Rights prohibits all laws establishing religion or interfering with the free exercise of religion. The Supreme Court's interpretation of that guarantee has led to various rulings designed to separate church and state. This view was reflected in *Engel v. Vitale* in 1962, when the court prohibited prayer in public schools. But in 1984, a majority of the court said that a city or town could include a *crèche,* or Nativity scene, in its annual Christmas display.

Controversy on the court

The Supreme Court has been sharply divided on some cases. This has been especially true of cases involving questions that have divided the American public, such as minority rights. The court's lack of complete agreement in such cases is not unexpected nor is it undesirable. It reflects the seriousness of the cases and the presence of different points of view.

Since the Supreme Court was established, a strong debate has continued concerning the extent of its power. One side has insisted that the court should interpret and apply the Constitution to agree with the meaning and intent of those who wrote it. But another group has insisted on a more creative role for the court. Members of this group would interpret the Constitution so that it would apply to the new and changing problems of the nation. The second group also draws support from the original intent of the founding fathers, but disagrees as to the scope and meaning of that intent.   Owen M. Fiss

See also **Constitution of the United States; Court.**

Web site

Supreme Court of the United States
http://www.supremecourtus.gov/
Official Web site of the U.S. Supreme Court.

© Alex Bartel, Uniphoto

The United States government has its headquarters in Washington, D.C. The United States Capitol in that city, *shown here,* is where Congress meets to make the nation's laws.

United States government

United States, Government of the. The government of the United States represents, serves, and protects the American people at home and abroad. Because the United States is a nation of great wealth and military strength, the actions of its government affect all parts of the world.

The Constitution of the United States establishes the basic structure of the U.S. government. The Constitution creates a *federal system,* in which political power is divided between the national government and the governments of each state. The national government is sometimes called the *federal* government. The Constitution also creates three separate branches of government—legislative, executive, and judicial—to share the work of creating, enforcing, and interpreting the laws of the nation. The branches are represented by Congress, the president, and the Supreme Court of the United States.

The national government of the United States is the country's largest government system. It employs about $2\frac{3}{4}$ million civilian workers and approximately $1\frac{3}{4}$ million military personnel. Each year, it collects about $2 trillion in taxes from American citizens and corporations to help finance its work.

From the United States capital in Washington, D.C., the national government conducts thousands of activities that affect the lives of Americans. It helps fund many state government services, including job training, welfare payments, roads, and health care. It manages a social security program that provides a pension plan and other benefits to the nation's retired or disabled workers. It sets standards for programs to aid poor, aged, or disabled people. It tests food and drugs for purity and safety, conducts research on such diseases as AIDS and cancer, and sets standards to control pollution. It con-

Roger H. Davidson, the contributor of this article, is Professor of Government and Politics Emeritus at the University of Maryland and coauthor of Congress and Its Members.

ducts and coordinates space exploration. It oversees air travel, forecasts the weather, and runs hospitals for veterans. It maintains national parks, forests, historic sites, and museums.

The national government also deals with the governments of other nations. It works in dozens of international organizations that promote cooperation among nations. Many of these organizations are associated with the United Nations. The government also operates numerous diplomatic and military posts around the world.

This article provides a broad overview of the system of national government in the United States. Separate *World Book* articles give detailed information on many of the topics discussed. For a list of these articles, see the *Related articles* at the end of this article.

Principles of American government

Constitutional authority. The national government gets its authority from the American people through a written document—the Constitution of the United States. The Constitution defines the goals of the national government and what it can and cannot do.

According to the Constitution, the national government's purpose is to "establish justice, insure domestic tranquility, provide for the common defense, promote the general welfare, and secure the blessings of liberty. ..." The Constitution grants the national government strong powers to work toward these goals. The government has direct authority over all citizens. It can collect taxes and pay debts, borrow money, negotiate with other governments, regulate trade between the states and with other countries, create armed forces, and declare war. It can also create and enforce all laws that are "necessary and proper" to carry out its constitutional goals and powers.

The Constitution also limits the authority of the government. It forbids certain laws and actions. The Bill of Rights in the Constitution describes certain basic freedoms and rights of all Americans and forbids the gov-

Cameramann International, Ltd.

The Supreme Court Building is where Supreme Court justices meet to interpret the laws that govern the nation.

Karen A. McCormack

The White House is the official residence of the president of the United States and also the place where the president works.

ernment to violate those rights. For example, the government must respect the people's freedoms of speech, religion, press, and peaceful assembly.

American citizens can change the Constitution. An amendment may be proposed by Congress or by a national convention called by Congress. The amendment becomes part of the Constitution after being *ratified* (approved) by the legislatures of three-fourths of the states or by conventions in three-fourths of the states. There have been 27 amendments to the Constitution.

Separation of powers. Three separate branches share the powers of the United States government. Each branch has both *expressed powers*—those specifically listed in the Constitution—and *implied powers*—those reasonably suggested by its expressed powers. In general, the legislative branch makes the nation's laws, the executive branch enforces the laws, and the judicial branch interprets the laws if questions arise.

A system of *checks and balances* makes sure that each branch acts only within its constitutional limits. Each branch has some powers that curb, or check, those of the other two. This prevents any single government group or official from becoming too powerful.

The Constitution ensures that the branches remain separate by forbidding members of Congress from serving in another branch. In addition, executive and judicial officials may not serve in Congress. The Constitution provides that the vice president officially preside over the Senate, one of the two bodies of Congress. However, the Senate presidency is mostly a ceremonial role, and the vice president rarely appears in Congress.

Federalism is the division of powers between a national or central government and local authorities. The Constitution divides powers between the national and state governments. In addition, the states share and divide powers with such local political subdivisions as counties, cities, and towns.

The national, or federal, government can exercise only those powers that are listed in the Constitution or implied by the Constitution. The states, or the people, retain all powers not denied them, or not given to the national government, by the Constitution. The federal

and state governments have some *concurrent* powers—that is, they both have authority to do some things. Concurrent powers include the right to tax, spend, and borrow money.

Each state has its own constitution, its own laws, and its own legislative, executive, and judicial branches. In general, state laws and activities must not conflict with the U.S. Constitution, acts of Congress, or U.S. treaties. The states take the lead in such areas as education, public safety, and consumer and environmental protection. Through the years, however, the role of the federal government has increased in these and other state government activities.

Representative democracy. The United States government relies on the consent of the people. The peo-

Symbols of the United States include the American flag and the Great Seal. The eagle holds an olive branch and arrows, symbolizing a desire for peace but the ability to wage war. The reverse side bears the Eye of Providence, representing God, and a pyramid dated 1776.

ple elect a certain number of their fellow citizens to represent them in making laws and in other matters. Federal, state, and local laws regulate elections.

Political parties play an important role in elections. They select candidates to run for public office, provide opposition to the party in power, and raise funds to conduct election campaigns. They also inform voters about public affairs and about problems they believe need government action.

The United States has a *two-party system*—that is, it has two major political parties, the Democratic and the Republican. Members of these two parties hold almost all the offices in the national and state governments.

Minor political parties in the United States rarely elect candidates to government offices. These parties serve chiefly to express discontent over problems that the major parties may have neglected. Often, one or both of the major parties moves toward solving such a problem. Then the third party may disappear or be absorbed by a major party.

The legislative branch

Congress creates, abolishes, and changes federal laws, which govern the nation. Congressional lawmakers also play an important role in establishing *public policy*—what the government does or says in response to political issues.

Organization. Congress consists of two chambers—the Senate and the House of Representatives. The two chambers have about equal power. Voters in each state elect the members of each chamber, or *house.* The Senate has 100 members, 2 from each state, who serve six-year terms. About a third of the seats come up for election every two years. The House of Representatives, usually called simply the *House,* has 435 members. House members, or *representatives,* serve two-year terms. The number of representatives from each state is based on the state's population. Each state has at least one representative. The Senate and House meet in separate wings of the Capitol in Washington, D.C.

Elections are held in November of even-numbered years. The members start each two-year Congress the following January. Beginning with the First Congress (1789-1791), each Congress has been numbered.

The legislative branch includes several agencies that provide Congress with information and services. For example, the General Accounting Office *audits* (closely examines) the financial records of various departments and agencies of the federal government and reports its findings to Congress. Other support agencies of Congress include the Congressional Budget Office, the Congressional Research Service of the Library of Congress, and the Government Printing Office.

In addition, each senator and representative has a personal staff to advise him or her on issues, answer mail from voters, handle publicity, and help in other ways. There are also staffs that assist committees in Congress and *aides* (assistants) for each house.

Functions. Making laws is the main job of Congress. During each two-year Congress, senators and representatives introduce up to 10,000 bills. In that period, Congress passes, and the president signs into law, about 600 bills.

Congress makes laws on all kinds of matters. Some laws are major policy decisions, such as taxing and spending measures. Others deal with administrative details, such as employee benefits or the purchase of land. Still others are *commemorative* laws, which honor a group, person, or event. In 1914, for example, Congress honored mothers with a law that declared the second Sunday in May as Mother's Day. All of these laws are called *public laws* if they apply to people in general. Congress also passes a few *private laws* that apply to specific individuals, such as immigration cases.

Congress does more than make laws. It investigates the actions of the executive branch and makes sure the laws are carried out. Congress also reviews the election, qualifications, and ethical behavior of its own members. It can remove federal officials from office, including members of Congress, for serious offenses. The House brings *impeachment* (misconduct) charges against an official, and the Senate tries the official.

Each chamber of Congress has some independent duties. The Senate approves or rejects the people that the president appoints to certain high-level federal positions. It also approves or rejects treaties that the president makes. All legislation that deals with taxes or spending must start in the House.

In addition, senators and representatives spend much time serving their *constituents*—the people who elected them. They answer individuals' questions or requests, meet with visitors, and inform the public of issues. They often travel to their home states to appear at public events, study area problems, and talk with voters and local officials. In addition, legislators, usually with the help of their parties, conduct their own election campaigns, including fund-raising.

Committee system. Congress does much of its work through committees. The House has 19 *standing* (permanent) committees, each with authority over bills in a certain area, such as agriculture or banking. The Senate has 16 standing committees. Most standing committees have subcommittees to handle particular topics. In addition, each house may form temporary *special committees* or *select committees,* usually to conduct investigations. *Joint committees*—made up of members from both the House and the Senate—handle mainly research and administrative details. Most legislators serve on several committees and subcommittees.

When committees or subcommittees study bills, they may hear testimony from experts and other interested people. Committees work out amendments to the bills and other details and recommend bills to the full House or Senate for passage.

Party leadership has an important influence on Congress. Democratic and Republican members of Congress choose official party leaders for each house. Party leaders plan the legislative strategy of the party, communicate their party's position on issues to other members, and encourage members to vote along party lines. When voting on major legislation, senators and representatives weigh their party loyalty against their own judgment or the interests of their constituents. On less important bills, legislators usually vote according to their party's position.

In each house, the *majority party*—that is, the party with the most members—chooses one of its members to lead the entire chamber. The House chooses a *speaker,* and the Senate chooses a *president pro tempore* (temporary president) to serve in the vice president's absence. In addition, majority-party members head congressional committees.

Each party in the House and Senate also elects a *floor leader* and an assistant leader called a *whip.* The floor leaders, known as *majority leaders* or *minority leaders* depending on their party, and the whips work for passage of their party's legislative program.

In the House, the majority party has strong control over the agenda. The speaker and the majority leader schedule the House's business and coordinate the committees' work on bills. House debate rules are formal and rigid, designed to let the majority have its way.

In the Senate, a smaller and less formal body, the majority party has less control. Debate rules allow senators opposed to a bill to make *filibusters*—long speeches or other tactics designed to slow down or block the legislative process or force the bill's sponsors to compromise on its content or abandon the bill.

The lawmaking process weeds out bills that lack sufficient support. At every stage in the process, a bill's backers must bargain for the support of their fellow lawmakers. A bill is debated by one or more committees and, if approved, by the full House or Senate. Both houses must approve a bill in exactly the same form before it is sent to the president. If they adopt different versions of a bill, a *conference committee,* made up of committee leaders from both houses, may be formed to work out the differences.

For a detailed description of the lawmaking process, see the chart *How a bill becomes a law in the United States* in this article. See also **Congress of the United States** (How Congress makes laws).

The executive branch

The executive branch carries out federal laws. It also creates and enforces regulations based on the laws. The president heads the executive branch. Fourteen executive departments and about 80 agencies handle the daily work of administering federal laws and programs.

The presidency. The president is elected to serve a four-year term. The 22nd Amendment to the Constitution, approved in 1951, provides that no one can be elected to the presidency more than twice.

A nationwide presidential election is held every four years in November. The people of each state elect delegates to the Electoral College. The delegates, or *electors,* then choose the president and vice president based on the popular votes in the states they represent. If no candidate receives a majority of Electoral College votes, the House elects the president and the Senate selects the vice president. If the president dies, is removed from office, or becomes unable to perform the duties of office, the vice president takes over the presidency until the next election. The president lives in the White House in Washington, D.C., and has offices there.

The president has many roles and duties. As chief executive, the president enforces federal laws, directs the preparation of the federal budget, and appoints many high-ranking officials. As commander in chief of the armed forces, the president directs foreign and national security affairs. As chief diplomat, the president negotiates treaties with other countries. As legislative leader, the president recommends laws to Congress and works to win their passage. The president may veto bills approved by Congress. The threat of a veto can influence the way Congress develops a bill.

Congress has the power to restrain most of the president's powers. Congress must approve the federal budget and the president's legislative plans. It can override a president's veto by a vote of a two-thirds majority of the members present in each house. In addition, all treaties and high-level appointments by the president require Senate approval.

For many Americans and people around the world, the president represents the United States government. Presidents can use their visibility in the news media to focus attention on their programs and to create public support for their policies. However, their visibility is a double-edged sword. People often blame presidents for problems, such as an economic depression or a foreign crisis, that the president may not have caused and can do little to solve.

The Executive Office of the President consists of a number of staff agencies that provide the president with information, ideas, and advice on a wide range of issues. One agency, the Office of Management and Budget (OMB), helps plan the federal budget. The OMB also advises the president on proposed laws and regulations, shaping its recommendations to promote the president's goals. Another key unit, the White House Office, includes the president's personal aides, policy advisers, speechwriters, and lawyers.

Executive departments and agencies carry out laws and create and enforce detailed regulations based on laws. Congress creates departments and agencies to deal with particular matters. It controls the basic structure and authority of each. The Office of Management and Budget and Congress control the funding of departments and agencies. Presidents cannot create, eliminate, or reorganize departments or agencies without the approval of Congress.

Executive departments are vast organizations that conduct a wide range of government activities. Each is divided into bureaus, divisions, offices, or other units. The president, with the approval of the Senate, appoints the head of each department. The department heads form the president's Cabinet, an informal advisory group that helps the president.

Independent agencies. The executive branch includes dozens of agencies that perform government functions. These agencies are called *independent agencies* because they are not part of an executive department. Some independent agencies, such as the National Aeronautics and Space Administration and the Peace Corps, carry out programs or provide services. Others, called *regulatory agencies* or *regulatory commissions,* enforce laws dealing with aspects of American economic life. For example, the Federal Trade Commission works to protect consumers from unfair trade practices.

Government corporations are independent agencies that are organized in ways similar to businesses. They conduct commercial activities, perform services, or raise funds for the public. For example, the Tennessee Valley Authority works to develop the natural resources of the Tennessee Valley. The U.S. Postal Service provides mail services.

Control of departments and agencies. Except for high-level officials appointed by the president, executive departments and independent agencies are made up of permanent staffs of civil service workers. They establish their own ways of carrying out programs and policies. Departments and agencies may be influenced by powerful interest groups. For example, the Forest Service, a division of the Department of Agriculture, manages the national forests. It must juggle the often-conflicting needs of such groups as campers, environmentalists, ranchers, and logging companies. In addition, departments and agencies must cooperate with Congress, especially with the committees that write their laws and approve funds for their programs.

Because of these influences, presidents may find it difficult to push departments and agencies and their programs in new directions. To have an effect, presidents may find it necessary to create wide public support for their policies. They can also influence departments and agencies by shaping the federal budget to reflect their goals and by making sure their policies are reflected in new regulations.

The judicial branch

The judicial branch interprets the nation's laws. It is made up of a system of federal courts and judges. The Supreme Court of the United States is the highest court in the nation.

Authority of the courts. Federal courts settle disputes among citizens involving the Constitution or federal laws, and disputes between citizens and the federal government. They also hear cases involving treaties or *maritime* (sea) laws. In addition, federal courts may decide certain cases between individuals or groups from different states, and cases involving other countries or their citizens.

The courts' most important power is *judicial review* that is, their authority to overturn laws they judge unconstitutional. Any court in the United States can declare laws or the actions of public officials illegal if they

How a bill becomes law in the United States

The drawings on this page and the next three pages show how federal laws are enacted in the United States. Thousands of bills are introduced during each Congress, which lasts two years, and hundreds become law. All bills not enacted by the end of the two-year period are killed.

Ideas for new laws come from many sources. The president, members of Congress, and other government officials may propose laws. Suggestions also come from individual citizens; special-interest groups, such as farmers, industry, and labor; newspaper editorials; and public protests. Congressional committees, in addition to lawyers who represent special-interest groups, actually write most bills. Specialists called *legislative counsels* in both the Senate and House of Representatives also help prepare many bills for congressional action.

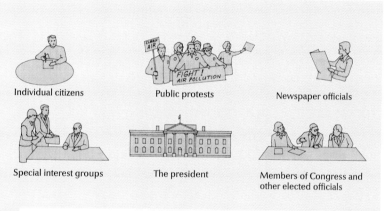

Individual citizens   Public protests   Newspaper officials

Special interest groups   The president   Members of Congress and other elected officials

Each bill must be sponsored by a member of the House or Senate. Any number of senators or representatives may co-sponsor a bill. A bill may originate in either house of Congress unless it deals with taxes or spending. The Constitution provides that all revenue bills must be introduced in the House. By tradition, spending bills begin there also. This practice came from England.

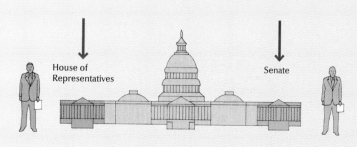

House of Representatives   Senate

WORLD BOOK illustrations by David Cunningham

Continues on the next page.

How a bill moves through Congress

The drawings on this page and the next show the normal path of a bill introduced in the House of Representatives. The process is the same for a bill introduced in the Senate, except that the House action comes after the Senate action. A bill may die at almost any stage of the process if no action is taken on it. A majority of the bills introduced in Congress fail and never become law.

Introduction in the House. A sponsor introduces a bill by giving it to the clerk of the House or placing it in a box called the *hopper.* The clerk reads the title of the bill into the *Congressional Record* in a procedure called the *first reading.* The Government Printing Office prints the bill and distributes copies.

Assignment to committee. The speaker of the House assigns the bill to a committee for study. The House has 19 *standing* (permanent) committees, each with jurisdiction over bills in a certain area.

The bill goes to the Senate to await its turn. Bills normally reach the Senate floor in the order that they come from committee. But if a bill is urgent, the leaders of the majority party might push it ahead.

Committee action. The committee or one of its subcommittees studies the bill and may hold hearings. The committee may approve the bill as it stands, revise the bill, or table it.

Assignment to committee. The presiding officer of the Senate assigns the proposed law to a committee for study. The Senate has 16 standing committees.

The Senate considers the bill. Senators can debate a bill indefinitely, unless they vote or agree to limit discussion. When there is no further debate, the Senate votes. Most bills must have a simple majority to pass.

A conference committee made up of members of both houses works out any differences between the House and Senate versions of the bill. The revised bill is sent back to both houses for their final approval.

The committee studies the bill and hears testimony from experts and other interested people. In many cases, a subcommittee conducts the study. The committee may release the bill with a recommendation to pass it, revise the bill and release it, or lay it aside so that the House cannot vote on it. Releasing the bill is called *reporting it out,* and laying it aside is called *tabling.*

The bill goes on a calendar, a list of bills awaiting action. The Rules Committee may call for quick action on the bill, limit debate, and limit or prohibit amendments. Undisputed bills may be passed by unanimous consent, or by a two-thirds vote if members agree to suspend the rules.

Consideration by the House begins with a second reading of the bill, the only complete reading in most cases. A third reading, by title only, comes after any amendments have been added. In most cases, if the bill passes by a *simple majority* (at least one more than half the votes), it goes to the Senate.

Introduction in the Senate. To introduce a bill, a senator must be recognized by the presiding officer and announce the introduction of the bill. A bill that has passed either house of Congress is sometimes called an *act,* but the term usually means legislation that has passed both houses and become law.

The bill is printed by the Government Printing Office in a process called *enrolling.* The clerk of the house of Congress that originated the bill certifies the final version.

The speaker of the House signs the enrolled bill, and then the vice president signs it. Finally, Congress sends the proposed new legislation to the White House for consideration by the president.

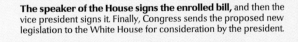

Action by the president

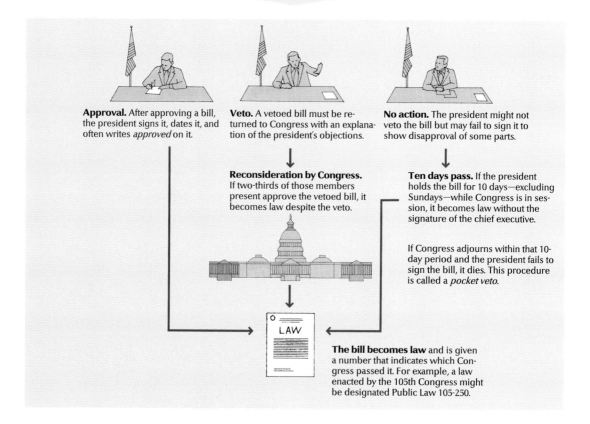

A bill passed by Congress goes to the president, who has 10 days—not including Sundays—to sign or veto it. The president may also let a bill become law by letting 10 days pass without acting.

Approval. After approving a bill, the president signs it, dates it, and often writes *approved* on it.

Veto. A vetoed bill must be returned to Congress with an explanation of the president's objections.

No action. The president might not veto the bill but may fail to sign it to show disapproval of some parts.

Reconsideration by Congress. If two-thirds of those members present approve the vetoed bill, it becomes law despite the veto.

Ten days pass. If the president holds the bill for 10 days—excluding Sundays—while Congress is in session, it becomes law without the signature of the chief executive.

If Congress adjourns within that 10-day period and the president fails to sign the bill, it dies. This procedure is called a *pocket veto*.

LAW

The bill becomes law and is given a number that indicates which Congress passed it. For example, a law enacted by the 105th Congress might be designated Public Law 105-250.

---

conflict with the U.S. Constitution. The Supreme Court, however, is the final authority on such matters. Judicial review provides an important check on the executive and legislative branches, as well as on state and local governments. The Supreme Court first established the power of judicial review in the famous case of *Marbury v. Madison* (1803), which struck down part of an act of Congress. Since then, the court has overturned all or parts of more than 125 federal laws and over 1,000 state laws.

Lower court system. The Constitution gives Congress the job of creating a system of lower courts. In 1789, Congress passed the Judiciary Act, which established the federal court system. Today, the system includes both *trial courts,* which conduct the first hearing of a case, and *appellate courts,* which review a trial court's decision at the request of the losing party. Most federal courts hear a wide variety of cases. Several specialized courts deal only with particular matters.

District courts are trial courts with general federal jurisdiction. There are 94 district courts in the United States and its possessions. Each state has at least one. Most federal cases begin in a district court.

Courts of appeals are appellate courts that review district court decisions on matters of law. A court of appeals can change a ruling if it decides the lower court incorrectly applied the law to the case. Courts of appeals also hear appeals of decisions made by federal agencies. The United States is divided into 12 judicial areas called *circuits,* each of which has one court of appeals. A 13th court, the United States Court of Appeals for the Federal Circuit, has nationwide jurisdiction.

Special courts. The federal court system includes several courts that deal with particular matters. For example, the United States Court of Federal Claims hears cases involving claims against the federal government. The

Court of International Trade settles disputes over imports. The Tax Court of the United States handles conflicts between taxpayers and the Internal Revenue Service. The Court of Military Appeals hears appeals from rulings by *courts-martial* (military courts).

The Supreme Court, the nation's highest court, is mainly an appellate court. It can review appeals from federal appellate courts and, in certain cases, appeals directly from district courts. It can also review appeals from the highest court in each state, providing the case involves an important federal question. In certain cases, the Supreme Court is a trial court. It tries disputes involving diplomats from other countries or conflicts between states.

The Supreme Court has one chief justice and eight associate justices. Four justices must agree to hear a case. At least six justices hear the cases chosen and decide each case by a majority vote. If a tie occurs, the lower court decision stands. The Supreme Court meets regularly in the Supreme Court Building in Washington, D.C.

Caseload. The court receives thousands of appeals each year, but it can choose which ones it will hear. Each year, it hears about 100 cases. Justices select cases that raise important questions about the government system or the rights of Americans. For example, the court hears many cases about the First Amendment guarantees of free speech and religion and about the Fourteenth Amendment's declaration that all citizens are entitled to equal protection under the law. Justices may choose a case because it involves a question that two or more lower appellate courts have decided differently.

Effects of decisions. A Supreme Court decision has great importance. Once the court rules on a constitutional question, all other courts throughout the United States are required to follow the decision in similar cases. In this way, the Supreme Court helps guarantee legal equality to all Americans.

Supreme Court decisions are not always carried out. The court must rely on the executive and legislative branches, as well as state and local officials, to enforce its decisions. Government officials may be slow to act on rulings with which they disagree. For example, the court ruled in the 1954 case of *Brown v. Board of Education of Topeka* that public school segregation was unconstitutional. But many Southern communities moved slowly in desegregating their schools after that landmark decision. Congress or state legislatures can pass laws that bypass the Supreme Court's ruling. If a ruling is extremely unpopular, the Constitution itself can be amended to override the court's decision.

Judges. The president appoints all federal judges with the approval of the Senate. Most federal judges may remain in office for life. This lifetime appointment protects them from political control and helps ensure their independence from the other branches of government. However, Congress can remove judges from office through impeachment for corruption or other abuses of office.

Because of the importance of Supreme Court decisions, the political opinions of each justice are of great public interest. Presidents generally nominate individuals to the Supreme Court who share their views on important issues. Before approving each nomination, the Senate carefully examines the nominee's qualifications.

Supreme Court nominees with extreme views on key issues usually face fierce opposition.

Growth of the federal government

Background. The American Colonies won their independence from the United Kingdom in the Revolutionary War in America (1775-1783). They founded the first national government of the United States in 1781 under a document called the Articles of Confederation. Under the Articles, however, the states kept much of their independence. The national government could not collect taxes, regulate trade, or force states to fulfill their obligations. Such leaders as George Washington, Benjamin Franklin, James Madison, and Alexander Hamilton feared that the weak national government would collapse. This concern about the Articles of Confederation led to the Constitutional Convention of 1787 in Philadelphia.

The state delegates at the convention wanted a strong national government but feared that it would not respect the independence of the states and the liberties of the people. In framing the Constitution, they used ideas from the constitutions of New York, Massachusetts, and other states. The delegates also drew on political theories set forth by philosophers of the 1600's and 1700's. Such thinkers as England's John Locke and France's Baron Montesquieu, for example, had urged separate governmental branches as a way to prevent tyranny.

The delegates created a bold new system of government—the Constitution of the United States. The document went into effect on June 21, 1788, when New Hampshire became the ninth state to ratify it. The first 10 amendments, called the Bill of Rights, were ratified in 1791. The Constitution is the oldest written national charter still in force. It establishes a broad framework of government, flexible enough to change as the nation changes. Through the years, government leaders have worked out the details as required by economic, political, and social conditions.

Early years. The federal government was tiny when it began operating in 1789. That year, Congress created the first three executive departments—foreign affairs (later the Department of State), treasury, and war—and the office of the attorney general. Only a few hundred clerks served the departments and Congress.

Alexander Hamilton, the nation's first secretary of the treasury, strongly influenced the early development of the U.S. government. He believed the Constitution should be interpreted loosely to give the federal government broad power. Hamilton pushed bills through Congress that helped pay the nation's debt from the Revolutionary War. He also launched plans that provided for such internal improvements as roads and canals, and aided the nation's struggling new industries.

In 1803, the United States almost doubled its area in a transaction with France known as the Louisiana Purchase. The government sold much of the new land to canal and railroad companies, greatly enriching its treasury. During the mid-1800's, the United States gained control of Texas, California, and other lands, extending its boundaries westward to the Pacific Ocean. Because of revenue from land sales, as well as taxes on imported goods, the government often collected more money than it spent during the 1800's.

76

Government of the United States

The chart on this page shows the basic structure of the government of the United States. The U.S. Constitution creates three separate branches—legislative, executive, and judicial—to share government powers. In general, the legislative branch makes the nation's laws, the executive branch carries out the laws, and the judicial branch interprets the laws.

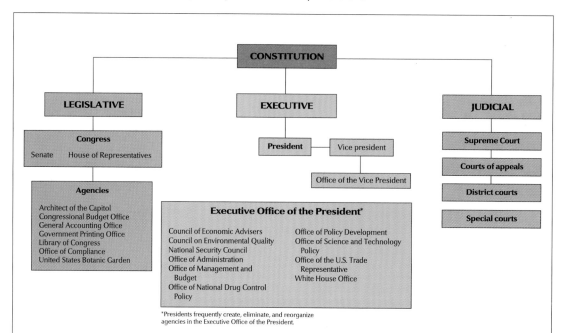

CONSTITUTION

LEGISLATIVE — **EXECUTIVE** — **JUDICIAL**

Congress
Senate · House of Representatives

President — **Vice president**
Office of the Vice President

Supreme Court
Courts of appeals
District courts
Special courts

Agencies
Architect of the Capitol
Congressional Budget Office
General Accounting Office
Government Printing Office
Library of Congress
Office of Compliance
United States Botanic Garden

Executive Office of the President*
Council of Economic Advisers
Council on Environmental Quality
National Security Council
Office of Administration
Office of Management and Budget
Office of National Drug Control Policy
Office of Policy Development
Office of Science and Technology Policy
Office of the U.S. Trade Representative
White House Office

*Presidents frequently create, eliminate, and reorganize agencies in the Executive Office of the President.

Executive departments
Department of Agriculture
Department of Commerce
Department of Defense
Department of Education
Department of Energy
Department of Health and Human Services
Department of Housing and Urban Development
Department of the Interior
Department of Justice
Department of Labor
Department of State
Department of Transportation
Department of the Treasury
Department of Veterans Affairs

Independent agencies
The executive branch includes about 80 agencies that are not part of an executive department. This chart lists some of the best-known independent agencies.

Central Intelligence Agency
Commission on Civil Rights
Consumer Product Safety Commission
Environmental Protection Agency
Equal Employment Opportunity Commission
Export-Import Bank of the United States
Federal Communications Commission
Federal Deposit Insurance Corporation
Federal Election Commission
Federal Maritime Commission
Federal Mediation and Conciliation Service
Federal Reserve System
Federal Trade Commission
General Services Administration
International Trade Commission
National Aeronautics and Space Administration
National Archives
National Foundation on the Arts and the Humanities
National Labor Relations Board
National Mediation Board
National Science Foundation
Nuclear Regulatory Commission
Peace Corps
Railroad Retirement Board
Securities and Exchange Commission
Small Business Administration
Social Security Administration
Tennessee Valley Authority
United States Postal Service

The rise of big government. The size and role of the government grew as the United States expanded westward and developed into an industrial nation. Certain crises and events caused major spurts of government growth.

The American Civil War (1861-1865) led to a great increase in the size of the U.S. government. The war forced the government to build up its military forces. At the beginning of the conflict, the Regular Army of the United States consisted of about 16,000 soldiers, most of whom fought for the Union. By the last year of the war, the Army had more than 1,000,000 troops. The government also had to increase its administrative activities to arm, transport, feed, and clothe the troops. After the war, the government required record keeping and paperwork on a scale never before achieved to process pensions for war veterans.

During the late 1800's and early 1900's, federal regulations increased as the government began to actively supervise the marketplace. For example, the government passed laws curbing the power of *trusts,* large business organizations that limited competition. New laws were created to set railroad rates, improve workplace conditions, and ensure the purity of food and drugs. In addition, the government began to set aside national parks and forests, help farmers grow crops more effectively, and train students for vocational trades.

During the 1930's, the Great Depression caused the government to greatly increase its role in supervising the economy. Under the New Deal programs of President Franklin D. Roosevelt, Congress established many agencies to regulate and influence financial, business, agricultural, and industrial practices. Congress also passed laws to provide jobless benefits and old-age pensions, known as Social Security. In addition, the government spent billions of dollars on relief and on public works projects to create jobs. Citizens built thousands of schools, hospitals, and other public facilities.

After the Great Depression, the government continued to sponsor public works. For example, the Army Corps of Engineers and the Tennessee Valley Authority dammed rivers to provide flood control and electric power. The interstate highway program, started in 1956, was one of the largest public works projects in history.

During the 1960's, the federal government expanded again. It passed strong new civil rights laws and began to set environmental standards. It also increased its role in matters that were once handled only by state and local governments, such as education, job training, health care, and transportation.

World power. During the 1900's, the activities of the federal government spread throughout the world. Both World War I (1914-1918) and World War II (1939-1945) thrust the United States into vast multinational military campaigns in other countries.

Cold War tensions greatly influenced the federal government's foreign policy and spending for many years. The Cold War was a struggle for international power between Communist nations, led by the Soviet Union, and non-Communist nations, led by the United States. During the Cold War, which began after World War II, the United States government kept its armed forces in a state of military readiness and invested in a massive build-up of nuclear weapons. It also provided billions of dollars in aid to many non-Communist nations. The United States fought two wars, the Korean War (1950-1953) and the Vietnam War (1957-1975), in an effort to stop the spread of Communism in Asia.

During the late 1980's and the early 1990's, Communist rule collapsed in most countries, and the Cold War ended. In 1991, the Soviet Union broke apart. As a result, the United States government shifted much of its attention from foreign affairs to domestic issues, especially the economy.

Domestic challenges. Since the early 1990's, a long list of national problems has demanded the U.S. government's attention. Many of the nation's industries have struggled to compete with industries in other countries. Many measures of educational achievement are not as high as they once were. In addition, Americans have been concerned about racial conflict, crime, drug abuse, and poverty, especially in the nation's cities.

Current issues in U.S. government

Current issues in United States government include debates over how much the federal government should do, how effective it is, and how democratic it is.

How much should the federal government do? People disagree on what the federal government should do about the nation's problems, and whether it has been doing too much or too little. In general, people with *liberal* political views call for the government to increase its efforts to solve economic and social problems. Those with *conservative* views believe economic and social problems are best solved when government interference is kept to a minimum. But they want the government to promote traditional values.

How effective is the government? The complex system of checks and balances between the executive and legislative branches makes it difficult for government officials to take quick action. Power is constantly shifting between the president and Congress. Strong presidents can use their position to arouse widespread public support for their plans and thus push them through Congress. The president assumes a dominant role during a crisis, especially a war or a severe economic depression, when the nation wants a strong leader. But in the absence of a crisis, the president must bargain and compromise with Congress.

In a *divided government*—when one political party wins the presidency and another controls Congress—bargaining may be especially difficult. For example, the president may want to lower taxes. But if the majority party in Congress plans to increase social programs that are funded by taxes, Congress may reject the president's proposed tax cut.

Even when one political party controls both branches, *factions* (groups) within the party can stall government action. Elected officials also may be influenced by many powerful special-interest groups who constantly strive for policies that benefit their members. Achieving clear-cut results or sweeping reforms under such a system is usually difficult and sometimes impossible.

How democratic is the government? Some people feel that certain features of the national government system are undemocratic and block majority rule. For example, the indirect election of the president by the Electoral College has resulted in some candidates winning with only a minority of the popular vote. Other features sometimes considered undemocratic include the appointment—rather than the election—of federal judges and the equal representation of each state in the Senate. In addition, many people believe the expense of election campaigns gives wealthy donors an unfair degree of influence on public officials.

Since the federal government began in 1789, Americans have disagreed on how their government should operate and how much it should do. Historians, political scientists, and other experts agree that no system of government can be perfect. Citizens have a right—and even a duty—to ask how their government is doing and to work to improve the system.   Roger H. Davidson

Related articles include:
Congress of the United States
Court
Democracy
Electoral College
House of Representatives
Political action committee
Political party
President of the United States
Presidential succession
Senate
Supreme Court of the United States
Term limits
Veto
Vice president of the United States
Voting

Outline

I. Principles of American government
  A. Constitutional authority
  B. Separation of powers
  C. Federalism
  D. Representative democracy

II. The legislative branch
  A. Organization
  B. Functions
  C. Committee system
  D. Party leadership
  E. The lawmaking process

III. The executive branch
  A. The presidency
  B. The Executive Office of the President
  C. Executive departments and agencies
  D. Control of departments and agencies

IV. The judicial branch
  A. Authority of the courts
  B. Lower court system
  C. The Supreme Court
  D. Judges

V. Growth of the federal government
  A. Background
  B. Early years
  C. The rise of big government
  D. World power
  E. Domestic challenges

VI. Current issues in U.S. government
  A. How much should the federal government do?
  B. How effective is the government?
  C. How democratic is the government?

Questions

What are the three branches of the United States government?
How does each branch of the government exercise its powers of checks and balances?
What is the source of the United States government's authority?
What are the two major political parties in the United States? What role do they play in elections?
How did the American Civil War enlarge the U.S. government?
How is the president of the United States elected?

It's a fact

The 27th Amendment to the Constitution, which prevents Congress from passing immediate salary increases for itself, was proposed on Sept. 25, 1789, but not ratified until more than 200 years later, on May 7, 1992.

Who appoints nearly all federal judges?
What is *judicial review*? Why is it important?
What types of courts make up the federal court system? What does each type of court do?
What are some features of the national government system that may be considered undemocratic?

Additional resources

Level I
American Government in Action. Enslow, 1996-   . Multivolume work. Titles include *The Presidency of the United States,* by Karen Judson (1996); and *Political Parties of the United States,* by Michael Kronenwetter (1996).
Democracy in Action. Watts, 1992-   . Multivolume work. Titles include *How Democratic Is the United States?* by Michael Kronenwetter (1994); and *Next in Line: The American Vice Presidency,* by Barbara S. Feinberg (1996).
Feinberg, Barbara S. *The National Government.* Watts, 1993.
Words in the News: A Student's Dictionary of American Government and Politics. 1993.

Level II
Barone, Michael, and Ujifusa, Grant. *The Almanac of American Politics.* National Journal, published biennially.
Biskupici, Joan, and Witt, Elder. *Guide to the U.S. Supreme Court.* 2 vols. 3rd ed. Congressional Quarterly, 1990.
Guide to Congress. 4th ed. Congressional Quarterly, 1991.
Nelson, Michael, ed. *Guide to the Presidency.* 2 vols. 2nd ed. Congressional Quarterly, 1996.
Shafritz, Jay M. *The HarperCollins Dictionary of American Government and Politics.* HarperPerennial, 1992.
The United States Government Manual. U.S. Government Printing Office, published annually.

Web sites

Constitution for the United States of America
http://Constitution.by.net/
U.S. Constitution, Bill of Rights, and links to state constitutions.

Federal Constitutions
http://Constitution.by.net/uSA/
Information about the Articles of Confederation, Constitution of the U.S., Bill of Rights, and Amendments to the Constitution.

U.S. Government Hypertexts
http://sunsite.unc.edu/govdocs.html
Government documents pertaining to the U.S. Executive Branch, including presidential speeches.

Topic for study

Look at the Executive departments *box in the chart in the article* United States, Government of the, *in this volume. Trace the growth of the executive branch of the United States government by finding out when each department was established. Report on some of the chief responsibilities given to recently created executive departments.*

Understanding the Electoral Process

The road to the White House begins with an effort to win the presidential nomination of a political party. This section features 16 *World Book* articles that provide a comprehensive look at seeking the nomination, campaigning, and voting. In this section's articles, you will learn:

❏ *what are the main activities at a national political convention.*

❏ *why the multiparty system tends to produce a less stable govern-ment than does the two-party system.*

❏ *how the Electoral College functions and has voted since 1804, when the present system was adopted.*

❏ *how many of the states of the United States use voting machines.*

Ballot is the means by which voters indicate their choices in an election. The ballot may be a printed form that lists the candidates and describes issues that voters are to decide. It may also be set up on a voting machine. The voting machine was first used in 1892, and is now used by over half the voters in the United States.

In the United States, the written ballot was used in Massachusetts as early as 1634. By the time the Constitution was ratified, nearly all the original 13 states used written ballots. Before 1800, political groups distributed tickets that listed the names of candidates they favored. Voters could use these tickets as ballots but found it hard to vote for candidates not on the list. Sometimes they *scratched* the ticket, crossing off the party's choice and writing in another name.

Voters did not always have the privilege of a secret ballot, and coercion and bribery were common. To correct these evils, Kentucky and Massachusetts adopted the *Australian ballot* system in 1888. In this system, each voter receives a printed ballot at the polling place, and then marks it in secret in a curtained booth.

Some states use the *party column* ballot. On this ballot, candidates are listed according to party. This ballot makes it easier for voters to *vote a straight ticket* (vote for candidates of one party only). Other states use the *office-block* ballot. This ballot lists candidates according to the office they seek, making it easier for voters to vote for candidates from different parties.

Since the 1960's, people in many election districts have voted by punching holes in *punch-card ballots,* which are mounted on voting machines and counted by computer. The small piece of paper that is punched out of the card is called a *chad.* This method allows high-speed processing of election totals. But critics have argued that confusing ballot layouts can cause voters to accidentally punch their ballots incorrectly. In addition, computers may not properly count ballots if the chad has not been completely punched out. In 2000, debates regarding partially punched chads and a "butterfly" ballot layout—in which candidates' names were arranged on both sides of the chad-punching area—were largely responsible for a delay in the outcome of the presiden-

tial election. Some districts have switched to newer voting methods, such as touch-screen computer systems and optical-scanning ballot systems.

Older customs. The word *ballot* comes from the French word *ballotte,* meaning a *little ball.* In ancient Athens, judges of the highest court generally gave their verdicts by dropping stone or metal balls into boxes. Balls that were pierced in the center or colored black stood for verdicts of condemnation. Unpierced or white balls meant acquittal.

The Romans generally used wooden tickets, or *tabellae.* When a change in law was proposed, those in favor marked the ballot with the letters *U R,* for *Uti rogas,* meaning *as you ask.* A vote against the change was indicated by the letter *A* for *Antiquo,* meaning *for the old.* In an election for public office, the names of the candidates were written on ballots. During the Middle Ages, voting fell into disuse but was revived in the Italian communes in the 1200's. Ballots were used in England in the 1500's and in the Netherlands in the 1600's.

Robert Agranoff

See also **Voting; Voting machine.**

Web site

Voting rights
http://www.usdoj.gov/kidspage/crt/voting.htm
The Civil Rights Division of the Department of Justice provides information on the Voting Rights Act of 1965.

Caucus is any gathering of individuals to nominate candidates for office or to endorse a policy or program. In many countries, the members of a political party hold a caucus to develop party policy and to nominate candidates for leadership positions. In the United States, for example, the members of each party in Congress traditionally hold a caucus to select congressional leaders.

Another type of caucus, called a *participatory caucus,* is prominent in the United States in presidential election years. The best-known participatory caucuses are those held in Iowa by the Republican and Democratic parties. The Iowa caucuses are the first major events in a series of state caucuses and primary elections that end in the nomination of each party's presidential candidate. For this reason, the Iowa caucuses receive a great deal of coverage from newspapers, television, and other media.

A participatory caucus may be attended by any eligible voter who is willing to acknowledge association with the party that holds it. People who attend such caucuses in presidential election years help elect delegates to a political convention that covers a larger region, such as a county. Typically, each delegate selected has promised to support a particular candidate at the convention.

During the early history of the United States, small groups of party leaders chose candidates for office in meetings called *party caucuses.* But the party caucus system became unpopular because it gave other party members little voice in the selection of candidates.

Since the 1830's, major U.S. political parties have used national conventions to nominate their candidates for president. During much of the 1800's, delegates to these conventions were selected by party officials at state conventions. These officials were typically selected, in turn, by party officials at local conventions. This arrangement became known as the *party convention system.* In the

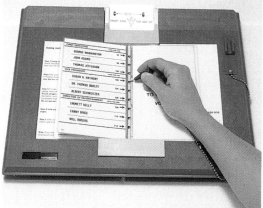

Larry Korb, Business Records Corporation

A computerized voting system uses a computer card. The voter punches holes in the card, as shown with this mock ballot. A computer later counts the votes and prints the results.

late 1800's, some Western states began using participatory caucuses instead of conventions at the lowest level of this process, usually in individual voting districts. This change opened local participation to anyone who turned out at the caucus. Other states, including Iowa, eventually adopted this *caucus-convention system.*

The party convention system has been in decline since the early 1900's and the caucus-convention system since the 1960's. Most states now use primary elections instead. Some states still use caucuses to select or endorse candidates for public office at the local or state level.   Byron E. Shafer

See also **House of Representatives** (Organization of the U.S. House); **Political convention; Primary election; Senate** (The leaders of the Senate).

Conservatism is an attitude or philosophy that places great emphasis on tradition. Conservatives want to *conserve* (save) traditional institutions, values, and ideas, and they rely on them as a guide to wisdom and goodness. Therefore, they seek progress in line with proven values of the past. But the word *conservatism* is confusing because its meaning varies with time, place, and circumstance.

Political conservatism. Political conservatives take a limited view of what politics can achieve. They believe that the aim of politics, or government, is to help promote a good life for people in society. Most conservatives, however, doubt that the good life can be brought about mainly by political means. They believe that all political problems are basically moral problems, and that legislation cannot significantly change human attitudes. Conservatives believe that the human potential for evil is as great as the potential for good. They doubt that evil will disappear with social reform or education.

Conservatives emphasize the performance of duties as the price of rights. They also believe in the desirability of maintaining social classes. Conservatives believe that all people have equal protection under the law, but they deny that all are born with equal advantages and influence in society. Conservatives maintain that only a few are natural leaders, and that the leadership provided by these few is essential to social order. For these reasons, conservatives consider political and economic leveling foolish and bound to fail.

Conservatives see a link between freedom and private ownership of factories and other means of economic production. They maintain that abolishing such private ownership would destroy individual liberty. Therefore, many conservatives believe that socialism and Communism are the greatest threats to modern society.

History. As early as the 1700's, the British statesman Edmund Burke expressed conservative ideas in his writings and speeches. Early conservatives in the United States included John Adams and Alexander Hamilton. The name *Conservative* was first used around 1830, applied to the descendants of the old British Tory Party. The words *Tory* and *Conservative* are used interchangeably in the United Kingdom today. Conservatism arose partly as a reaction to the excesses of the French Revolution and to the belief that human nature could become perfect through social change and political revolution.

A true conservative should also be distinguished from a *reactionary.* Reactionaries want to revolutionize existing society according to a model in past history. True conservatives want to preserve the best in the past and continue it into the future.

The word *conservative* as used in the United States today is often confusing. Many Americans who call themselves conservatives advocate a return to the principles and theories of liberalism of the 1800's. They oppose almost all government regulation of the economy, and are economic liberals in the tradition of Adam Smith. Traditionally, however, conservatives have opposed both economic liberalism and socialism. They have tried to steer a middle course between the extremes of individualism and collective ownership, and have generally favored a strong central government.

Today, many U.S. conservatives believe that economic and social problems are solved best when government interference in the economy is kept to a minimum. They also believe that the need to protect society justifies some restriction of the rights of people accused of crime. Some conservatives oppose abortion, and some support state-sponsored prayer in public schools. In foreign policy, U.S. conservatives tend to regard military power as the basis of world peace.   Carl L. Davis

See also **Liberalism.**

Web site

Traditionalist Conservatism Page
http://www.geocities.com/antitechnocrat/trad.html
A discussion of traditionalist conservatism.

Election is the process by which people vote for the candidate or proposal of their choice. The basis of democratic government is that citizens have the right to choose the officials who will govern them. Elections thus rank as one of the most important political activities. Elections also serve as a means of peacefully transferring power from one person or group to another.

In addition to public elections, nongovernmental elections are also held to select the officials of many organizations. Labor unions, social clubs, and the student bodies of schools hold elections to select their officers.

Elections in a democracy

Election procedures differ from country to country. However, certain principles characterize elections in democratic nations. In the United States, Canada, and other democratic countries, nearly all adults can vote. Those not permitted to vote include certain criminals and people with severe mental illness or mental retardation. Citizens vote by secret ballot so that they can vote without fear of how others will react. The mass media—which include radio, television, magazines, and newspapers—freely discuss the candidates and issues.

In most democratic countries, political parties select candidates for public office and propose public policies. But in some countries and in parts of the United States, local elections are *nonpartisan*—that is, candidates appear on the ballot without being identified by party.

Voters elect officials by either *direct* or *indirect* elections. In direct elections, the people themselves vote for public officials. In the United States, for example, citizens vote for members of Congress and for state and local officials in this way. In indirect elections, people elect representatives called *electors* to choose public officials. The U.S. president and vice president are chosen in an indirect election. The voters of each state select electors, who make up the Electoral College. The electors in turn choose the president and the vice president based on the popular vote in the states they represent.

Under a parliamentary system of government, also called a *cabinet system,* citizens elect members of the legislature. The head of state—the king or queen of a monarchy or the president of a republic—then selects a prime minister from the members of the legislature. Australia, Canada, and certain other Commonwealth nations regard the British ruler as head of state. In such nations, the governor general makes the appointment, acting as the representative of the monarch. In most countries, the head of state can appoint only the leader of the majority party in the legislature or the head of a coalition of parties.

Elections in the United States

Election regulations. The Constitution of the United States requires that a congressional election be held every two years. At that time, voters elect all the members of the House of Representatives for a two-year term and about one-third of the Senate members for a six-year term.

The Constitution also requires the election of a president and a vice president every four years. Federal law states that national elections are to be held on the first Tuesday after the first Monday of November.

State laws regulate all elections, including national and local ones. Such laws establish the eligibility requirements for state officials and the date on which state and local elections are to be held. They also establish the qualifications for voters. However, the Constitution gives Congress the right to change state voter requirements if they violate constitutional guarantees.

Nomination of candidates. At one time, political parties nominated nearly all candidates at national, state,

Florida election results by county This map and table show the distribution of Florida's popular votes in the 2000 election. On November 26, the state certified a win for George W. Bush by 537 votes. Al Gore contested this result and continued legal battles to win the state's 25 electoral votes, which both candidates needed to win the election.

WORLD BOOK map

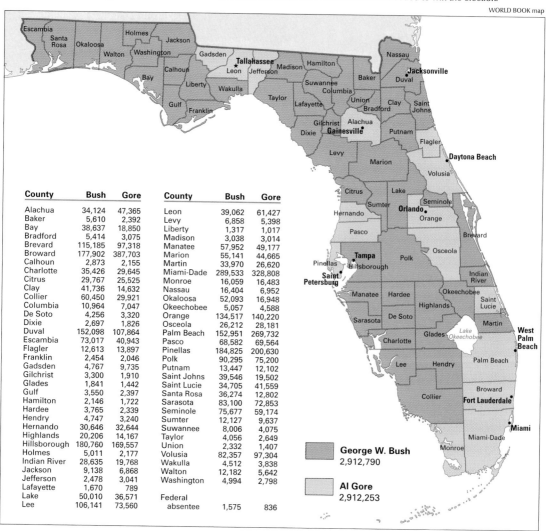

County	Bush	Gore	County	Bush	Gore
Alachua	34,124	47,365	Leon	39,062	61,427
Baker	5,610	2,392	Levy	6,858	5,398
Bay	38,637	18,850	Liberty	1,317	1,017
Bradford	5,414	3,075	Madison	3,038	3,014
Brevard	115,185	97,318	Manatee	57,952	49,177
Broward	177,902	387,703	Marion	55,141	44,665
Calhoun	2,873	2,155	Martin	33,970	26,620
Charlotte	35,426	29,645	Miami-Dade	289,533	328,808
Citrus	29,767	25,525	Monroe	16,059	16,483
Clay	41,736	14,632	Nassau	16,404	6,952
Collier	60,450	29,921	Okaloosa	52,093	16,948
Columbia	10,964	7,047	Okeechobee	5,057	4,588
De Soto	4,256	3,320	Orange	134,517	140,220
Dixie	2,697	1,826	Osceola	26,212	28,181
Duval	152,098	107,864	Palm Beach	152,951	269,732
Escambia	73,017	40,943	Pasco	68,582	69,564
Flagler	12,613	13,897	Pinellas	184,825	200,630
Franklin	2,454	2,046	Polk	90,295	75,200
Gadsden	4,767	9,735	Putnam	13,447	12,102
Gilchrist	3,300	1,910	Saint Johns	39,546	19,502
Glades	1,841	1,442	Saint Lucie	34,705	41,559
Gulf	3,550	2,397	Santa Rosa	36,274	12,802
Hamilton	2,146	1,722	Sarasota	83,100	72,853
Hardee	3,765	2,339	Seminole	75,677	59,174
Hendry	4,747	3,240	Sumter	12,127	9,637
Hernando	30,646	32,644	Suwannee	8,006	4,075
Highlands	20,206	14,167	Taylor	4,056	2,649
Hillsborough	180,760	169,557	Union	2,332	1,407
Holmes	5,011	2,177	Volusia	82,357	97,304
Indian River	28,635	19,768	Wakulla	4,512	3,838
Jackson	9,138	6,868	Walton	12,182	5,642
Jefferson	2,478	3,041	Washington	4,994	2,798
Lafayette	1,670	789			
Lake	50,010	36,571	Federal		
Lee	106,141	73,560	absentee	1,575	836

George W. Bush
2,912,790

Al Gore
2,912,253

and local conventions or in closed meetings of party members called *caucuses*. Today, candidates for most state and local offices are nominated in *direct primary elections*. A direct primary is a contest in which voters choose the candidates who will represent each political party in the upcoming general election. Other candidates may run in the general election, where voters make their final choice. However, only the candidates who win the primaries become official party nominees. A *runoff election* may be held if no candidate in the original primary receives more than half the vote. The two candidates with the most votes run against each other, and the winner becomes the party nominee.

The qualifications for voting in a direct primary election vary according to whether the primary is closed or open. In a *closed primary,* voters must declare a choice of party, either when registering to vote or when receiving their ballot. They must then choose from among the candidates on their party's ballot. In an *open primary,* voters may cast their ballot for candidates of any party. Voters receive ballots for all parties in the election, mark one in the voting booth, and discard the rest.

Each party holds a national convention to nominate its presidential and vice presidential candidates. Many states hold special primary elections to choose delegates to those conventions. In some states, the ballot lists presidential candidates. In others, it lists proposed delegates, who may have promised to support a certain candidate. Voters can support a candidate by voting for that person's delegates. In still other states, local caucuses choose delegates to the national convention.

Election procedures. Most elections are supervised on the local level by county election officials, who divide each county or ward into voting districts called *precincts*. Election officials determine the place where votes will be cast, called the *polling place* or the *polls*. They also check voters' names against registration lists, hand out ballots, and supervise the depositing of marked ballots in ballot boxes. In most states, the officials at each polling place must represent the two major parties.

Voters indicate their choices privately in an enclosed voting booth. Every state allows certain citizens to vote by absentee ballot before the election. These citizens include people in the armed services, college students, sick persons, and certain travelers.

The polls generally remain open from early morning until evening on Election Day. After the polls close, election officials count the votes for each candidate, including absentee votes. Then, all ballots and tally sheets are sent, under seal, to city or county officials or to the board of elections. All state and national election results are filed with the chief election official, the secretary of state in most states. State and local officials then declare the winners in each of the races. Federal and state laws define dishonest voting practices and provide severe penalties for them. Such practices include bribing voters, impersonating another voter, stuffing a ballot box with forged votes, and tampering with voting machines.

Robert Agranoff

Related articles include:

Ballot
Election campaign
Election Day
Electoral College

Primary election
Term limits

Voting
Voting machine

Web site

Federal Election Commission
http://www.fec.gov/
The home page of the Federal Election Commission provides information about elections, voting, and election campaign donations.

Election campaign is a series of operations designed to win votes for a certain candidate, party, or proposal. In the United States, the best-known campaign is the one for president held every four years. However, thousands of other campaigns—including those for Congress, state legislatures, city councils, and school boards—take place in a year. Still other campaigns involve a *referendum,* the process of submitting a proposal to the voters for approval.

What a candidate needs to campaign

A campaign organization consists of paid staff members and consultants, and unpaid volunteers. A presidential campaign may involve as many as 500 staff members and millions of volunteers. A campaign director heads the organization and coordinates all activities. Other officials of a large campaign include a general manager, a research director, a finance director, and a *media director,* who supervises advertising and publicity. Most candidates visit a number of communities, and specialists called *advance people* travel ahead to make the arrangements. Professional consultants help plan and conduct various operations. For example, many candidates employ a polling organization to take public opinion polls. Many also hire an advertising agency to create advertisements and a direct-mail marketing firm to raise funds and target appeals to voters.

Volunteers distribute leaflets, prepare mailings, call voters, and perform many other tasks. In small campaigns, volunteers also fill many of the top positions. A campaign headquarters has office machines, telephones, and computers for workers to use.

Campaign funds are necessary to pay personnel and to finance advertising, travel, and other needs. The chief sources of funds are personal solicitations, appeals by direct mail, fund-raising events, and matching funds.

Personal solicitations are individual requests by the candidate or a campaign worker. The majority of candidates raise most of their funds by soliciting donations from supporters, associates, and friends, and from members of their own family. Candidates also receive gifts of money from many organizations, but federal law prohibits corporations and labor unions from making direct political contributions. Instead, many such organizations establish panels called *political action committees* (PAC's). A PAC collects voluntary contributions from the organization's employees or members and gives the money to candidates it favors.

Appeals by direct mail involve fund-raising letters

Topic for study

Review biographies of the early presidents and compare their campaigning techniques with campaigns today.

sent to party members, people who have contributed to past campaigns, and members of groups likely to agree with the candidate's views. Automatic typewriters run by computers print hundreds of "personal" letters an hour.

Fund-raising events include bake or book sales, cocktail parties, dinners, and concerts. Most such activities make less money than personal solicitation or direct mail, but they provide opportunities for personal appearances and help build support for a candidate.

Matching funds are available to presidential candidates. Candidates can qualify for the funds by raising at least $5,000 in individual contributions of $250 or less in each of 20 states. The federal government then gives the candidate an amount of money equal to the total of each individual contribution of $250 or less.

Stages of a campaign

Most election campaigns start months before the public knows the candidates are running. A candidate asks community and party leaders and possible contributors if they will give their support. In major campaigns, polls also indicate the possible support for a candidate. If the candidate and his or her advisers think they have enough backing, they begin to develop strategy.

Planning campaign strategy. Most campaign strategy is based on information provided by research. Campaign planners study such economic and social conditions as the area's industrial production and the age distribution of the people. Planners use such information, along with data from public opinion polls and the results of previous elections, to determine the key issues and areas of possible strength and weakness. Then the planners choose their *targets*—the people at whom the campaign will be aimed. The candidate and his or her advisers develop positions on issues that are likely to be discussed during the campaign. They also begin to raise funds, recruit volunteers, and buy advertising.

Announcing the candidacy marks the official start of a campaign. Most candidates hold a news conference to make their announcement. Candidates may tour their state or district and repeat their declaration several times through the *media* in different geographic areas. The media include newspapers, radio, and television.

Developing support. The pace quickens after the announcement of candidacy, and the campaign becomes more apparent to the public. The campaign organization holds meetings and fund-raising events. Signs and bumper stickers appear. The candidates and their workers strive to develop voter support through publicity, advertising, and personal appearances.

Candidates reach the greatest number of people through the media. Men and women who run for office receive free publicity in various ways. For example, they issue news releases, grant interviews, hold news conferences, and appear on televised debates and talk shows. Candidates also buy advertising, including appeals on billboards, commercials on television and radio, and advertisements in newspapers.

A candidate spends much time making speeches and other personal appearances. Campaign officials encourage newspaper and television coverage of each appearance. Candidates also exchange views and debate their qualifications throughout the campaign on short TV and radio commercials. In addition, they may present themselves and their ideas in large blocks of program time that they have purchased on radio or TV.

Winning the nomination. Most major presidential candidates seek to be nominated for president by a political party. These candidates must run against one or more other members of their party to win the nomination. The two major U.S. parties, the Democrats and the Republicans, hold national conventions to officially select their nominees for president and vice president. In some states, a state or district convention of party members selects delegates to the national convention. To get the support of national delegates from those states, a presidential candidate must first win the backing of delegates to the state or district convention. Some states hold local party meetings called *caucuses* to select national, state, or district delegates.

Many states hold primary elections to choose delegates to each party's national convention (see **Primary election**). But changes in state laws and party rules have encouraged the direct selection of presidential nominees by primary voters. Presidential primaries are held early in election years, and candidates must gain voter support in primaries to contend for the nomination. Primary elections also determine who will represent the party in contests for most other offices.

Getting out the vote. As Election Day approaches, the pace of the campaign becomes hectic. Candidates issue daily news releases and flood the media with advertising. Rallies are held continually.

Much of the activity during this period is devoted to getting out the vote. In a process called *canvassing,* volunteers call or visit voters to ask which candidates they favor. The campaign workers then try to make sure that the probable supporters of their candidate will vote.

On Election Day, campaign workers provide transportation and baby-sitting service for voters. Volunteers at the polls keep track of supporters who have voted and contact those who have not done so.

Changes in election campaigns

Running for office has changed as the result of technological, political, and legal changes. The campaign methods of the past—including torchlight parades, bus tours, and "whistle-stop" tours by train—are less important today. However, they are still sometimes used, primarily to attract the attention of the media.

Technological changes have enabled candidates to reach more voters directly. For example, a person running for a national office may appear on television before huge audiences. Air travel allows candidates to visit many places in one day. Many candidates have Web sites on the Internet that provide information about their campaign positions and other topics. In addition, many campaign workers use computers to track voter trends, direct voter-contact activities, review records, and manage the campaign in general.

Political changes. In the past, local party leaders often won votes by assisting people in many ways. For example, they helped immigrants become citizens, found jobs for the unemployed, and sometimes provided charity. Today, welfare programs and greater prosperity have made people less dependent on such help. Also, civil service reforms have eliminated many *patronage jobs,* which the bosses gave out as rewards for service to the party. These changes have reduced the great influence that the political parties once had.

In the 1940's, about 85 percent of U.S. voters reported a loyalty to one of the two major parties. Today, only about half of the voters describe themselves as Democrats or Republicans. Also, many people vote for candidates of more than one party. These changes show that many citizens vote on the basis of candidates and issues, rather than for a party.

Legal changes have affected campaign financing and spending. Since 1940, federal law has limited the size of campaign contributions. For years, however, the law was difficult to enforce and generally ineffective. Many people became concerned about excessive campaign spending and the candidates' dependence on large contributions from wealthy people.

The Revenue Act of 1971 encouraged small contributions by allowing an income tax credit for them. This law also enabled taxpayers to specify that $1 of their federal income tax each year be used for public financing of presidential election campaigns.

The Federal Election Campaign Act of 1971 required detailed reporting of both campaign contributions and expenses. In 1974, amendments to the act established public financing of presidential campaigns and created the Federal Election Commission to enforce the rules. The amendments limited the amount an individual or group could contribute to any one candidate and put a ceiling on presidential and congressional campaign spending in each state. However, there are few limits on state and local party spending for candidates, and large contributions are channeled legally into general party funds. These contributions are sometimes referred to as *soft money*. In 1976, the U.S. Supreme Court ruled that only presidential candidates who accept public financing must stay within the spending limits.

Many states also enacted stricter regulation of campaign funds during the 1970's. However, state laws are generally less strict than federal ones. A few states finance campaigns.

Legal changes have led to many other changes in campaigns. In the past, for example, most candidates depended chiefly on large donations from the wealthy. Today candidates must raise more small contributions. Direct-mail appeals and fund-raising events, which usually attract small contributions, have become increasingly important. Contributions that can be matched with federal funds early in presidential campaigns also have become increasingly important indicators of voter support. Bank loans are now another common source of campaign money.

Candidates also must rely more on volunteer help because they have less money to pay campaign workers. Campaign organizations now must keep detailed records of contributions and expenses.   Robert Agranoff

Related articles include:

Caucus
Election
Political action committee
Political convention
Political party
President of the United States
  (The presidential election;
  pictures)
Primary election

Additional resources

Congressional Quarterly's Guide to U.S. Elections. 3rd ed. Congressional Quarterly, 1994.
Grey, Lawrence. *How to Win a Local Election.* M. Evans & Co., 1994.
Johnston, Richard, and others. *Letting the People Decide: The Dynamics of a Canadian Election.* Stanford, 1992.

Topic for study

Interview a local elected official concerning that person's most recent campaign. Build your interview around the factors discussed in the sections "What a candidate needs to campaign" and "Stages of a campaign" in the article Election campaign. *Prepare a report on what the official thought were the most important factors in winning the election, and why.*

Election Day in the United States is the day on which national elections for presidential electors take place. The U. S. Congress established the first Tuesday after the first Monday in November as Election Day. It is a legal holiday in most of the states and in all territories. Many state elections are also held on this day. Many states forbid the sale of liquor while the polls are open.

Originally, Congress did not set a specific date for national elections. Each state could appoint its electors on any day within 34 days before the date in December set for the convening of electors. In 1845, Congress established Election Day to correct abuses caused by the lack of a standard election day.   Robert Agranoff

Web site

Committee for the Study of the American Electorate
http://www.gspm.org/csae/
Information on election issues, including research material on voter participation, campaign financing, and the impact of media on elections.

Electoral College

The Electoral College is a group chosen by the voters of each state to elect the president of the United States. This chart shows how the college has voted since 1804, when the present system was adopted. The House of Representatives decided the 1824 election because no one won a majority. In 1872, the electoral votes of Arkansas and Louisiana were disputed and not counted.

| 5 | Democratic |
| 5 | Republican |

Year	Candidate elected	Winner's total	Total vote	Ala.	Alaska	Ariz.	Ark.	Calif.	Colo.	Conn.	Del.	D.C.	Fla.	Ga.	Hawaii	Ida.	Ill.	Ind.	Iowa	Kans.	Ky.	La.	Me.	Md.	Mass.	Mich.	Minn.	Miss.	Mo.	Mont.	Nebr.	Nev.	N.H.
1804	Jefferson	162	176							9	3			6							8			/	19								7
1808	Madison	122	175							9	3			6							7			/	19								7
1812	Madison	128	217							9	4			8							12	3		/	22								8
1816	Monroe	183	217							9	3			8				3			12	3		8	22								8
1820	Monroe	231	232	3						9	4			8			3	3			12	3	9	11	15			2	3				/
1824	J. Q. Adams	84	261							8	1						1					2	9	3	15								8
1828	Jackson	178	261	5						8	3			9			3	5			14	5	/	/	15			3	3				8
1832	Jackson	219	286	7						8	3			11			5	9			15	5	10	/	14			4	4				7
1836	Van Buren	170	294	7			3			8	3			11			5	9			15	5	10	10	14	3		4	4				7
1840	W. Harrison	234	294	7			3			8	3			11			5	9			15	5	10	10	14	3		4	4				7
1844	Polk	170	275	9			3			6	3			10			9	12			12	6	9	8	12	5		6	7				6
1848	Taylor	163	290	9			3			6	3		3	10			9	12	4		12	6	9	8	12	5		6	7				6
1852	Pierce	254	296	9			4	4		6	3		3	10			11	13	4		12	6	8	8	13	6		7	9				5
1856	Buchanan	174	296	9			4	4		6	3		3	10			11	13	4		12	6	8	8	13	6		7	9				5
1860	Lincoln	180	303	9			4	4		6	3		3	10			11	13	4		12	6	8	8	13	6	4	7	9				5
1864	Lincoln	212	233					5		6	3						16	13	8	3	11		7	7	12	8	4		11			2	5
1868	Grant	214	294	8			5	5		6	3		3	9			16	13	8	3	11		7	7	12	8	4		11		3	3	5
1872	Grant	286	349	10				6		6	3		4	/			21	15	11	5	/		7	8	13	11	5	8	/		3	3	5
1876	Hayes	185	369	10			6	6	3	6	3		4	11			21	15	11	5	12	8	7	8	13	11	5	8	15		3	3	5
1880	Garfield	214	369	10			6	/	3	6	3		4	11			21	15	11	5	12	8	7	8	13	11	5	8	15		3	3	5
1884	Cleveland	219	401	10			7	8	3	6	3		4	12			22	15	13	9	13	8	6	8	14	13	7	9	16		5	3	4
1888	B. Harrison	233	401	10			7	8	3	6	3		4	12			22	15	13	9	13	8	6	8	14	13	7	9	16		5	3	4
1892	Cleveland	277	444	11			8	/	4	6	3		4	13		3	24	15	13	10	13	8	6	8	15	/	9	9	17	3	8	3	4
1896	McKinley	271	447	11			8	/	4	6	3		4	13		3	24	15	13	10	/		6	8	15	14	9	9	17	3	8	3	4
1900	McKinley	292	447	11			8	9	4	6	3		4	13		3	24	15	13	10	13	8	6	8	15	14	9	9	17	3	8	3	4
1904	T. Roosevelt	336	476	11			9	10	5	7	3		5	13		3	27	15	13	10	13	9	6	/	16	14	11	10	18	3	8	3	4
1908	Taft	321	483	11			9	10	5	7	3		5	13		3	27	15	13	10	13	9	6	/	16	14	11	10	18	3	8	3	4
1912	Wilson	435	531	12		3	9	/	6	7	3		6	14		4	29	15	13	10	13	10	6	8	18	15	12	10	18	4	8	3	4
1916	Wilson	277	531	12		3	9	13	6	7	3		6	14		4	29	15	13	10	13	10	6	8	18	15	12	10	18	4	8	3	4
1920	Harding	404	531	12		3	9	13	6	7	3		6	14		4	29	15	13	10	13	10	6	8	18	15	12	10	18	4	8	3	4
1924	Coolidge	382	531	12		3	9	13	6	7	3		6	14		4	29	15	13	10	13	10	6	8	18	15	12	10	18	4	8	3	4
1928	Hoover	444	531	12		3	9	13	6	7	3		6	14		4	29	15	13	10	13	10	6	8	18	15	12	10	18	4	8	3	4
1932	F. Roosevelt	472	531	11		3	9	22	6	8	3		7	12		4	29	14	11	9	11	10	5	8	17	19	11	9	15	4	7	3	4
1936	F. Roosevelt	523	531	11		3	9	22	6	8	3		7	12		4	29	14	11	9	11	10	5	8	17	19	11	9	15	4	7	3	4
1940	F. Roosevelt	449	531	11		3	9	22	6	8	3		7	12		4	29	14	11	9	11	10	5	8	17	19	11	9	15	4	7	3	4
1944	F. Roosevelt	432	531	11		4	9	25	6	8	3		8	12		4	28	13	10	8	11	10	5	8	16	19	11	9	15	4	6	3	4
1948	Truman	303	531	11		4	9	25	6	8	3		8	12		4	28	13	10	8	11	10	5	8	16	19	11	9	15	4	6	3	4
1952	Eisenhower	442	531	11		4	8	32	6	8	3		10	12		4	27	13	10	8	10	10	5	9	16	20	11	8	13	4	6	3	4
1956	Eisenhower	457	531	/		4	8	32	6	8	3		10	12		4	27	13	10	8	10	10	5	9	16	20	11	8	13	4	6	3	4
1960	Kennedy	303	537	/	3	4	8	32	6	8	3		10	12	3	4	27	13	10	8	10	10	5	9	16	20	11	8	13	4	6	3	4
1964	L. Johnson	486	538	10	3	5	6	40	6	8	3	3	14	12	4	4	26	13	9	7	9	10	4	10	14	21	10	7	12	4	5	3	4
1968	Nixon	301	538	10	3	5	6	40	6	8	3	3	14	12	4	4	26	13	9	7	9	10	4	10	14	21	10	7	12	4	5	3	4
1972	Nixon	520	538	9	3	6	6	45	7	8	3	3	17	12	4	4	26	13	8	7	9	10	4	10	14	21	10	7	12	4	5	3	4
1976	Carter	297	538	9	3	6	6	45	7	8	3	3	17	12	4	4	26	13	8	7	9	10	4	10	14	21	10	7	12	4	5	3	4
1980	Reagan	489	538	9	3	6	6	45	7	8	3	3	17	12	4	4	26	13	8	7	9	10	4	10	14	21	10	7	12	4	5	3	4
1984	Reagan	525	538	9	3	7	6	47	8	8	3	3	21	12	4	4	24	12	8	7	9	10	4	10	13	20	10	7	11	4	5	4	4
1988	G. H. W. Bush	426	538	9	3	7	6	47	8	8	3	3	21	12	4	4	24	12	8	7	9	10	4	10	13	20	10	7	11	4	5	4	4
1992	Clinton	370	538	9	3	8	6	54	8	8	3	3	25	13	4	4	22	12	7	6	8	9	4	10	12	18	10	7	11	3	5	4	4
1996	Clinton	379	538	9	3	8	6	54	8	8	3	3	25	13	4	4	22	12	7	6	8	9	4	10	12	18	10	7	11	3	5	4	4
2000	G. W. Bush	271	538	9	3	8	6	54	8	8	3	/	25	13	4	4	22	12	7	6	8	9	4	10	12	18	10	7	11	3	5	4	4

	Democratic-Republican		National Republican		Progressive	/	Split vote
5		**5**		**5**			
5	Federalist	**5**	Whig	**5**	Other parties	☐	Not voting

N.J.	N.Mex.	N.Y.	N.C.	N.Dak.	Ohio	Okla.	Ore.	Pa.	R.I.	S.C.	S.Dak.	Tenn.	Tex.	Utah	Vt.	Va.	Wash.	W.Va.	Wis.	Wyo.	Year
8		19	14		3			20	4	10		5			6	24					1804
8		/	/		3			20	4	10		5			6	24					1808
8		29	15		7			25	4	11		8			8	25					1812
8		29	15		8			25	4	11		8			8	25					1816
8		29	15		8			24	4	11		7			8	25					1820
		26								4						7					1824
8		/	15		16			28	4	11		11			7	24					1828
8		42	15		21			30	4	11		15			7	23					1832
8		42	15		21			30	4	11		15			7	23					1836
8		42	15		21			30	4	11		15			7	23					1840
7		36	11		23			26	4	9		13			6	17					1844
7		36	11		23			26	4	9		13	4		6	17			4		1848
7		35	10		23			27	4	8		12	4		5	15			5		1852
7		35	10		23			27	4	8		12	4		5	15			5		1856
/		35	10		23		3	27	4	8		12	4		5	15			5		1860
7		33			21		3	26	4						5			5	8		1864
7		33	9		21		3	26	4	6		10			5			5	8		1868
9		35	10		22		3	29	4	7		12	8		5	11		5	10		1872
9		35	10		22		3	29	4	7		12	8		5	11		5	10		1876
9		35	10		22		3	29	4	7		12	8		5	11		5	10		1880
9		36	11		23		3	30	4	9		12	13		4	12		6	11		1884
9		36	11		23		3	30	4	9		12	13		4	12		6	11		1888
10		36	11	/	/		/	32	4	9	4	12	15		4	12	4	6	12	3	1892
10		36	11	3	23		4	32	4	9	4	12	15	3	4	12	4	6	12	3	1896
10		36	11	3	23		4	32	4	9	4	12	15	3	4	12	4	6	12	3	1900
12		39	12	4	23		4	34	4	9	4	12	18	3	4	12	5	7	13	3	1904
12		39	12	4	23	7	4	34	4	9	4	12	18	3	4	12	5	7	13	3	1908
14	3	45	12	5	24	10	5	38	5	9	5	12	20	4	4	12	7	8	13	3	1912
14	3	45	12	5	24	10	5	38	5	9	5	12	20	4	4	12	7	/	13	3	1916
14	3	45	12	5	24	10	5	38	5	9	5	12	20	4	4	12	7	8	13	3	1920
14	3	45	12	5	24	10	5	38	5	9	5	12	20	4	4	12	7	8	13	3	1924
14	3	45	12	5	24	10	5	38	5	9	5	12	20	4	4	12	7	8	13	3	1928
16	3	47	13	4	26	11	5	36	4	8	4	11	23	4	3	11	8	8	12	3	1932
16	3	47	13	4	26	11	5	36	4	8	4	11	23	4	3	11	8	8	12	3	1936
16	3	47	13	4	26	11	5	36	4	8	4	11	23	4	3	11	8	8	12	3	1940
16	4	47	14	4	25	10	6	35	4	8	4	12	23	4	3	11	8	8	12	3	1944
16	4	47	14	4	25	10	6	35	4	8	4	/	23	4	3	11	8	8	12	3	1948
16	4	45	14	4	25	8	6	32	4	8	4	11	24	4	3	12	9	8	12	3	1952
16	4	45	14	4	25	8	6	32	4	8	4	11	24	4	3	12	9	8	12	3	1956
16	4	45	14	4	25	/	6	32	4	8	4	11	24	4	3	12	9	8	12	3	1960
17	4	43	13	4	26	8	6	29	4	8	4	11	25	4	3	12	9	7	12	3	1964
17	4	43	/	4	26	8	6	29	4	8	4	11	25	4	3	12	9	7	12	3	1968
17	4	41	13	3	25	8	6	27	4	8	4	10	26	4	3	/	9	6	11	3	1972
17	4	41	13	3	25	8	6	27	4	8	4	10	26	4	3	12	/	6	11	3	1976
17	4	41	13	3	25	8	6	27	4	8	4	10	26	4	3	12	9	6	11	3	1980
16	5	36	13	3	23	8	7	25	4	8	3	11	29	5	3	12	10	6	11	3	1984
16	5	36	13	3	23	8	7	25	4	8	3	11	29	5	3	12	10	/	11	3	1988
15	5	33	14	3	21	8	7	23	4	8	3	11	32	5	3	13	11	5	11	3	1992
15	5	33	14	3	21	8	7	23	4	8	3	11	32		3		11		11	3	1996
15	5	33	14	3	21	8	7	23	4	8	3	11	32	5	3	13	11	5	11	3	2000

Electoral College is a group of representatives chosen by the voters of each state to elect the president and vice president of the United States. The U.S. Constitution created the Electoral College.

Every state has as many votes in the Electoral College as the total of its senators and representatives in Congress. Amendment 23 to the U.S. Constitution, ratified in 1961, gave the District of Columbia three electoral votes. The table with this article shows how the size of the college has changed. It also shows how the states have voted since 1804, when the present system of electing the president was adopted. State committees or conventions of each political party usually select the candidates for presidential electors. In some states, the ballots list the presidential and vice presidential candidates, but do not list the proposed electors. For this reason, many voters do not realize they do not vote directly for the president and vice presi-

Splits in state electoral votes

In most elections, the candidate who wins the highest number of a state's popular votes receives all the state's electoral votes. In some elections, however, Electoral College members from the same state have voted for different candidates. This situation is shown by a slash mark (/) in the table on these two pages. Since 1804, the following splits in electoral votes have occurred:

Election	State's total vote and split
1804	Maryland 11 (Jefferson 9, Charles C. Pinckney 2).
1808	Maryland 11 (Madison 9, Pinckney 2); New York 19 (Madison 13, George Clinton 6); North Carolina 14 (Madison 11, Pinckney 3).
1812	Maryland 11 (Madison 6, Clinton 5).
1820	New Hampshire 8 (Monroe 7, J. Q. Adams 1).
1828	Maine 9 (J. Q. Adams 8, Jackson 1); Maryland 11 (J. Q. Adams 6, Jackson 5); New York 36 (Jackson 20, J. Q. Adams 16).
1832	Maryland 8 (Henry Clay 5, Jackson 3).
1860	New Jersey 7 (Lincoln 4, Stephen A. Douglas 3).
1872	Georgia 8 (Benjamin G. Brown 6, Charles J. Jenkins 2); Kentucky 12 (Thomas A. Hendricks 8, Brown 4); Missouri 15 (Brown 8, Hendricks 6, David Davis 1).
1880	California 6 (Winfield Scott Hancock 5, Garfield 1).
1892	California 9 (Cleveland 8, B. Harrison 1); Michigan 14 (B. Harrison 9, Cleveland 5); North Dakota 3 (Cleveland 1, B. Harrison 1, James B. Weaver 1); Ohio 23 (B. Harrison 22, Cleveland 1); Oregon 4 (B. Harrison 3, Weaver 1).
1896	California 9 (McKinley 8, William Jennings Bryan 1); Kentucky 13 (McKinley 12, Bryan 1).
1904	Maryland 8 (Alton B. Parker 7, T. Roosevelt 1).
1908	Maryland 8 (Bryan 6, Taft 2).
1912	California 13 (T. Roosevelt 11, Wilson 2).
1916	West Virginia 8 (Charles E. Hughes 7, Wilson 1).
1948	Tennessee 12 (Truman 11, Strom Thurmond 1).
1956	Alabama 11 (Adlai E. Stevenson 10, Walter B. Jones 1).
1960	Alabama 11 (Harry F. Byrd 6, Kennedy 5); Oklahoma 8 (Nixon 7, Byrd 1).
1968	North Carolina 13 (Nixon 12, George C. Wallace 1).
1972	Virginia 12 (Nixon 11, John Hospers 1).
1976	Washington 9 (Ford 8, Reagan 1).
1988	West Virginia 6 (Michael S. Dukakis 5, Lloyd Bentsen 1).
2000	D.C. 3 (Al Gore 2; one elector did not vote).

dent. In the election, the candidate who wins a *plurality* (the highest number) of a state's popular votes usually receives all the state's electoral votes. Thus, a candidate may be elected to the presidency without a majority of the popular votes.

The College in action. In the December following the presidential election, on a day set by law, the presidential electors in each state and the District of Columbia assemble. State electors usually meet in their state's capital. The electors then cast their ballots for president and vice president. Either by custom or, in a few states, by law, electors vote for their party's choices for the two offices. The lists of these elections are sent under seal to the president of the U.S. Senate and to the Administrator of General Services in Washington, D.C.

In January, at a joint session in the House of Representatives, the president of the Senate opens the certificates. Then one Democrat and one Republican from each house count the votes in the presence of both houses of Congress. The candidate who gets a majority of the electoral votes for president is declared elected.

If no candidate has a majority, the state delegations in the House of Representatives choose the president from the three candidates with the highest number of electoral votes. Each state has one vote in such an election. If no candidate wins a majority of the electoral votes for vice president, the Senate elects the vice president. It chooses between the two people with the most votes.

Reasons for the Electoral College. The manner of electing the president was a major problem at the Constitutional Convention of 1787. The convention rejected the proposal that Congress elect the chief executive, on the grounds that the president would then be under the control of the legislature. The proposal that the people elect the president also was rejected. To solve this problem and promote calm deliberation, the convention agreed on the method of indirect popular election, which became the Electoral College.

History. From 1789 to 1801, each elector voted for two persons on the same ballot. In 1789, all 69 electors voted for George Washington, and 34 voted for John Adams. The rest of the votes were for other candidates. Adams became vice president because in those days the runner-up took that position.

By 1800, two political parties had emerged. In that year, two Democratic-Republican candidates, Thomas Jefferson and Aaron Burr, both got a majority of the electoral vote and tied for first place. The election went to the House of Representatives, where each state had one vote. Jefferson was elected president, and Burr became vice president. That election led to Amendment 12 to the Constitution, ratified in 1804, providing that electors should designate their votes for president and vice president on separate ballots.

The House had to settle another presidential election in 1824. Andrew Jackson received more electoral votes than any of the other three candidates but failed to win a majority. John Quincy Adams was the runner-up. In the House, Henry Clay, another candidate, threw his support to Adams. Adams became president in spite of Jackson's bigger popular vote.

According to the United States Constitution, each state legislature decides how that state's electors shall be chosen. At first, most states allowed their legislatures to choose the electors. After 1800, more and more states began choosing electors in popular elections. Today, all states and the District of Columbia use this method.

The development of political parties over the years has reduced the Electoral College to a routine ceremony. Electors have made an implied pledge to vote for their party's nominees, instead of the candidate that they personally think is best qualified for office. This implied pledge has seldom been broken.

Frequent proposals have been made for abolishing the Electoral College and for the direct election of the president. These amendments would tend to reduce the importance of the states in the federal system. It has been claimed that direct election might encourage third and fourth parties. But this, in turn, might often result in the election of a president who received only a minority of the popular votes. Opponents of the Electoral College point out that the system allowed four candidates to become president whose closest opponent received more popular votes. The four were John Quincy Adams in 1824, Rutherford B. Hayes in 1876, Benjamin Harrison in 1888, and George W. Bush in 2000.   Robert Agranoff

Related articles include:

Constitution of the United States (Article II; Amendment 12)	President of the U.S. Primary election Vice president of the United States
Electoral Commission	

Additional resources

Henry, Christopher E. *The Electoral College.* Watts, 1996. Younger readers.
Longley, Lawrence D., and Peirce, Neal R. *The Electoral College Primer 2000.* Yale, 1999.

Web sites

U.S. Electoral College
http://www.nara.gov/fedreg/elctcoll
The official home page of the Electoral College.

The Electoral College
http://freedom.house.gov/electoral/
Information on the Electoral College and election laws, including essays and historical documents, from the U.S. House of Representatives.

Is it Time to Abolish the Electoral College?
http://www.lwv.org/where/promoting/electoral_college.html
Extensive information on the election process from The League of Women Voters, including an essay explaining the league's reasons for seeking the abolishment of the Electoral College.

Topic for study

Review the arguments for and against keeping the Electoral College that are discussed in Section One *and in the article* Electoral College *in this section. Explain your position in the debate.*

Liberalism is a political and economic philosophy that emphasizes freedom, equality, and opportunity. The philosophy called *conservatism,* in contrast, stresses order, tradition, and ownership of private property. Liberals have generally urged more rapid social change than conservatives have favored. But liberalism is a confusing term, because its meaning and emphasis have changed considerably over the years.

Early liberalism. The right to rebel against a government that severely restricts personal freedom was one of the chief doctrines of early liberalism. Liberal ideas inspired England's Glorious Revolution of 1688, the Revolutionary War in America (1775-1783), and the French Revolution (1789-1799). Liberal revolutions led to the establishment of many governments based on rule by law and by the consent of the governed. Many such constitutional governments had detailed bills of rights that proclaimed the individual's right to freedom of speech, the press, assembly, and religion. The bills of rights also attempted to provide safeguards against the abuse of police and judicial power. The liberal philosophy is clearly stated in the Declaration of Independence and in the writings of Thomas Jefferson. Jefferson, in turn, was influenced by the English philosopher John Locke.

Early liberals favored constitutional government, but they usually distrusted democracy. They tried to restrict the exercise of political power to members of the property-owning middle class. But as the industrial working class grew larger, it adopted the liberal principle that government should rest on the consent of the governed. By the late 1800's, a liberal was a person who favored democracy and voting rights for adult citizens.

Political and economic liberalism were closely connected until the 1900's. Early liberals argued that all people benefit most when each individual is allowed to follow his or her own self-interest. They believed that the economy is self-regulating if left alone to operate according to its own rules. Therefore, they concluded, government regulation is unnecessary. The ideas of economic liberalism were arranged into a system by the Scottish economist Adam Smith. This system was called *capitalism,* or *free enterprise.*

Liberalism today. Liberalism underwent a major change of emphasis after 1900. In the late 1800's, many liberals began to think of freedom less in terms of freedom from restriction, and more in terms of freedom of opportunity. They became convinced that government action is often necessary to provide the conditions under which individuals can realize their potentials.

Today, liberals favor government regulation of the economy in the public interest. They support government programs to provide economic security and ease human suffering. Such programs include unemployment insurance, minimum-wage laws, old-age pensions, health insurance, civil rights legislation, and antipoverty measures. Modern liberals believe in the importance of individual freedom. But they maintain government must remove obstacles to the enjoyment of that freedom. Supporters of the earlier ideas of economic liberalism are now frequently called *conservatives.* Some former liberals often called *neoliberals* favor less government regulation of the economy. They also express a sense of limits about government in general.   Alonzo L. Hamby

See also **Conservatism.**

Additional resources

Garry, Patrick M. *Liberalism and American Identity.* Kent State Univ. Pr., 1992.
Gray, John. *Liberalism.* 2nd ed. Univ. of Minn. Pr., 1995.
Johnston, David. *The Idea of a Liberal Theory.* Princeton, 1994.

Web site

Liberalism
http://plato.stanford.edu/entries/liberalism/
Information on liberalism from the Stanford Encyclopedia of Philosophy.

Political action committee is a group set up by a labor union, corporation, or other organization to contribute money to candidates for federal and state offices in the United States. Political action committees, often called *PAC's,* are formed largely because U.S. law forbids certain organizations to make contributions directly to candidates. PAC's get their money from individuals, in most cases from employees or members of the group that formed the PAC. The first PAC's were established in the 1940's.

Federal law and some state laws limit the amount of money a PAC may contribute to each candidate in any single election. But the contributions may be repeated for each election, whether it is a primary, runoff, or general election. A PAC may also donate unlimited amounts to a political party.

Many people think PAC's have too much influence in American politics. They say that to raise campaign funds, officeholders may give more attention to issues that concern PAC's than to those that concern ordinary citizens. Also, PAC's donate mostly to candidates seeking reelection. Many people therefore believe PAC's reduce the competitiveness of elections by making it harder for challengers to win. Defenders of PAC's say they help citizens exercise their right to support political candidates and to communicate their concerns to public officials.

Bruce I. Oppenheimer

Web site

Federal Election Commission
http://www.fec.gov/
The home page of the Federal Election Commission provides information about elections, voting, and campaign donations.

Political convention is a gathering at which major political parties in the United States formally nominate their candidates for president and vice president. At one time, the conventions actually selected, as well as formally nominated, the party's candidates. Today, however, the presidential nominees of the major parties are normally determined before the convention takes place. Nonetheless, the conventions of the Democratic and Republican parties—the two major political parties—play an important role in the U.S. presidential election process. The conventions allow the party to unify around its nominees. Equally important, the conventions provide wide public exposure for the party's candidates and goals. A successful convention can dramatically boost the public's support for the party and its candidates.

The Democratic and Republican national conventions are four-day events that take place every four years. The two conventions are held at separate times during the summer of each presidential election year. They are typically held in separate cities, and in different cities from year to year.

Huge crowds gather at each convention. The people in attendance include thousands of party delegates, who nominate a candidate they hope can win the presidential election the following November. An even larger number of magazine, newspaper, radio, and television reporters come to the convention. They provide coverage of the gathering for millions of voters throughout the nation. Many other people attend conventions, in-

At a national political convention, delegates nominate their party's candidates for president and vice president. Arkansas Governor Bill Clinton, *shown here,* speaks at the 1992 Democratic Party convention in New York City, where he became the party's presidential nominee.

cluding *lobbyists* (representatives of interest groups), people who contribute money to the party or its candidates, and alternate delegates. The first national political conventions in the United States assembled in the early 1830's. The presidential candidate was both selected and nominated at the convention until the mid-1900's. Today, the candidate is normally selected before the convention in a series of state elections and other contests. These contests determine the number of supporters each candidate will have at the convention as delegates. The candidate with the most delegates is formally nominated at the convention. The delegates then nominate a vice presidential candidate, who normally has been hand-picked by the presidential candidate.

Other business is also handled at the convention. For example, the party adopts a *platform*—a statement of its goals and principles in the presidential campaign. The platform is designed to win votes for the presidential and vice presidential nominees, and for party candidates who are running for other political offices in the same election year.

Political conventions are lively events. Delegates support their choice for president and vice president by waving banners and cheering wildly. Parades, parties, and other celebrations promote the political party and its nominees. On the last day of the convention, the presidential and vice presidential nominees give speeches that launch the party's election campaign. The speeches are broadcast on television throughout the country.

Preconvention activities

The process of nominating a presidential candidate begins months before the convention. The most important step in the process is the selection of convention delegates. At the convention, each delegate votes for a presidential candidate. The candidate who gets a majority of the delegate votes wins the party's nomination.

Delegate selection takes place in elections and other state contests that occur during the late winter and spring of each presidential election year. Washington, D.C., Puerto Rico, and the Virgin Islands and other U.S. territories also send delegates to the conventions.

The national committee of each party decides how many delegates each state may send to the convention. The number is based on the party's strength in the state in recent elections. Thousands of delegates attend each convention, but exact numbers vary from year to year.

The method of choosing people to run as delegate candidates is different in different states. In many states, these candidates are chosen by the state party organization, by the presidential campaign organizations, or by mass meetings of supporters of a presidential candidate.

There are two main methods of choosing which delegate candidates will attend the convention as delegates. They are (1) the *primary election system* and (2) the *caucus-convention system.* Some states allow each party to choose which of the two systems it will use.

Most states require both parties to use the primary election system. As a result, primary elections determine more than two-thirds of all convention delegates.

Some states hold a *delegate primary,* in which voters elect the delegates. In most delegate primaries, the names of the delegate candidate and the presidential candidate whom the delegate supports are printed together on the ballot. In this way, voters know which delegate candidate supports which presidential candidate.

Other states hold a *candidate primary,* in which only the names of the presidential candidates appear on the ballot. The number of votes each candidate receives in the primary determines the number of delegates he or she is allowed to send to the national convention.

The caucus-convention system was once the main method of selecting delegates to national conventions. Today, less than one-third of all delegates are chosen in this way. The caucus-convention process begins with local meetings called *caucuses.* At each meeting, delegates are chosen to attend a convention that covers a larger region, such as a county. This convention, in turn, selects delegates to a state convention, where the state's national convention delegates are then chosen.

The caucus-convention process may begin with either of two types of caucuses—*party caucuses* or *participatory caucuses.* In a party caucus, the delegates sent to the regional convention are chosen by local party officials. In a participatory caucus, anyone who attends the caucus can take part in choosing the delegates.

Most states do not require individual delegates to vote for the candidates the delegates have pledged to support. But delegates rarely change their vote unless their candidate drops out of the race.

Certain primaries and caucuses are more influential than others in determining who the presidential nominee will be. The early contests provide the first indications of which candidates may have a chance to win the nomination. Candidates who do not win support in the early contests are unlikely to raise campaign funds, gather campaign workers, or attract media attention. These candidates often drop out of the presidential race early. The Iowa caucuses and the New Hampshire primary are examples of important early delegate contests.

The large states account for the most delegate votes at each party's convention. As a result, the candidates remaining after early contests try especially hard to win votes in big states, such as California and Texas.

Organizing the convention is done by the party's national committee. The committee chooses a permanent chairperson for the convention. It also designates a person to kick off the convention with a rousing speech called the *keynote address.* Members of Congress or other key party members usually are chosen for these positions. The committee also picks a convention site.

Much of the convention's official business is carried out by special committees. Most of the committees consist of delegates and other party members, including some elected government officials. The special committees meet in the months before the convention. One committee prepares a report that establishes procedures for the convention, and another makes sure the state delegate contests have conformed to party rules. Yet another committee drafts a party platform.

Convention activities

The main purpose of a national convention is to nominate candidates for president and vice president. But the convention also serves other purposes. Today, one of its most important functions is to present the party's platform and candidates to the nation's voters. To reach the voters, the party encourages television, newspaper, and other reporters to cover key events at the convention.

Introducing the campaign. Much of a national convention of the Democratic or Republican parties is devoted to speeches. These speeches include the keynote address. This speech, made by an important party member, sets out themes for the presidential campaign. It is also intended to inspire party members for the hard

work needed to win the November election.

The presidential candidates who will not receive the party's nomination often deliver speeches. In most cases, they use their speeches to announce their support for the person who will become the nominee.

Also at the convention, the special convention committees present their reports for adoption by the convention delegates. Most reports are drafted before the convention and do not change once it begins. But some reports are adopted only after debate. General party reaction to the reports can influence the presidential race. For example, the report that presents the party's platform must appeal to a wide range of voters—as well as to party members. Disagreement on the platform at the convention may reveal a lack of party unity and thus make the party and its nominees less attractive to the nation's voters.

Making nominations. The presidential nomination is one of the highlights of the convention. Delegates officially recommend the nomination of candidates in *nominating speeches,* in which the speaker praises the accomplishments of the candidate. Each speech may build to a climax that triggers a massive demonstration in the convention hall. Supporters of the candidate parade, wave banners, throw confetti, and cheer.

The *roll call* begins after all nominating speeches have been made. In the roll call, each state and territory casts a ballot that indicates how many of its delegate votes it is awarding to each candidate. The candidate who gets a majority of the votes of all the delegates at the convention formally becomes the party's nominee.

If no candidate receives a majority, more ballots would be cast until enough delegates switch their votes to give one candidate a majority. However, a second ballot has not been required at any Democratic or Republican national convention since the early 1950's.

To nominate a candidate for vice president, the party uses the same procedure that it used for the presidential nomination. The likely nominee for president normally chooses the vice presidential nominee before the convention begins. The delegates then approve the choice at the convention.

The nominees for vice president and president make *acceptance speeches* near the end of the convention. These speeches are viewed on television by millions of people. The speeches outline the issues that will be emphasized during the campaign and are designed to win the confidence of voters. With their speeches, the nominees also try to rally the enthusiasm of party members who may have supported other candidates during the nominating campaign.

Other convention activities. Numerous other activities also take place at a national convention. For example, state party leaders attend the convention to discuss issues affecting the party in their state. Also, many of the party's candidates for election to Congress or to state or local offices campaign at the convention. Lobbyists attend the convention to try to influence delegates and party leaders or to use news coverage of the convention to further their causes.

Attracting publicity. National news coverage of the presidential candidate and the party has become a major goal of the organizers of political conventions. Both major parties rely on newspaper articles, television stories, and other press coverage to generate public support for their nominees.

All national conventions of the Democratic and Republican parties have been televised since 1952. The parties often schedule convention events to occur at peak TV viewing hours.

Measuring convention success. A convention's success was once measured chiefly by how well it promoted party unity. The convention was judged successful if it ended with party members from the various states supporting a single presidential candidate.

Today, however, the success of a convention is more often measured in terms of how much the convention contributes to the public image of the nominee. The party compares opinion polls taken before and after the convention to determine how the convention has affected the nominee's public approval rating. Because of media coverage of the convention, the nominee's rating almost always rises. But the extent of this rise can vary a great deal from convention to convention. A large upward "bounce" in the nominee's approval rating is the sign of a successful convention.

The history of national conventions

The writers of the Constitution of the United States did not outline a procedure for nominating a president. Until the early 1830's, a party's supporters in Congress or in state legislatures usually nominated the party's candidate for president.

The Anti-Masonic Party held the first national nominating convention in September 1831. The first convention that closely resembled today's gatherings was that of the Democratic-Republican Party in 1832. Soon, the convention became the established procedure in the United States for nominating presidential candidates.

The changing role of conventions. Until the mid-1950's, almost all presidential nominees were not only formally nominated at the convention, but they also fought there for the support required to win the nomination. Usually, strong candidates assembled some support before the convention. Then, at the convention, they competed with one another to win a majority of the delegates' votes. Party leaders often had significant influence in maneuvering the votes of the delegates. At many conventions, multiple ballots were needed to reach a majority. In 1924, the Democrats took 103 ballots to nominate John W. Davis—the largest number of ballots ever needed at a Democratic or Republican presidential convention.

By the mid-1950's, however, delegate majorities had begun to form before the convention. The last time a major party had to go to a second ballot was in 1952, when the Democrats needed three ballots to nominate Adlai E. Stevenson.

Various factors contributed to this change. For example, the ability of party bosses to influence the nomination had diminished because of new laws on delegate selection in the early 1900's. This legislation included several state laws that required the parties to select their convention delegates in primary elections.

As a result of these and other changes, candidates increasingly turned to campaigning among voters for support. The spread of TV after 1945 helped these candidates achieve national recognition and aided the

formation of earlier and earlier nominating majorities.

Further reforms of the convention system took place soon after the 1968 Democratic convention. Many people viewing the convention, in which Hubert H. Humphrey won the nomination, disliked the political maneuvering they saw on the convention floor. Consequently, the Democrats appointed a commission to reform their rules for selecting convention delegates.

One result of the reforms was greater representation of minority groups and women among the delegates. The reforms also resulted in many states adopting laws that required the use of primary elections by both Republicans and Democrats. Although primaries had appeared in the early 1900's, they did not become the main method of delegate selection until after 1968.

Other types of conventions

State and local party conventions may be held to select party leaders, adopt local and state party platforms, or endorse nonpresidential candidates in primary elections. In addition, the constitutions of most states provide for a constitutional convention, often called a *con-con*. The purpose of such a convention is to rewrite or revise the state constitution. The people of the state elect the con-con delegates. In most states, the people must approve the new or revised constitution before it can take effect.   Byron E. Shafer

Related articles in *World Book* include:

Caucus	President of the	Vice president of
Election campaign	United States	the United
Electoral College	Primary election	States
Political party		

Web sites

The Democratic National Committee
http://www.democrats.org/index.html
The official Web site of the Democratic Party's National Committee.

The Republican National Committee
http://www.rnc.org/
The official Web site of the Republican National Committee.

Political party is an organized group of people who control or seek to control a government. In democratic countries, political parties compete against one another in elections to keep or gain control of a government. In the United States and Canada, political parties are active on the national, state or provincial, and local levels.

Political parties are absolutely necessary to democratic government. Most modern democracies are *representative* democracies. That is, the people elect representatives to act as their agents in making and enforcing laws. In a representative democracy, some means is needed for nominating candidates for public office and for selecting issues for public debate. Political parties perform these functions. At election time, the people vote into office the candidates of their choice. Political parties are voluntary organizations and want as many members as possible. Some of these parties have rules and membership dues. Others have practically no rules and require no dues.

Most dictatorships allow only one political party—the party that controls the government. That party also tightly controls who may run for election.

Party functions

In democratic countries, political parties perform several important tasks. (1) They select candidates to run for public office. (2) They help organize the government. (3) They provide opposition to the party in power. (4) They raise funds to conduct election campaigns. Other functions of parties in democratic countries include informing voters about public affairs and about problems that need government action. In one-party nations, the chief functions of political parties are to select candidates for office and organize the government.

Selecting candidates. In one-party nations, the candidates the party selects to run for office automatically win election because they have no opposition. In China, for example, the Communist Party—the only party allowed—chooses the candidates for office.

In nations that have two or more parties, each party selects candidates for the various public offices. The voters then decide which candidates among the parties win office. Party leaders try to select candidates who have voter appeal and experience for the office.

During the early history of the United States, party leaders selected candidates for office in meetings called *caucuses.* But the caucus system became unpopular because it gave other party members little voice in the selection of candidates. In addition, one person or a small group of persons sometimes gained control of a caucus and used it for private gain. See **Caucus.**

By about 1840, the *convention system* for nominating candidates was in general use. Under this system, party members chose delegates to represent them at nominating conventions. But party bosses and *political machines* (organizations within a party) gained control of many conventions. Many delegates voted the way they were told or paid to vote. Today, conventions are held in only a few states to make some nominations for state and local offices and to discuss party affairs. The two major U.S. political parties—the Democratic and Republican parties—still hold a national convention every four years to officially nominate candidates for president and vice president. See **Political convention.**

During the early 1900's, many states began to replace the convention system with primary elections to select candidates for office. The aim was to reduce party control in the selection of candidates. Today, all states hold either *open* or *closed* primary elections for state offices. In an open primary, each voter receives the ballots of all parties holding primaries. In the voting booth, the voter selects which ballot to use. In a closed primary, voters receive only the ballot of the party to which they belong. In recent years, the Republican and Democratic parties have relied on primary elections—and, in some states, caucuses—to select their presidential candidates. The parties then formally nominate the candidates at their national conventions. See **Primary election.**

Organizing the government is a major function of political parties. But how the parties do this depends on the government's established structure and on how the powers of government are divided.

Unitary and federal systems. In countries that have a *unitary* system of government, such as France, Italy, and the United Kingdom, the central government has most governmental powers, including control over local governments. In countries that have a *federal* system of government, such as Canada and the United States, the powers of government are divided between the central government and the state or provincial governments. The political parties in countries with a unitary system concentrate on gaining control of and organizing the central government. The parties are thus basically national in their activities and are so organized. The political parties in countries with a federal system try to gain power to organize both the central government and the state or provincial governments. The parties are thus both national and state in their activities and organization.

The presidential system. In the United States, the Constitution provides for the separation of powers among the executive, legislative, and judicial branches. The president, therefore, is not a member of Congress, nor are the Cabinet members. The president is elected by the people through the Electoral College and may be of a different political party than the party that controls Congress. Often, the president is forced to rely on leaders from both parties to get programs passed. Under the presidential system, Congress may refuse to pass legislation the president wants. On the other hand, the president may *veto* (reject) legislation passed by Congress—and Congress seldom overrides a veto.

The president serves a four-year term. The president has to deal with a House of Representatives whose total membership is elected every two years and with a Senate in which a third of the members face election every two years. These staggered elections make for shifting alliances and may increase or decrease support for the president's policies. The *bicameral* division of Congress into two independent bodies—the House of Representatives and the Senate—also complicates the president's role. Traditionally, each body jealously guards its powers against executive interference.

The parliamentary system. In such parliamentary democracies as the United Kingdom, the head of the government—the prime minister—faces fewer problems in organizing the government. The prime minister must be a member of Parliament and usually also is leader of the majority party in the House of Commons. The prime minister usually chooses a Cabinet from leaders of the majority party who are members of Parliament.

In the United Kingdom, the prime minister and Cabinet thus have both executive and legislative authority. They are members of the legislature and responsible to it. If the prime minister's program fails to win parliamentary support, the opposition party may demand an election. This election is called for by the government but must occur within five years of the previous election. The people will vote either to keep the present government in power or to give the opposition party the opportunity to form a new government.

Organizing the U.S. Congress. The Democratic and Republican parties organize their members in Congress according to the established structure of the House of Representatives and the Senate. At the beginning of each new session of Congress, both parties in the House and the Senate hold meetings to elect various officers and committee members. In the House, each party nominates a candidate for Speaker, the body's presiding officer. But most representatives vote for their party's candidate, and so the majority party actually chooses the Speaker. In the Senate, the vice president of the United States presides. The majority party elects a president *pro tempore* (temporary) to preside in the absence of the vice president.

Each party in the House and Senate also elects a *floor leader* and a *whip*. The floor leaders direct their party's activities during debates on proposed legislation. The whips help the floor leaders by letting them know how party members feel about bills coming up for vote. The whips—with the help of assistant whips—also try to assure as much party discipline as possible by persuading members to vote along party lines.

The majority party in each house has the most seats on House and Senate committees. In addition, the committee heads belong to the majority party. Congressional committees and subcommittees have great influence in speeding or slowing the passage of legislation. They are often called "little legislatures." See **Congress of the United States; House of Representatives; Senate.**

Providing opposition. In a democratic nation, the party or parties out of power have the duty of criticizing the policies of the party in power and offering alternative programs. In France, Italy, and other countries that have many parties, the opposition parties may represent various points of view—from those favoring a monarchy to those preferring Communism. In most two-party nations, the party out of power usually provides unified opposition. But in the U.S. Congress, this is not always true. Some members of the party that does not control the presidency may support the president's program against the wishes of their party leaders.

Raising funds for election campaigns is an important activity of political parties in democratic nations. Campaigns are expensive, but parties must wage them to win elections. United States parties spend much more money on election campaigns than do parties in other nations, partly because most U.S. campaigns last longer and employ television and other costly means of communication. It can cost millions of dollars to finance a campaign for a U.S. Senate seat in a large state, and many millions more to finance a presidential campaign. The cost of nominating and electing all U.S. public officials in a presidential-election year is over $1 billion.

Most campaign expenditures are for television and radio advertising, campaign consultants, polls, printing charges, telephone bills, campaign buttons, posters, and salaries. Some campaign funds come from the small contributions of thousands of party members and supporters. But most of the money comes from large donations by wealthy people and institutional groups called *political action committees (PAC's).*

In the United States, several federal and state laws regulate campaign spending and contributions. But the laws have been difficult to enforce and have been generally ineffective in controlling expenditures because so many groups are involved in waging campaigns and raising funds. See **Election campaign.**

Other functions. In democracies, each party uses newspapers, radio, television, and other means to tell the people about its program. In so doing, a party hopes to win—or stay in—office. The party in power tries to justify its program. The minority party, on the other hand, points out what it considers weaknesses in the majority party's program and offers voters an alternative one. In publicizing their views, political parties thus help keep the voters informed on important issues.

Political parties also simplify complicated issues for

Important political parties of the United States

This chart shows the time spans of some of the important political parties of the United States. A question mark means the date is disputed by political historians. For charts showing when each of the two major parties was in and out of office, see the articles **Democratic Party** and **Republican Party.**

Republican Party (1854-   )

Democratic Party (1830?-   )

National Republican Party (1825 - 1834)

Democratic-Republican Party (1792?-1825?)

Federalist Party (1787? - 1816?)

Greenback Party (1874 - 1887?)

Anti-Federalist Party (1787? - 1792?)

Whig Party (1832 - 1860)

| 1788 | 1796 | 1804 | 1812 | 1820 | 1828 | 1836 | 1844 | 1852 | 1860 | 1868 | 1876 | 1884 |

the voters by reducing the issues to choices between candidates for office. In order to win votes, political candidates also look for problems that have not received public attention and that affect many people. In this way, political parties help force the government to act on neglected problems.

Party systems

The number of political parties that win a significant share of votes in major elections determines the kind of *party system* that a country has. A country may thus have a one-party, two-party, or multiparty system.

One-party systems are often associated with dictatorships. Most dictatorships allow only one party—the party that controls the government. Some dictatorships permit other parties, but only as long as they create no threat to the government.

In China, the Communist Party forms the government. No other party may exist. Party membership is considered a privilege and is granted only after a person meets certain standards. Only about 4 percent of the Chinese people belong to the party. The party performs many more functions than political parties in democracies. For this reason, it has elaborate organization for recruiting members and leaders, developing policy, indoctrinating the people, and maintaining discipline.

Most one-party dictatorships have elections. The elections are held chiefly to generate enthusiasm for the party. In China, for example, the candidates of the Communist Party tell the nation's people how wonderful Communism is. Party leaders explain what the party has done, what it plans to do, and what it expects of the people.

Two-party systems are most common in English-speaking nations. These two-party countries include the United Kingdom, with its Conservative and Labour parties; and the United States, with its Democratic and Republican parties. Although these nations also have other parties, one of the two major parties in each country usually controls the government.

Similar voting patterns also exist in most two-party countries. Generally, industrial areas of a nation support the more liberal party, and rural areas vote for the more conservative party.

Although a nation may have a two-party system, one party may control politics in certain areas of the country. The party has this control because most voters in such areas always vote for its candidates. In the United Kingdom, for example, certain *constituencies* (voting districts) always support the Conservative Party. Some of the country's other constituencies always support the Labour Party. In national elections, each party considers certain constituencies "safe." If party leaders want to be sure that a candidate will win a seat in Parliament, they have the candidate run in a safe constituency. In the United Kingdom, candidates for national office do not have to be a resident of the constituency they hope to represent.

In many states of the United States, both the Democratic Party and the Republican Party have considerable strength. In other states, one of those two parties has traditionally controlled politics. From the American Civil War (1861-1865) until the 1960's, for example, Democrats strongly controlled most of the Southern States. During that same period, the Republicans controlled—though less strongly—some of the New England and Midwestern states. Since the 1960's, however, the Republicans have won increasing support in the South and West, and the Democrats have made gains in New England and in the Midwest.

Large industrial and commercial cities in the United States, such as Chicago and New York City, generally vote for the Democratic Party. Rural and suburban areas usually support Republican candidates.

Multiparty systems are found in many nations that have parliaments. Countries with multiparty systems include Belgium, Denmark, France, Italy, Japan, and Sri Lanka.

Most multiparty nations have four or five major parties. In addition, a nation may also have many minor parties. In most cases, each party seeks a particular economic or social goal. Multiparty systems vary from country to country. But most systems consist of one or two *left-wing* parties, which hold liberal or radical views; one or two *center* parties, which have moderate views; and one or two *right-wing* parties, which support conservative views.

WORLD BOOK chart

American Party (1968 - 1976)

Populist Party (1891-1908?)

Libertarian Party (1971 -   )

Progressive Party (1948 - 1957?)

Reform Party (1995-   )

Progressive Party (1924 - 1946?)

Progressive Party (1912 - 1916)

| 1892 | 1900 | 1908 | 1916 | 1924 | 1932 | 1940 | 1948 | 1956 | 1964 | 1972 | 1980 | 1988 | 1996 | 2004 |

In multiparty nations, one party rarely wins enough seats in the legislature to form a government. Consequently, two or more parties join forces and form a *coalition government* to direct the nation's affairs. But often, the coalition parties fail to agree on policies and programs, and so the government falls. The multiparty system thus tends to produce a less stable government than does the two-party system.

Party membership in the United States

Political parties in the United States have no strict requirements for membership. People are considered members of the party to which they consider themselves to belong. Therefore, neither the Republican Party nor the Democratic Party maintains accurate membership lists.

Some of the best evidence regarding party affiliation comes from voting surveys and public opinion polls. Such surveys and polls show that the majority of American voters who identify with a political party consider themselves Democrats. But party identification has never meant straight party voting. In the 1980 and 1984 presidential elections, for example, Republican Ronald Reagan received the votes of many people who normally thought of themselves as Democrats. These same people may have voted for Democratic candidates at the state and local levels. Such ticket-splitting is much more common in the United States than in other major countries.

Party organization in the United States

The Democratic and Republican parties are complicated organizations. Both parties are organized at the national, state, and local level. At each level, each party has three basic units. These units are the mass meeting, the committee, and specific leaders. The relationship between the three units varies at the three levels of government. It also varies from one state or community to another.

National conventions and committees. In theory, the national convention of each major political party has final authority in party matters. Actually, however, the convention has little power. Each party's national convention meets only once every four years, when it nominates the party's candidates for president and vice president. The national convention also goes through the formality of electing the national committee, which acts for the party between conventions. In reality, each state party chooses its representatives on the committee. To learn about the organization and activities of the national conventions and how the delegates to the conventions are chosen, see the *World Book* article on **Political convention.**

The national committee of both major parties consists of party representatives from the states, the District of Columbia, and the territories. The Republicans elect a committeeman and committeewoman from each area, and include each area's party chairperson. The Democrats have a much larger committee. Its representatives are apportioned by a complicated formula that is designed to include many special groups and to reflect party strength. Men and women must be equally represented on the committee.

Both the Democratic and Republican national committees have their headquarters in Washington, D.C. They meet only once, twice, or three times a year. One of the main tasks of each committee is to organize its party's next national convention. It chooses the city where the convention will meet and makes arrangements for a smoothly run convention. But most of the work of the party's national organization is done by the committee's national chairman and staff.

Each party's presidential candidate selects the national chairman at the end of the national convention. The national committee then formally elects that person. The chairman acts for the national committee in managing party affairs. He or she may assist the president in *patronage* matters by recommending appointees for federal jobs. During presidential elections, the chairman directs the party's fund-raising and other activities in the national campaign.

The national chairman also organizes the party's national headquarters and is the chief decision maker within the national organization. But the headquarters has a sizeable staff that does the detailed work. It has campaign, fund-raising, public relations, and research divisions.

State committees. Both the Democratic and Republican parties have a state committee in each state. In most states, the committee members are chosen in party primaries or at conventions. The state committees organize and manage campaigns for state offices and assist in local campaigns. They also raise money, make arrangements for primary elections, and organize the state conventions.

The leader of the state committee is the official head of the state party. The committee formally elects the leader. But the governor, a U.S. senator from the state, or a group of powerful local officials actually hand-pick the leader. In most states, these officials are also powerful enough to lead the party and control the state committee. In some states, however, the committee leader effectively directs the party and controls or even chooses key state party officers.

Local organizations. Each of the two major parties has a county committee in most counties of the United States. Committee members are chosen by county conventions or in primaries. The county committee elects the county leader, who maintains communication with the state party organization and, in most states, is a delegate to the state committee. Some county leaders retain patronage power, which they use to sway the votes of delegates at state and national conventions.

Below the county committees are the city, ward, and precinct organizations, whose leaders have the closest contact with the voters. City and ward committeemen and committeewomen are selected in local conventions or primaries. In some states, precinct committeemen and committeewomen or captains are also chosen in primaries. In others, the county committee selects them.

The United States has more than 146,300 election precincts. In most of them, either one or both major parties have a precinct captain, committeeman, or committeewoman. This official prepares the party *poll book,* which lists the names of the voters in the precinct and which party—if any—they belong to. Precinct captains and their assistants try to make sure that all members of their party are registered to vote.

In the past, precinct captains or committeemen and committeewomen frequently won votes by assisting voters and would-be voters. For example, they helped immigrants become citizens, bailed out prisoners under arrest, found jobs for unemployed persons, and sometimes gave out charity. But in many cities, local party leaders and bosses have lost the great influence they once had. Government welfare programs and rapid economic growth have made many voters less dependent on their help.

Development of parties in the United States

Early history. American leaders met in Philadelphia in 1787 to draw up the Constitution. This document makes no mention of political parties. In fact, George Washington, who presided over the Constitutional Convention, and many other early political leaders opposed their development. Nevertheless, common economic, political, and social interests brought people together to form political organizations. A group called the Federalists supported strong national government. Their opponents were called the Anti-Federalists. These political organizations began to take shape before Washington became president in 1789. Soon after, the two groups developed into the first American political parties, the Federalist Party and the Democratic-Republican Party. The Federalists, led by Alexander Hamilton, wanted a strong central government. The Democratic-Republicans, led by Thomas Jefferson, supported a weak central government.

After the 1816 presidential election, the Federalist Party broke up as a national organization, and the Democratic-Republican Party split into several groups. One of the Democratic-Republican groups came under the leadership of Andrew Jackson. By about 1830, Jackson and his followers were known as Democrats.

The Democratic Party is the oldest existing political party in the United States. Some historians believe it began in the 1790's as Jefferson's Democratic-Republican Party. Most historians trace its origin to the campaign organization that formed after the 1824 presidential election to win the presidency for Jackson in 1828.

From 1828 to 1860, the Democratic Party won all but two presidential elections—those of 1840 and 1848—even though its members often disagreed on several issues. They fought, for example, over banking policies, the slavery issue, and tariff rates. Democrats also met bitter opposition from outside the party. About 1832, several groups that opposed Jackson combined to form the Whig Party. But the Whigs never united sufficiently to propose a program with as much popular appeal as that of the Democrats.

During the 1850's, the Democrats split over whether to oppose or support the extension of slavery. In 1860, the party even had two nominees for president—John C. Breckinridge and Stephen A. Douglas. Both lost to the Republican candidate, Abraham Lincoln.

From 1860 to 1932, only two Democrats won the presidency—Grover Cleveland in 1884 and 1892 and Woodrow Wilson in 1912 and 1916. The Republican Party had gained so much strength during the Civil War that the Democrats had great difficulty winning control of the government. In addition, the Republicans repeatedly charged the Democrats with having caused the war

and having been disloyal to the Union.

The situation changed after 1929. Just as the Republicans had blamed the Democrats for the Civil War, so the Democrats blamed the Republicans for the stock market crash of 1929 and the Great Depression of the 1930's. The Democratic candidate won the presidency in 1932, and Democrats continued to win every election from 1932 through 1948.

In the last half of the 1900's, however, neither the Democrats nor the Republicans dominated the presidential elections to any great extent. The Democrats won about half of the 12 elections during that period—in 1960, 1964, 1976, 1992, and 1996. For more information, see **Democratic Party.**

The Republican Party started as a series of antislavery political meetings in the Midwest in 1854. At that time, the Whig Party was breaking up. Many Whigs—as well as Northern Democrats—opposed the extension of slavery. The Republican Party represented this viewpoint and thus gained followers rapidly. The party's first presidential candidate, John C. Frémont, ran in the 1856 election. He was not elected president, but he carried 11 Northern states.

From 1860, when Lincoln was elected, through 1928, when Herbert Hoover was elected, the Republican Party candidate won 14 of the nation's 18 presidential elections. The policies of the Republican Party appealed to many groups, including farmers, industrialists, and merchants.

In 1912, President William Howard Taft was the leader of a divided Republican Party. Progressive Republicans wanted Theodore Roosevelt, who had been president from 1901 to 1909, to run again. But conservative Republicans renominated Taft at the party's 1912 national convention. Roosevelt then withdrew from the party and formed the Progressive, or "Bull Moose," Party. This split helped the Democratic candidate, Woodrow Wilson, win the election. The Republicans lost to Wilson again in 1916. They regained the presidency in 1920, and won in 1924 and 1928. But their popularity declined after the stock market crash of 1929.

During World War II (1939-1945), the Republicans began to show signs of recovery. In 1952, World War II military leader Dwight D. Eisenhower brought the Republicans their first presidential victory in 24 years. Eisenhower won reelection in 1956.

The Republicans lost to the Democrats in the 1960 and 1964 presidential elections but regained the presidency in 1968 and held it in 1972. They lost to the Democrats in 1976, but then were victorious in the next three elections—1980, 1984, and 1988. They were defeated in 1992 and 1996 but won again in 2000. For more information, see **Republican Party.**

Third parties. There have been many third parties in the United States. None of them ever won the presidency. But many of their proposals gained such widespread public support that the two major parties were forced to adopt them. These proposals included the convention system of nominating presidential candidates and the direct election of U.S. senators.

Third parties in the United States can be divided into five types, according to their origins and goals. The first type consists of groups that broke away from the two major parties. For example, the Liberal Republicans in

1872 and the Roosevelt Progressives in 1912 broke away from the Republican Party. Third parties that were formed by groups leaving the Democratic Party include the Gold Democrats, who left the party in 1896; the Dixiecrats, who left in 1948; and the American Independent Party, which broke away from the Democratic Party in 1968.

The second type of third party consists of organizations formed chiefly to help a specific group of people. For example, debt-ridden farmers established the Greenback Party in the 1870's and formed the Populist Party in the 1890's.

The third type is made up of left wing protest groups. They include the Socialist Party, which was founded in 1901, and the American Communist Party, which was organized in 1919.

The fourth type consists of parties that have only one goal. These single-issue parties include the nation's oldest existing third party—the Prohibition Party, which was founded in 1869. The Prohibition Party seeks to prevent the manufacture and sale of alcoholic beverages in the United States.

The fifth type of third party consists of groups that have broad programs and attempt to gain national favor. Examples of this type of third party include the Progressive parties of 1924, 1948, and 1952; the Libertarian Party, which was founded in 1971; and the Reform Party, established in 1995.

Political parties in Canada

Canada has a combined parliamentary and federal system of government. Thus, the organization of its political parties resembles that of both the United Kingdom and the United States. Canada—like the United Kingdom—has a prime minister, who usually belongs to and is the leader of the majority party in the House of Commons. But the political parties in Canada—like those in the United States—are both national and provincial (state) in their activities and organization.

Oldest parties. The two oldest parties in Canada are the Conservative Party and the Liberal Party. Historically, they have also been the strongest parties. Both parties trace their origins to before 1867, when the British North America Act established the Dominion of Canada. In 1942, the Conservatives changed the name of their party to the Progressive Conservative Party. But most Canadians still call it the Conservative Party.

In 1867, John A. Macdonald, leader of the Conservative Party, became the first prime minister of Canada. He held office until 1873, when Alexander Mackenzie, head of the Liberal Party, became prime minister. The Conservatives regained control of the government in 1878 and held it until 1896. Between 1896 and 1935, one of the two parties—or a Conservative-Liberal coalition—controlled the government. But since 1935, the Liberals have been the dominant party in Canada.

Traditionally, the Liberals have favored the expansion of social programs and provincial rights. Conservatives have supported tighter controls on government spending.

Other parties in Canada have never won enough public support to control the federal government. The Liberals and the Conservatives have tried to make their programs broad enough to appeal to other parties.

The Progressive Party was the only Canadian party other than the Liberals and Conservatives to win more than 20 percent of the vote in a general election. In 1921, it gained 64 seats in the House of Commons. But by 1930, this farmer-supported party was no longer an effective organization.

In the 1930's, during the Great Depression, two groups of dissatisfied Canadians founded new parties—the left-wing Co-operative Commonwealth Federation (CCF) and the right-wing Social Credit Party. The CCF was formed in Alberta in 1932. It supported the establishment of a planned economy in Canada. The CCF controlled the government of Saskatchewan from 1944 to 1964. The party achieved its greatest national strength in 1945, with 28 members in the House of Commons.

In 1961, the CCF joined with the Canadian Labour Congress to form the New Democratic Party (NDP). The NDP has considerable influence in British Columbia, Manitoba, Ontario, Saskatchewan, and the Yukon Territory. It governed Saskatchewan during the early 1960's and from 1971 to 1982. It regained control there in 1991. The party held power in Manitoba from 1969 to 1977, from 1981 to 1988, and beginning again in 1999. It headed British Columbia's government from 1972 to 1975 and regained power there in 1991. The NDP won control of the Yukon Territory's government in 1985 and controlled Ontario's from 1990 to 1995. The party made its largest gains at the national level in 1963, 1968, 1972, 1979, 1980, and 1988. After 1988, its strength in the House of Commons declined.

The Social Credit Party, established in Alberta in 1935, supports the free enterprise system. This party controlled the government of Alberta from 1935 to 1971. It governed British Columbia from 1952 to 1972 and from 1975 to 1991. In 1962, the party won 30 seats in the House of Commons. But since then, its strength at the national level has fallen sharply.

Another party, the Reform Party, was established in Manitoba in 1987. By the early 1990's, it had gained much support across Canada—especially in the West.

In the 1990's, the Reform Party was one of two new parties that sharply increased their number of seats in the House of Commons. The other party was the Bloc Québécois. Founded in 1990 and based in Quebec, it supports sovereignty for Quebec. In the national elections of 1993, the two new parties' gains nearly eliminated the Conservatives from the House of Commons. The Conservatives, however, later regained some of their lost strength in the House.

In 2000, members of the Reform Party voted to dissolve their party and join the newly created Canadian Reform Conservative Alliance. The new party, commonly called the Canadian Alliance, favors such reforms as reducing the national debt and establishing a single-rate income tax. It strongly supports the free-enterprise system.   Charles O. Jones

Related articles in *World Book* include:

Caucus	Green party	Political conven-
Congress of the	Reform Party	tion
United States	Republican Party	Primary election
Democratic Party		

Outline

I. Party functions
   A. Selecting candidates

B. Organizing the government
C. Providing opposition
D. Raising funds
E. Other functions

II. Party systems
A. One-party systems
B. Two-party systems
C. Multiparty systems

III. Party membership in the United States

IV. Party organization in the United States
A. National conventions and committees
B. State committees
C. Local organizations

V. Development of parties in the United States
A. Early history
B. The Democratic Party
C. The Republican Party
D. Third parties

VI. Political parties in Canada
A. Major parties
B. Other parties

Questions

What are the chief functions of political parties in democratic nations?

Why does the multiparty system tend to produce a less stable government than the two-party system?

Which is the oldest existing political party in the United States?

Why is fund-raising an important activity of political parties?

Why do most one-party dictatorships hold elections?

What advantages does the majority party have over the minority party in organizing the U.S. Congress?

What difficulties might a U.S. president face in trying to get a legislative program passed into law by Congress?

What are Canada's two oldest political parties?

How did the Republican Party start in the United States?

In democracies, what are the duties of parties out of power?

Additional resources

Bibby, John F. *Politics, Parties, and Elections in America.* 3rd ed. Nelson-Hall, 1996.

Klingemann, Hans-Dieter, and others. *Parties, Policies, and Democracy.* Westview, 1994.

Kronenwetter, Michael. *Political Parties of the United States.* Enslow, 1996.

Reichley, A. James. *The Life of the Parties: A History of American Political Parties.* Free Pr., 1992.

Web sites

Green Parties of North America
http://www.greens.org/
The official Web site of the Green Party.

Socialist.org: Socialists on the Internet
http://socialist.org/
Information about the socialist movement.

It's a fact

Wisconsin passed the first statewide primary election law in 1903.

In the United States, some groups are more likely to vote than others. In general, more women vote than men, and people between the ages of 55 and 75 are more likely to vote than people of other ages.

The Democratic National Committee
http://www.democrats.org/index.html
The official Web site of the Democratic Party's National Committee.

The Libertarian Party
http://www.lp.org/
The official Web site of the U.S. Libertarian Party.

The Republican National Committee
http://www.rnc.org/
The official Web site of the Republican National Committee.

Primary election is a method of selecting candidates to run for public office. In a primary election, a political party, in effect, holds an election among its own members to select the party members who will represent it in the coming general election. Any number of party members can run for an office in a primary. But only the winning candidate can represent the party in the general election. Parties learn from the primary votes which candidates the members of their parties prefer. When several candidates enter a primary, the winner may receive less than 50 percent of the vote. Some states, especially in the South, then hold a *run-off primary,* in which the two candidates with the highest number of votes run against each other.

Direct and indirect. The *direct primary* is the most common form of primary election. In the direct primary, party members who want to run for office file petitions to have their names placed on the ballot. Voters then vote directly for the candidates of their choice. In an *indirect primary,* party members vote for delegates to party conventions, where candidates are chosen.

Open and closed. A primary election is considered *closed* when each voter must declare a choice of party, either when registering to vote or when voting. Party members can vote only for candidates on their party's ballot, and their party's contest is closed to members of other parties. In an *open primary,* the voter receives ballots for all the parties in the election, and chooses both party and candidates in the voting booth. A few states hold a primary called a *blanket primary,* in which voters may choose candidates from different parties.

Nonpartisan primaries are often used for judicial, school board, and local elections. Candidates are listed on the ballot with no indication of political affiliation. The voters choose the best candidates on the basis of their individual merits, not their party membership. The candidates with the greatest numbers of votes become the opposing candidates in the general election.

The presidential primary is used in more than half of the states to choose delegates to the national party conventions. Each candidate who enters the election lists a slate of delegates who have promised to support the candidate at the convention. The party members show their choice for the presidential nomination by voting for the slate of delegates committed to that candidate. Primaries that select about two-thirds of the delegates are held in the first six months of presidential election years.

History. Before primary elections were used, political parties nominated candidates for office at party conventions and caucuses. Political bosses often hand-picked candidates, making shady deals in order to win enough votes. People gradually turned against this system as being undemocratic and open to corruption. Reform movements urged "No More Boss Rule" and "Down with King Caucus!" In 1903, Wisconsin passed the first statewide primary law. Within 10 years, most states did likewise. Today, every state uses some form of primary election for statewide offices. Several states still use caucuses to nominate presidential candidates.

Robert Agranoff

See also **Caucus; Election**.

Web site

Campaigns
http://www.washingtonpost.com/wp-dyn/politics/elections/2000
This *Washington Post* site features news coverage of the 1998 and 2000 election campaigns.

Term limits prevent elected officials from serving more than a specified number of terms, and therefore years, in office. Some term limits prohibit all service in an office after the limit is reached. Other term limits only require a break in service.

Term limits are typically specified in a constitution. For example, the 22nd Amendment to the Constitution of the United States says that the nation's president cannot be elected to more than two four-year terms. The constitutions of many U.S. states set similar limits on the terms of the states' governors.

People disagree on whether term limits are needed. Supporters of such limits maintain that an *incumbent* (person who holds office) has an unfair advantage in an election. They claim that incumbents can use their power as elected officials to promote themselves politically and thus ensure their reelection. Supporters of term limits believe that there are many people who could do a good job in office, and that special experience is not needed.

Opponents of term limits believe that limits are undemocratic because they restrict voter choice. They argue that elections themselves allow sufficient control over the length of time officials remain in office. In addition, they claim that term limits remove expert people from office and shift power away from elected officials and toward bureaucrats and other nonelected staff members.

In the early 1990's, a widespread movement emerged in the United States to set term limits for members of the U.S. Congress and for state and local legislators. Twenty-three states eventually amended their constitutions to limit the terms of their senators and representatives in Congress. In 1995, however, the Supreme Court of the United States ruled that it was unconstitutional for states to set term limits for members of Congress.

Gerald Benjamin

It's a fact

Franklin D. Roosevelt, who served as president longer than any other person, vetoed 635 bills passed by Congress. Seven presidents did not veto any bills.

Web site

U.S. Term Limits
http://www.termlimits.org/
Information on legislation regarding term limits.

Veto is a Latin word which means *I forbid*. In American government, the word *veto* usually refers to the president's power to kill a law that the legislative branch has already passed.

The president of the United States has a *limited* veto power. It is not absolute. A vote of a two-thirds majority of the members present in each house of Congress can override it. The sovereign of the United Kingdom still holds the power of *absolute* veto. But no British king or queen has used this power since 1707.

Vetoing a bill. When the two houses of Congress pass a bill or joint resolution, it is sent to the president. Then one of four things must happen:

(1) The president may approve the bill. If so, the president signs it and it becomes law.

(2) The president may allow the bill to become law without signing it. This can take place under the clause in the Constitution which provides that "if any bill shall not be returned by the president within 10 days (Sundays excepted) after it shall have been presented to him, the same shall be a law in like manner as if he had signed it, unless the Congress by their adjournment prevent its return, in which case it shall not be a law."

(3) The president may retain the bill, expecting that Congress will adjourn within 10 days—not including Sundays—and thus the bill will be defeated. This method, called the *pocket veto,* is used by presidents who oppose a bill but do not want to veto it openly.

(4) The president may veto the bill. In that case, the president must send a message to Congress stating the reasons. Vetoing a bill defeats all parts of the bill. All provisions and "riders" attached to the bill are vetoed with it.

Presidents' use of the veto. When the Constitution was adopted, Alexander Hamilton declared that presidents would veto bills only with great caution. Seven presidents—John Adams, Thomas Jefferson, John Quincy Adams, William H. Harrison, Zachary Taylor, Millard Fillmore, and James A. Garfield—did not veto any bills. Franklin D. Roosevelt, who served as president longer than any other person, vetoed the most bills. He used 372 regular vetoes and 263 pocket vetoes. Grover Cleveland ranks second, with 346 regular vetoes and 238 pocket vetoes.

Congress has overridden only about 4 percent of all presidential vetoes of bills. For example, 11 of the presidents who vetoed bills had no vetoes overridden by Congress. Congress reversed only 9 of Roosevelt's 372 regular vetoes. But it overrode 15 of Andrew Johnson's 21 regular vetoes. Presidential veto power serves as a major check on Congress.

Governors' veto power. All state governors have a power to veto bills. But in some states, the governor's veto may be overridden by a simple majority of the members present in the houses of the legislature, rather than by a required two-thirds majority. Most governors also can veto parts of spending bills.   Peter Woll

See also **President of the United States** (Legislative leader); **United States, Government of the** (diagram: How a bill becomes law).

Voting is a method by which groups of people make decisions. In many countries, people vote to choose their leaders and to decide public issues. People also vote to make decisions in such groups as juries, labor unions, corporations, and social clubs. This article deals with voting on public issues and in political elections.

In most countries, citizens have the right to vote in elections. But nations that do not have a democratic form of government usually do not allow their citizens any real choice in voting. In a number of these countries, people may vote, but only for candidates named by the country's leadership.

Citizens of democratic countries consider voting one of their chief rights because it allows them to choose who will govern them. In almost all of these countries, most candidates seek office as members of a political party. Voters may elect their public officials either directly or indirectly. In *direct elections,* the citizens themselves vote for the officials. In *indirect elections,* the voters elect representatives, who then choose the officials.

In democracies, people vote on many issues besides elections for public officials. For example, they may vote on whether to build a school, expand the police force, or impose a tax. In some governments, voters may approve or reject proposed laws through elections called *referendums.* A *recall election* allows the voters to remove elected officials from office before the end of their term. See **Initiative and referendum; Recall.**

Who may vote. Since the 1800's, democratic nations have extended *suffrage* (the right to vote) to many people. The Constitution of the United States has been amended several times for this purpose. The 15th Amendment was adopted in 1870, five years after the American Civil War ended. It prohibited the states from denying a citizen the right to vote because of race. Women were not allowed to vote in most states until the ratification of the 19th Amendment in 1920. The 23rd Amendment, ratified in 1961, gave citizens living in Washington, D.C., the right to vote in national elections. In 1971, the 26th Amendment lowered the voting age to 18 for all state and national elections. Before then, only 10 states had allowed citizens under age 21 to vote.

In Canada, citizens 18 or older may vote in national elections. Provinces set voting rules for their elections.

Registration is the process by which a person's name is added to the list of qualified voters. In the United States, voters may register in person, or, in some states, by mail. To vote in a primary election, voters in some states must register as members of a party.

In 1993, Congress passed a law requiring most states to allow registration by mail for federal elections and to provide a voter registration form with each driver's license application. The law requires states to provide for federal voter registration at welfare offices and military recruiting offices. Most states allow voters to register for state and local elections by these methods as well. The law prohibits states from removing people from the rolls for failure to vote. It applies to all states except Idaho, Minnesota, New Hampshire, North Dakota, Wisconsin, and Wyoming. North Dakota does not require voter registration. The other five states have adopted laws to allow voters to register at the polls on Election Day. The federal law took effect in most states in 1995.

Restrictions on voting. All democracies limit the right to vote in special cases. In the United States, for example, people serving a prison sentence for committing certain crimes are not allowed to vote.

After adoption of the 15th Amendment, several states used means to deprive blacks of voting rights. Between 1890 and 1910, some Southern States added *grandfather clauses* to their constitutions. These clauses set voting requirements that few blacks could meet. In 1915 and 1939, the Supreme Court of the United States declared such clauses unconstitutional.

In addition, certain states required citizens to pay a *poll tax* to gain the right to vote. Officials in some of these states applied poll tax laws only to blacks and poor whites to prevent them from voting. The 24th Amendment to the U.S. Constitution, adopted in 1964, banned the states from requiring citizens to pay a poll tax to vote in national elections. In 1966, the Supreme Court outlawed the use of poll taxes in state and local elections. Many states denied voting rights to citizens who could not pass a literacy test. Election officials often employed these tests to disqualify blacks.

To protect the voting rights of blacks and members of other minority groups, the United States Congress passed the Voting Rights Act of 1965. Under its terms, people who attempt to deprive others of their voting rights are subject to severe penalties. The Voting Rights Act outlaws the use of literacy tests and gives the national government the power to use federal examiners to ensure that minorities are not prevented from registering to vote. It also requires that ballots be printed in two languages in areas where many people do not speak English as their first language. The act has been renewed several times and extended to the year 2007.

Voting districts. In the United States, each county, township, or ward of a state is divided into voting districts called *precincts.* Citizens may vote only at the polling place in the precinct in which they live. Election officials at the polling places certify voters and tabulate the votes after the polls close.

Beginning in 1962, the Supreme Court made a series of decisions concerning *redistricting*—that is, the redrawing of the boundaries of districts from which representatives are elected. The court has held that congressional districts—as well as state districts for the election of local, municipal, and state representatives—must be approximately equal in population. These rulings were designed to ensure that each vote would have equal power in the election process.

Methods of voting. In the 1700's, most of the American Colonies conducted oral elections. Later, some states used written ballots but required voters to sign them. Gradually, people came to feel that these practices restricted the freedom of voters. Some citizens feared that others would react negatively if they voted as they wished. As a result, states began using secret ballots so that each voter could choose freely.

Today, the United States and Canada use the Australian ballot system. Under this system, each voter marks a printed ballot while alone in a screened booth. Currently, a large majority of voters in the United States use voting machines that provide secrecy and simplify vote counting. Some U.S. states have experimented with other methods of voting. These include conducting elections entirely by mail and allowing voters to cast bal-

102

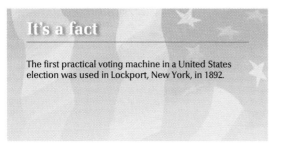

lots over the Internet. See **Ballot; Voting machine.**

Every U.S. state and Canadian province allows *absentee voting* for citizens who cannot go to their polling places. These citizens include people in the armed forces, college students, sick people, and travelers who are abroad on business or vacations. Citizens who wish to vote by absentee ballot must first apply through a state or local official. Qualified absentee voters receive a ballot, envelope, and instructions. They must mark their ballots in the presence of a *notary public* (licensed witness) and return them before Election Day.

Voting behavior. Many qualified voters in the United States rarely—or never—vote. During the 1970's and 1980's, about 55 percent of all qualified voters voted in presidential elections. In congressional, state, and local elections, the turnout is normally lower. In many other democracies, at least 80 percent of all voters vote in national elections. Some nations ensure high voter turnouts by fining or imprisoning citizens who do not vote.

In general, people vote if they believe they have something to gain or lose from an election. Some groups of people vote more often than others. More women vote than men, and people between the ages of 55 and 75 are more likely to vote than people of other ages. The higher an individual's income or education, the more likely the person is to vote. Family and social background also affect how people vote. Many people adopt the political party preferences of their parents.

Dramatic national or world events may cause shifts in voting patterns. During the Great Depression of the 1930's, for example, party loyalties in the United States shifted greatly to the Democratic Party.   George W. Carey

See also **Congress of the United States** (Passing a bill); **Election; Election campaign** (Getting out the vote).

Additional resources

Scher, Linda. *The Vote: Making Your Voice Heard.* Raintree Steck Vaughn, 1993. Younger readers.
Teixeira, Ruy A. *The Disappearing American Voter.* Brookings, 1992. Examines the reasons for declining voter participation.

Web sites

Voting Rights
http://www.usdoj.gov/kidspage/crt/voting.htm
The Civil Rights Division of the Department of Justice provides information on the Voting Rights Act of 1965.

Committee for the Study of an American Electorate
http://www.gspm.org/csae/
Information on election issues, including research material on voter participation, campaign financing, and the impact of media on elections.

Voting machine is a mechanical device for recording and counting votes during an election. The machine provides an absolutely secret ballot and records it auto-

matically, with accuracy, speed, and economy. Most voters in the United States use voting machines.

Operation. The voter stands in front of the machine and moves a master lever that closes a set of curtains around the voter and unlocks the voting machine. In front of the voter are the names of all the candidates, arranged in rows according to their political party. The candidates are listed next to the titles of the offices they seek. The voter turns a pointer next to the name of each candidate he or she chooses for an office.

In some states, a voter may vote a *straight ticket* simply by pulling a *party lever* at one end of the party's row of candidates. The machine will then register a vote for each candidate in the row. The machine does not register or count any votes until the voter moves the master lever back. This registers and counts the vote and opens the curtains. Voting machines also provide for ballots on bond issues or other proposals. The machine registers a *yes* or *no* vote for each proposal.

Many election districts in the United States use computerized voting machines. Instead of pulling a lever, the voter marks a square or punches a hole on a computer card. The small piece of paper that is punched out of the card is called a *chad.* A computer totals all valid votes for each candidate or issue.

Advantages. A voting machine is automatic and impartial. Dishonest officials cannot change it or tamper with its records, although they might "stuff" a ballot box with paper ballots. Fewer election officials are needed, and the cost of printing paper ballots is reduced. The machine allows for high-speed processing of vote totals.

Disadvantages. Critics of voting machines argue that confusing ballot layouts can cause voters to accidentally vote for the wrong candidate or to vote for more than one candidate. In addition, computers may not properly count votes if the chads have not been completely punched out from the cards. Debates regarding partially punched chads and complaints about confusing ballot layouts were largely responsible for a delay in the decision of the 2000 presidential election. Due to the shortcomings of voting machines and punch-card ballots, some election districts switched to touch-screen computer systems and optical-scanning ballot systems.

Legislative voting machines record votes for and against proposals in many state legislatures. These electric and mechanical devices reduce the time needed for a roll-call vote of the legislators. Each lawmaker's desk has buttons with which the lawmaker can vote either yes or no. When a button is pressed, the vote appears on a counting device at the clerk's or speaker's desk. Many legislatures also have a counting board on one wall of the chamber. As each legislator votes, a colored light is lit opposite the legislator's name on the board.

History. Thomas Edison invented the first legislative voting machine in 1868. Election voting machines developed more slowly. The first practical voting machine used in an election was put into service in Lockport, New York, in 1892. Today, voting machines are in use in more than three-fourths of the states. Many states now require the use of voting machines in all elections, including primary elections.

The United States was the first country to conduct elections by machine. Since the 1960's, other countries have begun using voting machines.   D. Craig Short

Section Four

Historic U.S. Presidential Elections

The United States has experienced a number of famous presidential elections. The seven *World Book* articles in this section chiefly highlight the biographies of the men involved in four of the most historic presidential races in United States history. These contests were the elections of 1800, 1824, 1876, and 1888. In this section's articles, you will learn:

❏ *why many Americans believed John Quincy Adams should follow James Monroe as president.*

❏ *who was the former president and first congressman to assert the right of the government to free slaves during wartime.*

❏ *why Rutherford B. Hayes was formally announced as the winner of the Election of 1876 only 56 hours before Inauguration Day.*

❏ *why the procedures of the Electoral College were changed in 1804.*

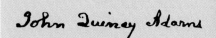

**6th president of
the United States 1825-1829**

Monroe
5th president
1817-1825
Democratic-
Republican

J. Q. Adams
6th president
1825-1829
Democratic-Re-
publican

Jackson
7th president
1829-1837
Democrat

**John C.
Calhoun**
Vice president
1825-1829

Oil painting on canvas (1824) by Thomas Sully; National Gallery of Art, Washington, D.C., Andrew W. Mellon Collection

Adams, John Quincy (1767-1848), was elected the sixth president of the United States 29 years after his father had been elected the second president. Like his father, John Adams, he failed to win a second term. But soon afterward, he was elected to the U.S. House of Representatives. This pleased him more, he said, than his election as president.

Before entering the presidency, Adams held several important diplomatic posts. He took part in the negotiations that ended the War of 1812. As secretary of state, he helped develop the Monroe Doctrine. Quarrels within his party hampered Adams as president, and he made little progress with his ambitious legislative program. His years in the White House were perhaps the unhappiest period of Adams's life.

Adams was short and stout, and his shrill voice often broke when he became excited. Yet he spoke so well he was nicknamed "Old Man Eloquent." He was affectionate with close friends, but more reserved toward others. He once referred to himself as "an unsocial savage."

During Adams's administration, Noah Webster brought out his two-volume *American Dictionary of the English Language,* and James Fenimore Cooper published his famous novel *The Last of the Mohicans.* The American labor movement began in Philadelphia.

Early life

Childhood. John Quincy Adams was born on July 11, 1767, in the family home in Braintree (now Quincy), Massachusetts. He was the second child and eldest son of the second president of the United States. During the 1770's, his father was away much of the time serving in the Continental Congresses. John Quincy had to help his mother manage a large farm. In February 1778, Congress sent his father to France. John Quincy, although

not yet 11, pleaded to go along on the dangerous voyage. His father proudly wrote in his diary: "Mr. Johnny's behavior gave me a satisfaction I cannot express. Fully sensible of our danger, he was constantly endeavoring to bear it with a manly patience, very attentive to me, and his thoughts constantly running in a serious vein."

Education. Adams attended schools in Paris, Amsterdam, and Leiden as his father moved from one diplomatic assignment to another. At 14, he went to St. Petersburg as private secretary to Francis Dana, the first American minister to Russia. The boy rejoined his father in 1783 and served as his private secretary.

When the elder Adams became minister to the United Kingdom in 1785, the boy returned home and entered Harvard College. He said later: "By remaining much longer in Europe I saw the danger of an alienation from my own country." His previous studies enabled him to join the junior class at Harvard. He graduated in 1787.

Lawyer and writer. Adams read law for three years and began his own practice in 1790. But he had few clients and soon turned to political journalism.

Important dates in Adams's life

1767 (July 11) Born in Braintree (now Quincy), Massachusetts.
1794 Became minister to the Netherlands.
1797 (July 26) Married Louisa Catherine Johnson.
1803 Elected to the United States Senate.
1809 Appointed minister to Russia.
1814-1815 Helped negotiate peace with the United Kingdom.
1815 Became minister to the United Kingdom.
1817 Appointed secretary of state.
1825 Elected president of the United States.
1830 Elected to the U.S. House of Representatives.
1848 (Feb. 23) Died in Washington, D.C.

The Erie Canal, completed in 1825, linked Lake Erie with the Hudson River. It enabled freight to be shipped between the Atlantic Ocean and the Great Lakes.

The world of President John Quincy Adams

The first women's labor union was organized in 1825. The union was formed by women working in the garment industry in New York City.

Czar Nicholas I of Russia crushed the Decembrist uprising, a revolt of discontented nobles, in 1825. As a result of wars fought during the late 1820's, Russia expanded its borders to include important territory on the Black Sea.

July 4, 1826, marked the 50th anniversary of the adoption of the Declaration of Independence. In a remarkable coincidence, the deaths of two of the nation's Founding Fathers, Thomas Jefferson and John Adams, occurred that same day.

The Last of the Mohicans, one of James Fenimore Cooper's most popular works, was published in 1826.

The first overland expedition from Utah to California was led by trader and explorer Jedediah Smith in 1826. Smith crossed Indian territories, the Mojave Desert, and the High Sierras in search of trade routes to California and the Northwest.

The Creek Indians signed treaties in 1826 and 1827 that transferred land in western Georgia to the U.S. government.

Artist and naturalist John James Audubon published the first part of his masterpiece, *Birds of America,* in 1827. The work, eventually completed in 1838, consisted of 435 life-sized, color engravings of Audubon's water colors.

Noah Webster published *An American Dictionary of the English Language* in 1828. The two-volume work included about 12,000 words and 40,000 definitions that had never appeared in any other dictionary.

View on the Erie Canal, a water color (1832) by John William Hill; Stokes Collection, New York Public Library

In 1791, Thomas Paine published the first part of *Rights of Man.* Adams considered Paine's ideas too radical and replied with 11 articles that he signed with the name "Publicola." A second series, signed "Marcellus," defended President George Washington's policy of neutrality. A third series, signed "Columbus," attacked French minister Edmond Genêt, who wanted America to join France in a war against the United Kingdom.

Political and public career

Diplomat. In 1794, Washington appointed Adams minister to the Netherlands. The French invaded the country three days after Adams arrived and overthrew the Dutch Republic. On a special assignment in London, Adams met his future wife, Louisa Catherine Johnson (Feb. 12, 1775-May 15, 1852), the daughter of a merchant who became the American consul general to London.

In 1796, Washington appointed Adams minister to Portugal. Just before he left for Lisbon, his father was elected president. Both men felt it would be undesirable for the son to hold such a post during his father's Administration. But Washington urged that the younger Adams stay on, calling him "the most valuable public character now abroad." President Adams followed this recommendation and named his son minister to Prussia.

Adams's family. John Quincy married Johnson in 1797, just before leaving for Berlin. He served there more than four years. Adams and his wife had four children. Their only daughter, Louisa Catherine, died in infancy. George Washington Adams, the eldest son, died in 1829, at the close of his father's presidency. John, who was named for his grandfather, died five years later. The youngest son, Charles Francis, served as minister to the United Kingdom during the Civil War.

U.S. senator. Thomas Jefferson became president in 1801. John Quincy Adams soon returned home, and was elected to the Massachusetts Senate in 1802. He soon displayed the independence that marked his entire career. Fisher Ames, the Federalist leader in Massachusetts, described him as "too unmanageable."

In 1803, the Federalists chose Adams to fill a vacant seat in the United States Senate. Although a Federalist, he often voted with the Democratic-Republicans. He broke with his party completely in 1807, when Congress passed the Embargo Act. The Federalists in New England wanted to trade with the British, but Adams supported the embargo, believing that it benefited the nation as a whole.

Doris S. Oberg, Quincy Historical Society

John Quincy Adams's birthplace stands in Quincy, Massachusetts. His father, John Adams, was born in a nearly identical house next door. The two buildings are now historic sites.

Oil painting on canvas (1821) by Gilbert Stuart; © White House Historical Association (National Geographic Society)

Louisa Johnson Adams was born in London, the daughter of an American diplomat. She first came to the United States in 1801, four years after she married John Quincy Adams.

Federalist leaders in Massachusetts felt that Adams had betrayed them. They elected another man to his Senate seat several months before the 1808 elections. Adams resigned immediately and prepared for a career as professor of rhetoric and oratory at Harvard.

Again a diplomat. Adams intended to stay out of public life permanently. But in 1809, President James Madison persuaded him to accept an appointment as minister to Russia. From mid-1814 to early 1815, Adams served as one of the American commissioners who negotiated the Treaty of Ghent with the British, ending the War of 1812. The negotiations gained respect for the United States, as well as for Adams as a diplomat.

Madison next appointed Adams as minister to the United Kingdom, a post once held by his father. While in London, Adams began discussions that led to improved relations along the U.S.-Canadian border. The United Kingdom and the United States agreed to stop using forts and warships in the Great Lakes region, leaving the frontiers of the two countries unguarded and open.

Secretary of state. In 1817, President James Monroe called Adams home to serve as secretary of state. Adams made an agreement with the United Kingdom for joint occupation of the Oregon region. He negotiated a treaty that quieted Spanish claims to territory in the northwest and also acquired Florida. But his most important achievement as secretary of state was to help develop the Monroe Doctrine. Adams made the first declaration of this policy in July 1823, several months before Monroe formally announced it. He told the Russian minister that "the American continents are no longer subjects for any new European colonial establishments."

Austria, Prussia, and Russia had formed the Holy Alliance in 1815, after the fall of Napoleon. During and after the Napoleonic Wars, the countries of Central and South America had revolted against Spanish rule. When King Ferdinand VII regained the Spanish throne in 1823, many people feared that the Holy Alliance might help

Spain reconquer its former colonies. British Foreign Minister George Canning asked the United States to join in a declaration against any such move. But Adams insisted that the United States should make its own policy. He declared that America must not "come in as a cockboat (small rowboat) in the wake of the British man-of-war." Monroe followed Adams' advice, and the Monroe Doctrine became a part of U.S. foreign policy.

Election of 1824. Many Americans believed Adams should follow Monroe as president. Both Madison and Monroe became president after serving as secretary of state. Adams felt he also should be elected but did little to attract votes. Four Democratic-Republicans opposed him: John C. Calhoun, Henry Clay, William H. Crawford, and Andrew Jackson. Calhoun withdrew, and was elected vice president. Jackson received 99 electoral votes; Adams, 84; Crawford, 41; and Clay, 37. For votes by states, see **Electoral College** (table). None had a majority, so the House of Representatives had to choose one of the first three men. Clay then threw his support to Adams, who was elected in February 1825.

Adams's administration (1825-1829)

Democratic-Republican Party split. Even before the House elected Adams, followers of Jackson accused Adams of promising Clay a Cabinet post in return for his support. When Adams named Clay secretary of state, Jackson's powerful supporters in Congress charged that the two men had made a "corrupt bargain." This split the Democratic-Republican Party, and Adams's group became known as the National Republicans. Jackson's group fought Adams for the next four years.

Rebuff by Congress. Adams delivered his inaugural address in the Senate chamber of the unfinished Capitol. In this address, and in his first message to Congress, he recommended an ambitious program of national improvements. This program included the construction of highways, canals, weather stations, and a national university. He argued that if Congress did not use the powers of government for the benefit of all the people, it "would be treachery to the most sacred of trusts." But the majority in Congress disagreed. Adams's hopes for a partnership of government and science were not to be realized until after his lifetime.

The "tariff of abominations." By 1828, manufacturing had replaced farming as the chief activity in most New England states. These states favored high tariffs on imported goods. But high tariffs would make farmers in the South pay more for imported products. Southern leaders wanted a low tariff or free trade.

Jackson's supporters in Congress wrote a tariff bill that put high duties on manufactured goods. The bill also raised duties on raw materials so high that even New Englanders could be expected to oppose it. To everyone's surprise, enough New Englanders voted for the bill to pass it. The "tariff of abominations," as it became known, aroused bitter anger in the South.

Life in the White House. Adams threw all his energies into the presidency from the day he took office. Each day, he conferred with a steady procession of congressmen and department heads in his upstairs study in the White House. The president wrote in his diary: "I can scarcely conceive a more harassing, wearying, teasing condition of existence." He felt a lack of exercise, in spite

Vice president and Cabinet

Vice president	John C. Calhoun
Secretary of state	Henry Clay
Secretary of the treasury	Richard Rush
Secretary of war	James Barbour
	Peter B. Porter (1828)
Attorney general	William Wirt
Secretary of the Navy	Samuel L. Southard

of daily walks. In warm weather, Adams liked to swim in the Potomac River.

Mrs. Adams suffered ill health during her husband's term as president, but she overcame her sickness to serve as White House hostess. She was responsible for a brilliant series of parties during the visit of the Marquis de Lafayette in 1825.

Election of 1828. Adams had never been popular, chiefly because of his aloof manner. He had not even tried to defend himself against the attacks of Jackson and his followers, feeling it was below the dignity of the president to engage in political debate. At the same time, Jackson gained great popularity. In the election of 1828, Jackson won a popular vote proportionately larger than any other presidential candidate received during the rest of the 1800's. He and his running mate, Vice President Calhoun, won 178 electoral votes. Adams and Secretary of the Treasury Richard Rush had 83.

Back to Congress

Election to the House. Adams again planned to retire, but the people of Quincy asked him to run for Congress in 1830. He defeated two other candidates by large majorities and wrote in his diary: "My election as president of the United States was not half so gratifying." He took his seat in the House of Representatives in 1831 and served for 17 years.

Adams served at times as chairman of the House Foreign Affairs Committee and of the Committee on Manufactures. But he remained independent of party politics. He fought President Jackson's opposition to the second Bank of the United States. He also opposed Jackson's policy of recognizing the independence of Texas. But Adams supported Jackson's foreign policy and stern resistance to nullification.

The Gag Rules. Adams's greatest public role may have occurred during debates about slavery. Abolition-ists sent many petitions to Congress urging that slavery be abolished in the District of Columbia and in new territories. These petitions took much of the lawmakers' time. In 1836, the House adopted the first of a series of resolutions called the *Gag Rules* to keep the petitions from being read on the floor. Adams believed these rules violated the constitutional rights of free speech and petition. He was strongly criticized in the House for opposing the Gag Rules, but he finally succeeded in having them abolished in 1844.

Adams became the first congressman to assert the right of the government to free slaves during time of war. President Abraham Lincoln based the Emancipation Proclamation on Adams's arguments.

The Amistad Rebellion. In 1841, Adams again publicly showed his opposition to slavery when he defended the Amistad rebels before the Supreme Court of the United States. The rebels were black Africans who had been captured and enslaved by whites. In 1839, they attacked their captors while on a ship called *La Amistad* in the Caribbean Sea. They killed two whites and took control of the vessel. They were later arrested in the United States for the killings and mutiny. Their case ended up in the Supreme Court. There, Adams strongly defended the rebels, arguing that every person has the right to freedom. The rebels were found not guilty.

Death. On Feb. 21, 1848, he suffered a stroke at his House desk. Too ill to be moved from the building, he was carried to the Speaker's room. He died there two days later. Adams was buried in the churchyard of the First Unitarian Church in Quincy, Massachusetts. His wife died on May 15, 1852, and was buried at his side. Their remains were later moved to the church crypt.

Jack Shepherd

See also **President of the United States.**

Outline

I. Early life
  A. Childhood
  B. Education
  C. Lawyer and writer

II. Political and public career
  A. Diplomat
  B. Adams's family
  C. U.S. senator
  D. Again a diplomat
  E. Secretary of state
  F. Election of 1824

III. Adams's Administration (1825-1829)
  A. Democratic-Republican Party split
  B. Rebuff by Congress
  C. The "tariff of abominations"
  D. Life in the White House
  E. Election of 1828

IV. Back to Congress
  A. Election to the House
  B. The Gag Rules
  C. The Amistad Rebellion
  D. Death

Questions

How did Adams help develop the Monroe Doctrine?
Why did Adams become president even though Andrew Jackson received more electoral votes?
Why did Adams oppose the Gag Rules?
What honor pleased Adams more than his election as president?
How did Adams contribute to the Emancipation Proclamation?

Additional resources

Coelho, Tony. *John Quincy Adams.* Chelsea Hse., 1990. Younger readers.
Kent, Zachary. *John Quincy Adams.* Childrens Pr., 1987. Younger readers.

It's a fact

In the election of 1824, Andrew Jackson won the popular vote and the most votes in the Electoral College. However, no candidate received an electoral majority, and the House of Representatives elected his rival John Quincy Adams president.

President John Quincy Adams was affectionate with close friends but more reserved toward other people. He once referred to himself as "an unsocial savage."

Nagel, Paul C. *John Quincy Adams.* Knopf, 1997.
Parsons, Lynn H. *John Quincy Adams.* Madison Hse., 1998.

Web sites

Adams, John Quincy (1767-1848) Biographical Information
http://bioguide.congress.gov/scripts/biodisplay.pl?index=
A000041
The Biographical Directory of the United States Congress site on
John Quincy Adams.

John Quincy Adams (1767-1848)
http://www.law.cornell.edu/amistad/adamsbio.html
A biography of John Quincy Adams, sixth president of the
United States.

Burr, Aaron (1756-1836), was vice president of the United States from 1801 to 1805, under President Thomas Jefferson. Burr's brilliant career and promising future declined disastrously after he killed Alexander Hamilton, Jefferson's most famous political opponent, in a gun duel in 1804. Burr's reputation was hurt further when he was charged with working to make part of the southwestern frontier an independent nation.

Early years. Burr was born in Newark, New Jersey, and graduated from the College of New Jersey (now Princeton University) in 1772. He fought with the Continental Army in the Revolutionary War from 1775 to 1779, rising to lieutenant colonel. Burr distinguished himself at the Battle of Monmouth.

He became a lawyer in 1782 and practiced in Albany, New York, and New York City. Soon, he became a top U.S. lawyer. He served New York as a state legislator and as attorney general in 1789. He was elected to the U.S. Senate in 1791, defeating Alexander Hamilton's father-in-law, General Philip Schuyler.

Gains recognition. The Democratic-Republican Party chose Burr as Jefferson's vice presidential running mate in 1796 and in 1800. According to the voting procedures of the time, each Electoral College member voted for two people. The person with the most votes became president, and the person with the second most votes became vice president. Jefferson lost his bid for the presidency in 1796 but became vice president under President John Adams. In the 1800 election, Burr and Jefferson received the same number of electoral votes, tying for the presidency even though the electors who voted for them intended to elect Jefferson to the presidency and Burr to the vice presidency. The U.S. House of Representatives had to take 36 ballots to break the tie, finally electing Jefferson as president. Burr became vice president. Hamilton, who disliked Burr more than he did Jefferson, helped elect Jefferson.

It's a fact

Following the disputed election of 1876, an Electoral Commission appointed by Congress selected the president. It was the first and only time such an agency has chosen a chief executive.

Burr ran for governor of New York in 1804. Hamilton again opposed him. Burr lost the election. He then challenged Hamilton to a duel. On July 11, 1804, the men faced each other with pistols in Weehawken, New Jersey. Burr fatally wounded Hamilton. A New York coroner's inquest "found a verdict of wilful murder by Aaron Burr, vice president of the United States." A New Jersey grand jury indicted him for murder. Nevertheless, Burr presided over the Senate until his term ended.

Tried for treason. After his vice presidency, Burr engaged in a complex web of questionable activities. He traveled through the American West and recruited men. The commander in New Orleans, General James Wilkinson, whose patriotism has also been questioned, arrested Burr. The question was whether Burr was assembling a group to invade Mexico, whether he was scheming to detach part of the southwestern frontier from the United States, or both.

Burr was tried for treason in 1807 and was *acquitted* (declared innocent) of the charges. Burr later went to Europe and tried to arouse support for his Mexican scheme. When he returned to the United States in 1812, he entered the country under an assumed name, Adolphus Arnot. He again prospered as a lawyer in New York City, using his own name.   William W. Freehling

See also **Jefferson, Thomas** (The Burr conspiracy).

Additional resources

Kline, Mary-Jo, and Ryan, J. W., eds. *Political Correspondence and Public Papers of Aaron Burr.* 2 vols. Princeton, 1983.
Lomask, Milton. *Aaron Burr.* 2 vols. Farrar, 1979, 1982.
Nolan, Charles J., Jr. *Aaron Burr and the American Literary Imagination.* Greenwood, 1980.

Web site

Burr, Aaron (1756-1836) Biographical Information
http://bioguide.congress.gov/scripts/biodisplay.pl?index=
B001133
The Biographical Directory of the United States Congress site on
Aaron Burr.

Electoral Commission was a group created by Congress in 1877 to decide who won the presidential election of 1876. Both Republicans and Democrats claimed victory. Samuel J. Tilden, the Democratic candidate, had 184 electoral votes, or one short of a majority in the Electoral College. Rutherford B. Hayes, the Republican candidate, had 165 votes. Twenty votes were disputed.

To settle the matter, Congress created the Electoral Commission. The commission was made up of 15 members: five senators, five representatives, and five Supreme Court justices. Congress carefully arranged that three senators and two representatives were to be Republicans, while two senators and three representatives were to be Democrats. Of the justices, two Democrats and two Republicans were named, and these four had power to choose a fifth. They would probably have chosen David Davis of Illinois, an independent in politics. However, his decision to accept election to the United States Senate left only Republican justices from whom to choose. As a result, the Electoral Commission had a Republican majority of eight to seven. By a strict party vote, the commission gave all the disputed votes, and the election, to Hayes.   H. Wayne Morgan

See also **Electoral College; Hayes, Rutherford Birchard** (The election dispute); **Tilden, Samuel Jones.**

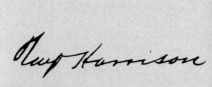

23rd president of the United States 1889-1893

Cleveland
22nd president
1885-1889
Democrat

Harrison
23rd president
1889-1893
Republican

Cleveland
24th president
1893-1897
Democrat

Levi P. Morton
Vice president
1889-1893

Oil portrait (1895) by Eastman Johnson; © White House Historical Association (photography by the National Geographic Society)

Harrison, Benjamin (1833-1901), was the only grandson of a president who also became president. He defeated President Grover Cleveland in 1888, but Cleveland regained the presidency by beating Harrison in 1892.

Harrison's grandfather was William Henry Harrison, the hero of the Battle of Tippecanoe. Both Harrisons ran for the presidency two times, winning once and losing once. Before being elected president, both had been successful army commanders and had served in the United States Senate. Benjamin Harrison won the presidency with the help of a Republican campaign song called "Grandfather's Hat Fits Ben."

Harrison did more than any other president to increase respect for the flag of the United States. By his order, the flag waved above the White House and other government buildings. Harrison also urged that the flag be flown over every school in the land.

Congress passed the Sherman Antitrust Act during Harrison's administration, and provided for the building of a two-ocean navy of steel ships. The American frontier disappeared as pioneers took over the last unsettled areas of the West. Six new states joined the Union. Women squeezed into whalebone corsets so they could wear the new "hourglass" fashions. James A. Naismith originated basketball, and a lively tune called "Ta-ra-ra-boom-de-ay" helped usher in the period of the Gay Nineties.

Early life

Childhood. Benjamin Harrison was born on Aug. 20, 1833, on his grandfather's farm in North Bend, Ohio. He was named for his great-grandfather, a signer of the Declaration of Independence. Ben was the second of the 10 children of John Scott Harrison and Elizabeth Irwin Harrison. His father, a farmer, served two terms in Congress. Ben, a short, stocky boy, spent his youth on the farm.

Education. Harrison attended Farmers' College in a Cincinnati suburb for three years. While a freshman, he met his future wife, Caroline Lavinia Scott (Oct. 1, 1832-Oct. 25, 1892). She was the daughter of John W. Scott, the president of a women's college in the town. In 1849, Scott moved his college to Oxford, Ohio. The next year Harrison followed the Scotts to Oxford, where he graduated from Miami University in 1852.

Harrison's family. Harrison and "Carrie" Scott were married in 1853. They had two children, Russell Benjamin (1854-1936) and Mary (1858-1930).

Lawyer. After reading law with a Cincinnati firm, Harrison was admitted to the bar in 1854. He moved to Indianapolis that same year. In his first big court case, a single candle stood on the table where Harrison had his notes. He vainly shifted the candle back and forth to get more light, but finally threw the notes away. Harrison not only discovered that he was a good speaker, but he also won the case. Harrison bolstered his income by earning $2.50 a day as court crier, proclaiming the orders of the court.

Political and public activities

Political beginnings. As the son of a Whig congressman and the grandson of a Whig president, Harrison's name was familiar to many voters. Although his father wrote him that "none but knaves should ever enter the political arena," Harrison ran successfully for city attorney of Indianapolis in 1857. He became secretary of the Republican state central committee in 1858, and was

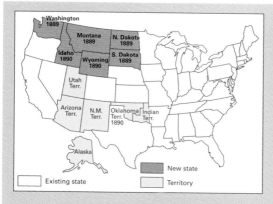

Six states—North Dakota, South Dakota, Montana, Washington, Idaho, and Wyoming—joined the Union during Harrison's term. The Oklahoma Territory was also formed.

The United States flag had 38 stars when Harrison took office in 1889. Five stars were added to the flag in 1890. Another was added in 1891, making a total of 44 stars, *left.*

The world of President Harrison

The Eiffel Tower was dedicated in Paris in 1889.
The Johnstown flood in Pennsylvania in 1889 killed more than 2,000 people and caused over $10 million in damage.
Mark Twain's satire on the King Arthur legend, *A Connecticut Yankee in King Arthur's Court,* was published in 1889.
A land rush into what had been Indian Territory in Oklahoma opened about 2 million acres (810,000 hectares) to white settlement in 1889.
Nellie Bly, a newspaper reporter, set a record by traveling around the world in 72 days 6 hours 11 minutes, beginning in November 1889.
The first Carnegie public library in the United States was established in 1890 in Allegheny City, Pennsylvania.
The Battle of Wounded Knee took place in South Dakota in 1890. It was the last major fight on the northern plains between Indians and U.S. troops. The soldiers massacred as many as 300 Indians.
Yosemite National Park was created by Congress in 1890.
Wyoming entered the Union in 1890 as the first state with women's voting rights.
Basketball was invented in 1891 by James A. Naismith, a physical education instructor in Springfield, Massachusetts.
Ellis Island, an island in New York Harbor, became a reception center for immigrants in 1892.
Inventions included the diesel engine, patented in 1892 by a German engineer named Rudolf Diesel, and the zipper, patented in 1893 by Whitcomb L. Judson of Chicago.

WORLD BOOK map

elected reporter of the state supreme court in 1860. He was reelected twice.

A deeply religious man, Harrison taught Sunday school. He became a deacon of the Presbyterian Church in 1857, and was elected an elder of the church in 1861.

Army commander. In 1862, Governor Oliver P. Morton asked Harrison to recruit and command the 70th Regiment of Indiana Volunteers in the Civil War. As he and Morton walked down the steps of the state Capitol, Harrison recruited his first soldier—his former law partner, William Wallace.

Colonel Harrison molded his regiment into a well-disciplined unit that fought in many battles. His soldiers called him "Little Ben" because he was only 5 feet 6 inches (168 centimeters) tall. A fearless commander, Harrison rose to the rank of brigadier general.

National politics. After the war, Harrison won national prestige as a lawyer. In 1876, he ran unsuccessfully for the governorship of Indiana. President Rutherford B. Hayes appointed him to the Mississippi River Commission in 1879, and he held this post until 1881. Harrison turned down a post in the Cabinet of President James A.

Garfield because he had been elected to the U.S. Senate in January 1881.

During his term in the Senate, Harrison supported civil service reform, a protective tariff, a strong navy, and regulation of railroads. He criticized President Grover Cleveland's vetoes of veterans' pension bills. Indiana's

Important dates in Harrison's life

1833	(Aug. 20) Born in North Bend, Ohio.
1853	(Oct. 20) Married Caroline Lavinia Scott.
1862-1864	Commanded a regiment of the Union Army.
1881	Elected to the United States Senate.
1888	Elected president of the United States.
1892	Caroline Harrison died. Defeated for reelection.
1896	(April 6) Married Mary Dimmick.
1901	(March 13) Died in Indianapolis.

President Benjamin Harrison Home

Harrison lived in Indianapolis, in this house, from 1872 until his death in 1901 except when he was in Washington. No picture of his birthplace in North Bend, Ohio, is known to exist.

Library of Congress

Caroline Scott Harrison worked hard as first lady despite poor health. She died in 1892, two weeks before the election in which her husband lost his bid for a second term as president.

Harrison's election

Place of nominating convention . . . .Chicago
Ballot on which nominated 8th
Democratic opponent . . . . .Grover Cleveland
Electoral vote* . . . . .233 (Harrison) to 168
    (Cleveland)
Popular vote . . . . .5,534,488 (Cleveland) to
    5,443,892 (Harrison)
Age at inauguration 55

*For votes by states, see **Electoral College** (table).

Vice president and Cabinet

Vice president	Levi P. Morton
Secretary of state	James G. Blaine
	John W. Foster (1892)
Secretary of the treasury	William Windom
	Charles Foster (1891)
Secretary of war	Redfield Proctor
	Stephen B. Elkins (1891)
Attorney general	William H. H. Miller
Postmaster general	John Wanamaker
Secretary of the Navy	Benjamin F. Tracy
Secretary of the interior	John W. Noble
Secretary of agriculture	Jeremiah M. Rusk

Democratic legislature defeated Harrison's bid for a second term by one vote.

Election of 1888. James G. Blaine, who had lost the 1884 presidential election to Cleveland, refused to run in 1888. The Republicans nominated Harrison, partly because of his war record and his popularity with veterans. Levi P. Morton, a New York City banker, was nominated for vice president. The Democrats renominated Cleveland and named Allen G. Thurman, a former Ohio senator, as his running mate.

Harrison, in a "front porch" campaign from his home, supported high tariffs. Cleveland called for lower tariffs, but did not campaign actively because he felt it was beneath the dignity of the presidency.

In the election, Harrison trailed Cleveland by more than 90,000 popular votes. But, by carrying Indiana, New York, and several "doubtful states," Harrison won the election in the Electoral College.

Harrison's administration (1889-1893)

The Republicans held a majority in both houses of Congress during the first half of Harrison's term. As a result, the president won enactment of his legislative program. In the congressional elections of 1890, the Democrats won control of the House of Representatives and the Republican majority in the Senate was reduced to six. The change partly reflected public disapproval of vast congressional appropriations, which reached almost a billion dollars. When Democrats accused the Republicans of wastefulness, Thomas B. Reed, speaker of the House, replied by saying: "This is a billion-dollar country!"

Domestic affairs. During the campaign, Harrison had promised to extend the civil service law to cover more jobs. He kept his promise by increasing the number of classified positions from 27,000 to 38,000.

The four most important laws of Harrison's administration were all passed in 1890.

The Sherman Antitrust Act. During the period of rapid industrialization in the late 1880's, many corporations formed *trusts* that controlled market prices and destroyed competition. Farmers and owners of small businesses demanded government protection from these trusts. The Sherman Antitrust Act, fulfilling one of Harrison's campaign pledges, outlawed trusts or any other monopolies that hindered trade.

The Sherman Silver Purchase Act met another demand of farm voters. Farm prices were falling, and farmers asked the government to put more money into circulation, either paper money or silver coins. Farmers felt that this action would increase farm prices and thus make it easier for farmers to pay their debts. The owners of the silver mines naturally favored a demand that would boost their own profits. The Sherman Silver Purchase Act increased the amount of silver that could be coined. The government purchased this silver, and paid for it with Treasury notes that could be redeemed either in silver or gold. Because most people chose to redeem their notes in gold, the fear of a resulting drain on the Treasury's gold reserves helped cause a financial panic in 1893.

The McKinley Tariff Act was designed mainly to protect U.S. industries and their workers. Its sponsors tried to make the law attractive to farmers by raising tariffs on imported farm products. But the McKinley Tariff Act set tariffs at record highs, and farmers regarded it chiefly as a benefit to business.

The Dependent Pension Bill broadened pension qualifications to include all veterans of the Civil War who could not perform manual labor. The cost of pensions soared from $88 million in 1889 to $159 million in 1893.

Foreign affairs. Harrison launched a program to build a two-ocean navy and expand the merchant marine. Both actions helped shape the new and vigorous foreign policy developed by Harrison and Secretary of State James G. Blaine.

Latin America. In 1889, the first Pan-American Conference met in Washington. The delegates began expanding the meaning of the Monroe Doctrine by promoting cooperation among the nations. The Pan American Union was created at this conference.

Trade with other nations was being threatened by U.S. tariffs that constantly grew higher. Harrison began to negotiate reciprocal trade agreements. This was a constructive attempt to compromise between manufacturers who wanted free competitive markets and those who favored protective tariffs.

Hawaii. Early in 1893, Queen Liliuokalani had lost her throne in a revolution led by American planters. The new Hawaiian government asked the United States to make Hawaii a territory. Harrison had been defeated for reelection the previous November, but he rushed a treaty of annexation to the Senate before his term ended. Cleveland returned to the presidency before the Senate could act on the treaty, and withdrew it. He declared that the whole affair was dishonorable to the United States.

Other developments. The Harrison administration also settled a number of old quarrels. The government agreed to arbitrate the long-standing dispute with the United Kingdom over fur seals in the Bering Sea. In 1889, a quarrel over the ownership of the Samoa Islands seemed likely, and the United States joined Germany and the United Kingdom in establishing a protectorate over the islands. In 1892, Congress passed the Oriental Exclusion Act, which long remained a sore spot in America's relations with China and Japan.

Life in the White House was thoroughly photographed for the first time during Harrison's term. Electric lights and bells were installed in the mansion in 1891. But the Harrisons, fearing shocks, often used the old-style gas lights, or asked the White House electrician to turn the switches on and off.

Despite poor health, Mrs. Harrison worked hard as official hostess. She once told a reporter that "there are only five sleeping rooms and there is no feeling of privacy." Members of the Harrison family usually occupied these rooms. Mrs. Harrison's father lived in the White House, as did Mary Dimmick, a widowed niece who served as her secretary. The Harrisons' daughter, Mary McKee, and her husband and two children lived there most of the time.

Bid for reelection. The Republicans renominated Harrison in 1892, and chose Whitelaw Reid, editor of the *New York Tribune,* as his running mate. The Democrats again nominated Cleveland for president, and named Adlai E. Stevenson, a former Illinois congressman, for vice president.

Discontented farmers turned from the Republicans to the new Populist Party, which had been formed in protest against falling farm prices. Angry factory workers deserted the Republicans, charging hostile interference by the federal and state governments in the bloody Homestead Strike and other labor disputes. Opposition to the McKinley Tariff Act also helped defeat Harrison, who received 5,182,690 popular votes to Cleveland's 5,555,426. The Populist candidate, James B. Weaver, received more than a million votes. This gave Cleveland 277 electoral votes to Harrison's 145. Weaver received 22 electoral votes.

Personal tragedy struck Harrison just two weeks before the national elections of 1892. His wife died on October 25.

Later years

Harrison returned to Indianapolis and the practice of law. In 1896, he married Dimmick (April 30, 1858-Jan. 5, 1948), who had nursed his wife during her last illness. They had one child, Elizabeth (1897-1955).

In 1897, Harrison wrote *This Country of Ours,* a book about the federal government. In 1899, he represented Venezuela in the arbitration of a dispute with the United Kingdom over the British Guiana boundary. Harrison died in his home on March 13, 1901, and was buried in Indianapolis.   H. Wayne Morgan

See also **President of the United States.**

Outline

I. Early life
   A. Childhood   C. Harrison's family
   B. Education   D. Lawyer
II. Political and public activities
   A. Political beginnings   C. National politics
   B. Army commander   D. Election of 1888
III. Harrison's administration (1889-1893)
   A. Domestic affairs
   B. Foreign affairs
   C. Life in the White House
   D. Bid for reelection
IV. Later years

Questions

Who was the only man whose father and son both became president of the United States?

What was unusual about the results of the 1888 presidential election?

How did Harrison please Civil War veterans?

Why did he decline a post in Garfield's Cabinet?

What reforms did farmers and persons who owned small businesses seek? Why?

How did the United States show its interest in Latin America during Harrison's administration?

What factors led to Harrison's defeat in 1892?

How was the White House modernized during Harrison's administration?

Additional resources

Clinton, Susan. *Benjamin Harrison: Twenty-Third President of the United States.* Childrens Pr., 1989. Younger readers.

Sievers, Harry J. *Benjamin Harrison.* 3 vols. 1952-1968. Reprint. Am. Political Biography Pr., 1996.

Socolofsky, Homer E., and Spetter, A. B. *The Presidency of Benjamin Harrison.* Univ. Pr. of Kans., 1987.

Stevens, Rita. *Benjamin Harrison: 23rd President of the United States.* Garrett Educational, 1989. Younger readers.

Web site

Benjamin Harrison
http://www.whitehouse.gov/WH/glimpse/presidents/html/bh23.html
Official White House biography of Benjamin Harrison.

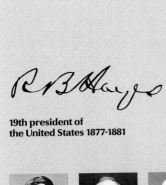

**19th president of
the United States 1877-1881**

Grant
18th president
1869-1877
Republican

Hayes
19th president
1877-1881
Republican

Garfield
20th president
1881
Republican

**William A.
Wheeler**
Vice president
1877-1881

Detail of an oil portrait (1884) by Daniel Huntington;
© White House Historical Association (photography by the National Geographic Society)

Hayes, Rutherford Birchard (1822-1893), was elected president by a margin of only one electoral vote. His victory over Samuel J. Tilden in 1876 climaxed one of the most disputed presidential elections in United States history. Congress had to create a special Electoral Commission to decide the winner.

Hayes was a studious, good-natured man who enjoyed books more than politics. Ohio Republicans nominated him for Congress while he was fighting in the Civil War. Hayes refused to campaign. He declared that any officer who "would abandon his post to electioneer for a seat in Congress, ought to be scalped." Hayes won the election. He later served three terms as Ohio's governor.

When Hayes became president, the nation was suffering from a business depression and the political scandals of the previous administration of Ulysses S. Grant. The unsolved problem of Reconstruction in the South still divided the American people, even though the Civil War had ended 12 years before. Hayes was not popular at first. Democrats charged he had "stolen" the election. His fellow Republicans were bitter because he refused to give special favors to party politicians.

However, by the time Hayes left office, most Americans respected him for his sincerity and honesty. He had promised to end Reconstruction, and he did. Within two months after he took office, the last federal troops marched from the South. Hayes also put the government on the path toward civil service reform. Throughout his career, Hayes tried to live by his motto: "He serves his party best who serves his country best."

During Hayes's administration, the United States continued its remarkable growth. The nation became more industrialized than ever before, and labor unions gained thousands of new members. The population of New York City soared above a million. Civil War General Lew

Wallace won nationwide fame for his novel *Ben-Hur.* And Thomas A. Edison visited the White House to demonstrate his favorite invention, the phonograph.

Early life

Rutherford Birchard Hayes was born on Oct. 4, 1822, in Delaware, Ohio. He was the fifth child of Rutherford Hayes, Jr., and Sophia Birchard Hayes. The family had migrated to Ohio from Dummerston, Vermont, in 1817. Hayes had two brothers and two sisters, but only he and his sister Fanny grew to adulthood. Hayes's father, a successful store owner, died two months before Rutherford, or "Rud," was born. A bachelor uncle, Sardis Birchard, became the children's guardian.

Education. Hayes was a champion speller in elementary school. He later boasted that "not one in a thousand could spell me down!" Hayes prepared for college at private schools in Norwalk, Ohio; and Middletown, Connecticut. In 1838, he entered Kenyon College in Gambier, Ohio. He graduated in 1842 at the head of his class. Hayes entered Harvard Law School the next year. He graduated and was admitted to the bar in 1845.

Lawyer. Hayes began practicing law in Lower Sandusky (later Fremont), Ohio, where his uncle lived. In 1850, he opened a law office in Cincinnati. At first, Hayes had so few clients and was so poor that he slept in his office to save money. Hayes's law practice gradually increased. In 1852, he won statewide attention as a criminal lawyer in two widely publicized murder trials. His brilliant defense arguments saved his clients from receiving the death penalty. In 1858, the Cincinnati City Council elected Hayes to fill a vacancy as city solicitor. He held this influential political and legal post until shortly before the Civil War began three years later.

Hayes's family. On Dec. 30, 1852, Hayes married Lucy

Railroad workers rioted during a nationwide strike in 1877. Hayes called out federal troops to restore order.

The first practical incandescent lamp was developed by Thomas Edison in 1879. In 1877, Edison had invented a phonograph.

The U.S. flag gained a 38th star in 1877, marking Colorado's entry into the Union in 1876 as the 38th state.

The world of President Hayes

Reconstruction ended in 1877, when the last federal occupation troops were withdrawn from the South.
Flag Day was first officially celebrated on June 14, 1877.
The first black cadet to graduate from the United States Military Academy at West Point was H. O. Flipper, in 1877.
Henry M. Stanley, a Welsh explorer, reached the mouth of the Congo River in 1877, after a nearly three-year journey across Africa. He became the first white person to trace the river from Central Africa to its mouth on the Atlantic coast.
Famous books published during Hayes's presidency included *Black Beauty* (1877), a novel by Anna Sewell protesting cruel treatment of horses; *Ben-Hur: A Tale of the Christ* (1880), a novel by Lew Wallace; and *Uncle Remus: His Songs and His Sayings* (1880), a collection of Southern black folk tales by Joel Chandler Harris.
The Russo-Turkish War of 1877-1878 gave Russia control of important areas in the Caucasus region, near the Black Sea.
The first commercial telephone exchange opened in New Haven, Conn., in 1878. It had 21 subscribers.
The woman suffrage amendment was proposed in the United States Congress for the first time in 1878.
The first journalism course was given at the University of Missouri in 1879.
The first woman lawyer to practice before the Supreme Court of the United States was Belva Ann Lockwood, in 1879.
Wilhelm Wundt, a German philosopher, established one of the first laboratories of experimental psychology in 1879.

The Rutherford B. Hayes Presidential Center; Consolidated Edison Company of New York, Inc.

Ware Webb (Aug. 28, 1831-June 25, 1889). They had eight children, but three died in infancy.

Lucy Hayes was the daughter of a Chillicothe, Ohio, physician. She had graduated in 1850 from the Wesleyan Female College in Cincinnati, and was the first president's wife to have a college degree. Her intelligence and social grace helped Hayes throughout his career. Mrs. Hayes championed many of the leading moral causes of the day. She supported the abolition of slavery, prohibition of alcohol, and aid to the poor.

Soldier. When the Civil War began in 1861, the Literary Club of Cincinnati formed a military drilling company, and elected Hayes captain. He was later appointed a major of a regiment of Ohio volunteers. Hayes distinguished himself in several battles, and earned rapid promotion during his four years in the Army. He was wounded four times and had four horses shot from under him. On June 8, 1865, two months after the war ended, Hayes resigned from the Army with the rank of brevet major general.

Political career

Congressman. Hayes was nominated for the U.S. House of Representatives in 1864. He received the news while fighting in the Shenandoah Valley under General Philip H. Sheridan. He refused to campaign for the office

because the outcome of the war was still in doubt. Hayes won the election, but did not take his seat in Congress until December 1865. He won reelection in 1866, but resigned in July 1867, a month after he was nominated for governor of Ohio.

While in Congress, Hayes did outstanding work as chairman of the Joint Committee on the Library of Congress. Under his leadership, Congress transferred the scientific library of the Smithsonian Institution to the Library of Congress.

Governor. In 1867, Hayes won election to the first of three terms as governor of Ohio. His election was a per-

Important dates in Hayes's life

1822	(Oct. 4) Born in Delaware, Ohio.
1852	(Dec. 30) Married Lucy Ware Webb.
1864	Elected to the U.S. House of Representatives.
1867	Elected governor of Ohio.
1876	Elected president of the United States.
1893	(Jan. 17) Died in Fremont, Ohio.

Brown Bros.

Hayes's birthplace, a brick house in Delaware, Ohio, *above,* was later used as a store. The building was torn down in 1928, and a bronze tablet now marks the site.

Detail of an oil portrait (1881) by Daniel Huntington;
© White House Historical Association
(photography by the National Geographic Society)

Lucy Webb Hayes was the first president's wife to have a college degree. She became a supporter of social causes, including help for the disadvantaged.

sonal triumph because he campaigned in favor of an unpopular black suffrage amendment to the state constitution. Hayes planned to retire from politics at the end of his second term in 1872. But Republican leaders persuaded him to run for Congress. He was defeated, and spent the next three years at his home near Fremont, Ohio, where he lived quietly and dealt in real estate. In 1875, he won a third term as governor.

Hayes gained nationwide attention as a courageous administrator. He worked hard for economy in government and for a strong civil service program based on merit rather than political influence. He also helped establish the college that became Ohio State University.

Campaign of 1876. As President Grant's second term drew to a close, the corruption-torn Republican Party split into two main factions. The *Stalwarts,* who were led by Senator Roscoe Conkling of New York, favored a third term for Grant. The *Half-Breeds,* who were led by Representative James G. Blaine of Maine, opposed the Stalwarts. Grant refused to run for a third term, but neither the Stalwarts nor the Half-Breeds had enough votes to nominate a presidential candidate. Many of the party leaders supported Hayes as a compromise candidate. At the Republican National Convention in June 1876, Hayes won the presidential nomination on the seventh ballot. The delegates nominated Representative William A. Wheeler of New York for vice president.

Samuel J. Tilden, who had gained fame as a reform governor of New York, was Hayes's Democratic opponent. The Democrats chose Governor Thomas A. Hendricks of Indiana for vice president. The new Greenback Party nominated Peter Cooper for president.

The Republicans seemed to have little chance for victory. The Democrats had increased their voting strength since 1874, when they gained control of the U.S. House

of Representatives. As election day approached, however, President Grant sent federal troops to South Carolina and Louisiana to protect the rights of black voters, and gain support for the Republicans. Tilden received 4,288,546 popular votes to 4,034,311 for Hayes.

The election dispute. Four states—Louisiana, South Carolina, Florida, and Oregon—submitted two sets of electoral returns, one by the Democrats and one by the Republicans. As a result, both parties claimed victory. On December 6, the Electoral College met and voted. Hayes received 165 unquestioned votes. Tilden got 184 votes, one short of a majority. Twenty electoral votes, from the four states that submitted conflicting returns, were disputed. In January 1877, Congress appointed a 15-member Electoral Commission to settle the matter (see **Electoral Commission**). Its decisions were to be final, unless both houses of Congress voted otherwise. During the debate in Congress, members of both parties threatened to seize the government by force.

As Inauguration Day neared, leaders of both parties feared the nation might be left without a president. In a private meeting, Southern Democrats in Congress agreed not to oppose the decision of the Electoral Commission. This agreement gave Hayes the presidency because the commission had a Republican majority. In exchange, the Republicans promised to end Reconstruction and pull federal troops from the South. Southerners thus regained complete political control over their state and local governments for the first time since the war. On March 2, 1877, just 56 hours before Inauguration Day, Hayes was formally announced as the winner.

Hayes's administration (1877-1881)

The end of Reconstruction. One of Hayes's first acts as president was to withdraw federal occupation forces from the South, as promised. On April 10, 1877, the soldiers left South Carolina, and on April 24, the last federal troops marched from Louisiana. Hayes hoped that the end of Reconstruction would restore the two-party system in the South. But the Democrats won back their solid hold on the South.

Civil service reform. Hayes had announced that he intended to serve only one term as president so he could strive for civil service reform. Hayes based his appointments on merit rather than on the spoils system. He even appointed a Southern Democrat, David M. Key, to his Cabinet. This and other Cabinet appointments angered members of his own party. Hayes also forced the removal of three fellow Republicans from their jobs in the New York Custom House. One of the men was Chester A. Arthur, who became the 21st president.

Congress refused to act on the civil service legislation

Hayes's election

Place of nominating convention	Cincinnati
Ballot on which nominated	7th
Democratic opponent	Samuel J. Tilden
Electoral vote*	185 (Hayes) to 184 (Tilden)
Popular vote	4,288,546 (Tilden) to 4,034,311 (Hayes)
Age at inauguration	54

*For votes by states, see **Electoral College** (table).

that Hayes proposed, but Hayes was the first president to fight Congress on this issue. His struggle gained wide public support and opened the way for later presidents to make civil service reforms.

Money problems. Because of the depression of the 1870's, many people demanded *cheap money.* Farmers and business owners, for example, believed that putting more money into circulation would raise the prices of their products and thus help them pay off their debts. They wanted the government to issue more paper and silver money even though the money could not be backed by gold in the Treasury. Hayes favored a conservative money policy and resisted their demands.

In 1878, Hayes vetoed the Bland-Allison Act, which required the Treasury to buy and coin between $2 million and $4 million worth of silver a month. Congress passed the bill over his veto. But the Treasury coined only the minimum amount required in an attempt to limit the inflationary effect of putting more money into circulation.

In 1879, the Hayes administration resumed payment of *specie* (metal coin) for *greenbacks* (paper money issued to finance the Civil War). Secretary of the Treasury John Sherman gathered enough gold in the Treasury to redeem all of the greenbacks that were likely to be brought in. As soon as this became known, no one was anxious to exchange notes for gold. This policy helped restore financial confidence, and business improved.

Life in the White House. Rutherford and Lucy Hayes tried to set a good example for every American family. They quickly gained respect for their hospitality, simplicity, and modesty. They were both concerned about the problem of alcoholism, as were many other people in the country. As a symbol of the temperance cause, the Hayeses stopped the practice of serving alcoholic drinks at the White House, even at formal dinners and receptions. Some critics called Mrs. Hayes "Lemonade Lucy" because of her stance against alcohol.

A typical day in the White House began with morning prayers. Early in the evening, the family often gathered for music and singing. Mrs. Hayes held public receptions almost every evening and welcomed everyone who wished to visit the White House. In 1878, she and President Hayes introduced the custom of Easter egg rolling by children on the White House lawn.

Later years

"Nobody ever left the Presidency with less regret … than I do," Hayes said when his term ended in 1881. No one seemed sorry that he did not run for a second term. But Hayes believed that the public showed its approval

Vice president and Cabinet

Vice president	William A. Wheeler
Secretary of state	William M. Evarts
Secretary of the treasury	John Sherman
Secretary of war	George W. McCrary
	Alexander Ramsey (1879)
Attorney general	Charles Devens
Postmaster general	David M. Key
	Horace Maynard (1880)
Secretary of the Navy	Richard W. Thompson
	Alexander Ramsey (1880)
	Nathan Goff, Jr. (1881)
Secretary of the interior	Carl Schurz

of his administration by electing James A. Garfield, his friend and political supporter, as president.

Hayes returned to his home at Spiegel Grove, near Fremont, Ohio, and completely withdrew from politics. He devoted himself to philanthropic work in education, prison reform, Christianity, and veterans' affairs.

Mrs. Hayes died in June 1889. Hayes became ill while visiting friends in Cleveland in January 1893. His friends urged him to remain in bed. But Hayes insisted on returning home, saying: "I would rather die at Spiegel Grove than to live anywhere else." He died on Jan. 17, 1893, and was buried in Fremont. Spiegel Grove is now open to the public. It includes the Rutherford B. Hayes Library and Museum.   H. Wayne Morgan

See also **President of the United States.**

Outline

I. **Early life**
   A. Education   C. Hayes's family
   B. Lawyer   D. Soldier
II. **Political career**
   A. Congressman   C. Campaign of 1876
   B. Governor   D. The election dispute
III. **Hayes's administration (1877-1881)**
   A. The end of Reconstruction
   B. Civil service reform
   C. Money problems
   D. Life in the White House
IV. **Later years**

Questions

What were Hayes's outstanding personal qualities?
How did Hayes influence future civil service laws?
Why did the Republicans turn to Hayes as their presidential candidate in 1876?
How did Congress settle the dispute that resulted from the 1876 election?
What did Hayes expect to accomplish by ending Reconstruction? What actually happened?

Additional resources

Barnard, Harry. *Rutherford B. Hayes and His America.* 1954. Reprint. Am. Political Biography Pr., 1992.
Hoogenboom, Ari. *Rutherford B. Hayes.* Univ. Pr. of Kans., 1995.
Kent, Zachary. *Rutherford B. Hayes.* Childrens Pr., 1989. Younger readers.

Web site

Rutherford B. Hayes
http://www.whitehouse.gov/WH/glimpse/presidents/html/rh19.html
Official White House biography of Rutherford B. Hayes. Includes a link to a biography of Lucy Webb Hayes.

**3rd president of
the United States 1801-1809**

Adams
2nd president
1797-1801
Federalist

Jefferson
3rd president
1801-1809
Democratic-
Republican

Madison
4th president
1809-1817
Democratic-
Republican

Aaron Burr
Vice president
1801-1805

George Clinton
Vice president
1805-1809

Detail of an oil portrait on canvas (1800) by Rembrandt Peale; © White House Historical Association (photography by the National Geographic Society)

Jefferson, Thomas (1743-1826), is best remembered as a great president and as the author of the Declaration of Independence. He also won lasting fame as a diplomat, a political thinker, and a founder of the Democratic Party.

Jefferson displayed a wide range of interests and talents. He became one of the leading American architects of his time and designed the Virginia Capitol, the University of Virginia, and his own home, Monticello. He greatly appreciated art and music and tried to encourage their advancement in the United States. He arranged for the famous French sculptor Jean Houdon to come to America to make a statue of George Washington. Jefferson also posed for Houdon and for the famous American portrait painter Gilbert Stuart. Jefferson also enjoyed playing the violin in chamber music concerts.

In addition, Jefferson served as president of the American Philosophical Society, an organization that encouraged a wide range of scientific and intellectual research. Jefferson invented a decoding device, a lap desk, and an improved type of moldboard plow. His collection of more than 6,400 books became a major part of the Library of Congress. Jefferson revised Virginia's laws and founded its state university. He developed the decimal system of coinage that allows Americans to keep accounts in dollars and cents. He compiled a *Manual of Parliamentary Practice* and prepared written vocabularies of Indian languages. Jefferson also cultivated one of the finest gardens in America.

Jefferson did not consider himself a professional politician. Instead, he regarded himself as a public-spirited citizen and a broad-minded, practical thinker. He preferred his family, his books, and his farms to public life. But he spent most of his career in public office and made his greatest contribution to his country in the field of politics.

The tall, red-haired Virginian believed that "those who labor in the earth are the chosen people of God." His ideal society was a nation of landowning farmers living under as little government as possible. The term *Jeffersonian democracy* refers to such an ideal and was based on Jefferson's faith in self-government. He trusted the majority of people to govern themselves and wanted to keep the government simple and free of waste. Jefferson loved liberty in every form, and he worked for freedom of speech, press, religion, and other civil liberties. Jefferson strongly supported the addition of the Bill of Rights to the Constitution of the United States.

Jefferson molded the American spirit and mind. Every later generation has turned to him for inspiration. Through about 40 years of public service, he remained faithful to his vow of "eternal hostility against every form of tyranny over the mind of man."

During Jefferson's two terms as president, the United States almost doubled in area with the purchase of the vast Louisiana Territory. America preserved its hard-won neutrality while France, led by Napoleon's armies, battled most of Europe. Congress passed a law banning the slave trade. It took travelers two days to go from New York City to Philadelphia by stagecoach. But the first successful voyage of Robert Fulton's steamboat, which became famous as the *Clermont,* signaled a promising new era in the history of transportation.

Early life

Boyhood. Thomas Jefferson was born on April 13, 1743, at Shadwell, the family farm in Goochland (now Albemarle) County, Virginia. (The date was April 2 by the

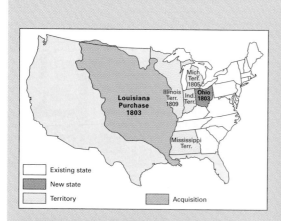

The world of President Jefferson

War with Tripoli, a Barbary State of northern Africa, broke out in 1801 after Barbary sea raiders attacked American shipping. The United States won the war in 1805.
The Louisiana Purchase, territorial agreement with France, doubled the size of the United States in 1803.
Dalton's Theory of the Atom, one of the foundations of chemistry, was developed in 1803. English chemist John Dalton proposed that all matter was made up of atoms.
Marbury v. Madison, a landmark Supreme Court ruling, established the court's right to declare laws unconstitutional.
The Lewis and Clark Expedition crossed the Rocky Mountains to the Pacific Ocean and mapped much of the vast northwestern wilderness. The explorers left in 1804 and returned in 1806.
Napoleon crowned himself emperor of the French in 1804.
The Steam Age revolutionized transportation. Richard Trevithick, an English engineer, invented the steam-powered locomotive in 1804. American inventor Robert Fulton began the first commercially successful steamboat service in 1807.
The Romantic Movement dominated literature. Sir Walter Scott's *The Lay of the Last Minstrel* (1805) and William Wordsworth's *Poems in Two Volumes* (1807), stressed imagination, passionate feeling, and unusual experiences.
The Embargo Act of 1807 prohibited ships from entering or leaving U.S. harbors. It sought to end interference with U.S. shipping by France and the United Kingdom, who were at war.
The importation of slaves was prohibited by Congress in 1808.

The United States doubled its area in 1803 with the Louisiana Purchase. Ohio became the 17th state in 1803. Congress extended the Mississippi Territory and created the Michigan and Illinois territories.

WORLD BOOK map

calendar then in use.) He was the third child in the family and grew up with six sisters and one brother. Two other brothers died in infancy. His father, Peter Jefferson, had served as surveyor, sheriff, colonel of militia, and member of the House of Burgesses. Thomas' mother, Jane Randolph Jefferson, came from one of the oldest families in Virginia.

Thomas developed the normal interests of a country boy—hunting, fishing, horseback riding, and canoeing. He also learned to play the violin and to love music.

Jefferson was 14 years old when his father died. As the oldest son, he became head of the family. He inherited more than 2,500 acres (1,010 hectares) of land and at least 20 slaves. His guardian, John Harvie, managed the estate until Jefferson was 21.

Education. Thomas began his studies under a tutor. At age 9, he went to live with a Scottish clergyman, who taught him Latin, Greek, and French. After his father died, Thomas entered the school of James Maury, an Anglican clergyman, near Charlottesville.

Important dates in Jefferson's life

1743	(April 13) Born in Goochland (now Albemarle) County, Virginia.
1772	(Jan. 1) Married Martha Wayles Skelton.
1776	Wrote the Declaration of Independence.
1779	Elected governor of Virginia.
1782	Mrs. Martha Jefferson died.
1785	Appointed minister to France.
1789	Became United States secretary of state.
1796	Elected vice president of the United States.
1801	(Feb. 17) Elected president of the United States.
1804	Reelected president.
1819	Founded the University of Virginia.
1826	(July 4) Died at Monticello, his Virginia home.

In 1760, when he was 16, Jefferson entered the College of William and Mary at Williamsburg. The town had a population of only about 1,000. But as the provincial capital, it had a lively social life. There, young Jefferson met two men, William Small and Judge George Wythe, who would have a great influence on him. Small was a professor of mathematics at the college. "From his conversation," Jefferson later recalled, "I got my first views of the expansion of science and of the system of things in which we are placed." Small introduced his eager young disciple to Wythe, one of the most learned lawyers in the province.

Through Small and Wythe, Jefferson became friendly

Jefferson Birthplace Memorial Park Commission

Jefferson's birthplace was this house at Shadwell, a family estate of more than 2,500 acres (1,010 hectares) in central Virginia. Jefferson inherited the property when he was 14 years old.

with Governor Francis Fauquier. The four spent many evenings at the governor's mansion, talking and playing chamber music. Jefferson felt that "... to the habitual conversation on these occasions I owed much instruction." The young student also met Patrick Henry.

Jefferson spent two years at William and Mary. His studies and the companionship of cultured men stimulated his eager mind. He formed many of his ideas about humanity and God. Jefferson had been reared in the Anglican Church, but he developed a distrust of organized religion. His views resembled those of the Unitarians. In his old age, he wrote: "To love God with all thy heart and thy neighbor as thyself is the sum of religion."

Lawyer. After finishing college in 1762, Jefferson studied law with George Wythe. He watched with concern as tension grew between the American Colonies

Thomas F. Kelsey, CC Ae.

Jefferson collected clever devices throughout his lifetime. The swivel chair shown here and other items Jefferson gathered are on display at Monticello.

Robert Lightfoot, Atoz Images

Monticello, the home Jefferson designed and built between 1768 and 1809, is a 35-room brick mansion on a hilltop near Charlottesville, Virginia. It attracts thousands of visitors yearly.

and the United Kingdom. In 1765, Jefferson heard Patrick Henry give his famous speech against the Stamp Act.

Jefferson was admitted to the bar in 1767. He practiced law with great success until public service began taking all his time. He divided his time between Williamsburg and Shadwell. At Shadwell, he designed and supervised the building of his own home, Monticello, on a nearby hill.

Jefferson's estate, like that of his father, lay in the rolling hills of Virginia's Piedmont region. The Scotch-Irish and German immigrants of this section had hacked their small farms out of the wilderness. Their ideas conflicted with the aristocratic beliefs of the wealthy landowners of the Tidewater region. Jefferson was related to many Tidewater aristocrats and was accepted in their society. But his political sympathies tended to be closer to those of his Piedmont neighbors.

Jefferson's family. In 1772, Jefferson married Martha Wayles Skelton (Oct. 19, 1748-Sept. 6, 1782), a widow. She was the daughter of John Wayles, a prominent lawyer who lived near Williamsburg. According to legend, Jefferson's love of music helped him win his bride. Two rival suitors came to call one day but left without a word when they saw the couple playing a duet on the harpsichord and violin.

The Jeffersons settled at Monticello, which was not yet completed. They had one son and five daughters, but only two children lived to maturity—Martha (1772-1836) and Mary (1778-1804). Mrs. Jefferson died in 1782, after only 10 years of marriage. Jefferson reared his two daughters. He never remarried.

Jefferson and Sally Hemings. Like many landowners of the time, Jefferson kept slaves. For many years, some historians thought that Jefferson might have had children with one of his slaves, Sally Hemings. In 1998, scientists conducted a DNA study to help learn if this was so. The study compared the DNA of male descendants of Sally Hemings with DNA from male descendants of Jefferson's uncle. The study could not include male descendants of Jefferson and his wife because they had no sons who lived to adulthood. Certain characteristics of Jefferson's DNA and that of his uncle, brother, and their descendants would be the same. The study suggested that Jefferson or one of his relatives fathered at least one of Hemings's children, Eston Hemings.

The Thomas Jefferson Memorial Foundation, which oversees Monticello, appointed a committee to review the study. Committee members examined historical and scientific documents and interviewed descendants of Monticello slaves and others. In early 2000, the foundation reported its findings. The likelihood is very strong, the foundation said, that Jefferson and Sally Hemings had a long-term relationship and that Jefferson was the father of one, if not all six, of Hemings's children.

Colonial statesman

Revolutionary leader. Jefferson was elected to the House of Burgesses in 1769 and served there until 1775. He was not a brilliant speaker but proved himself an able writer of laws and resolutions. Jefferson often showed a talent for clear and simple English that the more experienced legislators quickly recognized.

Jefferson became a member of a group that included Patrick Henry, Richard Henry Lee, and Francis Lightfoot

Lithograph (1876) by Currier & Ives; Library of Congress (Granger Collection)

The Declaration of Independence was written by Jefferson, a member of the committee named to draft it. The committee consisted of, *left to right,* Jefferson, Roger Sherman, Benjamin Franklin, Robert R. Livingston, and John Adams.

Lee. These men challenged the control that Tidewater aristocrats held over Virginia politics. They also took an active part in disputes between the colonies and the United Kingdom. Together with other patriots, they met in the Apollo Room of Williamsburg's Raleigh Tavern in 1769 and joined against the United Kingdom in a nonimportation association. The members protested the import duties set up by the Townshend Acts.

After a brief lull, the controversy resumed in 1774. Jefferson took the lead in organizing another nonimportation agreement. He also called for the colonies to meet and consider their grievances. He was chosen to represent Albemarle County at the First Virginia Convention, which in turn was to elect Virginia delegates to the First Continental Congress. He became ill and could not go to the meeting, but he sent a paper giving his views.

Jefferson argued that the British Parliament had no control over the American Colonies. He declared that when the original settlers came to America, they had used their "natural rights" to emigrate. Jefferson claimed the colonies still owed allegiance only to the king, to whom the original settlers had freely chosen to remain loyal. Jefferson said the first English settlers in America were like the first Saxons who had settled in England hundreds of years before. The Saxons had come from the area of present-day Germany. Jefferson claimed the British Parliament had no more right to govern America than the German rulers had to govern England. Most Virginians at the convention found Jefferson's views too extreme. But his views, supported by able legalistic argument, were printed in 1774 in a pamphlet called *A Summary View of the Rights of British America.*

Jefferson attended the Second Virginia Convention in the spring of 1775. The members of this convention chose Jefferson as one of the delegates to the Second Continental Congress. Before he left for Philadelphia, the Virginia Assembly asked him to answer a message of peace from Lord North, the U.K. prime minister. North had proposed that Parliament would not try to tax the settlers if they would tax themselves. Jefferson's *Reply to Lord North* was more moderate than the *Summary View.* But he rejected North's proposals. Jefferson insisted that a government had been set up in America for the colonists, not for the British. The Continental Congress approved Jefferson's letter to North.

The Declaration of Independence. Jefferson took a leading part in the Continental Congress. After the Revolutionary War began, he was asked to draft a "Declaration of the Causes and Necessity of Taking up Arms." The Congress found this declaration "too strong." The more moderate John Dickinson drafted a substitute, which included much of Jefferson's original version.

During the spring of 1776, sentiment rapidly grew stronger in favor of independence. On June 7, Richard Henry Lee of Virginia introduced his famous resolution that "these United Colonies are, and of right ought to be, free and independent States." Congress appointed a committee to draw up a declaration of independence. On the committee were Jefferson, John Adams, Benjamin Franklin, Roger Sherman, and Robert Livingston. The committee unanimously asked Jefferson to prepare the draft and approved it with few changes. Congress began debating the declaration on July 2 and adopted it on July 4. Congress made some changes, but, as Richard Lee said: "the Thing in its nature is so good that no cookery can spoil the dish for the palates of freemen."

The Declaration of Independence remains Jefferson's best-known work. It set forth with moving eloquence, supported by strong legal argument, the position of the American revolutionaries. It affirmed belief in the natural rights of all people. Few of the ideas were new. Jefferson said his object was "to place before mankind the common sense of the subject, in terms so plain and firm as to command their assent … Neither aiming at originality of principle or sentiment, nor yet copied from any particular and previous writing, it was intended to be an expression of the American mind. …"

Virginia lawmaker. In September 1776, Jefferson resigned from Congress and returned to the Virginia House of Delegates. He had no interest in military life and did not fight in the Revolutionary War. He felt that he could be more useful in Virginia as a lawmaker. His first moves toward social reform involved land distribution. A few wealthy slaveholders controlled Virginia. The people in this largest colony suffered from uneven distribution of land. The colonial government closely restricted voting privileges and limited educational opportunities. In practice, a great deal of religious tolerance existed. But the Anglican Church was established by law.

Jefferson sponsored a bill abolishing *entail,* which requires property owners to leave their land to specified descendants, rather than disposing of it as they wish. Jefferson then succeeded in outlawing *primogeniture,* whereby all land passes to the eldest son. Without entail and primogeniture, great estates could be broken up. Jefferson described the purposes of land reform when he wrote: "instead of an aristocracy of wealth … to make an opening for the aristocracy of virtue and talent."

At this time in Virginia, only people who owned land could vote. After large estates were broken up, more people owned property. As a result, more people could vote. The legislature passed another bill introduced by Jefferson providing that immigrants could become naturalized after living in Virginia for two years.

Even more important were Jefferson's bills designed to assure religious toleration and to abolish the special privileges of the Anglican Church in Virginia. Jefferson aroused hostility not only among Anglicans, but also among other denominations, which feared that a separation of church and state would loosen all religious ties. Virginia ended the Anglican Church's position as a state church in 1779. It took the church's clergymen off the public payroll and exempted Virginians from paying taxes to support the church. In 1786, when Jefferson was in France, the assembly passed his Statute of Religious Freedom, which guaranteed religious liberty in Virginia.

Jefferson also worked to revise Virginia's legal system. He pushed through many reforms, especially in land law and criminal law. The legislature defeated his plan for a system of free public education with a state-supported university, but parts of this plan later became law.

Jefferson considered attempting to end slavery in Virginia. But he took no strong stand because he felt the people of his state were not ready for such a major step. Jefferson had numerous slaves, but he believed slavery was morally wrong and could not permanently exist in the United States. He hoped the younger generation would end society's dependence on this system. He wrote, "Nothing is more certainly written in the book of fate than that these people are to be free."

Governor. The Virginia Assembly elected Jefferson governor for one-year terms in 1779 and 1780. During his administration, the state suffered severely from the effects of the Revolutionary War. At the request of General George Washington, Jefferson had stripped Virginia of its defenses to aid the American army. James Monroe was among those who recruited Virginians for military service. He and Jefferson formed a lasting friendship.

British troops under Benedict Arnold and Lord Cornwallis invaded Virginia in 1781. The state could put up little resistance. Jefferson himself barely escaped capture on June 4 when troops led by Lieutenant Colonel Banastre Tarleton swept down on Monticello.

Jefferson's term had ended on June 2. The Virginia legislature chose Thomas Nelson, Jr., the top officer of the state militia, to succeed Jefferson. Jefferson was criticized for the state's lack of resistance against the British invasion. An official investigation cleared him of blame. But many years passed before Jefferson regained prestige in his own state. The criticism wounded him deeply, and he left public office with genuine relief.

Congressman. Jefferson returned to Monticello embittered and determined to give up public life forever. He soon began writing his *Notes on the State of Virginia* (1784-1785). This book included much information on Virginia and on his own beliefs and ideals.

The death of Jefferson's wife in September 1782 left him stunned and distraught. For several months, he spoke to few people and wrote to none. His daughter Martha wrote many years later: "... the violence of his emotion ... to this day I dare not describe to myself." In referring to his wife's death, Jefferson told a friend: "A single event wiped out all my plans and left me a blank which I had not the spirits to fill up."

Jefferson was elected to Congress in 1783. He accepted the office because he felt it would take his mind off his personal tragedy. During his year in Congress, he devised a decimal system of currency that Congress approved. He also piloted through Congress the Treaty of Paris, which ended the Revolutionary War. Most important was Jefferson's work on the Ordinance of 1784 and the Land Ordinance of 1785. These measures formed the basis for all later American land policies.

The problem of western lands had troubled the colonies from the beginning of the war. Several colonies claimed land west of the Appalachian Mountains. Virginia, under Jefferson's leadership, gave up its claims in 1784. Other states followed, and the Northwest Territory was created.

Problems of how to govern the area and how to dispose of its land then arose. Congress appointed two committees to consider the issues and made Jefferson chairman of both. In 1784, Jefferson submitted a draft of an ordinance for the political organization of the lands. It would have divided the region into several states. Each would eventually be admitted to the Union on a basis of complete equality with the original 13 states. Jefferson's provision forbidding slavery west of the Appalachians lost by one vote. The Ordinance of 1784 never went into effect, but it furnished the basis for the Northwest Ordinance of 1787.

Minister to France. In May 1784, Congress sent Jefferson to France to join John Adams and Benjamin Franklin in negotiating European treaties of commerce. The next year, Franklin resigned as minister to France, and Jefferson succeeded him in Paris. "It is you, sir, who replace Franklin?" he was asked. "No, sir, I succeed him; no one can replace him," Jefferson replied. Yet Jefferson came as close as anyone could to replacing the honored Franklin. The United States was suffering from a weak central authority under the Articles of Confederation. Jefferson found himself seriously handicapped by what he described as "the nonpayment of our debts and the want of energy in our government." But he did work out several commercial agreements.

At this time, revolution was approaching in France. French reformers regarded Jefferson as a champion of liberty because of his political writings and his legal reforms in Virginia. The Marquis de Lafayette, who had fought for American independence, and other moderates often sought his advice. Jefferson tried to keep out of French politics. But he did draft a proposed Charter of Rights to be presented to the king. This document and his other suggestions urged moderation because Jefferson felt that the French were not yet ready for a representative government of the American type. Jefferson was in Paris at the beginning of the French Revolution. He sympathized with the revolution, feeling it was similar in purpose to the Revolutionary War in America.

Jefferson had taken his daughter Martha to France with him, and Mary joined them in 1787. Both girls attended a convent school in Paris. Jefferson traveled widely in Europe. He broadened his knowledge of many subjects, especially architecture and farming. He applied for a leave in 1789 and sailed for home in October. He wanted to settle his affairs in America and to take his daughters back home. Jefferson expected to return to represent the United States in France.

National statesman

During Jefferson's stay in France, Americans at home were busy reorganizing the government. Statesmen assembled in a convention in 1787 and drew up what became the Constitution of the United States. Jefferson's friend James Madison sent him a draft, which he ap-

Culver

Jefferson was secretary of state under President George Washington, *right.* The Cabinet was, *left to right,* Henry Knox, Jefferson, Edmund Randolph, and Alexander Hamilton.

proved. But he objected strongly to the lack of a bill of rights and wrote letters urging one. Soon after the Constitution went into effect, Madison introduced the 10 amendments that became the Bill of Rights.

Secretary of state. Jefferson arrived in the United States in November 1789. A letter from President George Washington awaited him, asking Jefferson to be secretary of state in the new government. Jefferson received this invitation "with real regret," but he finally yielded to Washington's urging.

Jefferson and Hamilton. Sharp differences of opinion soon arose between Jefferson and the secretary of the treasury, Alexander Hamilton. Hamilton, though younger than Jefferson, had gained prominence as a spokesman for the Constitution. Although of humble origin, the New Yorker distrusted the common people. Hamilton believed that the United States would be best governed by an aristocracy of the rich and well-born. Jefferson, with his faith in the people, disagreed with Hamilton.

Hamilton's financial program embodied many of his principles, and brought these differences into the open. Jefferson supported Hamilton's plan for funding all the debts of the previous national governments. He reluctantly agreed that Congress should also accept responsibility for the debts taken on by the states during the Revolutionary War. This proposal aroused considerable opposition, especially in Virginia and other Southern States that had paid off much of their debt. These states did not want to pay the debts of other states. Some Southern members of Congress agreed to vote for paying the state debts in return for having the national capital located in the South. Jefferson helped carry out this

compromise, and the capital was located in the District of Columbia.

But Jefferson opposed Hamilton's plans to encourage shipping and manufacturing. Jefferson wanted the United States to remain a nation of farmers. Hamilton's proposed national bank also alarmed Jefferson. He feared that such a bank would encourage financial speculation and hurt farming interests. Jefferson also thought it would give the government too much power. Washington asked his Cabinet to submit opinions on the constitutionality of a national bank. Jefferson developed his "strict construction" theory, which held that the government should assume only the powers expressly given it by the Constitution. Hamilton replied with his "loose" interpretation of the Constitution, declaring that the government could assume all powers not expressly denied it. Washington generally favored Hamilton in domestic affairs and approved the bank.

The differences between Jefferson and Hamilton grew into a bitter personal feud. Neither man believed in the honesty or good faith of the other. Hamilton went so far as to call Jefferson a "contemptible hypocrite." Their conflicting points of view led to the development of the first political parties. The Federalists adopted Hamilton's principles. Jefferson led the Democratic-Republicans (called *Republicans* at the time, though some historians regard it as the origin of the modern Democratic Party).

Foreign affairs. Washington supported most of Jefferson's policies in foreign relations. Jefferson urged recognition of the new revolutionary government of France. But he reluctantly supported Washington's proclamation of neutrality, and agreed on demanding the recall of Citizen Genêt. Jefferson tried to persuade the British to abandon their forts in the Northwest Territory. He also worked for free navigation of the Mississippi River.

Vice president. Jefferson joined his fellow Cabinet members in urging Washington to accept a second term as president. But he himself was heartily weary of office and wanted to escape the "hated occupation of politics." Jefferson finally persuaded Washington to accept his resignation. In January 1794, Jefferson returned to Monticello. He hoped to find happiness "in the society of my neighbors and my books, in the wholesome occupations of my farm and my affairs ... owing account to myself alone of my hours and actions."

But a life of this kind did not last long. In 1796, his Democratic-Republican supporters nominated him as a candidate for president to run against John Adams, the Federalist candidate. Adams received 71 electoral votes in this first party contest for the presidency and was elected president. Jefferson received 68 electoral votes, the second largest number. By the law of the time, he became vice president.

Jefferson took no active part in the new administration because it was largely Federalist. As leader of the opposition, he strengthened the organization of the Democratic-Republican Party. He found strong support among small farmers, frontier settlers, and Northern laborers. His relations with Adams grew more and more strained, until the men broke completely in 1800.

Jefferson presided over the Senate with dignity and skill. To aid deliberations, he wrote his famous *Manual of Parliamentary Practice,* which is still in use.

In 1798, the XYZ Affair aroused great hostility to France. War hysteria led the Federalists to pass the Alien and Sedition Acts. These laws in effect deprived the Democratic-Republicans of freedom of speech and of the press. They aroused much opposition, and Jefferson led the attack against them. He prepared a series of resolutions that were passed by the Kentucky legislature, and his friend Madison prepared similar resolutions for Virginia. These Kentucky and Virginia Resolutions set forth the "compact" theory of the Union and asserted the right of the states to judge when this compact had been broken. They were later used by advocates of nullification and secession.

Election of 1800. The Democratic-Republicans again nominated Jefferson for president in 1800, and named former Senator Aaron Burr of New York for vice president. The Federalist Party renominated President Adams and chose diplomat Charles C. Pinckney of South Carolina as his running mate. The Federalists warned Americans that Jefferson was a revolutionary, an anarchist, and an unbeliever. One Connecticut clergyman wrote: "I do not believe that the Most High will permit a howling atheist to sit at the head of this nation." The Federalists

A MANUAL

OF

PARLIAMENTARY PRACTICE.

FOR THE USE

OF THE

SENATE OF THE UNITED STATES.

BY THOMAS JEFFERSON.

WASHINGTON CITY.

PRINTED BY SAMUEL HARRISON SMITH.

MDCCCI.

Jefferson's Manual of Parliamentary Practice, a handbook of rules for the Senate, was published in 1801. The Senate still uses the manual.

were divided among themselves. Hamilton had quarreled with Adams, and wrote a pamphlet attacking him. This party quarrel helped the Democratic-Republicans, as did the unpopular Alien and Sedition Acts.

Jefferson won the presidency by receiving 73 electoral votes to 65 for Adams. His followers celebrated with bonfires and patriotic speeches. But their spirits fell when they learned that each Democratic-Republican elector had cast one vote for Jefferson and the other for Burr. Although they had clearly intended to elect Jefferson to the presidency and Burr to the vice presidency, the result was a tie. Burr was technically also a candidate for president according to the voting procedures of the time. He failed to withdraw his name as a candidate, and the House of Representatives had to settle the election.

The Federalists still controlled the House because the newly elected Democratic-Republican Congress had not yet taken office. Many Federalist members of Congress preferred Burr to Jefferson because they thought Burr would be more manageable. But Hamilton distrusted Burr even more than he did Jefferson. He threw his influence to the support of Jefferson, who won election on the 36th ballot. The final vote occurred on Feb. 17, 1801. Burr became vice president. This election led to an amendment to the Constitution by which each elector in the Electoral College casts one vote for president and one for vice president (see **Constitution of the United States** [Amendment 12]).

Jefferson's first administration (1801-1805)

The election of 1800, Jefferson insisted, "was as real a revolution in the principles of our government as that of 1776 was in its form." He felt that the Democratic-Republican victory after 12 years of Federalism would save the nation from tyranny.

Jefferson spoke more moderately in his inaugural address than he did during the political campaign. He was the first president to be inaugurated in Washington. Jefferson declared in his speech that "every difference of opinion is not a difference of principle. We have called by different names brethren of the same principle. We are all republicans—we are all federalists." Actually, the government continued much as before. Within a short time, the Democratic-Republicans had adopted, or at least accepted, many ideas of the Federalists.

Jefferson, a poor public speaker, was the first president to send his annual message to Congress, rather than deliver it in person. Later presidents followed this procedure until 1913, when Woodrow Wilson resumed the practice of appearing before Congress.

Life in the White House. The so-called "President's House" was only partly built when Jefferson moved in. He felt somewhat lonely in what he described as "a great stone house, big enough for two emperors, one pope and the grand lama." He kept a pet mockingbird for company. Jefferson's wife had been dead 18$\frac{1}{2}$ years when he became president. His daughter Martha Randolph served as hostess of the White House from time to time. Jefferson's most popular hostess was Dolley Madison, the wife of his secretary of state. Jefferson's grandson, James Randolph, was the first child born in the White House.

Jefferson kept a French steward and chef, but he tried to eliminate some of the formality in White House proto-

Thomas Jefferson Memorial Foundation

Martha Randolph, Jefferson's older daughter, sometimes served as hostess at the White House. Jefferson's wife, Martha Wayles Skelton, died $18\frac{1}{2}$ years before he became president.

Highlights of Jefferson's administration

1801	(June 10) Tripoli declared war on America.
1802	(July 4) The U.S. Military Academy opened.
1803	(Feb. 24) The Supreme Court decided the case of *Marbury v. Madison.*
1803	(March 3) John Pickering became the first federal judge to be impeached.
1803	(May 2) The Louisiana Territory was purchased from France, by a treaty predated April 30.
1804	(May 14) The Lewis and Clark Expedition set out for the Northwest.
1804	(Sept. 25) Amendment 12 to the Constitution was adopted.
1805	(June 4) The United States and Tripoli signed a peace treaty.
1807	(Dec. 22) Congress passed the Embargo Act against international commerce.
1808	(Jan. 1) The act prohibiting the importation of black slaves became law.
1809	(March 1) The Non-Intercourse Act was passed, banning trade with France and Britain.

col. He began the practice of having guests shake hands with the president instead of bowing. He also placed dinner guests at a round table so that everyone would feel equally important. Always interested in architecture, Jefferson developed some ideas for the addition of east and west terraces and a north portico to the White House. He employed Benjamin H. Latrobe to carry out these ideas.

New policies. Jefferson believed that government should play the smallest possible role in national life. With the help of Secretary of the Treasury Albert Gallatin, he began a policy of strict economy. The government sharply reduced department expenditures, especially those for the Army and Navy. It made substantial payments on the national debt. It repealed excise taxes, which had aroused opposition under the Federalists.

The administration also reversed other Federalist policies. It repealed the Naturalization Act. The Alien Friends Act and the Sedition Act were not renewed. The Alien Enemies Act was greatly amended.

Jefferson believed that appointments to federal jobs should be based on merit. But Federalists held all the offices, and he quickly discovered that vacancies "by death are few; by resignation none." He removed some Feder-

alists, and generally appointed Democratic-Republicans to vacancies. By the end of Jefferson's second term, his party held most federal offices. In effect, Jefferson's actions foreshadowed the spoils system.

The courts. The administration asked Congress to repeal the Judiciary Act of 1801. This act had allowed President Adams to make more than 200 "midnight appointments" of judges and other court officials just before he left office. Some of these judges had no commissions,

Vice presidents and Cabinet

Vice president	Aaron Burr
	George Clinton (1805)
Secretary of state	James Madison
Secretary of the treasury .	Samuel Dexter
	Albert Gallatin (1801)
Secretary of war	Henry Dearborn
Attorney general	Levi Lincoln
	John Breckinridge (1805)
	Caesar A. Rodney (1807)
Secretary of the Navy	Robert Smith

Louisiana Historical Society

A ceremony honoring the Louisiana Purchase took place in New Orleans in 1803. The United States had bought French territory between the Mississippi River and the Rocky Mountains.

no duties, and no salaries. Jefferson told them to consider their appointments as never having been made.

William Marbury was one of 42 justices of the peace whom Adams had appointed to five-year terms in the District of Columbia. He applied to the Supreme Court for a writ of mandamus, ordering Secretary of State James Madison to deliver his commission. Marbury did this in accordance with the Judiciary Act of 1789, which gave the Supreme Court power to issue such writs. Marbury's action led to one of the most important Supreme Court decisions in American history, that of *Marbury v. Madison* in 1803. In its decision, the court declared unconstitutional the section of the Judiciary Act of 1789 that gave the court power to issue writs of mandamus. Therefore, the court refused to force Madison to deliver Marbury's commission.

On the surface, Chief Justice John Marshall's decision should have pleased Jefferson and his fellow Democratic-Republicans. The decision meant that the Jefferson administration did not have to deliver commissions to the "midnight judges" appointed by the Federalists. But the Democratic-Republicans were disturbed by the idea that the Supreme Court could declare unconstitutional a law passed by Congress. This principle placed a powerful weapon in the hands of the courts, which the Federalists still controlled. Many Democratic-Republicans feared that the Supreme Court would use its power to help the Federalists.

The Democratic-Republicans tried impeachment as a way of checking the federal courts. First they impeached John Pickering, a New Hampshire judge who was a victim of insanity. After the Senate had removed Pickering from office, the House brought impeachment charges against Justice Samuel Chase of the Supreme Court. The House charged that he had criticized the Jefferson administration unfairly. The Senate acquitted him, much to Jefferson's disappointment. This helped establish the precedent that political changes do not affect the tenure of judges. See **Impeachment** (History).

War with Tripoli. Ever since Jefferson had been minister to France, he had urged that the United States should act against the Barbary *corsairs* (sea raiders) of North Africa. These corsairs attacked trading ships, demanding tribute and ransom from all countries. The United States had paid Tripoli, the most unruly of the Barbary States, $2 million in 10 years. In 1801, Tripoli opened war on American shipping because it wanted more tribute money. The little United States Navy blockaded Tripoli's ports, bombarded fortresses, and eventually forced Tripoli to respect the American flag. The war with Tripoli did not end troubles with the Barbary States, but it brought prestige to the United States Navy.

Western expansion. Jefferson had shown great interest in the West since his days in Congress. He obtained a grant from Congress early in 1803 for exploration of the region all the way to the Pacific Ocean. He sent Meriwether Lewis and William Clark to the headwaters of the Missouri River, then across the Rockies to the Pacific.

The population of the Northwest Territory grew rapidly. Ohio joined the Union in 1803 as the 17th state. In 1804, the government encouraged western settlement by cutting in half, from 320 to 160 acres (130 to 65 hectares), the minimum number of acres of western

land that could be bought. Anyone with $80 in cash could make the first payment on a frontier farm.

The Louisiana Purchase ranks as one of Jefferson's greatest achievements. The Louisiana Territory, a vast region between the Mississippi River and the Rocky Mountains, had been transferred from France to Spain in 1762. Jefferson learned in 1801 that Spain planned to cede the area back to France. When Louisiana belonged to Spain, it offered no threat to the United States. Under Napoleon, it might block American expansion and threaten American democracy.

In 1803, Jefferson obtained $2 million from Congress for "extraordinary expenses." He sent James Monroe to Paris to help the American minister, Robert Livingston, negotiate with France. Jefferson hoped to buy New Orleans and the Floridas. He at least wanted to get a perpetual guarantee of free navigation of the Mississippi and various commercial privileges at New Orleans.

Before Monroe reached Paris, Livingston proposed a modest purchase of New Orleans. Talleyrand, the French foreign minister, astounded Livingston by asking: "What would you give for the whole of Louisiana?" After Monroe arrived, he and Livingston quickly struck a bargain. For the province of Louisiana, the United States paid $11,250,000 and gave up claims on France estimated at $3,750,000. So, for about $15 million, the government gained control of the Mississippi River and almost doubled the nation's size.

Jefferson was amazed when he learned about the purchase. He doubted whether the government had a right under the Constitution to add this vast new territory to the Union. But his doubts did not keep him from submitting the treaty to the Senate, which ratified it by a vote of 24 to 7. Jefferson later said that he had "stretched the Constitution till it cracked."

Election of 1804. There seemed little doubt that a prospering nation would reelect Jefferson in 1804. The Democratic-Republicans nominated Governor George Clinton of New York for vice president.

But a group of northeastern Federalists feared that the purchase of Louisiana would weaken New England's position and influence. They felt that the time had come to break up the Union and sought an ally in vice president Burr. The plotters wanted to elect Burr governor of New York so he could help take that state out of the Union along with New England. Alexander Hamilton helped to defeat the plot.

The election of 1804 completely defeated the Federalists. Even New England, except for Connecticut, went Democratic-Republican. The final electoral count gave 162 votes to Jefferson and only 14 to the Federalist candidate, Charles C. Pinckney, a lawyer from Charleston, South Carolina. For votes by state, see **Electoral College** (table).

Topic for study

Look at the Quotations from Jefferson *feature in this article. Prepare a report on some of Jefferson's views that you agree with and explain. Comment on any of his views with which you disagree.*

Quotations from Jefferson

The following quotations come from some of Thomas Jefferson's speeches and writings.

Ignorance is preferable to error: and he is less remote from the truth who believes nothing, than he who believes what is wrong.

Notes on the State of Virginia (1784-1785)

… were it left to me to decide whether we should have a government without newspapers, or newspapers without a government, I should not hesitate a moment to prefer the latter.

Letter to Colonel Edward Carrington, an American statesman, Jan. 16, 1787

I hold it that a little rebellion now and then is a good thing, and as necessary in the political world as storms in the physical.

Letter to the American statesman James Madison, Jan. 30, 1787

Determine never to be idle. No person will have occasion to complain of the want of time who never loses any. It is wonderful how much may be done if we are always doing.

Letter to his daughter Martha, May 5, 1787

The tree of liberty must be refreshed from time to time with the blood of patriots and tyrants. It is its natural manure.

Letter to Colonel William Stephens Smith, an American diplomat, Nov. 13, 1787

… delay is preferable to error.

Letter to President George Washington, May 16, 1792

… unmerited abuse wounds, while unmerited praise has not the power to heal.

Letter to Edward Rutledge, an American political leader, Dec. 27, 1796

The second office of the government is honorable and easy, the first is but a splendid misery.

Letter to the American statesman Elbridge Gerry comparing the vice presidency with the presidency, May 13, 1797

… I have sworn upon the altar of God, eternal hostility against every form of tyranny over the mind of man.

Letter to Benjamin Rush, American physician and political leader, Sept. 23, 1800

All, too, will bear in mind this sacred principle, that though the will of the majority is in all cases to prevail, that will, to be rightful, must be reasonable; that the minority possess their equal rights, which equal laws must protect, and to violate which would be oppression.

First Inaugural Address, March 4, 1801

… error of opinion may be tolerated where reason is left free to combat it.

First Inaugural Address, March 4, 1801

Sometimes it is said that man cannot be trusted with the government of himself. Can he, then, be trusted with the government of others? Or have we found angels in the forms of kings to govern him? Let history answer this question.

First Inaugural Address, March 4, 1801

1. Never put off till to-morrow what you can do to-day.
2. Never trouble another for what you can do yourself.
3. Never spend your money before you have it.
4. Never buy what you do not want, because it is cheap; it will be dear to you.
5. Pride costs us more than hunger, thirst and cold.
6. We never repent of having eaten too little.
7. Nothing is troublesome that we do willingly.
8. How much pain have cost us the evils which have never happened.
9. Take things always by their smooth handle.
10. When angry, count ten, before you speak; if very angry, an hundred.

Letter to his namesake Thomas Jefferson Smith, Feb. 21, 1825

Resistance to tyrants is obedience to God.

Saying found among Jefferson's papers, date unknown

Jefferson's second administration (1805-1809)

Jefferson's second term began, as he later put it, "without a cloud on the horizon." But a storm soon began to gather.

The Burr conspiracy. Aaron Burr, already discredited in politics, had further damaged his reputation by killing Alexander Hamilton in a duel in July 1804. He then became involved in a mysterious scheme, the purpose of which is still not clear. He may have wanted to take the West away from the United States, or perhaps to conquer the Spanish Southwest. In any case, Burr tried unsuccessfully to get support from the British, French, or Spanish against his own government. He then raised a small military force of his own. In 1806, Burr set off down the Ohio River for New Orleans, hoping to gather recruits along the way. General James Wilkinson, the governor of the Louisiana Territory, had encouraged Burr to expect his support. But he decided to expose Burr's plot and wrote to Jefferson about a "deep, dark, wicked, and widespread conspiracy."

Jefferson had Burr captured, taken to Richmond, and tried for treason. To the disgust of Jefferson and others, Chief Justice Marshall interpreted the charge of treason so narrowly that the jury had to acquit Burr. See **Burr, Aaron.**

The struggle for neutrality. War had broken out between the United Kingdom and France in May 1803. Jefferson found that his chief tasks were to keep the United States out of the war, and at the same time uphold the country's rights as a neutral.

The United Kingdom and France were destroying each other's merchant shipping. One result was that a large part of the West Indies-Europe trade fell into American hands. American shipbuilding and commerce grew rapidly, and thousands of sailors were needed. Most of these men came from New England, but many had deserted from British ships. The United Kingdom, desperately needing seamen, began stopping American ships on the high seas and removing sailors suspected of being British. But it was hard to tell British and Americans apart. Thousands of Americans were seized and forced into the British Navy.

The struggle in Europe soon became so intense that neither side cared much about the rights of neutral nations. In the Berlin and Milan decrees of 1806 and 1807, Napoleon announced his intention to seize all neutral ships bound to or from a British port. The United Kingdom issued a series of orders in council which blockaded all ports in the possession of France or its allies. In practice, this meant that the United Kingdom would try to seize any ship bound for the European continent, while the French would do their best to seize ships sailing almost anywhere else.

The crowning outrage occurred in June 1807, when the British warship *Leopard* launched an unprovoked attack on the American ship *Chesapeake*. The *Leopard* fired on the *Chesapeake* after the captain of the American vessel refused to let the British search his ship for deserters. This incident almost brought the two nations to war. Jefferson later wrote: "The affair of the *Chesapeake* put war into my hand. I had only to open it and let havoc loose."

Commercial retaliation. Jefferson knew that the

United States was not prepared for war. In any case, it would have been hard to decide whether to fight France or the United Kingdom. Jefferson believed that he could bring the warring nations to reason by closing American markets to them, and not selling them any American supplies. In 1807, he forced the Embargo Act through Congress. This law prohibited exports from the United States and barred American ships from sailing into foreign ports. The embargo injured the United States far more than it did either the United Kingdom or France. Ships lay idle, sailors and shipbuilders lost their jobs, and exports piled up in warehouses. Many Americans evaded the law, and smuggling flourished.

The government had to pass additional laws to increase the nation's coastal defenses and to enforce the embargo. Jefferson, who found himself favoring more and more federal control, commented: "This embargo law is certainly the most embarrassing one we have ever had to execute." After 14 months, it became clear that the embargo would force no concessions from either the United Kingdom or France. Public clamor against the measure grew overwhelming, and Congress repealed it in March 1809 by passing the milder Non-Intercourse Act.

Many people urged Jefferson to run for reelection again in 1808. But he chose to follow George Washington's example and retire from office after two terms. Jefferson made it clear that he expected James Madison to be the next president. Madison won election easily.

Later years

Jefferson was 65 when he retired from the presidency in 1809. He felt free at last to cultivate those "tranquil pursuits of science" for which, he said, nature had intended him. "Never did a prisoner, released from his chains, feel such relief as I shall on shaking off the shackles of power," he wrote.

The sage of Monticello. Leisure gave Jefferson a chance to enjoy his countless and varied interests. He turned to music, architecture, chemical experiments, and the study of religion, philosophy, law, and education. During his long absence, Monticello had run down, and Jefferson worked energetically to repair the damages of long neglect. He also experimented with new crops and new farming techniques, and improved his flower and herb gardens.

Jefferson carried on an immense correspondence with people in all parts of the world. He improved a copying device called the *polygraph,* which made file copies of the many letters he wrote. He entertained an endless stream of guests who came to pay their respects. In 1811, Jefferson was reconciled with John Adams, and the two men renewed their old friendship. Their letters ranged widely over the fields of history, politics, philosophy, religion, and science. The remarkable correspondence continued until they died—both on the same day, July 4, 1826.

Jefferson had withdrawn from politics, but he was consulted constantly on public affairs. Madison and Monroe, his successors in the White House, frequently sought his advice. Jefferson had little money. He had made additions to Monticello, entertained lavishly, and supported members of his family. In 1815, he sold his library of more than 6,400 volumes to Congress to replace the books that the British had destroyed when they burned the Capitol during the War of 1812 (1812-1815). Public contributions aided him in later years, but Monticello passed out of the hands of his family after his death.

University founder. Jefferson's most important contributions in his later years were probably in the field of education. As a young legislator, he had worked for reform of Virginia's system of public education. Later he had tried to improve William and Mary College. In time, he became convinced that the state needed an entirely new university.

After he returned to Monticello, Jefferson worked constantly to create the University of Virginia. He projected his character, interests, and talents in planning a university "based on the illimitable freedom of the human mind to explore and to expose every subject susceptible of its contemplation." Jefferson reorganized the curriculum, hired the faculty, and selected the library books. Jefferson also drew the plans for the buildings and supervised their construction. As a result of his efforts, scholars from other countries were persuaded to teach at the university. In March 1825, Jefferson had the joy of seeing the University of Virginia open with 40 students.

But his strength was failing. On July 4, 1826, just 50 years after the adoption of the Declaration of Independence, Jefferson died. He was buried beside his wife at Monticello. The inscription that Jefferson wrote for his grave marker reads: "Here was buried Thomas Jefferson, Author of the Declaration of American Independence, of the Statute of Virginia for religious freedom, & Father of the University of Virginia." These were accomplishments that he ranked higher than being president of the United States. Noble E. Cunningham, Jr.

See also **Burr, Aaron; President of the United States.**

Outline

I. Early life
   A. Boyhood
   B. Education
   C. Lawyer
   D. Jefferson's family
   E. Jefferson and Sally Hemings

II. Colonial statesman
   A. Revolutionary leader   D. Governor
   B. The Declaration of   E. Congressman
      Independence   F. Minister to France
   C. Virginia lawmaker

III. National statesman
   A. Secretary of state   C. Election of 1800
   B. Vice president

IV. Jefferson's first administration (1801-1805)
   A. Life in the White House   E. Western expansion
   B. New policies   F. The Louisiana Purchase
   C. The courts   G. Election of 1804
   D. War with Tripoli

V. Jefferson's second administration (1805-1809)
   A. The Burr conspiracy
   B. The struggle for neutrality
   C. Commercial retaliation

VI. Later years
   A. The sage of Monticello
   B. University founder

Questions

What three achievements are noted on Jefferson's grave marker?
How did Jefferson's political enemy help him become president in 1801? Why did he do this?

On what occasion did Jefferson "stretch the Constitution till it cracked"?

What is meant by *Jeffersonian democracy*?

How did Jefferson help advance democracy in Virginia?

In what case did the Supreme Court gain great power during Jefferson's first administration?

On what basis did Jefferson argue that Americans owed no allegiance to the British Parliament?

How did Jefferson's views affect the adoption of the Constitution? Why did he lose prestige as Virginia governor?

How did Jefferson's philosophy of government conflict with that of Alexander Hamilton?

Additional resources

Bedini, Silvio A. *Thomas Jefferson: Statesman of Science.* Macmillan, 1990.

Cunningham, Noble E., Jr. *In Pursuit of Reason: The Life of Thomas Jefferson.* La. State Univ. Pr., 1987. *The Process of Government Under Jefferson.* Princeton, 1978.

Giblin, James C. *Thomas Jefferson.* Scholastic, 1994. Younger readers.

Malone, Dumas. *Jefferson and His Time.* 6 vols. Little, Brown, 1948-1981.

Mayer, David N. *The Constitutional Thought of Thomas Jefferson.* Univ. Pr. of Va., 1994.

Meltzer, Milton. *Thomas Jefferson.* Watts, 1991.

Morris, Jeffrey. *The Jefferson Way.* Lerner, 1994. Younger readers.

Randall, Willard S. *Thomas Jefferson.* Henry Holt, 1993.

Web sites

Thomas Jefferson
http://www.whitehouse.gov/WH/glimpse/presidents/html/tj3.html
Official White House biography of Thomas Jefferson. Includes a link to a biography of Martha Wayles Skelton Jefferson.

Thomas Jefferson in Williamsburg
http://www.history.org/people/bios/biojeff1.htm
Thomas Jefferson's experiences in Williamsburg as student, burgess, and governor. The text provides links to people, events, and places that were important to Jefferson during that time. The site is hosted by the Colonial Williamsburg Foundation.

Thomas Jefferson Timeline
http://memory.loc.gov/ammem/mtjhtml/mtjtime1.html
The Library of Congress presents a chronological account of Jefferson's life.

Tilden, Samuel Jones (1814-1886), was the Democratic nominee in the 1876 presidential election, the most disputed in United States history. Despite winning more popular votes than his Republican opponent, Rutherford B. Hayes, Tilden lost by one electoral vote.

Tilden was born in New Lebanon, New York. He earned a law degree in 1841 from the University of the City of New York. In 1846, he served as a Democratic member of the New York state Assembly. In 1866, he became state party chairman. In that post, he led the attack on the "Tweed Ring." This group of politicians, led by William M. Tweed, had stolen millions of dollars from New York City through improvement schemes.

In 1874, Tilden won election as governor of New York, running as a reformer. In the 1876 presidential election, he received a majority of the popular votes, but the Democrats and Republicans disagreed over who should receive 20 of the 369 electoral votes. An Electoral Commission created by Congress awarded the disputed electoral votes to Hayes, whom Congress then declared the winner (see **Electoral Commission**).

James E. Sefton

Web site

Samuel J. Tilden
http://library.thinkquest.org/12587/contents/personalities/stilden/sjt.html
Biographical information about Samuel Tilden.

Topic for study

Compare the bitterly contested election of 2000, between George W. Bush and Al Gore, with the disputed election of 1876, between Rutherford B. Hayes and Samuel J. Tilden. Describe aspects of the elections that were similar and those that were different. Summarize the similarities and differences in a table.

It's a fact

Samuel J. Tilden, the loser of the disputed 1876 election, became a multimillionaire by investing in railroads and mining. In his will, he left a large part of his fortune to help establish the New York Public Library.

President Rutherford B. Hayes, a Republican, began his presidency with little backing after his victory in the disputed election of 1876. Democrats charged that he had "stolen" the election. Hayes himself wrote that he had "few supporters in Congress and among the newspapers." By the time he left office in 1881, however, most Americans respected him for his sincerity and honesty.

Lucy Hayes was the first president's wife to have a college degree. She graduated in 1850 from the Wesleyan Female College in Cincinnati, Ohio.

President Thomas Jefferson's most popular White House hostess was Dolley Madison, the wife of his secretary of state. Jefferson's wife had died more than 18 years before he became president in 1801.

Presidents Thomas Jefferson and John Adams carried on a wide-ranging correspondence after they left the White House. Their letters dealt with history, politics, philosophy, religion, and science. The correspondence continued until they died—both on the same day, July 4, 1826.

Section Five

The 2000 U.S. Presidential Election

The 2000 presidential election in the United States began with hard-fought primary elections. In time, Texas Governor George W. Bush won the Republican Party nomination for president, and Vice President Al Gore won the Democratic Party nomination. The presidential election campaign was also intense. After a number of legal battles, Bush emerged as the winner of the election.

The final results are reflected in many of the 24 *World Book* articles in this section, including full-length biographies of Bush and Gore. Also included are articles on the other candidates in the presidential election and their parties, along with new maps, graphs, and articles on other notable figures. In this section, you will learn:

❏ *why George W. Bush became linked in U.S. history with his father.*

❏ *why Al Gore became associated in U.S. history with Andrew Jackson, Samuel J. Tilden, and Grover Cleveland.*

❏ *what are the seven basic roles of the president.*

❏ *how John Tyler established the right of the vice president to succeed to the presidency on the death of the chief executive.*

Baker, James Addison, III (1930-), served as United States secretary of state under President George H. W. Bush from 1989 to 1992. As secretary, Baker helped form the coalition of countries that fought Iraq in the Persian Gulf War (1991). After the war, he helped coordinate relief efforts for Kurdish refugees in Iraq. The Kurds had fled their homes in Iraq after the Iraqi military put down a rebellion there. Baker promoted peace between Arab nations and Israel. In 2000, Baker represented the presidential campaign of Bush's son George W. Bush as an observer to a vote recount in Florida. The 2000 election was one of the closest presidential races in United States history.

© Dirck Halstead, Gamma/Liaison

James Baker

Baker served as secretary of the treasury under President Ronald Reagan from 1985 to 1988. In this post, Baker led the Reagan Administration's revision of the federal tax system.

Baker was born in Houston. He graduated from Princeton University in 1952 and from the University of Texas Law School in 1957. Baker practiced law in Houston from 1957 until 1975, when President Gerald R. Ford named him undersecretary of commerce. From 1981 to 1985, Baker served as Reagan's chief of staff. Baker managed President George Bush's campaigns in 1980, 1988, and 1992 and served as Bush's chief of staff in 1992 and 1993.   William J. Eaton

Bauer, Gary Lee (1946-), a conservative activist, was a candidate for the Republican presidential nomination in 2000. He dropped out of the race in early 2000 for lack of voter support in the primary elections.

Bauer was born in Covington, Kentucky. He earned a bachelor's degree from Georgetown College in Georgetown, Kentucky, in 1968 and a law degree from Georgetown University Law School, Washington, D.C., in 1973.

Bauer began working for a Washington trade association in 1973. In 1980, he worked on Ronald Reagan's successful campaign for the U.S. presidency. During Reagan's two terms in office, Bauer held various positions in the administration, including undersecretary of education and adviser on domestic policy. From 1988 to 1999, Bauer headed the Family Research Council (FRC), a small lobbying group. Under his leadership, the FRC grew into an influential conservative organization, known for its promotion of traditional family values. In early 2000, Bauer became chairman of the Campaign for Working Families, a political action committee he formed in 1996.

Bradley, Bill (1943-), a New Jersey Democrat, served in the United States Senate from 1979 to 1997. He did not run for reelection in 1996. In the Senate, Bradley was a leading supporter of tax reform. He first gained fame as an outstanding basketball player. In 1999, Bradley began campaigning for the 2000 Democratic presidential nomination, but he dropped out of the race in early 2000.

William Warren Bradley was born in Crystal City, Missouri. He won all-America honors in basketball at Prince-

ton University. After graduating from Princeton, he accepted a Rhodes Scholarship to Oxford University in England. Bradley began a professional basketball career in 1967 with the New York Knickerbockers of the National Basketball Association as a forward. He retired from basketball in 1977.

© Nik Kleinbere, Picture Group

Bill Bradley

As a U.S. senator, Bradley drew national attention for coauthoring the Bradley-Gephardt "fair tax" bill, which called for fewer income tax brackets and elimination of most tax deductions. These concepts were reflected in the Tax Reform Act of 1986. Bradley also supported the U.S. Strategic Petroleum Reserve, an oil stockpile designed to prevent future U.S. oil shortages.   Guy Halverson

Buchanan, Patrick Joseph (1938-), is a columnist, broadcaster, and former presidential adviser known for his conservative political views. He was a Reform Party candidate for United States president in 2000 but received less than 1 percent of the popular vote. He had campaigned for the Republican nomination in 1992 and 1996 but failed to win the nomination in either year.

Buchanan was born in Washington, D.C. He earned a bachelor's degree from Georgetown University in 1961 and a master's from Columbia University's School of Journalism in 1962. He then worked for the *St. Louis Globe-Democrat*. In 1966, he became an executive assistant to former U.S. Vice President Richard M. Nixon, who was preparing to run for president in 1968. After Nixon was elected, Buchanan served him as a special assistant and speechwriter and, later, as a special consultant. After Nixon resigned in 1974, Buchanan worked for President Gerald R. Ford. From 1985 to 1987, Buchanan was a communications director for President Ronald Reagan.

From 1975 to early 1999, Buchanan wrote a syndicated newspaper column of political and social commentary and acted as a commentator on radio and television talk shows. In 1993, Buchanan founded The American Cause, an educational foundation dedicated to promoting conservative political principles.

It's a fact

The popular vote in the 2000 presidential election was close, but not the closest in United States history. Al Gore won the popular vote in 2000 over George W. Bush by a margin of about 0.5 percent. The closest popular vote in a presidential election occurred in 1880, when James A. Garfield won 48.27 percent of the vote to Winfield Scott Hancock's 48.25 percent, a margin of 0.02 percent. For other close races, see the table *Closest elections in the popular vote* later in this section.

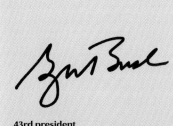

**43rd president
of the United States 2001-**

Clinton
42nd president
1993-2001
Democrat

Bush
43rd president
2001-
Republican

**Richard B.
Cheney**
Vice president
2001-

© Bob Daemmrich, Corbis/Sygma

Bush, George Walker (1946-   ), was elected president of the United States in 2000 in one of the closest presidential elections in U.S. history. Bush, a Republican and the governor of Texas, received a smaller number of popular votes in the election than his Democratic opponent, Vice President Al Gore. But Bush received more votes in the Electoral College. However, the outcome was in doubt for weeks after the election. It was not clear which candidate had carried Florida, where the vote was extremely close. Delays resulted from recounts of Florida ballots and court challenges to the recounts. Five weeks after the election, following a decision by the U.S. Supreme Court to halt the recounts, Gore conceded the election to Bush.

Bush's election marked the second time in U.S. history that the son of a former president was elected president. Bush's father, George Herbert Walker Bush (1924-   ), served as president from 1989 to 1993. The only other father and son to be elected president were John Adams and John Quincy Adams, who held office from 1797 to 1801 and from 1825 to 1829, respectively.

Bush was elected at a time of economic prosperity and low unemployment in the United States. Many Americans recognized that not everyone shared in the prosperity, however. They were concerned with high taxes and with the growing number of homeless people. They were also alarmed by the increase in violent crimes committed by children. Many were concerned about what they saw as a decline in moral values, particularly among the country's leaders.

During his presidential campaign, Bush emphasized

what he called "compassionate conservatism." He proposed to cut taxes and to use the nation's prosperity to help those in need. He pointed to his record as governor of Texas, which included reducing taxes, initiating school reform, and strengthening the state's criminal justice system.

Bush enjoys outdoor activities, especially fishing, hunting, and playing golf. He also likes country music. He wrote an autobiography, *A Charge to Keep* (1999).

Early life

Family background. George Walker Bush was born on July 6, 1946, in New Haven, Connecticut. His parents were living in New Haven while his father was a student at Yale University.

Bush's father, George H. W. Bush, grew up in Connecticut. After achieving financial success as an oilman in Texas, he turned to politics. His father, Prescott Sheldon Bush, had been a U.S. senator from Connecticut. George H. W. Bush served in the U.S. House of Representatives from 1967 to 1971 as a Republican from Texas. During the 1970's, he served successively as U.S. ambassador to the United Nations, U.S. envoy to China, and head of the Central Intelligence Agency. He was vice president of the United States under President Ronald

Important dates in Bush's life

1946 (July 6) Born in New Haven, Connecticut.
1968 Graduated from Yale University.
1968-1970 Served in the Texas Air National Guard.
1975 Graduated from Harvard Business School.
1977 (Nov. 5) Married Laura Welch.
1994 Elected governor of Texas.
1998 Reelected governor of Texas.
2000 Elected president of the United States.

Bill Minutaglio, the contributor of this article, is the author of First Son: George W. Bush and the Bush Family Dynasty.

Reagan from 1981 to 1989. He was U.S. president from 1989 to 1993.

George Walker Bush's mother, Barbara Pierce Bush (1925-   ), grew up in New York. Her father was the publisher of *McCall's* and *Redbook* magazines.

Barbara Pierce was 16 years old and George Herbert Walker Bush was 17 when the two met at a Christmas dance in Greenwich, Connecticut, in 1941. They married in 1945 while Bush was on leave from active duty in the U.S. Navy during World War II.

George Walker Bush was the first of the couple's six children. The second child, born in 1949, was Pauline Robinson, called Robin. She died of leukemia in 1953 at the age of 3. Young George also had three brothers— John, called Jeb (1953-   ), Neil (1955-   ), and Marvin (1956-   )—and another sister, Dorothy (1959-   ).

Boyhood. Bush grew up in Midland, in western Texas. His parents moved to the state from Connecticut when he was 2 years old. His father wanted to get involved in the booming oil business.

Bush was 7 years old when his little sister, Robin, died. He and his parents were grief-stricken. His parents later told friends that young George helped them deal with their sorrow. George tried to be cheerful and funny and make them laugh. As a child, he was known for his love of mischief and his joking remarks.

George Bush Presidential Library

As an airman in the Texas Air National Guard, Bush learned to pilot an airplane. He entered the National Guard in 1968, during the Vietnam War, after he graduated from Yale University.

School life. Bush attended Sam Houston Elementary School in Midland, then went on to San Jacinto Junior High. He spent one year, seventh grade, at San Jacinto.

In 1959, the Bushes moved to Houston. For the next two years, George attended Kinkaid School, a private academy. He was a member of the football team, and he was remembered as making friends easily.

Bush spent his final years of high school at the exclusive preparatory school his father had attended, Phillips Academy in Andover, Massachusetts. His grades were average, but his lively personality and quick tongue won him attention. He played basketball and baseball and was the head football cheerleader in his senior year.

College and military service

In 1964, Bush began his studies at Yale University, the college his father had attended. He majored in history. Classmates found him friendly and fun-loving. He enjoyed parties and sports, especially rugby, and was elected president of his fraternity, Delta Kappa Epsilon. He also belonged to Yale's elite secret society, Skull & Bones.

In 1968, as Bush was finishing up at Yale, the United States was deeply divided over the country's involvement in the Vietnam War (1957-1975). Just before college graduation, Bush applied and was accepted as an airman in the Texas Air National Guard. His commitment included 53 weeks of full-time training to become a pilot. He graduated in December 1969. He then continued flight training on the F-102 jet fighter. Bush attempted to sign up for a program that rotated pilots to Vietnam but was not accepted. He was not eligible for the program because he had not logged enough flight hours.

Business school

Bush completed his active duty with the Texas Air National Guard in 1970. He graduated from flight training school with a rank of lieutenant. In 1973, he entered Harvard Business School, where he received an M.B.A. degree in 1975.

Bush later described the three years between com-

George Bush Presidential Library

Bush as a baby is held by his parents, Barbara Pierce Bush and George H. W. Bush. George W. Bush was born in New Haven, Connecticut, where his father was a student at Yale University.

pleting active duty and entering business school as his "nomadic" period. He continued to fulfill his part-time commitment to the National Guard, but he did not find lasting, full-time employment. During this period, he applied for admission to law school but was not accepted. He was a management trainee with an agricultural firm. He worked on a political campaign in Alabama for a Republican candidate seeking a Senate seat. He also served as a counselor in a Houston program for disadvantaged youngsters.

Congressional candidate

Bush returned to Midland after graduating from Harvard Business School, and he began working in the oil business. In 1977, the congressional representative for the district that included Midland announced his retirement. Bush decided to seek the Republican nomination for the post.

Bush quickly assembled a campaign team, mostly made up of friends who volunteered to help him, and began raising funds. He campaigned tirelessly across the sprawling district. He won the nomination, but he lost the election to his Democratic opponent. The opponent, a native Texan, portrayed Bush as an "outsider." However, Bush received 47 percent of the vote in a district that had never elected a Republican to Congress.

Bush's family

In mid-1977, shortly after announcing his candidacy for Congress, Bush attended a cookout at the home of friends. There, he met Laura Welch (Nov. 4, 1946-   ). The couple started dating, and they married about three months later, on Nov. 5, 1977. The newlyweds put off their honeymoon to focus on Bush's campaign for office.

Laura Welch Bush, a native Texan, grew up in Midland as an only child. Her father, Harold, was a building

George Bush Presidential Library

Bush's career in the oil business included forming his own oil exploration firm in the late 1970's. He merged the firm with another company in the early 1980's when petroleum prices fell.

contractor, and her mother served as his bookkeeper. Laura was known as a reserved, quiet person who loved to read. She earned a bachelor's degree in education from Southern Methodist University and a master's degree in library science from the University of Texas at Austin. She was working as a librarian when she met Bush, and she had been a schoolteacher.

The Bushes had twin daughters, Barbara and Jenna. The children were born in 1981 and were named for their grandmothers.

Business career

Oil exploration. In the late 1970's, Bush set up an oil exploration company, Arbusto Energy Incorporated, later called Bush Exploration Company. The company searched for potentially profitable oil and gas fields. After his election loss, Bush turned his energies to running his company.

In the early 1980's, oil prices fell, and many oil companies went out of business. Bush merged his company with another small oil firm, Spectrum 7 Energy Corporation. Bush became Spectrum's chief executive officer.

The downturn in the energy field continued, however, and Spectrum began to falter. In 1986, the struggling

George Bush Presidential Library

The young Bush family lived in Midland, Texas, while Bush worked in the oil business. Bush's family includes his wife, Laura Welch Bush, and their daughters, Barbara, *left,* and Jenna.

firm was taken over by Harken Oil and Gas, Incorporated, later known as Harken Energy Corporation. Bush received Harken stock for his Spectrum shares and became a member of Harken's board of directors.

In the late 1980's, Bush returned to politics. His father, then vice president of the United States, was campaigning for president in the 1988 election. The younger Bush and his family moved to Washington, D.C., to help manage his father's political campaign. After the election, which his father won, Bush and his family returned to Texas and settled in Dallas.

In 1990, Bush sold most of his shares in Harken at a profit shortly before the company declared huge losses. The timing of the sale later prompted charges that Bush had known about Harken's poor financial condition. Bush said he was not aware of the firm's financial difficulties when he sold his shares. An investigation into the matter by the Securities and Exchange Commission ended in 1993 with no charges brought against Bush.

By the time Bush sold his Harken shares, he had already become involved in a new career. He was a part owner of a baseball team.

Baseball ownership. In late 1988, Bush learned that the Texas Rangers baseball team was for sale. The American League team was based in the nearby city of Arlington. Bush and a group of investors bought the team in 1989. Bush became a managing general partner of the team. He was an enthusiastic spectator at Ranger games, and he worked to promote the team and increase attendance. Bush helped win support for a controversial plan to have a new stadium built for the team. He was involved during the planning and construction stages of the new facility, called the Ballpark in Arlington. The stadium opened in April 1994. Later that year, Bush was elected to his first political office, and he stepped down from his post with the team.

Governor of Texas

Campaign. Bush's father lost his bid for reelection as president and left the White House in 1993. That year, the younger Bush announced his candidacy for governor of Texas. At the same time, his brother Jeb was campaigning for governor of Florida.

Bush's opponent was Ann W. Richards, the state's

AP/Wide World
Campaigning for governor of Texas, Bush talks with supporters. He won the Texas governorship by a wide margin in 1994 and was reelected by an even wider margin in 1998.

popular governor, who was seeking a second term. During the campaign, Richards said Bush was running on his family name. Bush made no personal attacks against Richards. Instead, he criticized the governor's record, and he focused on presenting his conservative views. He supported welfare reform. He called for *autonomy* (self-government) and increased state funding for public school districts. He stressed a need for stronger criminal laws, particularly against juvenile offenders. He promised reform of the Texas civil justice system, which was clogged with unimportant lawsuits. Bush won the election by a wide margin, receiving about 54 percent of the vote. His brother lost in Florida.

First term. As governor, Bush earned high approval ratings. He worked to get legislation passed on his proposed reforms. Bush's lieutenant governor was a Demo-

George Bush Presidential Library
In the Texas Rangers locker room, Bush and his father chat with broadcaster and former baseball star Joe Morgan. George W. Bush was part owner of the Rangers from 1989 to 1994.

George Bush Presidential Library
Fishing is a favorite pastime of the Bushes. Shown here on a 1980's fishing trip, *from left to right,* are Bush's father, George H. W. Bush, then vice president; Bush; and Bush's brother Jeb.

Bush and Richard B. Cheney, former U.S. secretary of defense, accept the Republican nomination for president and vice president at the Republican Party's 2000 convention in Philadelphia.

crat, and Democrats controlled both houses of the Texas Legislature. However, Bush became known for achieving success with a combination of personal charm and an ability to compromise. The lawmakers enacted legislation that put limits on welfare benefits, gave local school districts more authority, imposed stricter penalties on juvenile criminals, and placed limits on civil lawsuits.

In 1997, Bush presented a plan to restructure the Texas tax system and increase state funding for schools. At the time, Texas schools were supported by local property taxes. Bush proposed reducing property taxes and increasing the state's role in financing education. To make up for the lower property taxes, he called for an increase in the state sales tax and for a new tax on fees of doctors, lawyers, and other professionals.

Bush's proposal for new taxes received much criticism, particularly from conservative Republicans, and it was not accepted. However, the members of the Legislature did reduce property taxes by increasing the amount of a home's value that was exempt from taxes. They used surplus funds in the state budget to make up for the decreased property taxes.

Reelection. Bush's popularity remained high throughout his term. In 1998, he ran for reelection. He defeated his opponent, Texas Land Commissioner Garry Mauro, by a wide margin. Bush received about 69 percent of the vote. He drew support not only from traditional Republicans but also from the state's Hispanic Americans, who often vote Democratic. Also in 1998, Bush's brother Jeb was elected governor of Florida.

During Bush's second term, the state increased school funding and continued to adopt educational reforms. The Legislature also approved the largest tax cuts in Texas history. Bush was criticized for not doing more to combat racism, poverty, and pollution.

Bush received national attention. Even before his second term began, he was spoken of as a possible candidate for the presidency in 2000.

Election as president

In June 1999, Bush announced that he would seek the Republican nomination for president. He faced several rivals, including Elizabeth Dole, former president of the American Red Cross; newspaper and magazine publisher Steve Forbes; Alan Keyes, a former State Department official; Arizona Senator John McCain; and former Vice President Dan Quayle.

The campaign. Early in the campaign, critics brought up events from Bush's past. They questioned why he had been accepted in the Texas Air National Guard before others on a waiting list. They charged that Bush received favorable treatment because his father was a congressman at the time. Bush said that neither he nor his father had sought to influence his selection. Reporters asked Bush if he had used cocaine or other drugs in his youth, but Bush did not respond.

Senator McCain won the first of the primary elections, in New Hampshire in February 2000. By the time the March primaries ended, however, Bush had won enough delegates to secure the nomination.

At the Republican National Convention in Philadelphia in August 2000, Bush was named the Republican presidential nominee. At Bush's request, the delegates nominated Richard B. Cheney, a former congressman and U.S. secretary of defense, as their candidate for vice president. The Democrats nominated Vice President Al Gore for president and Senator Joseph I. Lieberman of Connecticut for vice president.

During the campaign, Bush labeled Gore "the candidate of the status quo." Bush emphasized what he called

Bush's election

Place of nominating convention . . Philadelphia
Ballot on which nominated 1st
Democratic opponent . . . . Al Gore
Age at inauguration 54

"compassionate conservatism." He said the nation's prosperity must be extended to those still struggling. He pledged to cut taxes and to strengthen and preserve the nation's Social Security system. He stressed the need to improve the performance of the public schools and to rebuild the nation's military strength.

Gore argued that Bush lacked the experience to be president. He said Bush's proposal to use a federal budget surplus to make up for reduced taxes was risky. Gore also pointed to the danger, under Bush's plan, that the Social Security and Medicare programs would be left without sufficient funding.

The election of 2000 was one of the tightest presidential contests in U.S. history. The outcome was in doubt for weeks after the election. It depended upon which candidate won Florida. Because the vote was extremely close there, the state ordered a machine recount. After that recount, Bush was ahead. Gore asked for manual recounts in certain counties, and Bush challenged in court the need for those recounts. Five weeks after the election, a decision by the U.S. Supreme Court brought an end to the recounts. Gore then conceded the election. Bush became the 43rd president of the United States.   Bill Minutaglio

See also **President of the United States.**

Outline

I. Early life
    A. Family background   B. Boyhood
    C. School life
II. College and military service
III. Business school
IV. Congressional candidate
V. Bush's family
VI. Business career
    A. Oil exploration   B. Baseball ownership
VII. Governor of Texas
    A. Campaign   C. Reelection
    B. First term
VIII. Election as president
    A. The campaign   B. The election of 2000

Questions

How did Bush campaign against Vice President Al Gore?
What were some of Bush's achievements as governor of Texas?
Where did Bush do his military service during the Vietnam War?
What were the two most important industries Bush worked in before becoming governor of Texas?
What political office is held by Bush's brother Jeb?
Where did Bush grow up?
What did Bush mean by the phrase "compassionate conservatism"?
Before Bush, who was the only other son to follow his father as president of the United States?
What was the first political office Bush held?
Why did Bush's sale of his shares in Harken Energy Corporation draw questions?

Additional resources

Bush, George W. *A Charge to Keep.* Morrow, 1999.
Cohen, Daniel. *George W. Bush.* Millbrook, 2000.
Minutaglio, Bill. *First Son: George W. Bush and the Bush Family Dynasty.* Times Bks., 1999.

Electoral votes in 2000 This map shows who won each state's electoral votes in the 2000 election. The candidate who wins the most popular votes in a state usually receives all the state's electoral votes. Each state has as many electoral votes as it has senators and representatives in Congress.

WORLD BOOK map

271 George W. Bush   266 Al Gore

Washington 11
Oregon 7
Montana 3
North Dakota 3
Minnesota 10
Vermont 3
Maine 4
N.H. 4
Mass. 12
Idaho 4
South Dakota 3
Wisconsin 11
Michigan 18
New York 33
R.I. 4
Conn. 8
Wyoming 3
Iowa 7
Pennsylvania 23
New Jersey 15
Nevada 4
Utah 5
Nebraska 5
Illinois 22
Indiana 12
Ohio 21
W.Va. 5
D.C. 3*
Delaware 3
Maryland 10
California 54
Colorado 8
Kansas 6
Missouri 11
Kentucky 8
Virginia 13
Arizona 8
New Mexico 5
Oklahoma 8
Arkansas 6
Tennessee 11
North Carolina 14
South Carolina 8
Mississippi 7
Alabama 9
Georgia 13
Texas 32
Louisiana 9
Florida 25
Alaska 3
Hawaii 4

*The 3 electoral votes from Washington, D.C. were split, with two votes for Al Gore and one ballot left blank.

Bush, Laura Welch (1946-   ), is the wife of George W. Bush, who was elected president of the United States in 2000. Born Laura Lane Welch in Midland, Texas, she grew up there as the only child of homebuilders Harold and Jenna Welch.

Laura Welch received a bachelor's degree in education from Southern Methodist University in 1968 and a master's degree in library science from the University of Texas at Austin in 1973. She worked as a public school teacher and librarian before marrying George W. Bush in 1977. The couple have twin daughters, Jenna and Barbara, who are named after their grandmothers.

After her husband became governor of Texas in 1995, Bush spent much of her time promoting literacy and the arts in the state of Texas. Working with her mother-in-law, former First Lady Barbara Bush, Laura Bush established several state literacy programs. She helped organize the annual Texas Book Festival, which raises thousands of dollars for the state's public libraries, and she displayed the work of Texas artists. She also aided organizations that promote breast cancer awareness.

Cheney, Richard Bruce (1941-   ), a Wyoming Republican, was elected vice president of the United States in 2000. He and his running mate, Texas Governor George W. Bush, defeated their Democratic opponents, Vice President Al Gore and Senator Joseph I. Lieberman, in an extremely close election.

Cheney, a former congressman, had served as U.S. secretary of defense under Bush's father, President George H. W. Bush, from 1989 to 1993. As secretary of defense, Cheney advised the president on military strategy against Iraq during the Persian Gulf War (1991). He also helped persuade other countries to join U.S.-led forces in the war.

© Reuters/Archive Photos
Richard B. Cheney

Early life. Cheney was born in Lincoln, Nebraska. He moved with his parents to Casper, Wyoming, while still a boy. He entered Yale University on a scholarship but returned home after three semesters. He took a job with an electric company, working on power lines. He then attended the University of Wyoming, earning a B.A. in 1965 and an M.A. in 1966, both in political science.

In 1964, Cheney married Lynne Ann Vincent, a graduate student who went on to earn a Ph.D. in English literature. Lynne Cheney became a college teacher, novelist, and magazine editor. She headed the National Endowment for the Humanities from 1986 to 1993. The couple have two daughters, Elizabeth and Mary.

Career. The Cheneys moved to the Washington, D.C., area after Richard Cheney received a congressional fellowship in 1968. In 1969, Cheney joined the staff of Donald H. Rumsfeld, then director of the Office of Economic Opportunity. Cheney worked for Rumsfeld in various jobs until 1973. In 1974 and 1975, Cheney was a deputy assistant to President Gerald R. Ford. Cheney served as White House chief of staff under Ford from 1975 to 1977.

In 1978, Cheney won election to the U.S. House of Representatives as a Republican from Wyoming. He was reelected five times. As a representative, Cheney was known for his conservative political views. In 1988, he became the Republican *whip* (assistant leader) in the House. He also served on several House committees, including the Select Committee on Intelligence and a committee that investigated the sale of arms by the United States to Iran. Cheney gave up his House seat in 1989 after accepting the post of secretary of defense.

After Cheney completed his stint as defense secretary in 1993, he left government service and joined the boards of several corporations. In 1995, he became the president and chief executive officer of Halliburton Company, a Dallas-based oil-field services and construction firm. In July 2000, George W. Bush asked Cheney to be his running mate.   Lee Thornton

Web site

SecDef Histories - Richard Cheney
http://www.defenselink.mil/specials/secdef_histories/bios/
    cheney.htm
Biographical information about Richard B. Cheney.

Christopher, Warren Minor (1925-   ), served as United States secretary of state under President Bill Clinton from 1993 to 1997. His roles as secretary included negotiations to settle disputes between warring sides in Bosnia. Christopher had served as deputy secretary of state under President Jimmy Carter from 1977 to 1981. In that position, he acted as chief negotiator for the release of a group of Americans held hostage in Iran. In 2000, Christopher represented Al Gore's presidential campaign as an observer to a vote recount in Florida. The 2000 election was one of the closest presidential races in United States history.

From 1967 to 1969, Christopher was deputy attorney general under President Lyndon B. Johnson. In that post, he managed federal efforts to restore order in Chicago and Detroit after riots broke out in predominantly black areas of those cities. In 1991, he headed a commission that investigated the use of force by the Los Angeles police against minorities. The investigation followed an incident in which white Los Angeles police officers beat Rodney G. King, a black motorist stopped after a pursuit.

Christopher was born in Scranton, North Dakota. He earned a bachelor's degree from the University of Southern California in 1945 and a law degree from Stanford University in 1949. He practiced law in Los Angeles when not in government service.   Andrew Bennett

Web site

Warren Christopher
http://www.health.state.nd.us/gov/rr/christopher.htm
Biographical information about Warren Christopher.

It's a fact

The Republican and Democratic parties each won 50 seats in the United States Senate in the election of 2000. It was the first such tie since the 47th Congress (1881-1883).

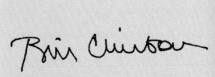

**42nd president of the
United States 1993-2001**

G. H. W. Bush
41st president
1989-1993
Republican

Clinton
42nd president
1993-2001
Democrat

G. W. Bush
43rd president
2001-
Republican

Al Gore
Vice president
1993-2001

Democratic National Committee

Clinton, Bill (1946-   ), was elected president of the United States in 1992 and reelected in 1996. Clinton, a Democrat, won the 1992 election while serving his fifth term as governor of Arkansas. President George Bush was his Republican opponent. Former Senator Robert Dole of Kansas was Clinton's Republican foe in 1996.

Clinton took office at a time when the nation's attention had shifted sharply from foreign affairs to domestic issues. The years before his election had seen a series of turbulent world events, including the end of the Cold War struggle between the United States and the Soviet Union, and—in 1991—the breakup of the Soviet Union itself. By 1992, Americans were troubled chiefly by fears about their country's economic health. The unemployment rate had climbed to the highest level since 1984. Many people were concerned about what they saw as a decline in U.S. productivity compared with that of other nations. Another concern involved the federal government's policy of *deficit spending,* or borrowing to finance expenditures, which over the years had resulted in a large national debt. In addition, Americans had become increasingly frustrated over signs of growing racial conflict, crime, and poverty.

During his two campaigns, Clinton argued that he was the best candidate to solve the country's economic and social problems. He promised to reduce the need for deficit spending and to expand the educational and economic opportunities of poor and middle-class Americans. Clinton's positions included both traditionally liberal and traditionally conservative ideas. He once de-

clared, "The change I seek ... isn't liberal or conservative. It's different and it's both."

In December 1998, the U.S. House of Representatives impeached Clinton for perjury and obstruction of justice. The charges developed out of Clinton's efforts to conceal an improper sexual relationship. The House sent its findings to the Senate, which conducted a trial. The Senate found Clinton not guilty. For more details, see the *Domestic events* section of this article.

Clinton, who was 46 when he took office, was the third youngest person ever to serve as president, after Theodore Roosevelt and John F. Kennedy. In 1978, Clinton had become one of the youngest Americans ever elected as a governor, when he won that office in Arkansas at the age of 32. Clinton became a skillful public speaker known for his ability to seize the attention of a wide variety of audiences. His hobbies include reading, solving crossword puzzles, playing the tenor saxophone, jogging, and golfing.

Important dates in Clinton's life

1946 (Aug. 19) Born in Hope, Arkansas.
1968 Graduated from Georgetown University.
1968-1970 Attended Oxford University as Rhodes scholar.
1973 Graduated from Yale Law School.
1975 (Oct. 11) Married Hillary Rodham.
1979-1980 Served first term as governor of Arkansas.
1982 Again elected governor of Arkansas, and later reelected three more times. Held office until 1992.
1992 Elected president of the United States.
1996 Reelected president.
1998 Impeached by U.S. House of Representatives.
1999 Tried by U.S. Senate on impeachment charges and found not guilty.

Ernest C. Dumas, the contributor of this article, is a political columnist for The Arkansas Times *and Journalist in Residence at the University of Central Arkansas.*

Early life

Boyhood. Clinton was born on Aug. 19, 1946, in Hope, Arkansas. His given and family name was William Jefferson Blythe IV. His parents were Virginia Cassidy Blythe (1923-1994) and William Jefferson Blythe III (1918-1946). His father, a traveling heavy-equipment salesman and former automobile dealer, was killed as a result of a car accident three months before Bill was born.

During the first years of his life, young Bill—called Billy—lived with his mother and her parents in Hope. When the boy was about 2, his mother left him in the care of his grandparents for a year while she studied in New Orleans to become a nurse-anesthetist. When Billy was 4, his mother married Roger Clinton (1909-1967), a car dealer. The family lived for a time in Hope, then moved to Hot Springs, Arkansas, in 1953. There, Virginia and Roger Clinton had another son, Roger, Jr. (1956-). Billy began using his stepfather's last name while in elementary school. He formally changed his name to William Jefferson Clinton when he was 15.

Virginia Clinton had a strong influence on her older son. She cared deeply about the problems of people she met in her hospital work, and she and Bill often had long conversations about situations one or the other considered unfair. But Clinton's life at home was not easy. Roger Clinton, Sr., was an alcoholic who sometimes verbally or even physically abused his wife. At least once, Bill stood up to his stepfather to protect his mother. Clinton later said that his troubled family life made him skilled at solving disagreements and avoiding conflicts. Clinton grew close to his stepfather shortly before the older man died of cancer in 1967.

School life. In Hot Springs, Clinton attended a Roman Catholic school for two years before enrolling in public school. The Clintons, who were Baptists, sent their son to the smaller Catholic school to ease his move to the large public school system of Hot Springs. In high school, he was active in a variety of clubs and held many offices. He also played tenor saxophone in the high school band and was band major as a senior.

Clinton early showed an interest in—and a gift for—politics. As a schoolmate recalled, Bill was always "running for something." Clinton became interested in politics in 1963, when, at the age of 17, he met President John F. Kennedy. He met Kennedy while visiting Washington, D.C., as a delegate to the American Legion Boys Nation, a citizenship training program in which young people form a model of national government.

College and law school. After graduating from high school in 1964, Clinton attended Georgetown University in Washington, D.C. He majored in international affairs. He served as class president during his freshman and sophomore years. From 1966 to 1968, he helped pay his college expenses through a job with the Senate Foreign Relations Committee.

Clinton had been strongly influenced by African Americans' fight for social justice during the civil rights movement of the 1950's and 1960's. In April 1968, the assassination of civil rights leader Martin Luther King, Jr., led to rioting in Washington. Clinton worked as a Red Cross volunteer during the rioting, helping to bring food and clothing to people whose homes had been burned. He graduated from college a few months later.

Following his graduation, Clinton entered Oxford University in Oxford, England, as a Rhodes scholar. He remained at Oxford for two years. Clinton entered Yale Law School in 1970. From August to November 1972, he worked in Texas as a state coordinator for the presidential nomination of George McGovern.

Clinton's family. At Yale, Clinton met fellow law student Hillary Rodham (Oct. 26, 1947-   ) of Park Ridge, Illinois. Hillary and Bill began to date in 1971 and were married on Oct. 11, 1975. The couple had one child—a daughter, Chelsea (1980-   ). After the marriage, Hillary continued to pursue her own career as an attorney, eventually becoming one of the nation's most prominent lawyers. She also played an active role in public affairs. She remained known as Hillary Rodham until 1982, when she adopted her husband's last name.

Entry into politics

After receiving his law degree in 1973, Clinton returned to Arkansas. There, he joined the faculty of the

Clinton Birthplace Foundation

The Clinton birthplace was this frame house in Hope, Arkansas. He lived in Hope from his birth in 1946 until 1953, when he and his family moved to Little Rock, Arkansas.

Clinton Campaign Headquarters

Seventeen-year-old Clinton shakes hands with President John F. Kennedy. Clinton's meeting with Kennedy helped persuade the youth to pursue a political career.

University of Arkansas Law School in Fayetteville. Soon afterward, he decided to run for a seat in the U.S. House of Representatives. In 1974, Clinton became the Democratic nominee to represent Arkansas's Third Congressional District, which includes Fayetteville. Representative John Paul Hammerschmidt, a popular Republican, narrowly defeated Clinton in the general election.

In 1976, Clinton won the Democratic primary for attorney general of Arkansas. He ran unopposed in the general election. As attorney general, Clinton became known as a supporter of consumers' interests. He opposed the construction by an Arkansas utility company of two large coal-burning power plants, demanding that the company promote efficiency and conservation instead. The plants were eventually built.

Clinton became a candidate for governor of Arkansas in early 1978. In his campaign, he partly focused on a need for economic development and improvements in the state's educational system. Clinton overwhelmed his four Democratic opponents in the primary, winning 60 percent of the vote. He easily defeated Republican Lynn Lowe in the general election. Clinton's impressive showing, combined with his liberal policies and his youth, brought him his first national attention.

Governor of Arkansas, 1979-1980

Early difficulties. Clinton was inaugurated governor in January 1979. Once in office, he began efforts to establish a wide range of programs and policies. But he failed to gather broad support for these efforts, and most of them met with little success. To pay for a road improvement program, Clinton pushed through the legislature a measure increasing various fees and taxes, including motor vehicle license fees. The increase in license fees was extremely unpopular. Clinton also came under attack by local leaders, who said he failed to attract industries to the state. In addition, the powerful wood-products industry began working against Clinton because his administration had condemned one of its timber-management practices, called *clearcutting*.

Reelection defeat. Clinton ran for reelection in 1980 against conservative Republican Frank D. White, a savings and loan executive. White stressed Clinton's unpopular license fee increase. White also profited from a federal government decision to hold about 18,000 Cuban refugees temporarily at Fort Chaffee, then a military reserve training facility, near Fort Smith, Arkansas. In May and June 1980, discontent among the Cubans led to breakouts and rioting. White claimed that Clinton had not done enough to persuade President Jimmy Carter to hold the Cubans elsewhere. In the election, White gained 52 percent of the vote to Clinton's 48 percent. Clinton then returned to private life, joining the law firm of Wright, Lindsey and Jennings in Little Rock, Arkansas. He began making plans to challenge White in 1982.

Governor of Arkansas, 1983-1992

Return to office. In his 1982 campaign, Clinton worked to convince voters that he understood his mistakes and had matured. He failed to win a majority of the votes in the Democratic primary, but he won the nomination in a runoff. In the general election, Clinton defeated White by 55 percent to 45 percent of the vote. Clinton returned to office in January 1983. In his second term, he

Reuters/Archive Photos

Clinton's family includes his wife, Hillary Rodham Clinton, and their daughter, Chelsea. The family greeted supporters from a train platform during the 1996 presidential campaign.

abandoned some strongly liberal positions. In addition, he decided to focus on two main problems—education and the economy—instead of a wide range of issues.

Clinton's opponents argued that his 1980 defeat had taught him to avoid taking stands that might be unpopular. But Clinton was reelected in 1984 and in 1986, each time by a wide margin. In 1984, Arkansas passed a constitutional amendment changing the governor's term of office from two years to four, beginning with the 1986 election. Clinton was elected to a fifth term in 1990.

Reforms in education. Beginning in 1983, Clinton set as his main goal the improvement of the Arkansas public school system. Arkansas had long ranked near the bottom of the states in many measures of educational achievement. During his first term, Clinton had taken steps toward improving education in Arkansas. In one such move, he proposed a bill—passed into law in 1979—that required new teachers to pass a certifying examination before being allowed to teach.

In 1983, at Clinton's urging, the legislature passed a series of educational reforms. These reforms included a requirement—the first of its kind in the nation—that teachers pass a basic skills test to keep their jobs.

Economic developments. Arkansas had traditionally been a state with few major resources and an underdeveloped economy. It had relied heavily on low-skill, low-paying manufacturing jobs. During his first term, Clinton had sought unsuccessfully to reduce the state's dependence on manufacturing jobs. After his reelection, he worked instead to broaden its industrial base. In 1985, at his urging, the legislature passed an economic package designed to attract businesses and capital to Arkansas. His actions helped Arkansas reduce unemployment and increase production in the late 1980's and early 1990's.

Steps to the presidency. Throughout his years as governor, Clinton played an active role in Democratic Party politics. In 1985, he was elected vice chairman of the National Governors' Association (NGA), made up of the governors of the 50 states and 5 U.S. territories. Clinton served as NGA chairman in 1986 and 1987. In 1990 and 1991, he headed the Democratic Leadership Council, an organization of moderate Democratic officeholders from all levels of government, as well as business and community members. In 1987 and 1988, Clinton worked to obtain the support of Congress and President Ronald Reagan for the NGA's proposals on welfare reform. The proposals led to passage of the Family Support Act of 1988, which required welfare mothers to work if they had no children under 3 years of age.

At the Democratic National Convention in 1988, Clinton gave the speech nominating Michael S. Dukakis as the party's candidate for president. Dukakis lost the election to Bush, then vice president.

Election as president

The Democratic nomination. In October 1991, Clinton formally announced his candidacy for the Democratic nomination for president. His chief challengers for the nomination were former Massachusetts Senator Paul E. Tsongas and former California Governor Edmund G. Brown, Jr., known as Jerry.

For a time, Clinton's campaign faltered over charges of marital infidelity. The Clintons acknowledged that they had encountered some difficulties in their relationship, but they said their marriage was strong. Clinton also came under attack for his actions during the early 1970's, which, his opponents charged, showed that he had sought to evade military service during the Vietnam War (1957-1975). Clinton denied that he had acted improperly, and his campaign rapidly regained ground. Tsongas, an early front-runner, suspended his campaign for lack of funds in March 1992. Clinton had already seized a commanding lead over Brown, and he soon had enough delegates to ensure the nomination.

At the Democratic National Convention in New York City in July 1992, Clinton was named the Democratic presidential nominee. At his request, Senator Al Gore of Tennessee was nominated for vice president. The Republicans renominated President Bush and Vice President Dan Quayle to oppose Clinton and Gore.

The 1992 election. During the presidential campaign, Clinton took advantage of many Americans' perception of Bush as unconcerned about domestic issues. He seized upon the high unemployment rate and the widespread belief that the gap between rich and poor had grown under Bush and his predecessor, Ronald Reagan. Clinton promised to stimulate the economy by encouraging business expansion in various ways, including tax breaks for new factories, new technology, and new small businesses. He proposed to reduce government spending and to raise taxes on wealthy Americans to help reduce the federal budget deficit.

Bush charged that Clinton lacked experience in foreign affairs. He defended his record on the economy, claiming that Congress—which was made up largely of Democrats—had rejected most of his proposals.

Texas businessman Ross Perot ran for president as an independent. Clinton defeated Bush and Perot.

Clinton's first administration (1993-1997)

National affairs. Clinton appointed more women and minority members to his Cabinet than had any previous president. Early in his presidency, he concentrated on the economy and other domestic issues.

In October 1993, Clinton sent Congress a plan for sweeping reform of the nation's health care system. A committee headed by Hillary Clinton had developed the plan. After much debate, Congress chose not to act on the proposal. In August 1996, however, Congress approved the Kennedy-Kassebaum bill, which included two important parts of Clinton's 1993 plan. The bill provided (1) that workers can change jobs without losing their medical insurance coverage, and (2) that workers cannot be denied medical insurance coverage because of a preexisting illness.

In November 1993, Congress approved the Brady bill, which Clinton backed strongly. The bill required people to wait five working days between the time they bought a handgun and the time they took possession of it. In August 1994, Clinton won a victory when Congress passed an anticrime law he supported. The law called for spending billions of dollars on crime prevention, law enforcement, and prison construction. It also outlawed the sale of certain types of *assault weapons,* guns that many people believe are designed specifically for killing or injuring people.

The unemployment rate declined after Clinton became president. Clinton's 1993 and 1994 budgets included cuts in government spending and tax increases that

Clinton's inauguration as governor of Arkansas in 1983 marked his return to office after two years in private life. Clinton had been elected governor in 1978 but lost a reelection bid in 1980. He was elected to a total of five terms as governor.

© *Arkansas Democrat-Gazette* from Sipa Press

Clinton's first election

Place of nominating convention	. . .New York City
Ballot on which nominated	. . . . .1st
Republican opponent	. . . . .George Bush
Independent opponent	. . . . .Ross Perot
Electoral vote*	. . . . .370 (Clinton) to 168 (Bush) and 0 (Perot)
Popular vote	. . . . .44,908,233 (Clinton) to 39,102,282 (Bush) and 19,721,433 (Perot)
Age at inauguration	46

*For votes by states, see **Electoral College** (table)

helped reduce the federal deficit. They were approved by Congress, which had a Democratic majority. In the elections of November 1994, however, the Democrats lost control of Congress to the Republicans. The Republicans called for larger spending cuts, with the goal of erasing the deficit by the year 2002. Clinton said some of the proposed cuts were too sharp, including those for spending on education, welfare, and Medicare. He responded with his own plan to wipe out the deficit.

By the start of the government's new fiscal year on Oct. 1, 1995, Congress had failed to pass some of the appropriations bills that fund the government's operations. It then passed a series of bills to allow spending to continue for short periods. But the bills included certain other provisions that Clinton opposed. For example, one bill increased Medicare premiums. Clinton vetoed bills with provisions he opposed, and Congress refused to remove the provisions. The resulting lack of funding forced many federal government operations to shut down for 6 days in November and for 21 days from December 1995 to January 1996.

As president, Clinton pressed for actions to keep young people from starting to smoke. He and his administration worked to persuade Congress to create federal restrictions on smoking by people under the age of 21.

In 1996, Congress created legislation to revise the welfare system. Clinton vetoed two bills, claiming they included changes that would harm the poor too much. But he approved a third welfare bill in August 1996, upsetting many in his own party. The bill placed limits on how long people can receive welfare benefits, and it shifted much responsibility for administering welfare from the federal government to the states.

Clinton called for an increase in the legal minimum wage. Congress approved an increase in August 1996.

During his presidency, Clinton struggled to clear himself of charges of financial misconduct. The charges centered on alleged illegal and unethical acts by the Whitewater Development Corporation, a small company that bought land in Arkansas for a vacation home development. The Clintons had invested in the company in 1978, shortly before Clinton was elected governor of Arkansas, and sold their interest in the company in 1992. They denied any wrongdoing and pointed out that they had lost a large sum of money on their investment. But Clinton promised a full investigation.

In January 1994, Attorney General Janet Reno appointed a Republican lawyer, Robert B. Fiske, as an independent counsel to investigate the Whitewater affair. In August 1994, a panel of federal judges appointed another Republican lawyer, Kenneth W. Starr, to take Fiske's place. Republicans had charged that Fiske was favoring the Clinton administration.

International affairs presented Clinton with many challenges. In August 1994, he ended a long-standing U.S. policy of accepting almost all refugees from Communist Cuba. He abandoned the old policy after thousands of Cubans set out for southern Florida on small boats and rafts to escape poverty in Cuba. Clinton's action was designed, in part, to avoid the cost of settling large numbers of refugees in the United States.

Since the last years of Bush's presidency, thousands of refugees from Haiti had also tried to reach the United States by sea. They left Haiti after Haiti's military overthrew Jean-Bertrand Aristide, the nation's first democratically elected president, in 1991. The new rulers set up a military dictatorship.

In September 1994, Clinton threatened to use armed force against Haiti's rulers if they did not allow Aristide to return to power. As U.S. forces prepared to invade Haiti, Haiti's top military leader, Lieutenant General Raoul Cédras, agreed to step down and allow Aristide's return. The agreement was negotiated by a U.S. team led by former President Jimmy Carter, whom Clinton had sent to Haiti as his representative. United States troops were sent to help ensure the transfer of power to Aristide.

Clinton achieved one of his major foreign policy goals in November 1993, when Congress approved the North American Free Trade Agreement (NAFTA). Clinton strongly supported the pact, which will gradually eliminate tariffs and other trade barriers between the United States, Mexico, and Canada. In December 1994, Clinton won Congress's approval of an expansion of the General Agreement on Tariffs and Trade (GATT). This expanded GATT plan called for large reductions in trade barriers among many nations.

The United States and other countries have long claimed that Japan's trade practices unfairly restrict imports to that country. In 1995, Clinton threatened increases in tariffs on Japanese luxury cars. Japanese car companies then agreed to try to improve their practices.

In 1992, a civil war began in Bosnia-Herzegovina between Bosnian Serb rebels and the country's government, which was dominated by Bosnian Muslims. Bos-

Vice president and Cabinet

Vice president	* Al Gore
Secretary of state	* Warren M. Christopher
	Madeleine K. Albright (1997)
Secretary of the treasury	Lloyd M. Bentsen, Jr.
	Robert E. Rubin (1995)
	Lawrence H. Summers (1999)
Secretary of defense	Les Aspin
	William J. Perry (1994)
	William S. Cohen (1997)
Attorney general	Janet Reno
Secretary of the interior	Bruce E. Babbitt
Secretary of agriculture	Mike Espy
	Dan Glickman (1995)
Secretary of commerce	Ronald H. Brown
	Mickey Kantor (1996)
	William M. Daley (1997)
	Norman Y. Mineta (2000)
Secretary of labor	Robert B. Reich
	Alexis M. Herman (1997)
Secretary of health and human services	Donna E. Shalala
Secretary of housing and urban development	Henry G. Cisneros
	Andrew M. Cuomo (1997)
Secretary of transportation	Federico F. Peña
	Rodney E. Slater (1997)
Secretary of energy	Hazel R. O'Leary
	Federico F. Peña (1997)
	Bill Richardson (1998)
Secretary of education	Richard W. Riley
Secretary of veterans affairs	Jesse Brown
	Togo D. West, Jr. (1998)
	†Hershel W. Gober (2000)

*Has a separate biography in this volume.   † Acting secretary.

nia-Herzegovina, sometimes simply called Bosnia, was formerly a republic of Yugoslavia. In 1991, the United Nations (UN) had approved an embargo against providing arms to any of the former Yugoslav republics to try to keep fighting from spreading in the area. The UN sent a peacekeeping force to Bosnia. The United States used its Air Force to help provide relief to Bosnian Muslims under siege and to try to stop Serb aggression.

Televised brutal actions by Serbs in the Bosnian civil war caused many people in the United States to favor providing arms to the Muslims. Clinton continued to follow the UN arms embargo policy, however. In August 1995, Congress voted to require Clinton to end U.S. participation in the arms embargo if the UN force in Bosnia pulled out. Clinton vetoed the legislation.

In late 1995, Clinton helped bring about a meeting of representatives of the sides in the Bosnian civil war. In December, they signed a peace plan that included a cease-fire. Under the plan, the cease-fire was to be policed by a force of troops from the North Atlantic Treaty Organization (NATO). Clinton agreed to send United States troops to Bosnia to serve in the force.

In 1991, a coalition of nations led by the United States had driven Iraqi forces out of Kuwait after the Iraqis had occupied that country. The coalition then placed restrictions on Iraq. But in September 1996, Iraqi forces attacked Kurds in northern Iraq in violation of the restrictions. In response, Clinton ordered the U.S. military to launch missiles against military targets in Iraq.

The 1996 election. At the Democratic National Convention in Chicago in August 1996, Clinton and Gore were renominated without opposition. The Republicans nominated Robert Dole of Kansas for president and Jack Kemp of New York for vice president. Ross Perot ran for president on the Reform Party ticket.

In the presidential campaign, Clinton pointed to his first-term record, emphasizing improvements in the economy and such laws as gun control measures and the minimum-wage increase. He also said he had kept Congress from cutting some government programs too deeply, including Medicare, welfare, and education. In November, the voters reelected Clinton and Gore.

Clinton's second administration (1997-2001)

International affairs. In 1998, Clinton visited China, where he urged its leaders to allow a greater degree of democracy. Also in 1998, Clinton called for increased controls on nuclear weapons after India and Pakistan tested such weapons. In August 1998, bombs planted by terrorists destroyed the U.S. embassies in Kenya and

AP/Wide World

Running mates Clinton and Al Gore accepted the Democratic nomination for president and vice president at the Democratic Party's 1996 national convention in Chicago.

Tanzania. American officials claimed that terrorists camped in Afghanistan and led by Osama bin Laden, a wealthy Saudi businessman, were responsible for the bombings. Clinton ordered missile strikes against the camps in Afghanistan and a plant in Sudan suspected of making deadly nerve gas for terrorists.

In December 1998, Clinton ordered U.S. forces to launch missile strikes against military and industrial sites in Iraq. Clinton said he ordered the attacks because Iraq had failed to cooperate with United Nations (UN) inspection of suspected weapons facilities. UN officials feared that the Iraqi facilities contained or could be used to produce chemical, biological, or other weapons of mass destruction. Iraq had agreed to such inspections after its defeat by U.S-led forces in 1991.

In March 1999, NATO began air strikes against Yugoslavia to halt Yugoslav attacks against ethnic Albanians in Kosovo, a province of the Yugoslav republic of Serbia. The air campaign used primarily U.S. aircraft and cruise missiles. Clinton said there was no alternative to military intervention because Yugoslavia refused to halt its attacks. But in June 1999, Yugoslav military leaders agreed to withdraw their troops. NATO stopped the bombing and sent an international peacekeeping force to Kosovo. The United States pledged 7,000 troops.

In 2000, Congress passed a bill calling for permanent normal trading relations with China. Clinton had campaigned tirelessly for the bill's passage. He said that opening markets between the United States and China would not only increase jobs and prosperity in the United States but help spread democratic values abroad.

Domestic events. The Republican Party kept control of both houses of Congress as a result of the 1996 elections. In August 1997, Clinton and the Republican-controlled Congress reached a compromise on the budget. The two sides agreed to a plan to end the deficit

Clinton's second election

Place of nominating convention	Chicago
Ballot on which nominated	1st
Republican opponent	Robert Dole
Reform Party opponent	Ross Perot
Electoral vote*	379 (Clinton) to 159 (Dole) and 0 (Perot)
Popular vote	47,402,357 (Clinton) to 39,198,755 (Dole) and 8,085,402 (Perot)
Age at inauguration	50

*For votes by states, see **Electoral College** (table).

by 2002. In 1998, however, the government beat the 2002 deadline. That year, a strong economy helped lead to a $70 billion budget surplus. The surplus was the first achieved by the federal government since 1969.

Clinton continued to appoint women and minorities to important posts. In 1996, he named Madeleine K. Albright secretary of state. Albright, who took office in 1997, became the first woman to head the Department of State. Bill Richardson, another Clinton appointee, became the first Hispanic American to serve as the head U.S. delegate to the United Nations. Norman Mineta, appointed secretary of commerce in 2000, was the first Asian American to serve in the Cabinet.

In 1994, a former Arkansas state employee named Paula Corbin Jones filed a sexual harassment suit against Clinton. Jones claimed that in 1991, when Clinton was governor of Arkansas, he had requested sexual favors from her. In April 1998, a federal judge dismissed the Jones case, ruling there was not enough evidence of sexual harassment to send the case to a jury. Jones appealed this verdict. In December 1998, while the appeal was being heard, Clinton agreed to a cash settlement for Jones, and Jones dropped the appeal.

While preparing Jones's case, her lawyers had tried to establish a pattern of sexual affairs between the president and female employees. As part of this effort, they took testimony from a former White House intern named Monica Lewinsky, whom they suspected of having an affair with Clinton from late 1995 to early 1997. In January 1998, Kenneth Starr, who was still investigating the Whitewater case, asked Attorney General Janet Reno to expand his authority to allow him to investigate the Lewinsky matter, and she consented. Linda Tripp, a friend of Lewinsky's, had given Starr audiotapes on which Lewinsky reportedly discussed an affair with Clinton. In sworn statements to Jones's lawyers, Clinton and Lewinsky both denied having a sexual relationship.

In July, Clinton agreed to submit to questioning before a grand jury about whether he had urged Lewinsky to lie. If proven, such an action eventually could have led to criminal charges of obstruction of justice and *subornation of perjury* (persuading a witness to lie in court). Clinton testified before the grand jury on August 17. That night, he told the nation on television that he had had a relationship with Lewinsky that was not appropriate. He said it was a personal failure.

Starr sent his final report to the House of Representatives. The report suggested that Clinton may have committed impeachable offenses in trying to conceal his relationship with Lewinsky. In December 1998, the House impeached Clinton for perjury and obstruction of justice. The Senate then conducted a trial to consider the charges and Clinton's removal from office. In February 1999, the Senate found Clinton not guilty, and Clinton remained in office.

In October 1999, Kenneth Starr stepped down as independent counsel. One of his assistants, Robert W. Ray, took over the task of completing a final report on the Whitewater investigation. Ray issued the report in September 2000, closing the investigation. No charges were brought against the Clintons. The report stated that the evidence was insufficient to prove any wrongdoing on the part of the president or Mrs. Clinton.

Ernest C. Dumas

See also **Clinton, Hillary Rodham; Democratic Party; Gore, Al; President of the United States.**

Outline

Questions

What was Clinton's original name? How did he get the name?
What difficulties did Clinton have in his first term as governor?
What were Americans' main concerns when Clinton became president?
How did Clinton work to improve education in Arkansas?
As president, how did Clinton promote international trade?
Why did young Clinton become skilled at avoiding conflicts?
When did Clinton decide to pursue a political career?
How did Clinton campaign in his presidential races?
As president, how did Clinton support gun control?
Why was Clinton impeached by the House of Representatives?

Additional resources

Landau, Elaine. *Bill Clinton and His Presidency.* Watts, 1997. Younger readers.
Maraniss, David. *First in His Class: A Biography of Bill Clinton.* Simon & Schuster, 1995.
Walker, Martin. *The President We Deserve: Bill Clinton, His Rise, Falls, and Comebacks.* Crown, 1996.

Web sites

ABCNews.com Bio: William Jefferson Clinton
http://www.abcnews.go.com/reference/bios/clinton.html
This profile from ABC News features a link to recent news stories about William Jefferson Clinton.

William J. Clinton
http://www.whitehouse.gov/WH/glimpse/presidents/html/bc42.html
Official White House biography of Bill Clinton. Includes a link to a biography of Hillary Rodham Clinton.

Clinton, Hillary Rodham (1947-   ), a Democrat, was elected in 2000 to represent New York in the United States Senate. Before being elected a senator, Mrs. Clinton, the wife of President Bill Clinton, was one of the most active first ladies in U.S. history. She was also known as a distinguished lawyer and a gifted speaker.

In 1993, Mrs. Clinton was the chief author of a Clinton administration plan to guarantee low-cost health care to all Americans. Congress chose not to act on the plan. Many people thought the plan would give the government too large a role in the health care system. But in 1996, Congress passed a bill that included key elements of the plan (see **Clinton, Bill** [National affairs]).Mrs. Clinton was born Hillary Diane Rodham in Chicago and grew up in the Chicago suburb of Park Ridge. She graduated from Wellesley College in 1969. In 1973, she earned a law degree from Yale University, where she met fellow student Bill Clinton.

In 1974, Rodham joined Clinton on the faculty of the University of Arkansas Law School in Fayetteville. She married Clinton in 1975. In 1977, she joined the Rose Law Firm in Little Rock, Arkansas. She was with the firm until 1992, when her husband was elected president.

The White House

Hillary Rodham Clinton

Mrs. Clinton became a key adviser in all of her husband's political campaigns. She helped devise some of his major programs while he was governor of Arkansas from 1979 to 1981 and from 1983 to 1992. In the early 1980's, for example, Mrs. Clinton played a leading role in reforming the public school system in Arkansas.

Mrs. Clinton developed a deep interest in problems faced by children who are neglected. From 1986 to 1992, she served as national chairperson of the Children's Defense Fund, an organization that promotes child welfare. Her book *It Takes a Village* (1996) calls for community participation in helping children develop.

In 1999, New York Senator Daniel P. Moynihan announced that he would not be seeking reelection. In February 2000, Mrs. Clinton declared her candidacy for Moynihan's Senate seat. Ernest C. Dumas

It's a fact

In 2000, First Lady Hillary Rodham Clinton was elected to the United States Senate from New York. She was the first wife of a president ever elected to public office.

Democratic Party is one of the two major political parties of the United States. The Republican Party is the other. The Democratic Party, the nation's oldest existing party, has played a vital role in the history and politics of the United States. From 1828 through 2000, Democrats won almost half of the 44 presidential elections. They dominated U.S. politics from 1828 through 1856, winning 6 of the 8 presidential elections. From 1860 through 1928, they won only 4 of the 18 presidential elections. But the Democratic candidate won 10 of the 18 presidential elections held from 1932 through 2000. Traditionally, the Democratic Party has drawn support from several groups, including many immigrants, Southerners, wage earners, and—since the 1930's—blacks.

The policies of the Democratic Party, like those of other parties, have changed with the flow of history. Until Woodrow Wilson became president in 1913, the Democrats generally approved a strict interpretation of the United States Constitution and favored a limitation on government powers. As president, Wilson expanded the role of government and mobilized the nation to help

From *Thomas Nast* by Albert Bigelow Paine, permission of Harper & Bros.

The donkey was used as a political symbol by Andrew Jackson after his opponents called him a "jackass" during the 1828 election campaign. By the 1880's, such cartoons as the one above by Thomas Nast had caught the public eye and established the donkey as the symbol of the Democratic Party.

defeat Germany in World War I (1914-1918). Franklin D. Roosevelt boldly took government action to pull the nation through the Great Depression of the 1930's. During World War II (1939-1945), Roosevelt again expanded government powers to fight Germany and Japan.

Some Democrats thought Roosevelt extended the government's powers too far. Others believed these powers had not been extended far enough. Ever since Roosevelt's presidency, Democrats have disagreed on how extensive the role of government should be.

This article chiefly describes the history of the Democratic Party. For information about the party's national convention and organization, see **Political convention; Political party**.

Origin of the Democratic Party is uncertain. Some historians trace its beginnings to the Democratic-Republican Party that Thomas Jefferson created during the 1790's. Most historians, however, regard Andrew Jackson's presidential campaign organization, formed in 1828, as the beginning of the Democratic Party as it is known today.

Jefferson served as president from 1801 to 1809, and other Democratic-Republicans held the presidency from 1809 to 1825. After 1816, the Democratic-Republican Party split into several groups and fell apart as a national organization. Jackson became the favorite of one of these groups and gained great popularity. He lost a bid for the presidency in 1824. But he easily won election in 1828 and swept to reelection in 1832. By about 1830, Jackson and his followers were called Democrats.

By the late 1830's, top Jacksonian Democrats had turned Jackson's loose organization into an effective national political party—the Democratic Party. One of these men, Martin Van Buren, became president in 1837.

Jacksonian policies appealed to a wide variety of voters. Small farmers, large plantation owners, city laborers, and state bankers joined in their support of the Democratic Party. They had in common a strong belief in states' rights and a firm faith in limited government. But Democrats also disagreed frequently. For example, they argued over banking policies, slavery, and tariff rates. In spite of their differences, Democrats won the presidential election of 1844 with James K. Polk. In 1852, they won with Franklin Pierce and in 1856 with James Buchanan. They also controlled Congress during most of the 1840's and 1850's.

The slavery issue, more than any other, divided the Democrats. During Polk's administration, from 1845 to 1849, vast new territories in the West became part of the United States. Southerners wanted to extend slavery into the new lands, but many Northerners urged Congress to prohibit it.

Fierce debates led to division within the party and to sectional hostility between North and South. Congressional leaders, such as Stephen A. Douglas of Illinois,

worked for legislation that would satisfy both Northerners and Southerners. They favored the Compromise of 1850, which, for a time, quieted both party and sectional differences.

Hostility flared again after Congress passed the Kansas-Nebraska Act in 1854. In this act, Douglas had provided for "popular sovereignty," which let settlers decide for themselves whether a new state would permit slavery. The act pleased few people. It led to renewed hostility between North and South and caused the Democratic Party to split apart.

In 1860, Northern Democrats nominated Douglas for president. Southern Democrats chose John C. Breckinridge. Both Democratic candidates lost to Abraham Lincoln, the candidate of the new Republican Party. In 1860 and 1861, 11 Southern states seceded from the Union. In April 1861, shortly after the seventh state had withdrawn, the American Civil War began.

During the Civil War, the Northern Democrats divided. The "War Democrats" supported Lincoln and the war. The "Peace Democrats," especially those known as "Copperheads," opposed Lincoln and the war. In the

Democratic presidential and vice presidential candidates

Year	President	Vice President	Year	President	Vice President
1828	*Andrew Jackson*	*John Calhoun*	1916	*Woodrow Wilson*	*Thomas R. Marshall*
1832	*Andrew Jackson*	*Martin Van Buren*	1920	James M. Cox	Franklin D. Roosevelt
1836	*Martin Van Buren*	*Richard M. Johnson*	1924	John W. Davis	Charles W. Bryan
1840	Martin Van Buren	Richard M. Johnson	1928	Alfred E. Smith	Joseph T. Robinson
1844	*James K. Polk*	*George M. Dallas*	1932	*Franklin D. Roosevelt*	*John Nance Garner*
1848	Lewis Cass	William O. Butler	1936	*Franklin D. Roosevelt*	*John Nance Garner*
1852	*Franklin Pierce*	*William R. D. King*	1940	*Franklin D. Roosevelt*	*Henry A. Wallace*
1856	*James Buchanan*	*John C. Breckinridge*	1944	*Franklin D. Roosevelt*	*Harry S. Truman*
1860	Stephen A. Douglas	Herschel V. Johnson	1948	*Harry S. Truman*	*Alben W. Barkley*
1864	George B. McClellan	George H. Pendleton	1952	Adlai E. Stevenson	John J. Sparkman
1868	Horatio Seymour	Francis P. Blair, Jr.	1956	Adlai E. Stevenson	Estes Kefauver
1872	Horace Greeley	B. Gratz Brown	1960	*John F. Kennedy*	*Lyndon B. Johnson*
1876	Samuel J. Tilden	Thomas A. Hendricks	1964	*Lyndon B. Johnson*	*Hubert H. Humphrey*
1880	Winfield S. Hancock	William H. English	1968	Hubert H. Humphrey	Edmund S. Muskie
1884	*Grover Cleveland*	*Thomas A. Hendricks*	1972	George S. McGovern	Sargent Shriver
1888	Grover Cleveland	Allen G. Thurman	1976	*Jimmy Carter*	*Walter F. Mondale*
1892	*Grover Cleveland*	*Adlai E. Stevenson*	1980	Jimmy Carter	Walter F. Mondale
1896	William Jennings Bryan	Arthur Sewall	1984	Walter F. Mondale	Geraldine A. Ferraro
1900	William Jennings Bryan	Adlai E. Stevenson	1988	Michael S. Dukakis	Lloyd M. Bentsen, Jr.
1904	Alton B. Parker	Henry G. Davis	1992	*Bill Clinton*	*Al Gore*
1908	William Jennings Bryan	John W. Kern	1996	*Bill Clinton*	*Al Gore*
1912	*Woodrow Wilson*	*Thomas R. Marshall*	2000	Al Gore	Joseph I. Lieberman

Names of elected candidates are in italics.

Administrations in office

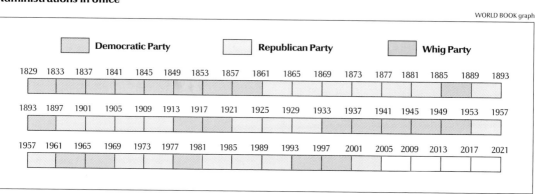

WORLD BOOK graph

election of 1864, many War Democrats supported Lincoln. They joined the Republican Party to form the Union Party. Andrew Johnson, a War Democrat, became Lincoln's vice presidential running mate. The Peace Democrats nominated General George B. McClellan. Lincoln won the election. Following Lincoln's assassination in April 1865—just five days after the war ended—Vice President Johnson became president.

After the Civil War. Republicans condemned the Democrats as disloyal to the Union during the Civil War. Unable to win the presidency or to gain control of Congress, the Democratic Party reached its lowest point.

Under Johnson's leadership, the Democrats attacked the Reconstruction plans of the Radical Republicans for the defeated South. Among other actions, the Republicans (1) denied the vote to Southerners who had fought against the Union and (2) gave the vote to Southern blacks. Enraged white Southerners deprived blacks of the vote after regaining power later. These white Southerners believed that the Republicans were opposed to most Southern beliefs. Thus, the Democratic "Solid South" was born. During the 1870's, meanwhile, Democrats demanded reforms that would end dishonest practices in business and in government.

A business depression swept the nation during the 1870's and helped change the party's fortunes. Many voters blamed the Republicans for the depression and vot-

United Press Int.

Franklin D. Roosevelt shakes hands with a coal miner—one of the "forgotten" men for whom he promised a "new deal" during his successful campaign for the presidency in 1932.

ed Democratic in the congressional elections of 1874. As a result, the Democrats gained control of the House of Representatives. In 1876, the Democrats made reform the central issue of their campaign. The Democratic candidate, Samuel J. Tilden, received more popular votes than did his Republican opponent, Rutherford B. Hayes. But Hayes won the election by one electoral vote.

As Civil War issues faded, there seemed to be less and less difference between the Democratic and Republican parties. However, the Democrats were distinguished by their support of lower tariffs and by their opposition to the prohibition of alcoholic beverages. The Democrats' image as supporters of states' rights and limited government appealed to white Southerners, small farmers, and many Northerners who associated strong government with prohibition and similar laws. Drawing on this appeal in 1884, Grover Cleveland became the first Democrat to be elected president since 1856. He narrowly lost the presidency to Benjamin Harrison in 1888, but he regained it in another close race in 1892.

Tremendous changes had reshaped the economy since the Civil War. Railroads had expanded to carry goods to farmers and farm products to city workers. Vast business and industrial empires had appeared. Politicians knew little about business growth, depressions, or economic theories. Democrats and Republicans favored a policy of *laissez faire* (nonregulation), and the government left business largely in the hands of businessmen. Neither party seemed aware of hardships that industrialization brought to many people.

In 1893, shortly after Cleveland began his second term as president, a major economic depression struck the nation. Farmers cried out against high railroad charges to send their goods to market. Many city workers demanded jobs, and others called for higher wages. Confused by the problems of an increasingly industrialized society, Cleveland followed a laissez-faire policy at the same time that farmers faced ruin, city workers went on strike, and the unemployment rate went up.

As president, Cleveland stood for a national currency backed by gold. By the election of 1896, many Democrats favored government action to increase the money

Reproduction of a lost color lithograph by T. J. Nicholl; Library of Congress

Grover Cleveland is shown "landing" the presidency for the Democratic Party in 1892. His Republican opponent, Benjamin Harrison, looks on after a narrow defeat for reelection.

in circulation by allowing the free coinage of silver. They believed that free coinage of silver would help solve the nation's economic problems. The money question became the major campaign issue. Most Democrats supported silver, but most Republicans favored gold.

In 1896, William Jennings Bryan won the Democratic presidential nomination with his famous "cross of gold" speech. He campaigned energetically and won wide support in the South and West—but ran poorly in the East and lost the election. Bryan lost again in 1900, and, after another Democratic defeat in 1904, he lost again in 1908.

Wilsonian democracy. In 1912, a split in the Republican Party enabled the Democratic candidate, Woodrow Wilson, to win the presidency. And, for the first time in 20 years, the Democrats gained control of both houses of Congress. Wilson won reelection in 1916, and the Democrats retained control of Congress.

Wilson wanted to eliminate monopoly and special privilege from American business, but without expanding the regulatory power of the federal government. He worked to restore fair competition and called for Americans to have a "new freedom" to prosper. During his first administration, he signed into law such reform legislation as the Clayton Antitrust Act, the Federal Trade Commission Act, and the Underwood Tariff Act.

During Wilson's second administration, World War I overshadowed his drive for reform legislation. Wilson directed the nation's energy to the defeat of Germany. After the war, he called for the United States to join the League of Nations. Wilson, the chief planner of the league, believed that the international organization would prevent future wars. Most Democrats supported the league, but some joined with conservative Republicans and blocked U.S. membership.

During the 1920's, the Democrats failed to win the presidency or to gain control of either house in Congress. The United States seemed prosperous. Business boomed, and industries expanded. But beneath the surface of prosperity lay much economic disorder. Neither business nor government took action in spite of danger signals occurring in 1927 and 1928.

In 1929, the worst business crash in United States history brought some government action. But the Republican administration of Herbert Hoover would only go so far. It provided aid for some failing banks, railroads, and agricultural organizations during the Great Depression that followed in the 1930's. But Hoover was committed to the concept of "rugged individualism," and he rigidly refused to offer direct government aid to people in need of relief from the economic disaster.

The New Deal. The Great Depression brought a revolution in the fortunes of the Democratic Party. Democrats won every presidential election of the 1930's and 1940's and controlled Congress for most of that period. Franklin D. Roosevelt won the elections of 1932, 1936, 1940, and 1944 and became the only man to win the presidency four times. Vice President Harry S. Truman became president after Roosevelt's death in 1945 and won the election in 1948.

Roosevelt was the dominating figure of the years of the Great Depression. He did even more than Wilson to convert the Democrats from a party of states' rights and limited government to one of national reform. During

the 1932 campaign, he had promised Americans a "new deal" that included economic relief, recovery, and reform and a better life for what he called the "forgotten man." Roosevelt's personality and confidence made him a hero to millions as he carried through promises of his New Deal program by greatly extending the role of government. Under the New Deal, the federal government imposed many business regulations and passed laws to help the needy.

Most farmers, intellectuals, unemployed workers, wage earners, and members of minority groups supported the New Deal and voted Democratic. Most Southerners and residents of big cities also backed the party. But conservatives—both Democrats and Republicans—believed that the federal government was taking far too great a role in people's lives. Conservatives' opposition to Roosevelt's 1937 plan to "pack" the U.S. Supreme Court with new members led many Southern Democrats to join Republicans in a conservative coalition. Until the 1960's, this coalition frequently blocked Democratic presidents' attempts at reform. During World War II (1939-1945), Roosevelt turned the nation's efforts toward defeating Germany and Japan.

The Fair Deal. President Truman continued the policies of the New Deal, calling his program the Fair Deal. He fought for civil rights for African Americans and for a national medical insurance plan. Southern Democrats often joined Republicans to block Truman's efforts.

In 1948, some Southern Democrats formed the States' Rights Democratic Party, or Dixiecrat Party, to oppose Truman. But Truman won a surprise victory over the Republican candidate, Thomas E. Dewey.

In both 1952 and 1956, the Democratic presidential candidate, Adlai E. Stevenson, lost to Dwight D. Eisenhower, one of the nation's greatest heroes of World War II. Yet the Democrats controlled Congress for the last six of Eisenhower's eight years in office.

The New Frontier. John F. Kennedy won the presidency in 1960, defeating Republican Richard M. Nixon. Kennedy called for many reforms in his program, which he named the New Frontier. Democrats outnumbered Republicans in both houses of Congress, but conservative Southern Democrats frequently joined conservative Republicans to defeat bills supported by Kennedy.

The Great Society. Vice President Lyndon B. Johnson became president after Kennedy was assassinated in November 1963. In 1964, Johnson won a full term as president with a landslide victory over his Republican opponent, Barry M. Goldwater.

A skillful politician, Johnson worked hard for the program begun by Kennedy. He called on the nation to join him in building what he termed the Great Society. Congress approved Johnson's requests for aid to cities and education, landmark civil rights legislation, greater Social Security benefits, and tax cuts.

Times of trouble. By 1966, the Vietnam War—and the nationwide dispute about it—overshadowed Johnson's Great Society program. The war divided many Americans into "hawks," who supported U.S. involvement in Vietnam, and "doves," who opposed it.

In 1968, Johnson announced that he would not run for reelection. The Democrats nominated Vice President Hubert H. Humphrey for the presidency. George C. Wallace, a Southern Democrat, became the candidate of a

It's a fact

Many people pronounce the last name of Vice President Richard B. Cheney to sound like *CHAY nee*, but Cheney himself prefers the pronunciation *CHEE nee*.

Former Governor Mel Carnahan of Missouri was elected to the U.S. Senate in the election of 2000. His victory marked the first time a dead person had ever been elected to the Senate. Carnahan had died in a plane crash shortly before the election, too late for his name to be removed from the ballot. After the election, Jean Carnahan, the former governor's widow, was appointed to fill the vacancy.

In the 2000 election, four Democrats won Senate seats who were multimillionaires and financed their own campaigns—Maria Cantwell of Washington, Jon S. Corzine of New Jersey, Mark Dayton of Minnesota, and Herbert Kohl of Wisconsin.

Senator Joseph I. Lieberman of Connecticut was the first Jewish vice presidential candidate of a major American political party. He ran with Democratic presidential candidate Al Gore in the 2000 election.

Following his graduation from Princeton University, former Senator Bill Bradley accepted a Rhodes Scholarship to Oxford University in England.

third party, the American Independent Party. The Republican candidate, Richard M. Nixon, won in 1968, but the Democrats kept control of Congress.

In 1969, a commission chaired by Senator George S. McGovern of South Dakota adopted a set of rules for the states to follow in selecting convention delegates. These rules reduced the influence of party leaders on the nominating process and provided greater representation for minorities, women, and youth. The reforms led most states to adopt laws requiring primary elections, instead of party leaders, to choose delegates.

In 1972, the Democrats nominated McGovern for the presidency, and the Republicans renominated Nixon. Nixon won a landslide victory, but the Democrats kept control of Congress. In 1974, Nixon resigned rather than face impeachment for the Watergate scandal (see **Watergate**). Vice President Gerald R. Ford succeeded him.

Mixed results. Jimmy Carter, the Democratic nominee, defeated Ford in the 1976 presidential election. The Democrats also retained control of Congress. In the 1980 election, however, Carter lost his bid for a second term. He was defeated by former Governor Ronald Reagan of California, the Republican candidate. The Democrats also lost the Senate to the Republicans, though they kept control of the House.

Walter F. Mondale, Carter's vice president, became the Democratic presidential nominee in 1984. His running mate, Representative Geraldine A. Ferraro of New York, was the first woman vice presidential candidate of a major American political party. The Republicans renominated Reagan, and he easily won a second term as president. The Republicans retained control of the Senate. But the elections of 1986 gave the Democrats control of both houses of Congress.

In 1988, Massachusetts Governor Michael S. Dukakis won the Democratic presidential nomination. He lost the election to Republican Vice President George H. W. Bush, but the Democrats retained control of Congress.

In 1992, Governor Bill Clinton of Arkansas, a Democrat, won the presidency, defeating Bush and independent candidate Ross Perot. In 1994, the Democrats lost control of both houses of Congress to the Republicans. In 1996, Clinton was reelected, defeating Republican Robert Dole. But the Republicans retained control of both houses of Congress in 1996 and 1998.

Vice President Al Gore was the Democratic candidate in the 2000 presidential election. His running mate, Senator Joseph I. Lieberman of Connecticut, was the first Jewish vice presidential candidate of a major American political party. Gore lost a close race to his Republican opponent, Texas Governor George W. Bush. The Republicans retained control of the House, but neither party won a majority in the Senate. After the election, the Senate had 50 Republican members and 50 Democratic members. Sidney M. Milkis

Related articles in *World Book* include:

Political convention
Political party
President of the United States

Additional resources

Chambers, William Nisbet. *The Democrats in American Politics: A Short History of a Popular Party.* 2nd ed. Van Nostrand, 1972.
Lindop, Edmund, and Thornton, J. C. *All About Democrats: Over 750 Questions and Answers.* Enslow, 1985.

Web site

The Democratic National Committee
http://www.democrats.org/index.html
Official web site of the Democratic Party's National Committee.

Forbes, Steve (1947-   ), is a newspaper and magazine publisher. He campaigned for the Republican nomination for United States president in 2000 but left the race for lack of voter support in the primaries. He had campaigned for the 1996 nomination but failed to win it. He is known for supporting a *flat tax,* which would eliminate the country's graduated income tax and require everyone to pay a flat percentage of income in taxes.

Malcolm Stevenson Forbes, Jr., was born in Morristown, New Jersey. He graduated from Princeton University in 1970. While he was in college, he founded *Business Today,* a quarterly business magazine. In 1971, he started as a researcher at *Forbes,* the business magazine founded by his grandfather and owned by his family. He began writing a column for the magazine in 1973, and he worked in various departments to learn the business.

In 1980, Forbes became president and chief operating officer of Forbes Inc., which owns a number of newspapers and magazines. Two years later, he was also named the deputy editor in chief of *Forbes* magazine. After his father died in 1990, Forbes became chief executive officer of the company and editor in chief of the magazine.

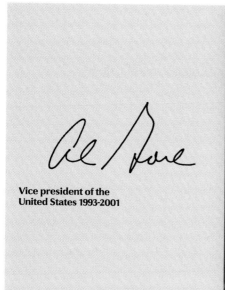

**Vice president of the
United States 1993-2001**

The White House

Gore, Al (1948-   ), vice president of the United States under President Bill Clinton, was the Democratic candidate for president in 2000. Gore lost to his Republican opponent, Texas Governor George W. Bush, in one of the closest presidential elections in U.S. history. Gore received more popular votes than Bush, but Bush received more votes in the Electoral College. However, the outcome was in doubt for weeks after the election. It was not clear which candidate had carried the state of Florida, where the vote was extremely close. Delays resulted from recounts of Florida ballots and court challenges to the recounts. Five weeks after the election, following a decision by the U.S. Supreme Court to halt the recounts, Gore conceded the election to Bush.

During Gore's campaign for the presidency, he pledged to maintain the nation's healthy economy. He focused on family and children's issues. He proposed making high-quality preschool education and affordable health-care insurance available to every child. He also called for medical coverage that would assist senior citizens in paying for prescription medicines.

Before becoming vice president in 1993, Gore represented his home state, Tennessee, in the United States House of Representatives and the U.S. Senate. He won recognition as an accomplished political leader. He was especially strong in his efforts to protect the environment.

Gore came from a political family. His father, Albert Gore, Sr., had served in the House of Representatives and then in the Senate. Albert Gore, Sr., a Tennessee Democrat, wanted to keep his roots in his home state.

Bill Turque, the contributor of this article, is a Washington correspondent for Newsweek *and the author of* Inventing Al Gore.

As a result, he never bought a home in Washington, D.C. Instead, he rented a suite in a Washington hotel. Al, Jr., therefore, lived in a hotel for much of his childhood.

Before he entered politics in 1976, Gore had a varied career. He worked as a journalist and a real estate developer, and he operated a small farm. Gore also served in Vietnam during the Vietnam War (1957-1975).

Gore is well-spoken but has a formal, even stiff, way of speaking. He often jokes about that characteristic.

An athletic man, Gore played basketball and football in high school and college and competed on the track team. When he was 50 years old, Gore ran in his first marathon. He still runs and plays basketball to keep fit.

Early life

Family background. Al Gore was born on March 31, 1948, in Washington, D.C. His full name is Albert Arnold Gore, Jr.

Important dates in Gore's life

1948	(March 31) Born in Washington, D.C.
1969	Graduated from Harvard University.
1969-1971	Served in the U.S. Army.
1970	(May 19) Married Mary Elizabeth (Tipper) Aitcheson.
1976	Elected to the U.S. House of Representatives. Gore was reelected three times and served until 1985.
1984	Elected to the U.S. Senate.
1988	Campaigned for the Democratic nomination for U.S. president but lost to Massachusetts Governor Michael S. Dukakis.
1990	Reelected to the U.S. Senate.
1992	Elected vice president of the United States.
1996	Reelected vice president.
2000	Unsuccessful in race for president of the United States.

Gore's father, Albert Gore, Sr., was born in rural middle Tennessee. He served in the United States House of Representatives from 1939 to 1944, when he entered active duty in the U.S. Army. He returned to the House in 1945 and remained a member until 1953. He then served in the United States Senate from 1953 to 1971.

Gore's mother was born Pauline LaFon in rural west Tennessee. She earned a college law degree from the Vanderbilt University School of Law in Nashville, Tennessee, in 1936. It was unusual for a woman to earn a law degree at that time. Pauline LaFon was one of the first women to earn a law degree at Vanderbilt.

LaFon and Al Gore, Sr., met in the restaurant where LaFon was working as a waitress to pay her way through school. Gore, also a law student, went there often for coffee. The couple married in 1937. Pauline Gore became one of the most important workers in her husband's campaigns and his congressional office.

Pauline Gore and Al Gore, Sr., had two children—Nancy and Al, Jr. Nancy was 10 years older than her brother, and Al was devoted to her. Nancy, who became a cigarette smoker as an adult, died of lung cancer in 1984. In a speech at the 1996 Democratic National Convention, Al Gore spoke out against smoking. The members of the audience could see his sadness as he spoke about the death of his sister 12 years earlier.

Boyhood. When Congress was in session, Al, Jr., lived in a hotel suite in Washington, D.C., with his parents. During the summer and at other times, he lived on his family's large farm near Carthage, Tennessee.

When his parents were away, Al stayed with the tenant farmers who lived on the property, William Thompson and his wife, Alota. Al Gore became a close friend of their son, Gordon. Gore and his friends enjoyed horseback riding, fishing, canoeing, and swimming on the farm and in the surrounding rural area. They also enjoyed playing with their dogs. Al's dog was a collie named Buff. When Al was 8 years old, his father gave him a pony, which he loved to ride.

Young Gore also worked on the farm. He helped harvest crops and take care of livestock.

Later in life, Gore commented on his two homes while a young boy. He said he enjoyed the family farm much more than the Washington, D.C., hotel suite.

School life. Gore attended school in Carthage through the third grade. He then entered St. Albans School, a highly rated private academic institution in Washington, D.C. He completed both elementary school and high school at St. Albans. In high school, he was a member of the debate club and the varsity basketball, football, and track teams. He also took part in the school's student government.

College and military service

In 1965, Gore enrolled at Harvard University in Cambridge, Massachusetts. Gore majored in government studies and earned a degree in 1969.

At the time of Gore's graduation from Harvard, the United States was deeply involved in the Vietnam War, and the country had become divided over U.S. participation in the conflict. Gore opposed the involvement, but he felt it was his duty to do military service. After graduation, he enlisted in the United States Army. He served in the Army until 1971. Gore spent about six months of

© *The Tennessean* from Sygma

Young Al Gore posed with his parents in this picture. His father served in Congress for many years. His mother was an important aide in her husband's campaigns and in his office.

© Martin Simon, Saba

Gore served in the United States Army during the Vietnam War from 1969 to 1971. He was stationed in Vietnam for six months. He worked as an Army journalist.

his service time in Vietnam and worked as an Army journalist there.

Early career

After leaving the Army, Gore became a reporter and editorial writer for the *The Tennessean,* a Nashville newspaper. He worked for the paper from 1971 to 1974 and again in 1975 and 1976.

During the same period, Gore operated a small farm and worked as a real estate developer. In addition, he attended Vanderbilt University in Nashville, his mother's alma mater. At Vanderbilt, Gore studied in the Divinity School in 1971 and 1972. He then attended the Law School from 1974 to 1976.

Gore's family

Gore met Mary Elizabeth Aitcheson (Aug. 19, 1948-) at a high school graduation party in 1965. Mary Elizabeth has been called Tipper since her infancy. She got this nickname because her mother sang her to sleep with the song "Tippy Tippy Tin." Tipper Aitcheson had come to the graduation party with someone else, but she and Gore talked briefly. They liked each other, and they began dating after that evening. They married on May 19, 1970.

Tipper Gore became an accomplished photographer. Her book, *Picture This: A Visual Diary* (1996), contains her photos and comments about her life as the vice president's wife. She also became a strong spokesperson against what she considered obscene lyrics in music aimed at young people.

Tipper and Al Gore had three daughters and a son. Their daughters are Karenna (1973-), Kristin (1977-), and Sarah (1979-). Their son is named Albert III (1982-).

Congressional career

In 1976, Gore decided to enter politics. He was elected to the United States House of Representatives in that year and took office in 1977. He won election to the House three more times, serving until 1985.

In 1984, Gore decided to seek a seat in the United States Senate. He was elected to the Senate that year and took office in 1985. He won reelection in 1990.

While in Congress, Gore gained a reputation as a moderate liberal. He became a specialist on the environment, nuclear arms control, and public health.

Gore became one of the leading congressional supporters of efforts to protect the environment. In 1980, while in the House of Representatives, he helped write the "Superfund" law, which provided funds to clean up unsafe hazardous waste dumps. This legislation is officially known as the Comprehensive Environmental Response, Compensation, and Liability Act. In June 1992, Gore led a Senate delegation to the United Nations Conference on Environment and Development, also known as the Earth Summit, in Rio de Janeiro, Brazil. He spoke out against threats to the environment, such as toxic wastes and global warming. Gore is the author of *Earth in the Balance: Ecology and the Human Spirit* (1992).

Nuclear arms control was another Gore specialty. An assistant to President Ronald Reagan, a Republican, called Gore the best expert in the Senate on nuclear arms control.

Gore became one of the most outspoken House leaders in the movement to strengthen health warning messages on cigarette packages. He also promoted a number of other public health bills.

Gore gained a reputation as an intelligent and hard-working member of Congress. He returned to his home district regularly to learn the views of the people he represented. Gore carefully studied legislative matters and strongly promoted his beliefs.

In Congress, Gore served on the Senate's Commerce, Science, and Transportation Committee and on its Armed Forces Committee. Gore also served as a member of Congress's Joint Economic Committee.

In 1987, when he was 39 years old, Gore announced he was running for the 1988 Democratic presidential nomination. He received widespread support in Southern States, but Michael Dukakis, the governor of Massachusetts, won the nomination.

Vice president

Election and reelection. In 1992, Bill Clinton, the governor of Arkansas, won the Democratic nomination

Gore campaigned in Tennessee for a seat in the United States House of Representatives, winning election in 1976. It was the same congressional seat that his father had won during his father's first successful campaign.

Gore and his family pose on the porch of their Washington, D.C., home. In the back row, *left to right,* are Albert Gore III, Al Gore, and Sarah and Kristin Gore. In the front are Andrew Schiff, Karenna Gore Schiff, and Tipper Gore.

The White House

for the presidency. At Clinton's request, the Democratic National Convention nominated Gore for vice president.

The Republicans renominated President George Bush and Vice President Dan Quayle to oppose Clinton and Gore. Ross Perot, a wealthy businessman, ran for president as an independent candidate.

Al and Tipper Gore campaigned hard in 1992. They took bus trips, often with the Clintons, to many parts of the country to talk to voters. During the campaign, Gore often criticized the Bush administration's environmental policies. Clinton and Gore were elected president and vice president of the United States in November 1992.

In 1996, the Democrats again nominated Clinton and Gore. The Republicans selected Bob Dole, a former United States senator from Kansas, to run for president. Jack Kemp, a former member of the United States House of Representatives from New York, became the Republican vice presidential candidate. In November 1996, Clinton and Gore were reelected.

Role in office. The role of the U.S. vice president is traditionally viewed as a weak one because the vice

president has almost no political power. However, Vice President Gore became an important force in the Clinton administration. He acted as an adviser to President Clinton on most major issues. He played a leading role in foreign affairs, trade policy, environmental protection, and efforts to improve U.S. technology. In 1993, Clinton made Gore head of the National Performance Review (now called the National Partnership for Reinventing Government), which studies ways to increase the federal government's efficiency and reduce its costs.

Scandals. In their second term in office, both Gore and Clinton received public criticism for certain actions. Gore was accused of improper fund-raising activities. Clinton was charged with having an affair with a White House intern and lying under oath about it.

In 1996, Gore had attended a fund-raising event at a Buddhist temple. The temple had a tax-exempt status and, therefore, should not have been used for a political fund-raising event. Gore had also made telephone calls from the White House to prospective donors, though political fund-raising is not permitted in government

AP/Wide World

At a UN conference on the environment in 1992, Gore spoke out against toxic wastes and global warming. He was a leading congressional supporter of efforts to protect the environment.

© Allan Tannenbaum, Sygma

Al Gore and Bill Clinton were nominated for vice president and president at the 1992 Democratic National Convention. They won election in both 1992 and 1996.

At the Gore family farm in Carthage, Tennessee, Al Gore jogs with his daughter Kristin. Gore ran in his first marathon when he was 50 years old.

AP/Wide World

buildings. An investigation into the Democratic Party's fund-raising activities for the 1996 campaign resulted in charges against several people concerning illegal donations. Gore admitted that he made mistakes, but no charges were brought against him.

In 1998, Gore faced the possibility that he might have to step into the presidency. In December of that year, the U.S. House of Representatives impeached Clinton for perjury and obstruction of justice. The charges developed out of Clinton's efforts to conceal a sexual relationship with a White House intern, Monica Lewinsky. The House sent its findings to the Senate, which conducted a trial. The Senate considered the charges and whether or not the president should be removed from office. In February 1999, the Senate found Clinton not guilty, and Clinton remained in office.

Election of 2000

In June 1999, Gore announced that he would seek the Democratic nomination for president. His chief rival was

Bill Bradley, a former senator from New Jersey. Gore defeated Bradley in a number of primary elections, and Bradley withdrew from the race in March 2000.

At the Democratic National Convention in Los Angeles in August 2000, Gore was named the Democratic presidential nominee. At Gore's request, the delegates nominated Senator Joseph I. Lieberman of Connecticut as their candidate for vice president. Lieberman became the first Jewish vice presidential candidate of a major American political party. The Republicans nominated George W. Bush, governor of Texas, as their candidate for president, and Richard B. Cheney, a former congressman and U.S. secretary of defense, as their candidate for vice president.

During the campaign, Gore vowed to maintain the nation's healthy economy. He also called for a number of changes to benefit children and families. Gore said, for example, that good preschool education should be available for every child and that parents should have access to affordable health-care insurance for their chil-

AP/Wide World

Running mates Gore and Senator Joseph I. Lieberman of Connecticut accept the Democratic Party's nomination for president and vice president at the party's national convention in Los Angeles in August 2000.

Closest elections in the Electoral College*

1876 Hayes 185, Tilden 184 (margin of 1)*

2000 Bush 271, Gore 266 (margin of 5)

1824 Jackson 99, Adams 84, Crawford 41, Clay 37 (margin of 15)

1916 Wilson 277, Hughes 254 (margin of 23)

1848 Taylor 163, Cass 127 (margin of 36)

1884 Cleveland 219, Blaine 182 (margin of 37)

1812 Madison 128, Clinton 89 (margin of 39)

1976 Carter 297, Ford 240, Reagan 1 (margin of 57)

*Note: This table does not include the results of the election of 1800, in which Thomas Jefferson and his running mate, Aaron Burr, each received 73 electoral votes. That election led to Amendment 12 to the Constitution, ratified in 1804, providing that electors should designate their votes for president and vice president on separate ballots, as they do today.

Closest elections in the popular vote

1880 Garfield 4,446,158 (48.3%), Hancock 4,444,260 (48.3%) (actual percentage: Garfield 48.27%, Hancock 48.25%) (0.02% margin)

1960 Kennedy 34,221,344 (49.7%), Nixon 34,106,671 (49.6%) (0.1% margin)

1884 Cleveland 4,874,621 (48.5%), Blaine 4,848,936 (48.3%) (0.2% margin)

2000 Gore 50,996,116 (48.4%), Bush 50,456,169 (47.9%) (0.5% margin). Gore lost the Electoral College vote.

1968 Nixon 31,785,148 (43.4%), Humphrey 31,274,503 (42.7%) Wallace 9,901,151 (13.5%) (0.7% margin)

1888 Cleveland 5,534,488 (48.6%), Harrison 5,443,892 (47.8%) (0.8% margin). Cleveland lost the Electoral College vote.

---

dren. He also proposed providing medical coverage that would help senior citizens pay for prescription drugs.

Gore's campaign statements also emphasized his many years in political office. He charged that Bush was not experienced enough to be president. He labeled as "risky" Bush's proposal to reduce taxes and use the federal budget surplus to make up the difference. Gore said that such a plan might leave the Social Security and Medicare programs without sufficient funds.

Bush hit at Gore's 1996 fund-raising tactics. Gore acknowledged that his fund-raising had gone too far and added to his campaign promises a pledge to overhaul the campaign finance system.

The election of 2000 was one of the tightest presidential contests in U.S. history. The outcome was in doubt for weeks after the election. It depended upon which candidate won Florida. Because the vote was very close there, the state ordered a machine recount. After that recount, Bush was ahead. Gore asked for hand recounts in certain counties, and Bush challenged in court the need for those recounts. Five weeks after the election, following a U.S. Supreme Court decision to halt the recounts, Gore conceded the election to Bush. Gore won the popular vote by a margin of .5 percent. But Bush had a 5-vote margin in the Electoral College, the group of representatives chosen by the voters of each state to elect the president and vice president.   Bill Turque

See also **Clinton, Bill; Democratic Party; President of the United States.**

Outline

I. Early life
   A. Family background   C. School life
   B. Boyhood
II. College and military service
III. Early career
IV. Gore's family
V. Congressional career
VI. Vice president
   A. Election and reelection   C. Scandals
   B. Role in office
VII. Election of 2000

Questions

Why did Gore have two boyhood homes?
How did Gore's political career resemble his father's?
What family tragedy led Gore to speak out against smoking?
Where did Gore meet his future wife, Tipper?

What are measures Gore has taken to protect the environment?
How did Gore serve in the Vietnam War?
What was Gore's career before he entered politics?
What role did Gore play as vice president?

Additional resources

Burford, Betty M. *Al Gore*. Enslow, 1994.
Turque, Bill. *Inventing Al Gore: A Biography*. Houghton, 2000.

Web site

Gore, Albert Arnold, Jr. (1948-   ) Biographical Information http://bioguide.congress.gov/scripts/biodisplay.pl?index= G000321
The Biographical Directory of the U.S. Congress site on Al Gore.

Gore, Tipper (1948-   ), is the wife of Al Gore, vice president of the United States under Bill Clinton and the Democratic candidate for president in 2000. During the Clinton administration, Tipper Gore served as mental

It's a fact

The winner of the 2000 election has reason to hope that it is mere coincidence that the presidents elected every 20 years die in office. Beginning with William H. Harrison, who won office in 1840, no president elected in a year ending with zero left the White House alive. Harrison, William G. Harding (1920), and Franklin D. Roosevelt (1940) died of natural causes. Abraham Lincoln (1860), James A. Garfield (1880), William McKinley (1900), and John F. Kennedy (1960) were assassinated. Finally Ronald Reagan, elected in 1980, survived his presidency and broke the string.

Most historians regard Andrew Jackson's presidential campaign organization, formed in 1828, as the beginning of the Democratic Party as it is known today.

Ronald Reagan received the greatest number of electoral votes of any president—525 in 1984.

A record number of women won election to the United States Senate in 2000. The 107th Congress had 13 women senators, more than ever before.

health policy adviser to the president. She has also been a photojournalist and political activist.

Born Mary Elizabeth Aitcheson in Washington, D.C., she has been called Tipper since her infancy. She married Al Gore in 1970. They have three daughters and one son—Karenna, Kristin, Sarah, and Albert Gore III.

Tipper Gore received a bachelor's degree from Boston University in 1970. She earned a master's degree from George Peabody College for Teachers, now part of Vanderbilt University, in 1976. Gore has been an outspoken supporter of several causes. She cofounded the Parents' Music Resource Center (PMRC), which campaigned against violent and explicit lyrics in popular music. She wrote a related book as a guide for parents, *Raising PG Kids in an X-Rated Society* (1987). She cofounded and chaired Families for the Homeless, an organization that works to raise public awareness of the plight of the homeless. She created a book of her photographs, *Picture This: A Visual Diary* (1996), which records her life as the vice president's wife.

Green party is any of a number of political parties that are most widely known for promoting environmental issues. Other issues advanced by Green parties include the rights of women and opposition to capitalism, modernism, the building of nuclear power plants, and the testing and production of nuclear weapons.

Green parties operate primarily in industrialized countries. Germany and other Western European nations have some of the strongest Green parties. In 1983, before the German unification, West Germany's Green Party became the first Green party in Europe to win seats in a national legislature. The United States has many Green parties, but none has many members. Other countries with Green parties include Australia, Austria, Finland, France, New Zealand, Spain, and Sweden.

Most existing Green parties were founded in the 1980's. But Green parties draw on the traditions of anarchist, socialist, and other left-wing movements that developed in Europe during the 1800's. Because of their diverse objectives, Green parties have had difficulty joining to challenge better-established parties. As a result, they have sometimes formed alliances with other kinds of parties, such as the Social Democratic Party in Germany.   Kim R. Holmes

Web site

Green Parties of North America
http://www.greens.org/
Information and documents defining the purpose of Green political parties.

Hagelin, John Samuel (1954-   ), a research scientist and educator, was a candidate of the Reform Party and the Natural Law Party for president of the United States in the 2000 election. He received less than 1 percent of the votes. Hagelin had also been the Natural Law Party's candidate in 1992 and 1996 .

Hagelin has won international recognition for his research in modern physics. As a candidate, he argued that scientific principles and science's common-sense approach could be used to solve society's problems.

Hagelin was born in Pittsburgh, Pennsylvania. He graduated from Dartmouth College in 1975. He then attended Harvard University, where he earned a master's degree in 1976 and a doctorate in nuclear physics in 1981. After leaving Harvard, he did scientific research at the European Laboratory for Particle Physics (CERN) in Geneva, Switzerland, and then at the Linear Accelerator Center at Stanford University.

In 1984, Hagelin joined Maharishi University of Management in Fairfield, Iowa, where he is a physics professor and director of the doctoral physics program. In 1992, he also became director of the Institute of Science, Technology, and Public Policy, a center for public policy study and research run by the university. The institute explores solutions to problems in such areas as crime prevention, education, the environment, and health care.

Keyes, Alan Lee (1950-   ), was one of the first African Americans to seek the Republican presidential nomination. He campaigned for the nomination in 1996 and in 2000 but did not win it.

Keyes held several governmental positions in the administration of Republican President Ronald Reagan in the 1980's. From 1983 to 1985, he served as ambassador to the United Nations Economic and Social Council. In 1988 and 1992, Keyes ran for the United States Senate from Maryland, but was defeated both times.

In his campaigns for the Republican presidential nomination, Keyes became known for his conservative views on such issues as abortion and the right to own guns. He also became known for his abilities as a public speaker. He was not a leading candidate in either campaign, but he gained the support of many conservative voters.

Alan Lee Keyes was born in New York City. He earned a doctoral degree in government from Harvard University in 1979. In addition to his public policy posts, Keyes also hosted a radio talk show, wrote a newspaper column, and was a paid public speaker.

Lieberman, *LEE bur muhn,* **Joseph Isadore** (1942-   ), a U.S. senator representing Connecticut, was the Democratic candidate for vice president of the United States in 2000. In an extremely close contest, he and his running mate, Vice President Al Gore, lost to their Republican opponents, Texas Governor George W. Bush and former U.S. Secretary of Defense Richard Cheney. Lieberman, an Orthodox Jew, was the first Jewish vice presidential candidate of a major U.S. political party.

In 1998, Lieberman was the first Democratic senator to publicly criticize President Bill Clinton for having an affair with White House intern Monica Lewinsky and trying to cover up his misconduct.

Early life. Lieberman was born in Stamford, Connecticut. He received a bachelor's degree in 1964 and a law degree in 1967, both from Yale University. After graduation, Lieberman began practicing law.

In 1965, Lieberman married Elizabeth (Betty) Haas, whom he had met when they both worked as summer interns for Connecticut Senator Abraham A. Ribicoff. The couple had two children, Matthew and Rebecca. They divorced in 1981. In 1983, Lieberman married Hadassah Freilich, who had a son, Ethan, from a previous

U.S. Senate

Joseph I. Lieberman

marriage. The couple had a daughter, Hana. Hadassah Lieberman has worked in public relations and health care consulting.

Political career. Lieberman ran for public office for the first time in 1970. He was elected to the Connecticut state Senate and served until 1981. From 1975 to 1981, he was the Senate majority leader. In 1980, Lieberman ran for the U.S. House of Representatives but lost. He served as Connecticut's attorney general from 1983 to 1988. In 1989, Lieberman began his service as a U.S. senator representing Connecticut.

As a member of the Senate, Lieberman became known for his criticism of violence on television and in rap music and video games. He encouraged those industries to voluntarily reduce such violence so that legislation to restrict it would not be necessary. He supported an increase in the legal minimum wage, which was passed by Congress and signed into law by President Clinton in 1996. Lieberman was a member of the Senate committees on Armed Services, Governmental Affairs, Small Business, and Environment and Public Works.

Lieberman has written several books, including *The Scorpion and the Tarantula* (1970), about the spread of nuclear weapons; *Child Support in America* (1986); and *In Praise of Public Life* (2000).   Lee Thornton

See also **Gore, Al; Vice President of the United States.**

Web site

Senator Joseph I. Lieberman
http://www.senate.gov/~lieberman/
The official United States Senate Web site of Joseph Lieberman.

McCain, John Sidney, III (1936-   ), a Republican from Arizona, has been a member of the United States Senate since 1987. He has chaired the committees on Indian Affairs and on Commerce, Science, and Transportation, and has served on the Armed Services Committee. In 1999, McCain began campaigning for the Republican presidential nomination for the 2000 election. But he withdrew from the race in early 2000.

In the mid-1990's, McCain worked with Daniel K. Inouye, a Democrat from Hawaii, on a bill to regulate casino gambling on Indian reservations. McCain and Russell Feingold, a Democrat from Wisconsin, cosponsored a bill to encourage limits on campaign spending.

McCain was born in the Panama Canal Zone, where his father was serving in the U.S. Navy. Both his grandfather and his father were Navy admirals. In 1958, McCain graduated from the U.S. Naval Academy. He then entered the Navy and served as a fighter pilot. In 1967, during the Vietnam War, his plane was shot down in Vietnam, and he was held prisoner there until 1973. In 1973 and 1974, McCain attended the National War College. From 1977 to 1980, he served as director of the Navy Senate Liaison Office. He retired from the Navy in 1981.

McCain was elected to the U.S. House of Representatives in 1982 and in 1984. In 1986, he won election to his first term in the U.S. Senate. His autobiography, *Faith of My Fathers,* was published in 1999.   Jackie Koszczuk

Web site

Senator John S. McCain III
http://www.senate.gov/~mccain/
The official United States Senate web site of John McCain.

Nader, *NAY duhr,* **Ralph** (1934-   ), an American lawyer, became famous for fighting business and government practices he felt endangered public health and safety. Nader also is an outspoken critic of the influence of large corporations on the American political system. In 1996 and 2000, he ran as the Green Party candidate for president of the United States. The Green Party's platform stresses community leadership, environmental responsibility, respect for diversity, improved health care, and social justice. Nader won only a small percentage of votes in either election, but his candidacy brought increased attention to the Green Party and its causes.

In his book *Unsafe at Any Speed* (1965), Nader argued that the U.S. automobile industry emphasized profits and style over safety. The National Traffic and Motor Vehicle Safety Act of 1966, which established safety standards for new cars, resulted largely from his work.

UPI/Bettmann Newsphotos
Ralph Nader

Nader's studies of the meat and poultry industries, coal mines, and natural gas pipelines also resulted in stricter health and safety laws. He publicized what he felt were the dangers of pesticides, food additives, radiation from color TV sets, and excessive use of X rays. He said the government was not strict enough in enforcing antipollution and consumer protection laws.

Nader's operating funds come mainly from his writings and speeches, from foundation grants, and from contributions. In 1971, Nader founded an organization called Public Citizen, Inc., which he headed until 1980. It specialized in energy problems, health care, tax reform, and other consumer issues. Nader and his staff conducted a major study of Congress in 1972. Their findings were published in a book, *Who Runs Congress?* In 1982, another Nader group published a study of the Reagan Administration called *Reagan's Ruling Class: Portraits of the President's Top One Hundred Officials.*

In 1988, Nader's efforts helped bring about the passage of California's Proposition 103, a law that provided for lowering some auto insurance costs. Nader won another battle in 1989 when General Motors announced it would make air bags standard equipment on many 1990 models. Nader had promoted the use of the safety feature for more than 10 years.

In the 1990's, Nader continued his struggle for consumer health and safety. He also spoke out on such issues as campaign finance reform, trade policy, globalization, corporate abuse, universal health care, and criminal justice reform.

Nader was born in Winsted, Connecticut, the son of Lebanese immigrants. He graduated from Princeton University and Harvard Law School.   Frederick E. Webster, Jr.

Web site

Nader 2000—Biography
http://www.votenader.org/biography.html
Information from the official Web site of Ralph Nader.

President of the United States

The seal of the president of the United States includes an eagle holding arrows and an olive branch. The branch symbolizes the desire for peace, and the arrows represent the ability to wage war. The 50 stars stand for the 50 U.S. states.

President of the United States is often considered the most powerful elected official in the world. The president leads a nation of great wealth and military strength. Presidents have often provided decisive leadership in times of crisis, and they have shaped many important events in history.

The Constitution of the United States gives the president enormous power. However, it also limits that power. The authors of the Constitution wanted a strong leader as president, but they did not want an all-powerful king. As a result, they divided the powers of the United States government among three branches—executive, legislative, and judicial. The president, who is often called the *chief executive,* heads the executive branch. Congress represents the legislative branch. The Supreme Court of the United States and other federal courts make up the judicial branch. Congress and the

Supreme Court may prevent or end any presidential action that exceeds the limits of the president's powers and trespasses on their authority.

The president has many roles and performs many duties. As chief executive, the president makes sure that federal laws are enforced. As commander in chief of the nation's armed forces, the president is responsible for national defense. As foreign policy director, the president determines United States relations with other nations. As legislative leader, the president recommends laws and works to win their passage. As head of a political party, the president helps mold the party's positions on national and foreign issues. As popular leader, the president tries to inspire the people of the United States to work together to meet the nation's goals. Finally, as chief of state, the president performs a variety of ceremonial duties.

A number of presidents became great leaders. The most admired ones include George Washington, Thomas Jefferson, Andrew Jackson, Abraham Lincoln, Theodore Roosevelt, Woodrow Wilson, Franklin D. Roosevelt, and John F. Kennedy. These leaders served as president when the United States faced extraordinary challenges. They also met those challenges with courage, determination, energy, imagination, and political know-how. Some of the most admired presidents at times ignored the U.S. Constitution or showed little regard for Congress. Nevertheless, their actions won public support. Therefore, like other great presidents, they broadened respect for the presidency and strengthened the office.

The presidency

Legal qualifications. The Constitution establishes only three qualifications for a president. A president must (1) be at least 35 years old, (2) have lived in the United States at least 14 years, and (3) be a natural-born citizen.

Courts have never decided whether a person born abroad to American parents could serve as president of the United States. However, many scholars believe that such a person would be considered a natural-born citizen.

Term of office. The president is elected to a four-year term. The 22nd Amendment to the Constitution

---

Facts in brief about the president

Qualifications: The United States Constitution provides that a candidate for the presidency must be a "natural-born" United States citizen. The candidate must also be at least 35 years old and must have lived in the United States for at least 14 years. No law or court decision has yet defined the exact meaning of *natural-born.* Authorities assume the term applies to citizens born in the United States and its territories. But they are not sure if it also includes children born to United States citizens in other countries.

How nominated: By a national political party convention.

How elected: By a majority vote of the Electoral College, held in December following the general election on the first Tues-

day after the first Monday in November of every fourth year.

Inauguration: Held at noon on January 20 after election. If January 20 is a Sunday, the ceremony may be held privately that day and again in public on January 21.

Term: The president is elected to a four-year term. A president may not be elected more than twice.

Income: Effective Jan. 20, 2001, the president receives a yearly salary of $400,000. In addition, the president receives a $50,000 annual allowance for expenses, and additional allowances for travel, staff support, and White House maintenance.

Succession: If a president dies, resigns, is disabled, or is removed from office, the vice president assumes the office.

Portrait gallery of the presidents

 1. George Washington

 2. John Adams

 3. Thomas Jefferson

 4. James Madison

 5. James Monroe

 6. John Quincy Adams

 7. Andrew Jackson

 8. Martin Van Buren

 9. William H. Harrison

 10. John Tyler

 11. James K. Polk

 12. Zachary Taylor

 13. Millard Fillmore

 14. Franklin Pierce

 15. James Buchanan

 16. Abraham Lincoln

 17. Andrew Johnson

 18. Ulysses S. Grant

 19. Rutherford B. Hayes

 20. James A. Garfield

 21. Chester A. Arthur

 22., 24. Grover Cleveland

 23. Benjamin Harrison

 25. William McKinley

 26. Theodore Roosevelt

 27. William H. Taft

 28. Woodrow Wilson

 29. Warren G. Harding

 30. Calvin Coolidge

 31. Herbert C. Hoover

 32. Franklin D. Roosevelt

 33. Harry S. Truman

 34. Dwight D. Eisenhower

 35. John F. Kennedy

 36. Lyndon B. Johnson

 37. Richard M. Nixon

 38. Gerald R. Ford

 39. Jimmy Carter

 40. Ronald W. Reagan

 41. George H. W. Bush

 42. Bill Clinton

 43. George W. Bush

The presidents of the United States

President	Born	Birthplace	Political party	Age at inaugur- ation	Served	Died	Age at death
1. George Washington	Feb. 22, 1732	Westmoreland County, VA	None	57	1789-1797	Dec. 14, 1799	67
2. John Adams	Oct. 30, 1735	Braintree, MA	Federalist	61	1797-1801	July 4, 1826	90
3. Thomas Jefferson	Apr. 13, 1743	Albemarle County, VA	Dem.-Rep.*	57	1801-1809	July 4, 1826	83
4. James Madison	Mar. 16, 1751	Port Conway, VA	Dem.-Rep.*	57	1809-1817	June 28, 1836	85
5. James Monroe	Apr. 28, 1758	Westmoreland County, VA	Dem.-Rep.*	58	1817-1825	July 4, 1831	73
6. John Quincy Adams	July 11, 1767	Braintree, MA	Dem.-Rep.*	57	1825-1829	Feb. 23, 1848	80
7. Andrew Jackson	Mar. 15, 1767	Waxhaw settlement, SC (?)	Democratic	61	1829-1837	June 8, 1845	78
8. Martin Van Buren	Dec. 5, 1782	Kinderhook, NY	Democratic	54	1837-1841	July 24, 1862	79
9. William H. Harrison	Feb. 9, 1773	Berkeley, VA	Whig	68	1841	Apr. 4, 1841	68
10. John Tyler	Mar. 29, 1790	Greenway, VA	Whig	51	1841-1845	Jan. 18, 1862	71
11. James K. Polk	Nov. 2, 1795	near Pineville, NC	Democratic	49	1845-1849	June 15, 1849	53
12. Zachary Taylor	Nov. 24, 1784	Orange County, VA	Whig	64	1849-1850	July 9, 1850	65
13. Millard Fillmore	Jan. 7, 1800	Locke, NY	Whig	50	1850-1853	Mar. 8, 1874	74
14. Franklin Pierce	Nov. 23, 1804	Hillsboro, NH	Democratic	48	1853-1857	Oct. 8, 1869	64
15. James Buchanan	Apr. 23, 1791	near Mercersburg, PA	Democratic	65	1857-1861	June 1, 1868	77
16. Abraham Lincoln	Feb. 12, 1809	near Hodgenville, KY	Republican, Union†	52	1861-1865	Apr. 15, 1865	56
17. Andrew Johnson	Dec. 29, 1808	Raleigh, NC	Union‡	56	1865-1869	July 31, 1875	66
18. Ulysses S. Grant	Apr. 27, 1822	Point Pleasant, Ohio	Republican	46	1869-1877	July 23, 1885	63
19. Rutherford B. Hayes	Oct. 4, 1822	Delaware, Ohio	Republican	54	1877-1881	Jan. 17, 1893	70
20. James A. Garfield	Nov. 19, 1831	Orange, Ohio	Republican	49	1881	Sept. 19, 1881	49
21. Chester A. Arthur	Oct. 5, 1829	Fairfield, VT	Republican	51	1881-1885	Nov. 18, 1886	57
22. Grover Cleveland	Mar. 18, 1837	Caldwell, NJ	Democratic	47	1885-1889	June 24, 1908	71
23. Benjamin Harrison	Aug. 20, 1833	North Bend, Ohio	Republican	55	1889-1893	Mar. 13, 1901	67
24. Grover Cleveland	Mar. 18, 1837	Caldwell, NJ	Democratic	55	1893-1897	June 24, 1908	71
25. William McKinley	Jan. 29, 1843	Niles, Ohio	Republican	54	1897-1901	Sept. 14, 1901	58
26. Theodore Roosevelt	Oct. 27, 1858	New York City	Republican	42	1901-1909	Jan. 6, 1919	60
27. William H. Taft	Sept. 15, 1857	Cincinnati, Ohio	Republican	51	1909-1913	Mar. 8, 1930	72
28. Woodrow Wilson	Dec. 29, 1856	Staunton, VA	Democratic	56	1913-1921	Feb. 3, 1924	67
29. Warren G. Harding	Nov. 2, 1865	near Blooming Grove, Ohio	Republican	55	1921-1923	Aug. 2, 1923	57
30. Calvin Coolidge	July 4, 1872	Plymouth Notch, VT	Republican	51	1923-1929	Jan. 5, 1933	60
31. Herbert C. Hoover	Aug. 10, 1874	West Branch, Iowa	Republican	54	1929-1933	Oct. 20, 1964	90
32. Franklin D. Roosevelt	Jan. 30, 1882	Hyde Park, NY	Democratic	51	1933-1945	Apr. 12, 1945	63
33. Harry S. Truman	May 8, 1884	Lamar, MO	Democratic	60	1945-1953	Dec. 26, 1972	88
34. Dwight D. Eisenhower	Oct. 14, 1890	Denison, TX	Republican	62	1953-1961	Mar. 28, 1969	78
35. John F. Kennedy	May 29, 1917	Brookline, MA	Democratic	43	1961-1963	Nov. 22, 1963	46
36. Lyndon B. Johnson	Aug. 27, 1908	near Stonewall, TX	Democratic	55	1963-1969	Jan. 22, 1973	64
37. Richard M. Nixon	Jan. 9, 1913	Yorba Linda, CA	Republican	56	1969-1974	Apr. 22, 1994	81
38. Gerald R. Ford#	July 14, 1913	Omaha, NE	Republican	61	1974-1977		
39. Jimmy Carter	Oct. 1, 1924	Plains, GA	Democratic	52	1977-1981		
40. Ronald W. Reagan	Feb. 6, 1911	Tampico, IL	Republican	69	1981-1989		
41. George H. W. Bush	June 12, 1924	Milton, MA	Republican	64	1989-1993		
42. Bill Clinton	Aug. 19, 1946	Hope, AR	Democratic	46	1993-2001		
43. George W. Bush	July 6, 1946	New Haven, CT	Republican	54	2001-		

*Democratic-Republican.
†The Union Party consisted of Republicans and War Democrats.

#Inaugurated Aug. 9, 1974, to replace Nixon, who resigned that same day.
‡The Union Party consisted of Republicans and War Democrats; Johnson was a War Democrat.

	College or university	Religion	Occupation or profession	Runner-up		Vice president	
1.		Episcopalian	Planter	John Adams	(1789, 1792)	John Adams	(1789–1797)
2.	Harvard	Unitarian	Lawyer	Thomas Jefferson	(1796)	Thomas Jefferson	(1797–1801)
3.	William and Mary	Unitarian*	Planter, lawyer	Aaron Burr	(1800)	Aaron Burr	(1801–1805)
				Charles C. Pinckney	(1804)	George Clinton	(1805–1809)
4.	Princeton	Episcopalian	Lawyer	Charles C. Pinckney	(1808)	George Clinton	(1809–1812)
				De Witt Clinton	(1812)	Elbridge Gerry	(1813–1814)
5.	William and Mary	Episcopalian	Lawyer	Rufus King No opposition	(1816)	Daniel D. Tompkins	(1817–1825)
6.	Harvard	Unitarian	Lawyer	Andrew Jackson	(1824)	John C. Calhoun	(1825–1829)
7.		Presbyterian	Lawyer	John Quincy Adams	(1828)	John C. Calhoun	(1829–1832)
				Henry Clay	(1832)	Martin Van Buren	(1833–1837)
8.		Dutch Reformed	Lawyer	William H. Harrison	(1836)	Richard M. Johnson	(1837–1841)
9.	Hampden-Sydney	Episcopalian	Soldier	Martin Van Buren	(1840)	John Tyler	(1841)
10.	William and Mary	Episcopalian	Lawyer			None	
11.	U. of N. Carolina	Methodist	Lawyer	Henry Clay	(1844)	George M. Dallas	(1845–1849)
12.		Episcopalian	Soldier	Lewis Cass	(1848)	Millard Fillmore	(1849–1850)
13.		Unitarian	Lawyer			None	
14.	Bowdoin	Episcopalian	Lawyer	Winfield Scott	(1852)	William R. King	(1853)
15.	Dickinson	Presbyterian	Lawyer	John C. Frémont	(1856)	John C. Breckinridge	(1857–1861)
16.		Presbyterian*	Lawyer	Stephen A. Douglas	(1860)	Hannibal Hamlin	(1861–1865)
				Geo. B. McClellan	(1864)	Andrew Johnson	(1865)
17.		Methodist*	Tailor			None	
18.	U.S. Military Acad.	Methodist	Soldier	Horatio Seymour	(1868)	Schuyler Colfax	(1869–1873)
				Horace Greeley	(1872)	Henry Wilson	(1873–1875)
19.	Kenyon	Methodist*	Lawyer	Samuel J. Tilden	(1876)	William A. Wheeler	(1877–1881)
20.	Williams	Disciples of Christ	Lawyer	Winfield S. Hancock	(1880)	Chester A. Arthur	(1881)
21.	Union	Episcopalian	Lawyer			None	
22.		Presbyterian	Lawyer	James G. Blaine	(1884)	Thomas A. Hendricks	(1885)
23.	Miami	Presbyterian	Lawyer	Grover Cleveland	(1888)	Levi P. Morton	(1889–1893)
24.		Presbyterian	Lawyer	Benjamin Harrison	(1892)	Adlai E. Stevenson	(1893–1897)
25.	Allegheny College	Methodist	Lawyer	William J. Bryan	(1896, 1900)	Garret A. Hobart	(1897–1899)
						Theodore Roosevelt	(1901)
26.	Harvard	Dutch Reformed	Author	Alton B. Parker	(1904)	Charles W. Fairbanks	(1905–1909)
27.	Yale	Unitarian	Lawyer	William J. Bryan	(1908)	James S. Sherman	(1909–1912)
28.	Princeton	Presbyterian	Educator	Theodore Roosevelt	(1912)	Thomas R. Marshall	(1913–1921)
				Charles E. Hughes	(1916)		
29.		Baptist	Editor	James M. Cox	(1920)	Calvin Coolidge	(1921–1923)
30.	Amherst	Congregationalist	Lawyer	John W. Davis	(1924)	Charles G. Dawes	(1925–1929)
31.	Stanford	Friend (Quaker)	Engineer	Alfred E. Smith	(1928)	Charles Curtis	(1929–1933)
32.	Harvard	Episcopalian	Lawyer	Herbert Hoover	(1932)	John N. Garner	(1933–1941)
				Alfred M. Landon	(1936)		
				Wendell L. Willkie	(1940)	Henry A. Wallace	(1941–1945)
				Thomas E. Dewey	(1944)	Harry S. Truman	(1945)
33.		Baptist	Businessman	Thomas E. Dewey	(1948)	Alben W. Barkley	(1949–1953)
34.	U.S. Military Acad.	Presbyterian	Soldier	Adlai E. Stevenson	(1952, 1956)	Richard M. Nixon	(1953–1961)
35.	Harvard	Roman Catholic	Author	Richard M. Nixon	(1960)	Lyndon B. Johnson	(1961–1963)
36.	Southwest Texas State	Disciples of Christ	Teacher	Barry M. Goldwater	(1964)	Hubert H. Humphrey	(1965–1969)
37.	Whittier	Friend (Quaker)	Lawyer	Hubert H. Humphrey	(1968)	Spiro T. Agnew	(1969–1973)
				George S. McGovern	(1972)	Gerald R. Ford**	(1973–1974)
38.	Michigan	Episcopalian	Lawyer			Nelson A. Rockefeller§	(1974–1977)
39.	U.S. Naval Acad.	Baptist	Businessman	Gerald R. Ford	(1976)	Walter F. Mondale	(1977–1981)
40.	Eureka	Disciples of Christ	Actor	Jimmy Carter	(1980)	George H. W. Bush	(1981–1989)
				Walter F. Mondale	(1984)		
41.	Yale	Episcopalian	Businessman	Michael S. Dukakis	(1988)	Dan Quayle	(1989–1993)
42.	Georgetown	Baptist	Lawyer	George H. W. Bush	(1992)	Al Gore	(1993–2001)
				Robert J. Dole	(1996)		
43.	Yale	Methodist	Businessman	Al Gore	(2000)	Richard B. Cheney	(2001–)

*Church preference; never joined any church.
**Inaugurated Dec. 6, 1973, to replace Agnew, who resigned Oct. 10, 1973.

§Inaugurated Dec. 19, 1974, to replace Ford, who became president Aug. 9, 1974.

Roads to the White House

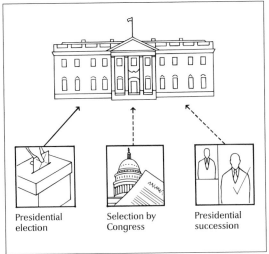

Presidential election

Selection by Congress

Presidential succession

WORLD BOOK illustration by David Cunningham

Presidential election

The chief road to the White House is the presidential election, which is held every four years. Political parties nominate their candidates for president and vice president at national conventions. The nation's voters cast their ballots on Election Day to determine the presidential electors. The Electoral College, made up of the electors chosen by all the states and the District of Columbia, officially elects the president and vice president.

Selection by Congress

If the Electoral College fails to give any candidate a majority, one of three procedures may be used. (1) The House of Representatives chooses the president from among the top three candidates. Each state's House delegation has only one vote, and the winner must receive a majority of the votes that are cast. (2) If the House fails to choose a president, the vice president, chosen by the Electoral College or the Senate, becomes president. (3) If both houses fail to choose a president or vice president, Congress shall by law deal with the situation. Congress would probably apply the terms of the Presidential Succession Act in that case. The Speaker of the House would then become president.

Presidential succession

If the president dies, resigns, or is removed from office, the vice president becomes president. If the president becomes unable to perform the duties of office, the vice president serves as acting president during the president's disability. Next in line to the presidency after the vice president are the following government officials:

1. Speaker of the House
2. President *pro tempore* of the Senate
3. Secretary of state
4. Secretary of the treasury
5. Secretary of defense
6. Attorney general
7. Secretary of the interior
8. Secretary of agriculture
9. Secretary of commerce
10. Secretary of labor
11. Secretary of health and human services
12. Secretary of housing and urban development
13. Secretary of transportation
14. Secretary of energy
15. Secretary of education
16. Secretary of veterans affairs

provides that no one may be elected president more than twice. Nobody who has served as president for more than two years of someone else's term may be elected more than once.

Before the 22nd Amendment was approved in 1951, a president could serve an unlimited number of terms. Franklin D. Roosevelt held office longest. He was elected four times and served from March 1933 until his death in April 1945. President William H. Harrison served the shortest time in office. He died a month after his inauguration in 1841.

The Constitution allows Congress to remove a president from office. The president first must be *impeached* (charged with wrongdoing) by a majority vote of the House of Representatives. Then, the Senate, with the chief justice of the United States serving as presiding officer, tries the president on the charges. Removal from office requires conviction by a two-thirds vote of the Senate.

Only two presidents, Andrew Johnson and Bill Clinton, have been impeached. Both remained in office, however, because the Senate failed to convict either man of the charges.

Salary and other allowances. Effective Jan. 20, 2001, the president receives a salary of $400,000 a year. The chief executive also gets $50,000 annually for expenses, plus allowances for staff, travel, and maintenance of the White House. Congress establishes all these amounts.

After leaving office, a president qualifies for a basic pension. In the early 2000's, the basic amount for a newly retiring president was $157,000 yearly. But a number of factors may affect the actual size of the pension. For example, it will be larger if the president has served in Congress. Other retirement benefits include allowances for office space, staff, and mailing expenses. Widowed spouses of former presidents get an annual pension of $20,000.

Roads to the White House

The chief road to the White House is the presidential election held every four years. However, a person may become president of the United States several other ways as well.

The presidential election. Certain people frequently become leading candidates for the presidency because of their experience. They include the vice president of the United States and governors of such large states as California and New York. A number of vice presidents and governors have become president.

Most top presidential candidates must first compete against fellow political party members to win the party's presidential nomination. The Democratic and Republican parties are the two main political parties in the United States. Each holds a national convention to nominate its presidential candidate. The conventions take place a few months before the presidential election.

The Democratic and Republican conventions are lively spectacles. Millions of Americans watch them on television. Delegates wave banners and cheer wildly to support their choice for president. See **Political convention.**

After the conventions, the presidential nominees campaign across the nation. Candidates for president face a number of challenges. They must raise millions of dollars for campaign expenses, attract many volunteers,

The inauguration is held on January 20 after the election. This picture shows Chief Justice Earl Warren administering the presidential oath to John F. Kennedy in 1961. Looking on were departing President Dwight D. Eisenhower, *far left,* and future Presidents Lyndon B. Johnson, *second from right,* and Richard M. Nixon, *far right.*

Wide World

and gain the support of voters throughout the country. The campaign continues until Election Day, the first Tuesday after the first Monday in November.

On Election Day, voters in each state and the District of Columbia mark a ballot for president and vice president. This balloting is called the *popular vote.* The popular vote does not directly decide the winner of the election. Instead, it determines the delegates who will represent each state and the District of Columbia in the Electoral College. These delegates officially elect the president and vice president.

The Electoral College has 538 delegates, each of whom casts one electoral vote. To be elected president, a candidate must win a majority, or 270, of the electoral votes. Each state has as many electoral votes as the total of its representatives and senators in Congress. The District of Columbia has three electoral votes.

The Electoral College voting takes place in the December following the presidential election. The results are announced in January. But the public usually finds out who the president will be a few hours after polls close on Election Day. This is because the candidate who gets the most popular votes in a state will receive by custom or law all the state's electoral votes. Thus, the press can forecast the winner.

The winner of the nationwide popular vote nearly always receives a majority of the electoral votes and becomes president. But the Electoral College elected three presidents who lost the popular vote. These presidents were Rutherford B. Hayes in 1876, Benjamin Harrison in 1888, and George W. Bush in 2000. A fourth president, John Quincy Adams, also lost the popular vote. But Adams was elected president by the House of Representatives after no candidate had received a majority of the electoral votes in the election of 1824. Ronald Reagan received the greatest number of electoral votes of any president—525 in 1984. See **Electoral College.**

The inauguration is the ceremony of installing the new or reelected president in office. It is held at noon on January 20 after the election. Up to 100,000 spectators attend the inauguration, which usually takes place outside the U.S. Capitol in Washington, D.C. Millions of other Americans see the event on television.

The highlight occurs when the new president takes the oath of office from the chief justice of the United States. With right hand raised and left hand on an open Bible, the new president says: "I do solemnly swear (or affirm) that I will faithfully execute the office of president of the United States, and will to the best of my ability, preserve, protect and defend the Constitution of the United States."

Other roads to the White House. A person may become president in other ways besides winning the presidential election. These procedures are established by Article II of the Constitution; the 12th and 20th amendments; and the Presidential Succession Act.

Article II provides that the vice president becomes president whenever the president dies, resigns, is removed from office, or cannot fulfill the duties of the presidency. Nine vice presidents became president by filling a vacancy. One of them, Gerald R. Ford, followed an unusual route to the White House. President Richard M. Nixon nominated him to succeed Spiro T. Agnew, who had resigned as vice president in 1973. In 1974, Nixon resigned as president, and Ford succeeded him. Ford was the only president who was not elected to either the vice presidency or the presidency.

The 12th Amendment permits Congress to act if no candidate for president wins a majority of the electoral votes. Then, the House of Representatives chooses the president. Each state delegation casts one vote. The House has elected two presidents, Thomas Jefferson in 1801 and John Quincy Adams in 1825.

The 20th Amendment allows leaders of the party of the popular-vote winner to select a new presidential candidate if the winner dies before the Electoral College meets. The college would then vote on that selection. If the popular-vote winner dies after the college meets but before the inauguration, the winning candidate for vice president becomes president. Neither of these provisions has ever been applied.

The Presidential Succession Act permits other high government officials to become president if vacancies exist in both the presidency and the vice presidency. Next in line is the speaker of the House. Then comes the *president pro tempore* (temporary president) of the Senate, usually the majority party member who has served the longest in the Senate. Next are members of the important presidential advisory group that is known as the Cabinet, with the secretary of state first. The Succession Act has never been applied. See **Presidential succession.**

The executive branch

The president heads the executive branch of the federal government. This branch consists of the Executive Office of the president, 14 executive departments, and about 80 independent agencies.

The Executive Office of the President consists of a number of agencies that work directly for the chief executive. One of them, the White House Office, includes the president's physician, secretaries, and a number of close, influential aides known as *presidential assistants*.

The other Executive Office agencies also provide ideas and suggestions concerning many national and international issues. These agencies include the Council of Economic Advisers, Council on Environmental Quality, National Security Council, Office of Administration, Office of Management and Budget, Office of National Drug Control Policy, Office of Policy Development, Office of Science and Technology Policy, and Office of the United States Trade Representative. Franklin D. Roosevelt created the Executive Office in 1939.

The executive departments directly administer the federal government. They are the departments of (1) State, (2) the Treasury, (3) Defense, (4) Justice, (5) the Interior, (6) Agriculture, (7) Commerce, (8) Labor, (9) Health and Human Services, (10) Housing and Urban Development, (11) Transportation, (12) Energy, (13) Education, and (14) Veterans Affairs.

The heads of all but one of the executive departments are called *secretaries*. The head of the Justice Department is the *attorney general*. The department heads belong to the president's Cabinet. The president nominates the department heads. All the appointments require approval of the Senate.

The independent agencies administer federal programs in many fields. These fields include aeronautics and space, banking, communications, farm credit, labor relations, nuclear energy, securities, small business, social security, and trade.

Independent agencies may issue rules, enforce penalties, and administer programs that have far-reaching effects on American life. Some independent agencies are known as *regulatory agencies*. Important regulatory agencies include the Federal Reserve System, the Federal Communications Commission, and the Equal Employment Opportunity Commission. The president picks the heads of nearly all the independent agencies. These people require the consent of the Senate.

Roles of the president

The only roles that the Constitution clearly assigns to the president are those of chief administrator of the nation and commander of its armed forces. But court decisions, customs, laws, and other developments have greatly expanded the president's responsibilities and powers. Today, the president has seven basic roles: (1) chief executive, (2) commander in chief, (3) foreign policy director, (4) legislative leader, (5) party head, (6) popular leader, and (7) chief of state.

Chief executive. As chief executive, the president has four main duties. They are (1) to enforce federal laws, treaties, and federal court rulings; (2) to develop federal policies; (3) to prepare the national budget; and (4) to appoint federal officials.

The president uses a variety of powers to carry out administrative duties. Federal laws give the president *emergency powers*—that is, special authority to prevent or end a national emergency. For example, the Taft-Hartley Act allows the president to delay a labor strike for 80 days if it might endanger "national health or safety." The president also may issue *executive orders*. Executive orders are directions, proclamations, or other statements that have the force of laws. They require no action by Congress. One of the most famous executive orders was the Emancipation Proclamation issued by Abraham Lincoln in 1863, during the American Civil War. It declared freedom for all slaves in the areas then under Confederate control.

The Office of Management and Budget, part of the Executive Office, helps the president plan the federal budget. Presidents often use their budgets to shape key programs. Lyndon B. Johnson did so in the mid-1960's to develop his War on Poverty program.

The president nominates Cabinet members, Supreme Court justices, and other high federal officials. All such top appointments require Senate approval. The president can appoint a number of personal aides and advisers and can fill hundreds of lower jobs in the executive branch without Senate approval.

The Constitution also allows the president to issue *reprieves* and *pardons* for crimes against the United States, except in impeachment cases. A reprieve delays the penalty for a crime. A pardon frees the offender from a sentence or the possibility of a sentence.

Commander in chief. The president's main duties as commander of the nation's armed services are to defend the country during wartime and to keep it strong during peacetime. The chief executive appoints all the nation's highest military officers and helps determine the size of the armed forces. Only the president can decide whether to use nuclear weapons.

The president shares some military powers with Congress. Top appointments in the armed services require

Abraham Lincoln quickly built up the Union Army after the Civil War began in 1861. After the Battle of Antietam in 1862, he visited General George B. McClellan on the battlefield, *shown here.*

congressional approval. Major military expenses and plans to expand the armed forces also need the consent of Congress. Only Congress can declare war. But presidents have sent American troops into conflicts that were equal to war though none was declared. In 1950, for example, Harry S. Truman ordered U.S. troops to fight in South Korea. The Korean War (1950-1953) was officially only a "police action."

Congress generally allows the president to exercise broad powers in wartime. During World War II (1939-1945), Franklin D. Roosevelt created many emergency agencies, took control of American manufacturing plants, and even imprisoned American citizens of Japanese descent.

Foreign policy director. The Constitution gives the president power to appoint ambassadors, make treaties, and receive foreign diplomats. The chief executive may refuse to recognize a newly formed foreign government. The president also proposes legislation dealing with foreign aid and other international activities.

Treaties and ambassadorial appointments require approval of the Senate. The president may also make *executive agreements* with foreign leaders. These agreements resemble treaties but do not need Senate approval.

Many presidents have allowed their secretaries of state to direct U.S. foreign policy. But Woodrow Wilson, Franklin D. Roosevelt, and others have mainly relied on their own judgment in this area.

Some presidents have helped settle disputes between foreign nations. Theodore Roosevelt and Wilson were among the first presidents to serve as peacemakers in foreign conflicts. Roosevelt won the Nobel Peace Prize for helping end the Russo-Japanese War (1904-1905). Wilson helped work out the peace treaty that ended World War I (1914-1918).

Legislative leader. The president greatly influences the development of many laws passed by Congress. At the beginning of each session of Congress, the chief executive delivers a State of the Union address to the lawmakers. In this message, the president discusses the major problems facing the nation and recommends a legislative program to solve them. The president also gives Congress detailed plans for new legislation at other times during the year.

Cabinet officers and other presidential aides work to win congressional support for the president's programs. However, the president also may become involved in a struggle over a key bill. In such cases, the president may speak to members of Congress several times to win their backing. This activity requires shrewd bargaining and in many cases fails in spite of the president's influence.

The Constitution allows the president to veto any bill passed by Congress. If both the House and the Senate repass the vetoed bill by a two-thirds majority, the bill becomes law despite the president's disapproval. But Congress has overturned only about 4 percent of all vetoes.

Party head. As leader of a political party, the president helps form the party's positions on all important issues. The president hopes these positions will help elect enough party members to Congress to give the party a majority in both the House and the Senate. Such a strong party makes it easier to pass the president's legislative program.

However, presidents cannot always control members of their party in Congress. Senators and representatives owe their chief loyalty to the people in their state and local district. They may vote against a bill favored by the president if it meets with opposition at home.

Presidents try to win the support of legislators in several ways. They often use *patronage power,* the authority to make appointments to government jobs. For example, a president can reward a loyal supporter by approving that person's choice for a federal judge. A president also may campaign for the reelection of a faithful party member or promise to approve a federal

Wide World

Theodore Roosevelt met with Russian and Japanese delegates in 1905 and helped end the Russo-Japanese War. In 1906, he became the first American to win the Nobel Peace Prize.

United Press Int.

Franklin D. Roosevelt explained his policies in informal radio reports that became known as "fireside chats," *shown here.* In 1939, he became the first president to appear on television.

project that will benefit a legislator's home district.

Popular leader. The president and the American people have a special relationship. The people rely on the chief executive to serve the interests of the entire nation ahead of those of any state or citizen. In turn, the president depends on public support to help push programs through Congress. The president seeks such support by explaining the issues and by showing the confidence and determination to deal with problems.

The president uses many methods to communicate with the public and provide strong national leadership. Woodrow Wilson pioneered the use of regular presidential press conferences to mold public opinion and to rally support. Franklin D. Roosevelt addressed the nation over radio in his "fireside chats." He was also the first president to speak on television. Since the 1960's, presidents have favored the use of televised addresses from the White House to reach large audiences.

Chief of state. As the foremost representative of the U.S. government, the president is expected to show pride in American achievements and traditions. In this role, the president attends historical celebrations, dedicates new buildings and national parks, and may throw out the first ball of the professional baseball season. The president also presents awards to war heroes and invites distinguished Americans to the White House.

In addition, the chief executive greets visiting foreign officials and often hosts formal White House dinners for them. The president also represents the United States in visits to other countries.

The life of the president

The president is almost always busy. During a typical day, the chief executive attends several meetings and so-

© Susan Biddle, The White House

The president's office, an oval-shaped room called the Oval Office, is in the west wing of the White House. The president meets here with many government officials and receives frequent briefings on national and world affairs.

cial affairs and may meet 100 or more people. The president works and lives in the White House in Washington, D.C., but makes many outside appearances and spends much time traveling.

The White House. The president's headquarters is the Oval Office, an oval-shaped room in the White House. There, the chief executive meets congressional leaders, foreign officials, and representatives of various groups. The president also spends much time in the Oval Office studying reports from aides and agencies.

The presidential family's main living quarters are on the second floor of the White House. The family also can relax in the mansion's swimming pool and at its bowling lanes and motion-picture theater. The White House grounds have some beautiful gardens.

In spite of its beauty and comfort, however, the White House lacks privacy. Every week, thousands of visitors tour the rooms that are open to the public. Partly as a result, most presidents enjoy recreation outside the White House.

Recreation. The president often spends weekends at Camp David, a retreat in the Maryland mountains that is reserved for the nation's leader. Through the years, presidents have favored various ways to relax. Theodore Roosevelt boxed, hiked, and hunted big game. Warren G. Harding played poker, and Dwight D. Eisenhower played golf. Lyndon B. Johnson and Ronald Reagan enjoyed horseback riding.

The president's family generally attracts wide interest. The wedding of a president's child is a major news event. An interesting relative also draws much attention. Even unimportant activities of members of the president's family sometimes appear in the newspapers.

Some presidents have had children who helped make the White House cheerful and lively. John Tyler had 15 children, more than any other president. Daughters of seven presidents were married in the White House. Grover Cleveland was the only president who had a child born in the White House.

Guarding the president. The United States Secret Service guards the president at all times. In addition, agents of the Secret Service continually check the president's food, surroundings, and travel arrangements.

At various times, the president travels in an official car, a private airplane, or a U.S. Navy ship. The chief executive usually flies long distances in a reserved jet called *Air Force One*.

Even though U.S. presidents get tight protection, four have been assassinated while in office. They were Abraham Lincoln in 1865, James Garfield in 1881, William McKinley in 1901, and John F. Kennedy in 1963. Others have survived attempted assassinations, including Harry S. Truman, Gerald R. Ford, and Ronald Reagan.

A day in the life of the president. The president might begin a typical day by reading a few newspapers. A breakfast conference might follow with such top aides as the press secretary and the White House chief of staff. In the Oval Office, the president signs documents and reads letters, reports, and proposed legislation. Later in the morning, the president might discuss plans with congressional leaders or meet with the vice president. In the afternoon, the president might see people from various organizations. The president also might take part in a bill-signing ceremony, officially signing into law an

Nixon Project, National Archives

Camp David is the official retreat of the president of the United States. It lies in a wooded mountain area in Maryland.

act passed by Congress.

In the evening, the president sometimes attends a social function. The White House might host a formal dinner for a foreign official. While dining, the leaders might discuss trade problems, environmental protection, or other issues. The president might spend the late evening reading, perhaps a speech scheduled for the next day or a report on a new foreign aid program.

Development of the presidency

The founding of the presidency. During and immediately after the Revolutionary War in America (1775–1783), the U.S. government operated under laws called the Articles of Confederation. The Articles gave the national government little authority over the states. Most Americans agreed that the nation needed to strengthen its federal government. In 1787, a group of state leaders gathered in Philadelphia to revise the Articles of Confederation. Instead, they wrote an entirely new document—the Constitution of the United States.

Under the Articles, the chief officer presiding over Congress had been called the president, and that title was chosen for the leader of the new government. The Constitution's authors described the presidency in fairly general language because they knew the nation's respected wartime leader, George Washington, would be the first president. They expected Washington to shape the responsibilities of the office for future presidents.

Washington brought extraordinary courage, prestige, and wisdom to the U.S. presidency. In 1793, he kept the young nation out of a war between the United Kingdom and France. In 1794, he used federal troops to end the Whiskey Rebellion, a tax protest in the state of Pennsylvania. This action helped establish the federal government's authority to enforce federal laws in the states.

Strengthening the office. During the early and mid-1800's, the nation had several bold and imaginative presidents. They interpreted the Constitution in new ways and greatly increased the power of the presidency. One of these leaders was Thomas Jefferson, the third president. Many scholars consider Jefferson the most brilliant person ever to have served in the White House.

Jefferson raised a constitutional question when he approved a treaty to buy the Louisiana Territory from France in 1803. The purchase almost doubled what was then the area of the United States. The Constitution did not specifically give the president power to buy new territory. But Jefferson decided that the purchase was constitutional under his treaty-making power.

Andrew Jackson strengthened the president's role as the nation's popular leader. In July 1832, Jackson vetoed a bill to renew the charter of the Second Bank of the United States. Jackson and many other Americans viewed the bank as a dangerous monopoly and criticized its failure to establish a reliable currency. Later in 1832, South Carolina declared federal tariff laws unconstitutional and refused to collect tariffs at its ports. Jackson declared that no state could cancel a federal law. The president received congressional approval to use federal troops in order to collect the tariffs. Jackson's actions helped force South Carolina to end its rebellion.

The American Civil War began in 1861, when Southern forces attacked Fort Sumter. Abraham Lincoln ordered a military draft, blockaded Southern ports, and spent funds without congressional approval. He knew he had used powers the Constitution reserved for Congress. But he believed his actions were needed to save the Union.

The decline of the presidency. After the Civil War ended in 1865, Congress moved quickly to increase its influence in the government. A power struggle broke out between Congress and Andrew Johnson. This struggle led to Johnson's impeachment by the House of Representatives. The prestige of the presidency was damaged, but it was saved from total destruction because the Senate failed, by one vote, to convict Johnson and remove him from office.

Few strong presidents emerged during the late 1800's. Most presidents of the period accepted the view that Congress, not the chief executive, had the responsibility to set the nation's basic policies.

The rebirth of presidential leadership. The United States became a world power during the late 1800's and early 1900's. This development helped bring increased power to the president. In the Spanish-American War (1898), the United States took control of Guam, the Philippines, and Puerto Rico. To protect these interests, Theodore Roosevelt built up U.S. military forces. He also warned European nations against interfering in Latin America. Roosevelt broadened the scope of executive power at home by leading a fight for reforms that limited the power of great corporations.

Woodrow Wilson enlarged the presidency during World War I (1914-1918). After the United States entered the conflict in 1917, Wilson rallied public support for the war effort. He won widespread praise for his pledge to help make the world safe for democracy. After the war, he led the drive to set up the League of Nations, an international organization dedicated to maintaining peace.

Perhaps no one expanded the powers of the presidency as much as Franklin D. Roosevelt. He became president during the Great Depression of the 1930's and took extraordinary measures to combat the severe business slump. Roosevelt won public acceptance of his view that the federal government should play a major role in the economy. Largely as a result of strong popular support, he got Congress to adopt a far-reaching program called the New Deal. This program created work for millions of Americans and strengthened the president's role as the nation's legislative leader.

The rapid growth of U.S. military strength during World War II (1939-1945) further increased the influence of the presidency in world affairs. Harry S. Truman's decision to use atomic bombs against Japan during the war showed the tremendous authority of the president.

Another example of this authority occurred in the Cuban missile crisis in 1962. In that crisis, John F. Kennedy carried out negotiations that led to the withdrawal of Soviet missiles from Communist Cuba. The Soviet Union had placed nuclear missiles in Cuba capable of striking U.S. cities. Kennedy demanded the missiles' removal and announced a naval blockade of Cuba. Several days later, the Soviets withdrew their missiles after the U.S. publicly promised to withdraw its nuclear missiles from Turkey and privately agreed not to invade Cuba.

The Vietnam War. The presidency lost much of its prestige during the Vietnam War (1957-1975). Lyndon B. Johnson, who became president in 1963, believed that non-Communist South Vietnam had to be defended against local Communist rebels and Communist North Vietnam. In 1964, Congress allowed him "to take all necessary measures" to protect U.S. bases in South Vietnam.

During the late 1960's and early 1970's, Johnson and his successor, Richard M. Nixon, sent hundreds of thousands of U.S. troops to support South Vietnam. Many Americans opposed United States participation in the Vietnam War. They argued that both Johnson and Nixon had abused presidential powers and misled Congress.

The Watergate scandal further damaged public regard for the presidency. It involved burglary, wiretapping, and other illegal activities designed to help Nixon win reelection in 1972. Attempts by Nixon's aides to cover up many of the activities led to an investigation by the House of Representatives. In 1974, the House Judiciary Committee recommended that Nixon be impeached.

That same year, Nixon lost an appeal to the Supreme Court involving the president's *executive privilege*—the right to keep records secret. The court ruled that executive privilege is not unlimited. It ordered Nixon to release recordings of conversations said to contain evidence for a criminal case in the Watergate scandal. By then, Nixon had lost nearly all support in Congress and faced possible impeachment. He resigned as president on Aug. 9, 1974, and was succeeded by vice president Gerald R. Ford. No other president has ever resigned.

Many Americans thought Nixon had violated federal laws and wanted him brought to trial. The nation became further divided in September 1974, when Ford pardoned Nixon for all federal crimes Nixon may have committed as president.

The impeachment of Bill Clinton. In 1998, the House impeached President Bill Clinton for perjury and

Interesting facts about presidents

Who was the only president who did not win election to either the office of vice president or president? Ford.

Who was the only president who had served as speaker of the House? Polk.

Who was the only president to serve two nonconsecutive terms? Cleveland.

Who held the first regular presidential press conferences? Wilson.

Which president was sworn into office on an airplane? Lyndon B. Johnson.

Who was the only person to serve as both president and chief justice? Taft.

Four presidents were elected whose closest opponent received more popular votes. Who were the presidents? John Quincy Adams, election of 1824; Hayes, 1876; Benjamin Harrison, 1888; and George W. Bush, 2000.

Who was the first president to visit a foreign country while in office? Theodore Roosevelt.

Which presidents are buried in Arlington National Cemetery? Taft and Kennedy.

Who were the only grandfather and grandson who both served as president? William Henry Harrison and Benjamin Harrison.

Who were the only presidents to be sworn into office by a former president? Coolidge and Hoover (by Taft).

Which president never married? Buchanan.

Two sons of former presidents became presidents themselves. Who were the sons and who were their fathers? John Quincy Adams, son of John Adams, and George W. Bush, son of George H. W. Bush.

Which two former presidents died on the same day? John Adams and Jefferson.

Which presidents lived past the age of 90? John Adams and Hoover.

Which president lived the shortest time? Kennedy, 46 years.

'ho was the only former vice president who became pres-'lent but did not succeed the president under whom he 'rved? Nixon.

vas the first president to live in the White House? Adams.

Who was the first president to be inaugurated in Washington, D.C.? Jefferson.

Who was the first president to speak on radio? Wilson.

Who was the first president to speak on television? F. D. Roosevelt.

What two presidents died in the White House? W. H. Harrison and Taylor.

Which president served the shortest time in office? W. H. Harrison, one month, 1841.

Which president served the longest? F. D. Roosevelt, 12 years, 1 month, 8 days.

Which president received the greatest number of electoral votes? Reagan in 1984, 525.

Which presidents signed the Constitution? Washington, Madison.

Who was the only president who had a child born in the White House? Cleveland, in 1893.

Which presidents were assassinated? Lincoln, Garfield, McKinley, Kennedy.

Which president had the most children? Tyler, 15.

Which other presidents died in office? W. H. Harrison, Taylor, Harding, Franklin D. Roosevelt.

Which presidents died on the Fourth of July? Jefferson, 1826; John Adams, 1826; and Monroe, 1831.

Who was the first president born after the adoption of the U.S. Constitution? Tyler.

Who was the first president to ride on a railroad train? Jackson.

Who was the only president to resign? Nixon.

Which presidents served as university presidents before their election to the U.S. presidency? Wilson (Princeton) and Eisenhower (Columbia).

Who was the first president nominated by a national political convention? Jackson.

Who was the youngest person ever to become president? T. Roosevelt, 42.

Who was the youngest person ever elected president? Kennedy, 43.

Who was the oldest person ever elected president? Reagan, 73 years and 274 days when he was elected to his second term.

obstruction of justice. The House charged Clinton with lying to a grand jury that was investigating an extramarital affair he had while in office. Other charges included hindering the investigation by lying to his aides and by encouraging others to lie and conceal evidence on his behalf. The Senate acquitted Clinton in 1999.

The presidency today is still strong and important. This is largely because the United States has powerful armed forces and ranks as a leader of the democracies. In addition, the president's ability to reach huge audiences on television adds to the prestige of the office.

Americans look to the president to build morale, recruit talented officials, and explain complex issues. They also expect the chief executive to champion the rights of all Americans regardless of their age, color, political party, religion, region, or sex. At the same time, some Americans dislike the great size and power of the national government and want the president to reduce federal influence over state and local affairs.

Congress and the Supreme Court sometimes act to prohibit or limit actions that they consider a misuse of presidential power. But such challenges have halted the expansion of presidential authority only for limited periods. The presidency will continue to have its ups and downs. But it will remain, as John F. Kennedy once said, "the vital center of action in our whole scheme of government."   Thomas E. Cronin

Related articles include:

Constitution of the United
   States (Article II)
Election
Election campaign
Electoral College
Impeachment
Political convention
Political party

Presidential succession
Primary election (The presidential primary)
Term limits
United States, Government of the (The executive branch)
Vice president of the U.S.
Veto

Outline

I. The presidency
  A. Legal qualifications
  B. Term of office
  C. Salary and other allowances
II. Roads to the White House
  A. The presidential election
  B. Inauguration
  C. Other roads to the White House
III. The executive branch
  A. The executive office of the president
  B. The executive departments
  C. The independent agencies
IV. Roles of the president
  A. Chief executive
  B. Commander in chief
  C. Foreign policy director
  D. Legislative leader
  E. Party head
  F. Popular leader
  G. Chief of state
V. The life of the president
  A. The White House
  B. Recreation
  C. The president's family
  D. Guarding the president
  E. A day in the life of the president
VI. Development of the presidency
  A. The founding of the presidency
  B. Strengthening the office
  C. The decline of the presidency
  D. The rebirth of presidential leadership
  E. The Vietnam War
  F. The Watergate scandal
  G. The impeachment of Bill Clinton
  H. The presidency today

Questions

What are the qualifications for a president?
Who succeeds a president who dies in office?
What are the executive departments?
How did Theodore Roosevelt enlarge the presidency?
What challenges does a presidential candidate face?
What are *executive orders*?
What was the Watergate scandal?
What is the president's *patronage power*?
What are the seven basic roles of the president?

Additional resources

Level I
Blassingame, Wyatt. *The Look-It-Up Book of Presidents.* Rev. ed. Random Hse., 1996.
Krull, Kathleen. *Lives of the Presidents.* Harcourt, 1998.
Rubel, David. *Scholastic Encyclopedia of the Presidents and Their Times.* Rev. ed. Scholastic, 1997.
Smith, Carter, ed. *A Sourcebook on the U. S. Presidency.* 6 vols. Millbrook, 1993.

Level II
Graff, Henry F., ed. *The Presidents.* 2nd ed. Scribner, 1996.

Brown Bros.

Presidential election campaigns have changed over the years. Warren G. Harding campaigned from his front porch in Marion, Ohio, in 1920, *left.* President Harry S. Truman toured the nation in a special railroad car during a "whistle-stop" campaign in 1948, *right.*

Levy, Leonard W., and Fisher, Louis, eds. *Encyclopedia of the American Presidency.* 2 vols. 1994. Reprint. Macmillan, 1998.

Nelson, Michael, ed. *Guide to the Presidency.* 2 vols. 2nd ed. Congressional Quarterly, 1996. *The Presidency A to Z.* 2nd ed. 1998.

Web sites

U.S. Presidents and the Presidency
http://www.worldbook.com/fun/presidents/html/intro.htm
An extensive report on the history of the presidency, including biographies of all the presidents, first ladies, and vice presidents, from World Book.

A White House History
http://www.whitehouse.gov/WH/glimpse/tour/html
An electronic tour of the U.S. president's home, from the official White House Web site.

Campaigns
http://www.washingtonpost.com/wp-dyn/politics/elections/2000
This *Washington Post* site features news coverage of the 1998 and 2000 election campaigns.

Hall of Presidents
http://www.npg.si.edu/col/pres/index.htm
Information on and images of the United States presidents.

Time and the Presidency
http://www.pathfinder.com/offers/presidents/
    related_features.html
Time magazine presents selected articles on Franklin Delano Roosevelt, Harry Truman, Dwight Eisenhower, John F. Kennedy, Lyndon B. Johnson, Gerald Ford, Jimmy Carter, Ronald Reagan, George H. W. Bush, and Bill Clinton.

Topic for study

Describe the roles of the president and discuss the variety of powers that the chief executive uses to carry out these roles.

Reform Party is a political party in the United States that promises to reform national politics. Ross Perot, a wealthy Texas businessman, founded the Reform Party in 1995. It quickly became the most successful third party since Theodore Roosevelt's Progressive or "Bull Moose" Party of 1912. But in 2000, arguments over the choice of a presidential candidate divided and weakened the party.

The party's platform calls for balancing the federal budget, repaying the national debt, and simplifying the nation's tax code. The platform urges stricter laws to regulate campaign financing and limit gifts to officeholders "to ensure that our elected officials owe their allegiance to the people whom they are elected to serve." The party also supports term limits, which would prevent elected officials from serving more than a specified number of terms. For example, U.S. senators would be allowed to serve no more than two terms, or 12 years.

The Reform Party also urges elimination of the United States trade deficit. It calls for trade policies that would protect home industries from outside competition. In addition, the party opposes free-trade agreements.

James I. Lengle

Web site

American Reform Party
http://www.americanreform.org/
The official Web site of the Reform Party.

Republican Party is one of the two principal political parties of the United States. The other is the Democratic Party. The Republican Party is often called the *G.O.P.,* which stands for *Grand Old Party,* a nickname Republicans gave their party in the 1880's.

The Republican Party has greatly influenced the nation's history and politics. It won 14 of the 18 presidential elections from 1860, when Abraham Lincoln was elected, to 1932. From 1932 through 2000, it won 8 of 18 presidential elections.

The policies of the Republican Party, like those of other political parties, have changed through the years. At first, Republican candidates got most of their support from people who opposed slavery. To gain wider support, the party passed land legislation that appealed to farmers. Republicans won the backing of business leaders by endorsing sound money policies and high tariffs. By the late 1800's, the Republican Party represented a firm alliance of the agricultural West and the industrial East.

The Republican Party dominated American politics in the 1920's. The economy boomed during much of the decade, and the party became known as the "party of prosperity." But the Republicans fell out of power in the 1930's, when the Great Depression, the worst economic downturn in U.S. history, hit the nation.

The Republican Party includes both strongly conservative members and less conservative members called *moderates.* During the 1950's, the party prospered under the moderate leader Dwight D. Eisenhower. Eisenhower won two terms as president—in 1952 and 1956. He was the first Republican to do so since William McKinley in 1896 and 1900. The conservatives of the Republican Party gained strength during the 1980's under the leadership of Ronald Reagan. Reagan also won two terms as president—in 1980 and 1984.

This article describes chiefly the history of the Republican Party. For information about the party's national convention and organization, see **Political convention** and **Political party.**

Origin of the Republican Party dates back to the strong antislavery opposition to the Kansas-Nebraska Bill of 1854. As passed by Congress in May 1854, the bill permitted slavery in the new territories of Kansas and Nebraska if the people there voted for it.

The Republican Party grew out of a series of antislavery meetings held throughout the North to protest the Kansas-Nebraska Bill. One such meeting was held by Alvan E. Bovay, a leading Whig, on Feb. 28, 1854, in Ripon, Wisconsin. This meeting passed a resolution declaring that a new party—the Republican Party—would be organized if the United States Congress passed the Kansas-Nebraska Bill.

Bovay held a second meeting in Ripon on March 20, after the Senate had passed the Kansas-Nebraska Bill. The 53 men at this meeting appointed a committee to form the new party. On July 6, 1854, at a party meeting in Jackson, Michigan, the delegates formally adopted the name *Republican.*

The new party had chiefly sectional appeal. Few

Southern voters supported the Republicans, because almost all Southerners wanted to expand slavery, not restrict it. Many Northerners supported the party. But some feared that the extreme antislavery views of such Republican leaders as Senator Charles Sumner of Massachusetts threatened the Union.

The election of 1856. As their first presidential candidate, the Republicans chose John Charles Frémont, a dashing young explorer and soldier. During the campaign, antislavery and proslavery groups fought in Kansas. The chief campaign issue became "bleeding Kansas." Democrats predicted that the South would secede from the Union if the antislavery Frémont won.

The voting reflected the sectional appeal of the Democratic and Republican parties. Frémont won 11 Northern states. His Democratic opponent, James Buchanan, carried 19 states—including every Southern state except Maryland—and won.

Changes in party policy. After the Republican defeat in 1856, party leaders realized that they could not win the presidency on just the slavery issue. To broaden their appeal, Republicans endorsed construction of a transcontinental railroad system and federal aid to improve harbors and rivers. They also promised to open Western land for settlement, to raise U.S. tariff rates, and to permit slavery where it already existed.

In 1860, the Republicans chose Abraham Lincoln, a lanky, self-educated Illinois lawyer, as their presidential candidate. Lincoln had received national attention by expressing moderate antislavery views in his debates with Illinois Senator Stephen A. Douglas, a Democrat.

Lincoln easily won the election, even though he received less than 40 percent of the popular vote. The Democrats had split over the slavery issue. Northern Democrats nominated Douglas, and Southern Democrats chose Vice President John C. Breckinridge.

The Civil War began in April 1861. Most Southerners believed the election of Lincoln justified secession. In 1860 and 1861—both before and after the shooting started—11 Southern states left the Union.

Above all, Lincoln wanted to save the Union. But many Republicans—the so-called Radical Republicans—made the abolition of slavery their main goal. Many Northern Democrats supported Lincoln and the war and were called War Democrats.

Lincoln tried to bring all groups of both parties together, but succeeded only partly. By 1864, his chances of reelection looked doubtful. To stress the war's national character—and to gain more supporters—the Republican Party used the name *Union Party* in the 1864 election. It nominated Andrew Johnson, a War Democrat, for vice president. With the help of Northern victories just before the election, Lincoln won a second term.

On April 9, 1865, shortly after Lincoln's second term began, the war ended when General Robert E. Lee surrendered to General Ulysses S. Grant. Five days later, Lincoln was assassinated.

The Radical Republicans and Reconstruction. Johnson hoped to follow Lincoln's moderate plan of Reconstruction. But the Radical Republicans in Congress favored harsh punishment for the South.

The Radicals dominated Congress after the congressional elections of 1866. They divided the South into five military districts, deprived former Confederate soldiers of the vote, and gave the vote to former slaves.

The dispute over Reconstruction hardened political loyalties along sectional lines. Most Northern Republicans supported the Radical Republicans who, by 1868, felt strong enough to drop the Union Party label. Many Northern Democrats also backed Republican policies. But Southerners rejected Republican leadership. As a result, Reconstruction led to the birth of the Democratic "Solid South."

The Republicans nominated Grant, the great Union war hero, for president in 1868, and he won an easy victory. Grant won reelection in 1872, but by this time many

From *Thomas Nast* by Albert Bigelow Paine, permission of Harper & Row

The elephant as a Republican symbol first appeared in this 1874 cartoon by Thomas Nast in *Harper's Weekly.* The elephant in the cartoon represented the Republican vote. Nast used the elephant many times as a Republican symbol, and it soon came to stand for the Republican Party.

voters had become alarmed over corruption in both business and government. A depression in 1873 helped the Democrats win a sweeping victory in the congressional elections of the next year.

In 1876, the Republicans nominated a cautious reformer, Rutherford B. Hayes. A group of conservative Republicans called *Stalwarts* opposed Hayes because he favored civil service reform and friendly relations with the South. Hayes and his followers became known as *Half-Breeds.* Samuel J. Tilden, the Democratic candidate, won more popular votes than Hayes, but the electoral vote was disputed. A special commission declared Hayes the winner by one vote. The Democrats accepted the verdict only because the Republicans had promised to end Reconstruction and withdraw federal troops from the South. Hayes kept the promise.

Political inactivity marked the 1880's and 1890's. Both major parties failed to face the problems resulting from the rapid industrialization that followed the Civil War. Many industrial monopolies set high prices for their products and services. Economic power became centered with a few wealthy business leaders, and farmers and wage earners suffered increasingly hard times.

In 1880, Republican James A. Garfield won the presidency. He was assassinated in 1881, only a few months after taking office, and Vice President Chester A. Arthur, a Stalwart, succeeded him. Arthur surprised his fellow Stalwarts by supporting civil service reform. In 1883, Congress passed the Pendleton Act, which established the merit system in the civil service.

In 1884, the Republican candidate, James G. Blaine, narrowly lost to Grover Cleveland. The party made the protective tariff its chief campaign issue in 1888 and won the presidency with Benjamin Harrison. In 1890, the McKinley Tariff pushed tariffs higher than they had ever been before. Dissatisfaction with the tariff helped Cleveland defeat Harrison in 1892.

The money issue dominated the election of 1896. A third party, the Populist Party, had appeared during the early 1890's. The Populists demanded that the government increase the amount of money in circulation by permitting unlimited coinage of silver. They believed such action would help farmers and wage earners and improve the nation's economy. Many Democrats joined the Populists in their demand for silver coinage. In 1896, the Democratic Party nominated William Jennings

Republican presidential and vice presidential candidates

Year	President	Vice President	Year	President	Vice President
1856	John C. Frémont	William L. Dayton	1932	Herbert Hoover	Charles Curtis
1860	*Abraham Lincoln*	*Hannibal Hamlin*	1936	Alfred M. Landon	Frank Knox
1864	*Abraham Lincoln*	*Andrew Johnson*	1940	Wendell L. Willkie	Charles L. McNary
1868	*Ulysses S. Grant*	*Schuyler Colfax*	1944	Thomas E. Dewey	John W. Bricker
1872	*Ulysses S. Grant*	*Henry Wilson*	1948	Thomas E. Dewey	Earl Warren
1876	*Rutherford B. Hayes*	*William A. Wheeler*	1952	*Dwight D. Eisenhower*	*Richard M. Nixon*
1880	*James A. Garfield*	*Chester A. Arthur*	1956	*Dwight D. Eisenhower*	*Richard M. Nixon*
1884	James G. Blaine	John A. Logan	1960	Richard M. Nixon	Henry Cabot Lodge, Jr.
1888	*Benjamin Harrison*	*Levi P. Morton*	1964	Barry M. Goldwater	William E. Miller
1892	Benjamin Harrison	Whitelaw Reid	1968	*Richard M. Nixon*	*Spiro T. Agnew*
1896	*William McKinley*	*Garret A. Hobart*	1972	*Richard M. Nixon*	*Spiro T. Agnew*
1900	*William McKinley*	*Theodore Roosevelt*	1976	Gerald R. Ford	Robert J. Dole
1904	*Theodore Roosevelt*	*Charles W. Fairbanks*	1980	*Ronald W. Reagan*	*George H. W. Bush*
1908	*William Howard Taft*	*James S. Sherman*	1984	*Ronald W. Reagan*	*George H. W. Bush*
1912	William Howard Taft	James S. Sherman	1988	*George H. W. Bush*	*Dan Quayle*
1916	Charles Evans Hughes	Charles W. Fairbanks	1992	George H. W. Bush	Dan Quayle
1920	*Warren G. Harding*	*Calvin Coolidge*	1996	Robert Dole	Jack Kemp
1924	*Calvin Coolidge*	*Charles G. Dawes*	2000	*George W. Bush*	*Richard B. Cheney*
1928	*Herbert Hoover*	*Charles Curtis*			

Names of elected candidates are in italics.

Administrations in office

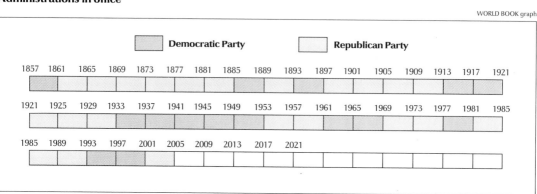

WORLD BOOK graph

Abraham Lincoln is about to devour his Democratic opponents, Stephen A. Douglas and John C. Breckinridge, in a political cartoon published during the 1860 presidential race.

Granger Collection

In the Republican Party split of 1912, "Teddy" Roosevelt and William Howard Taft pulled apart. The division of the party helped Woodrow Wilson, the Democratic candidate, win the presidency with about 40 percent of the popular vote.

Bryan, the main silver spokesman, for president. The Republican presidential candidate, William McKinley, supported a currency backed by gold and won the election.

Economic conditions improved rapidly in the late 1890's. The United States victory in the Spanish-American War also gained support for the Republicans. McKinley defeated Bryan again in 1900. But six months after beginning his second term, McKinley was assassinated. Vice President Theodore Roosevelt succeeded him.

The party splits. "Teddy" Roosevelt supported much reform legislation. He brought suits against several large monopolies and crusaded for honesty in government.

Roosevelt also sponsored a conservation policy, laws to protect the American public from impure food and drugs, and legislation to regulate railroad rates.

In 1908, Roosevelt chose his friend, Secretary of War William Howard Taft, to succeed him and continue his policies. Taft easily beat Bryan, who ran for the third time as the Democratic nominee.

Taft brought many more suits against monopolies than Roosevelt had. But Taft, by nature quieter and more conservative than Roosevelt, lost favor with Republican progressives. He faced open hostility from the progressives after signing into law the high Payne-Aldrich Tariff in 1909. By 1912, Taft no longer led a united party, and the progressives turned to Roosevelt, who wanted to be president again. After the Republicans renominated Taft, Roosevelt left the party and formed the Progressive, or "Bull Moose," Party. The Republican split helped Woodrow Wilson, the Democratic candidate, win the election.

The Republicans began to reunite after their defeat, and in 1916, most of them supported the party candidate, Charles Evans Hughes. But some backed Wilson because he had promoted progressive legislation and had kept the nation out of World War I, which had begun in 1914. Wilson won reelection by a close margin. A month after he took office for the second time, the United States went to war against Germany.

By the congressional elections of 1918, the Republicans had reunited, and they gained control of Congress. After the war, the Republican-controlled Senate rejected American membership in the League of Nations.

During the Roaring 20's, the Republicans won every presidential and congressional election. In 1920, the party's candidate, Warren G. Harding, promised a return to "normalcy." Americans, weary of wartime controls and world problems, wanted just that—and Harding won in a landslide.

The nation's economy boomed during the 1920's as business and industry expanded. Successive Republican administrations helped big business by keeping government spending and taxes low and by raising tariffs.

After Harding's death in 1923, congressional investigations revealed corruption in several government departments during his administration. But the exposures did not keep Harding's successor, Vice President Calvin Coolidge, from easily winning the 1924 election. Coolidge's conservative administration reflected the nation's largely antiforeign, anti-immigration, antilabor mood.

In 1928, the Republicans turned to Herbert Hoover, Coolidge's secretary of commerce. Hoover easily defeated his Democratic opponent, Alfred E. Smith, but Smith carried most of the largest cities.

Soon after Hoover took office in 1929, the worst stock-market crash in the nation's history occurred. The Great Depression followed. Hoover tried to stop the depression but failed. He lost badly in 1932 to the Democratic candidate, Franklin D. Roosevelt. Hoover's defeat reduced the Republican Party to a hard core of business leaders, Midwestern farmers, and conservative workers.

From 1933 to 1953, the Republican Party was the minority party. Roosevelt led the nation through the Great Depression with a massive federal program called the New Deal. The Republicans, far outnumbered in both houses of Congress, took little action against his policies. The 1936 Republican Party platform criticized the

New Deal, but Roosevelt won reelection by a landslide over Alfred M. Landon.

By the election of 1940, World War II (1939-1945) had started. The Republicans nominated Wendell L. Willkie and continued to attack the New Deal, but Roosevelt easily won a third term. The United States entered the war in 1941. Roosevelt defeated Thomas E. Dewey in 1944 and became the only candidate to be elected president four times.

In the 1930's and 1940's, many Republicans accepted the idea of federal welfare programs and of U.S. leadership in world affairs. They also accepted U.S. membership in the United Nations, formed in 1945. Vice President Harry S. Truman became president after Roosevelt's death in 1945. The Republicans expected to win the 1948 election easily, and they nominated Dewey again. But Truman won a surprise victory.

The Eisenhower years. Dwight D. Eisenhower easily won the 1952 election for the Republicans, defeating Adlai E. Stevenson. Eisenhower, a World War II hero, carried four Southern states and broke the Democratic Solid South for the first time in more than 20 years. Great numbers of voters turned to Eisenhower for reasons other than his popularity. Many voted Republican because of dissatisfaction with the government's conduct of the Korean War (1950-1953). Others believed charges that the Democrats had harbored Communists in high government posts. Eisenhower won reelection in 1956 by a landslide, again over Stevenson.

Eisenhower, a moderate Republican, won support from his own party and from many Southern Democrats. During his presidency, Congress extended Social Security benefits and passed the first civil rights act since Reconstruction.

Defeat, then victory. Vice President Richard M. Nixon won the Republican presidential nomination in 1960. He narrowly lost the election to his Democratic opponent, John F. Kennedy. After Kennedy's assassination in 1963, Vice President Lyndon B. Johnson succeeded to the presidency. In 1964, the Republicans nominated Barry M. Goldwater, who stood for an extreme form of conservatism. Johnson defeated him overwhelmingly.

At Johnson's urging, Congress passed additional civil rights legislation and other laws to help disadvantaged Americans. Conservative Republicans and conservative Southern Democrats joined forces to oppose many of Johnson's programs.

For the 1968 presidential election, the Republicans turned to Nixon again. The Democrats nominated Vice President Hubert H. Humphrey. A third party, the American Independent Party, nominated George C. Wallace, a Southern Democrat who strongly opposed civil rights

legislation. Nixon won even though he received only about 43 percent of the popular vote.

In 1972, the Republicans renominated Nixon. The Democrats nominated George S. McGovern. Nixon received over 17 $\frac{3}{4}$ million more popular votes than McGovern—the widest margin of any United States presidential election.

The Watergate scandal. In 1973, Nixon helped end U.S. involvement in the Vietnam War. His administration suffered a loss of public confidence later that year, however, because of the Watergate scandal and an unrelated criminal investigation that led to the resignation of Nixon's vice president, Spiro T. Agnew.

House Minority Leader Gerald R. Ford replaced Agnew as vice president. In July 1974, the House Judiciary Committee recommended that Nixon be impeached on charges related to the Watergate scandal. Nixon resigned in August, before the House voted on impeachment, and Ford became president. In 1976, Ford was defeated in his bid for a full term by Jimmy Carter, his Democratic opponent.

Victories in the 1980's. The Republicans won every presidential election during the 1980's. In 1980, they chose Ronald Reagan for president. The Democrats renominated Carter, and Representative John B. Anderson of Illinois ran as an independent. Reagan won by a wide margin. The Republicans also won control of the Senate. In the 1984 presidential election, Reagan defeated his Democratic opponent, Walter F. Mondale. In the 1986 elections, the Democrats regained control of the Senate. In 1988, Vice President George H. W. Bush won the Republican presidential nomination. He defeated his Democratic opponent, Michael S. Dukakis.

Control of Congress. In 1992, the Republicans renominated Bush for president. The Democrats nominated Bill Clinton, and Texas businessman Ross Perot ran as an independent. Bush and Perot lost the election to Clinton. In 1994, the Republicans won control of both houses of Congress. The party had not controlled both houses since 1955. In 1996, Senator Robert Dole of Kansas won the Republican presidential nomination. The Democrats renominated Clinton. Dole lost the election to Clinton. But the Republicans retained control of both houses of Congress in 1996 and 1998.

In the 2000 presidential election, Texas Governor George W. Bush, son of former President George H. W. Bush, defeated the Democratic candidate, Vice President Al Gore, in an extremely close race. The Republicans retained control of the House. However, the Senate became equally divided, with neither party winning a majority.   George H. Mayer

See also **Political convention; Political party; President of the United States.**

Additional resources

Connelly, William F., Jr., and Pitney, J. J., Jr. *Congress' Permanent Minority? Republicans in the U.S. House.* Rowman & Littlefield, 1994.
Foner, Eric. *Free Soil, Free Labor, Free Men: The Ideology of the Republican Party Before the Civil War.* 1970. Reprint. Oxford, 1995.

Web site

Republican National Committee
http://www.rnc.org/
Official Web site of the Republican Party.

An analysis of the popular vote in 2000

These graphs give a breakdown of the popular vote in the election of 2000. The graphs show how people voted by ethnic background, gender, urban and rural distribution, family income, and educational level for Republican candidate George W. Bush, Democratic candidate Al Gore, and Green Party candidate Ralph Nader. The information is based on what voters told interviewers as they left the polling places on Election Day, November 7, 2000.

Vote by ethnic background

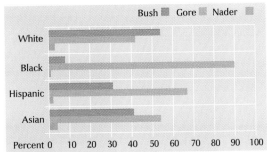

Figures based on nationwide exit polls taken November 7, 2000. Source: Voter News Service.

Vote by gender

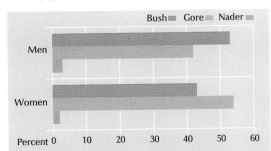

Figures based on nationwide exit polls taken November 7, 2000. Source: Voter News Service.

Vote by urban and rural distribution

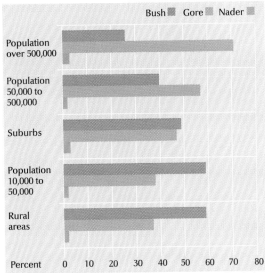

Figures based on nationwide exit polls taken November 7, 2000. Source: Voter News Service.

Vote by family income

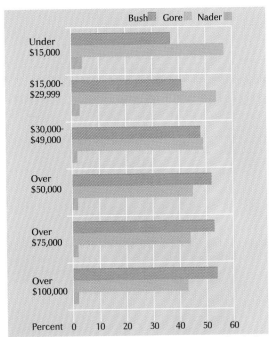

Figures based on nationwide exit polls taken November 7, 2000. Source: Voter News Service.

Vote by educational level

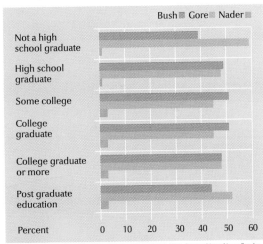

Figures based on nationwide exit polls taken November 7, 2000. Source: Voter News Service.

Total vote

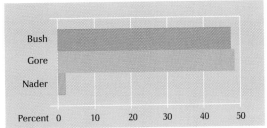

Source: Official final figures.

Vice president of the United States

Office of the Vice-President

The seal of the vice president of the United States includes an eagle holding arrows and an olive branch. The olive branch symbolizes the desire for peace, and the arrows represent the ability to wage war. The Latin words *E Pluribus Unum* mean *Out of Many, One* and refer to the unity of the United States.

Vice president of the United States is only a heartbeat away from the most powerful elective office in the world. The vice president must be ready to become president or acting president at a moment's notice if the president dies, resigns, is removed from office, or becomes unable to perform the duties of office.

Fourteen vice presidents have become president, eight because of the death of a president. These eight so-called "accidental presidents" were John Tyler, Millard Fillmore, Andrew Johnson, Chester A. Arthur, Theodore Roosevelt, Calvin Coolidge, Harry S. Truman, and Lyndon B. Johnson. The other vice presidents who became president were John Adams, Thomas Jefferson, Martin Van Buren, Richard M. Nixon, Gerald R. Ford, and George H. W. Bush. Of these six, all but Nixon became president immediately after serving as vice president. Ford was the only vice president to take office because of a president's resignation.

The United States Constitution also provides that the vice president shall become acting president if the president is disabled. In 1967, the 25th Amendment to the Constitution was ratified. It spelled out procedures in case of presidential disability and provided for vice

Portrait gallery of the vice presidents

The term of each vice president, as well as the name of the president under whom the vice president served, is listed under each picture. The asterisks identify those who later served as president.

*John Adams
1789-1797
Washington

*Thomas Jefferson
1797-1801
J. Adams

Aaron Burr
1801-1805
Jefferson

George Clinton
1805-1812
Jefferson-Madison

Elbridge Gerry
1813-1814
Madison

Daniel D. Tompkins
1817-1825
Monroe

John C. Calhoun
1825-1832
J. Q. Adams-Jackson

*Martin Van Buren
1833-1837
Jackson

Richard M. Johnson
1837-1841
Van Buren

*John Tyler
1841
W. H. Harrison

George M. Dallas
1845-1849
Polk

*Millard Fillmore
1849-1850
Taylor

William R. D. King
1853
Pierce

John C. Breckinridge
1857-1861
Buchanan

Hannibal Hamlin
1861-1865
Lincoln

*Andrew Johnson
1865
Lincoln

Schuyler Colfax
1869-1873
Grant

Henry Wilson
1873-1875
Grant

William A. Wheeler
1877-1881
Hayes

*Chester A. Arthur
1881
Garfield

Thomas A. Hendricks
1885
Cleveland

Levi P. Morton
1889-1893
B. Harrison

presidential succession (see **Constitution of the United States** [Amendment 25]). Presidents James A. Garfield, Woodrow Wilson, and Dwight D. Eisenhower all had serious illnesses. But their vice presidents carefully avoided assuming the duties of the president. In 1985, George Bush became the first vice president to serve as acting president. He held the office for about eight hours. President Ronald Reagan had designated Bush as acting president when Reagan had surgery.

The vice president serves as the presiding officer of the United States Senate and has the title of *president of the Senate*. The Constitution gives the vice president no other official duty. For more than 100 years, the job's lack of political importance caused it to be treated as somewhat of a joke. Some people had humorously suggested that the vice president be addressed as "Your Superfluous Excellency."

Yet the Founding Fathers had high hopes for the office of the vice presidency. James Iredell of North Carolina, who later served on the Supreme Court of the United States, explained that there would be "two men … in office at the same time; the president, who will possess, in the highest degree, the confidence of the country, and the vice president, who is thought to be

Facts in brief about the vice president

Qualifications: The Constitution provides that a candidate must be a "natural-born" U.S. citizen and must have lived in the United States for at least 14 years. The candidate must be at least 35 years old and must be eligible under the Constitution for the office of president. No law or court decision has defined the exact meaning of the term *natural-born*. Authorities assume that the term applies to all citizens born in the United States and its territories. But they are not certain if the term also includes children born to U.S. citizens in other countries.

How nominated: By a national political convention. If a vacancy in the vice presidency exists, the president nominates a new vice president, who takes office upon confirmation by a majority vote of both houses of Congress.

How elected: By a majority vote of the Electoral College, held in December after the general election held on the first Tuesday after the first Monday in November of every fourth year.

Inauguration: Held at noon, January 20, after election by the Electoral College. If the date falls on Sunday, the ceremony is held on Monday, January 21.

Term: The vice president is elected for four years and can serve any number of terms.

Income: $181,400 annual salary, $10,000 expense allowance, and an allowance for staff support.

Removal from office: Impeachment by a majority vote of the House of Representatives, and trial and conviction by a two-thirds vote of those present in the Senate.

Adlai E. Stevenson
1893-1897
Cleveland

Garret A. Hobart
1897-1899
McKinley

*Theodore Roosevelt
1901
McKinley

Charles W. Fairbanks
1905-1909
T. Roosevelt

James S. Sherman
1909-1912
Taft

Thomas R. Marshall
1913-1921
Wilson

*Calvin Coolidge
1921-1923
Harding

Charles G. Dawes
1925-1929
Coolidge

Charles Curtis
1929-1933
Hoover

John N. Garner
1933-1941
F. Roosevelt

Henry A. Wallace
1941-1945
F. Roosevelt

*Harry S. Truman
1945
F. Roosevelt

Alben W. Barkley
1949-1953
Truman

*Richard M. Nixon
1953-1961
Eisenhower

*Lyndon B. Johnson
1961-1963
Kennedy

Hubert H. Humphrey
1965-1969
L Johnson

Spiro T. Agnew
1969-1973
Nixon

*Gerald R. Ford
1973-1974
Nixon

Nelson A. Rockefeller
1974-1977
Ford

Walter F. Mondale
1977-1981
Carter

*George H.W. Bush
1981-1989
Reagan

Dan Quayle
1989-1993
G. H. W. Bush

Al Gore
1993-2001
Clinton

Richard B. Cheney
2001-
G. W. Bush

the next person in the Union most fit to perform this trust."

The prestige of the vice presidency has gradually increased since the early 1920's. Beginning in 1933 with the presidency of Franklin D. Roosevelt, vice presidents have regularly attended meetings of the president's Cabinet. Dwight D. Eisenhower and John F. Kennedy did more than any other presidents to establish the importance of the office of vice president. Eisenhower's vice president, Richard M. Nixon, and Kennedy's vice president, Lyndon B. Johnson, had important duties and responsibilities. When Kennedy was assassinated in 1963, many experts believed that Johnson was the best-prepared "accidental president."

The vice president has offices in the Capitol, the Richard B. Russell Office Building of the U.S. Senate, and the Executive Office Building. All these offices are in Washington, D.C. In 1974, Congress established a 33-room mansion on the grounds of Washington's Naval Observatory as the vice president's official residence. Secret Service agents guard the vice president.

Choosing a vice president

Nomination of the vice presidential candidate occurs at the party's national convention. The convention delegates usually nominate the person preferred by the presidential nominee. A contest develops only if the presidential nominee makes no choice. The vice presidential candidate is often called the presidential nominee's *running mate.*

Many factors may influence the selection of a vice presidential nominee. After a bitter campaign for the presidential nomination, the nominee may want a running mate who can help restore party harmony. The choice for vice president may be one of the losing candidates for the presidential nomination, or a supporter of one of the losers. In 1844, the Democrats nominated Senator Silas Wright of New York for vice president. They did this to appease former President Martin Van Buren, who had failed to win the Democratic presidential nomination. But Wright, a close friend of Van Buren, refused. In 1972, the Democratic vice presidential nominee, Senator Thomas F. Eagleton, became the only person ever to withdraw after having accepted a party's nomination at a national convention. He did so following the disclosure that he had received psychiatric treatment.

Often the vice president comes from one of the states considered to be especially important in the election. This may be a state in which the election outcome is expected to be very close, or it may simply be a state with a large electoral vote. By appealing to local loyalties, the vice presidential candidate may strengthen the party's vote in this "home" state.

Sometimes the vice presidential candidate is chosen because the person is thought to appeal to a large bloc of voters. In 1984, the Democrats nominated Representative Geraldine A. Ferraro of New York for vice president. She was the first woman and the first person of Italian descent ever chosen as the vice presidential candidate by a major American political party.

The vice presidential choice often is made to *balance the ticket.* If an older candidate is nominated for president, a younger person may be chosen for vice presi-

dent. A presidential nominee from the East may be balanced with a vice presidential nominee from the West. If the presidential nominee is known as a conservative, the vice presidential nominee may be a liberal. By balancing the ticket, party leaders hope to win the support of the largest possible number of voters.

The system of selecting a vice president helps the party win the election. It does not necessarily produce the person best qualified to serve as vice president. The custom of balancing the ticket with people of conflicting political beliefs has often been criticized. Theodore Roosevelt said early in his political career: "It is an unhealthy thing to have a vice president and president represented by principles so far apart that the succession of one to the place of the other means a change as radical as any party overturn." This occurred when John Tyler succeeded William Henry Harrison and when Roosevelt later succeeded William McKinley.

The campaign. The vice presidential candidate plays an active role in the election campaign. The vice presidential and presidential candidates usually map out separate campaign routes for maximum coverage of the country. They may later change places to cover all strategic areas with repeated campaigning.

Election. Voters select the same electors for the vice president when they choose presidential electors. They cannot split the ticket. That is, a person cannot vote for electors of the presidential candidate of the Republican Party and for electors of the vice presidential candidate of the Democratic Party. Citizens must vote for a slate of electors pledged to one party's candidates.

The Electoral College elects the president and vice president on separate ballots (see **Electoral College**). If the Electoral College fails to choose the vice president by a majority vote, the Senate elects one of the two leading candidates. At least two-thirds of the Senate must be present at the voting, and the winner must receive a majority vote of the entire membership.

The Senate has elected a vice president only once. In 1837, the Senate elected Richard M. Johnson, a Democrat, by a vote of 33 to 16 over Francis Granger, a Whig. Johnson had fallen one vote short in the Electoral College. He became so controversial that the Democrats refused to renominate him in 1840. In fact, they failed to nominate any vice presidential candidate—the only time any convention has done so.

Inauguration. Until 1933, the vice president took the oath of office in the Senate. Today, both president and vice president are inaugurated in the same ceremony in January after their election. The vice president is sworn into office immediately before the president is inaugurated. The vice president's oath may be administered by the retiring vice president, by a member of Congress, or by some other government official, such as a justice of the Supreme Court. In the early days, the vice president made an inaugural address. This custom has disappeared with the adoption of the combined ceremony in which the president gives the inaugural address.

The 25th Amendment spells out procedures for filling a vacancy in the vice presidency. The office becomes vacant if the vice president dies, resigns, or is unable to carry out the duties of office. Then the president appoints a new vice president. The appointment is subject to the approval of a majority of both the Senate and the

The vice presidents of the United States

Name	Birthplace	Occupation or profession	Political party	Age at inauguration	Served	President
1. Adams, John (a)	Braintree, MA	Lawyer	Federalist	53	1789-1797	Washington
2. Jefferson, Thomas (a)	Albemarle County, VA	Planter	Democratic-Republican	53	1797-1801	J. Adams
3. Burr, Aaron	Newark, NJ	Lawyer	Democratic-Republican	45	1801-1805	Jefferson
4. Clinton, George (c)	Little Britain, NY	Soldier	Democratic-Republican	65	1805-1809	Jefferson
				69	1809-1812	Madison
5. Gerry, Elbridge (c)	Marblehead, MA	Businessman	Democratic-Republican	68	1813-1814	Madison
6. Tompkins, Daniel D.	Fox Meadows, NY	Lawyer	Democratic-Republican	42	1817-1825	Monroe
7. Calhoun, John C. (d)	Abbeville District, SC	Lawyer	Democratic-Republican	42	1825-1829	J. Q. Adams
			Democratic	46	1829-1832	Jackson
8. Van Buren, Martin (a)	Kinderhook, NY	Lawyer	Democratic	50	1833-1837	Jackson
9. Johnson, Richard M.	Beargrass, KY	Lawyer	Democratic	56	1837-1841	Van Buren
10. Tyler, John (b)	Charles City County, VA	Lawyer	Whig	50	1841	W. H. Harrison
11. Dallas, George M.	Philadelphia	Lawyer	Democratic	52	1845-1849	Polk
12. Fillmore, Millard (b)	Locke, NY	Lawyer	Whig	49	1849-1850	Taylor
13. King, William R. D. (c)	Sampson County, NC	Lawyer	Democratic	66	1853	Pierce
14. Breckinridge, John C.	near Lexington, KY	Lawyer	Democratic	36	1857-1861	Buchanan
15. Hamlin, Hannibal	Paris, ME	Lawyer	Republican	51	1861-1865	Lincoln
16. Johnson, Andrew (b)	Raleigh, NC	Tailor	Union (e)	56	1865	Lincoln
17. Colfax, Schuyler	New York City	Auditor	Republican	45	1869-1873	Grant
18. Wilson, Henry (c)	Farmington, NH	Businessman	Republican	61	1873-1875	Grant
19. Wheeler, William A.	Malone, NY	Lawyer	Republican	57	1877-1881	Hayes
20. Arthur, Chester A. (b)	Fairfield, VT	Lawyer	Republican	51	1881	Garfield
21. Hendricks, Thomas A. (c)	near Zanesville, OH	Lawyer	Democratic	65	1885	Cleveland
22. Morton, Levi P.	Shoreham, VT	Banker	Republican	64	1889-1893	B. Harrison
23. Stevenson, Adlai E.	Christian County, KY	Lawyer	Democratic	57	1893-1897	Cleveland
24. Hobart, Garret A. (c)	Long Branch, NJ	Lawyer	Republican	52	1897-1899	McKinley
25. Roosevelt, Theodore (b) (a)	New York City	Author	Republican	42	1901	McKinley
26. Fairbanks, Charles W.	near Unionville Center, OH	Lawyer	Republican	52	1905-1909	T. Roosevelt
27. Sherman, James S. (c)	Utica, NY	Lawyer	Republican	53	1909-1912	Taft
28. Marshall, Thomas R.	North Manchester, IN	Lawyer	Democratic	58	1913-1921	Wilson
29. Coolidge, Calvin (b) (a)	Plymouth Notch, VT	Lawyer	Republican	48	1921-1923	Harding
30. Dawes, Charles G.	Marietta, OH	Lawyer	Republican	59	1925-1929	Coolidge
31. Curtis, Charles	Topeka, KS	Lawyer	Republican	69	1929-1933	Hoover
32. Garner, John N.	Red River County, TX	Lawyer	Democratic	64	1933-1941	F. Roosevelt
33. Wallace, Henry A.	Adair County, IA	Farmer	Democratic	52	1941-1945	F. Roosevelt
34. Truman, Harry S. (b) (a)	Lamar, MO	Businessman	Democratic	60	1945	F. Roosevelt
35. Barkley, Alben W.	Graves County, KY	Lawyer	Democratic	71	1949-1953	Truman
36. Nixon, Richard M. (a)	Yorba Linda, CA	Lawyer	Republican	40	1953-1961	Eisenhower
37. Johnson, Lyndon B. (a)	near Stonewall, TX	Teacher	Democratic	52	1961-1963	Kennedy
38. Humphrey, Hubert H.	Wallace, SD	Pharmacist	Democratic	53	1965-1969	L Johnson
39. Agnew, Spiro T. (d)	Towson, MD	Lawyer	Republican	50	1969-1973	Nixon
40. Ford, Gerald R. (f) (g)	Omaha, NE	Lawyer	Republican	60	1973-1974	Nixon
41. Rockefeller, Nelson A. (f)	Bar Harbor, ME	Businessman	Republican	66	1974-1977	Ford
42. Mondale, Walter F.	Ceylon, MN	Lawyer	Democratic	49	1977-1981	Carter
43. Bush, George H. W. (a)	Milton, MA	Businessman	Republican	56	1981-1989	Reagan
44. Quayle, Dan	Indianapolis	Lawyer	Republican	41	1989-1993	Bush, G. H. W.
45. Gore, Al	Washington, D.C.	Journalist	Democratic	44	1993-2001	Clinton
46. Cheney, Richard B.	Lincoln, Nebr.	Businessman	Republican	59	2001-	Bush, G. W.

(a) Elected to the presidency. (b) Succeeded to the presidency upon the death of the president. (c) Died in office. (d) Resigned. (e) The Union Party consisted of Republicans and War Democrats. Johnson was a War Democrat. (f) Became vice president by filling a vacancy. (g) Succeeded to the presidency upon the resignation of the president.

House of Representatives. In 1973, House Minority Leader Gerald R. Ford became the first vice president chosen under the terms of the 25th Amendment. Ford succeeded Vice President Spiro T. Agnew, who resigned.

Roles of the vice president

The vice president can be only as important as the president chooses. The vice president has almost no political power, unless the president asks for advice about party policy and political appointments. Even the vice president's role as a Cabinet member depends on the wishes of the president. But with the active support of the president, the vice president can exert a tremendous amount of influence. The vice president's attendance at conferences between the president and congressional leaders strengthens the vice president's power with the legislative branch. If the president gives the vice president important diplomatic missions, the vice president can help shape United States foreign policy.

A typical day for the vice president might begin with a breakfast conference called by the president. A legislative meeting might follow. The two officials confer with their party's congressional leaders about legislation being debated by the Senate and the House of Representatives. The vice president may then work at an office in the White House, the Executive Office Building, or the Senate wing of the Capitol. The vice president reads and answers mail and sees callers who have appointments. Tourists or unexpected visitors on emergency matters also may arrive. If the Senate is meeting that day, the vice president enters about noon to preside at the opening of the session. The vice president may remain at the session, depending on the nature of the day's business and the vice president's own schedule. If the vice president leaves, the president *pro tempore* or another senator takes over.

The vice president spends many evenings away from home. The vice president must make various kinds of public appearances, many of which require speeches. The vice president may go to the airport to greet dignitaries from other nations. Ceremonial duties may require the vice president to dedicate a public-works project, open an athletic tournament, or present an award to the winner of a contest.

President of the Senate. When presiding over the Senate, the vice president performs the duties of chairperson and cannot take part in any Senate debates. Nor can the vice president vote, except in the rare case of a tie. John Adams cast a deciding vote 29 times, more than did any other vice president.

The vice president enforces the rules established by the Senate for its own guidance. Senators can speak only after being recognized by the vice president or the president *pro tempore*. By using this power of recognition, the vice president can either aid or hold back legislation by permitting only certain senators to speak. The vice president also has the power to make rulings in disputes over procedure by interpreting the rules of the Senate. But the Senate can reject such rulings by a majority vote. In 1919, Vice President Thomas R. Marshall ruled three times in one day on a certain point. He was fighting to save the controversial Versailles Treaty and

U.S. membership in the League of Nations. The Senate overruled Marshall three times and defeated the treaty.

The president of the Senate also directs the counting of electoral votes for president and vice president. Early vice presidents could decide whether to count or disallow disputed votes. Congress has since assumed this power, leaving the vice president only formally in charge of counting electoral votes.

Administration and policymaking. The vice president attends meetings of the president's Cabinet and is a member of the National Security Council (NSC). The NSC is the highest advisory body to the president on matters of foreign and defense policies. The vice president also is a member of the Board of Regents of the Smithsonian Institution.

The president may assign the vice president general counseling and liaison activities. Such duties may involve trips abroad to spread good will, exchange information, and learn about the attitudes of various nations toward the United States. The vice president may also act as an intermediary between the president and their political party. The vice president attempts to build party support for the president's program.

Social duties. One of the oldest functions of the vice president is to serve as ceremonial assistant to the president. For example, the vice president attends many receptions and other social events at which the president cannot be present. The vice president often plays host to dignitaries from other countries.

Some vice presidents have enjoyed their ceremonial and social duties, but others have not. Calvin Coolidge took a characteristically philosophic approach. When his hostess at a dinner once remarked to him how annoying it must be to have to dine out so often, Coolidge replied: "Have to eat somewhere." John Nance Garner drew the line on social life. He went to bed early and refused to receive calls from 6 p.m. to 7 a.m., saying these hours "are my own."

History of the vice presidency

Early days. Most historians believe that Alexander Hamilton first proposed the office of vice president. Not all the delegates to the Constitutional Convention sup-

---

Interesting facts about the vice presidents

Who was the youngest vice president to be inaugurated? Breckinridge, 36. **The oldest?** Barkley, 71.

Which vice presidents were chosen under provisions of the 25th Amendment? Ford, Rockefeller.

Who was the first vice president to attend meetings of the Cabinet regularly? Coolidge.

Who was the first vice president to become a regular member of the National Security Council? Barkley.

Who was the first vice president to officially serve as acting president? Bush, for about eight hours during President Ronald Reagan's cancer surgery in 1985.

What president-elect died without ever performing the duties of office? King.

Who was the first vice president to succeed to the presidency, then win the office by election? T. Roosevelt.

Who was the first vice president to be assigned administrative duties by the president? Wallace.

Who was the only vice president to succeed to the presidency upon the resignation of the president? Ford.

Which vice presidents resigned? Calhoun, Agnew.

What vice president was selected by the Senate because the Electoral College failed to agree? R. Johnson.

Who was the first vice president nominated at a national political convention? Van Buren.

What state has produced the most vice presidents? New York.

What vice presidents died while in office? G. Clinton, Gerry, King, Wilson, Hendricks, Hobart, Sherman.

Who was the youngest vice president to succeed to the presidency upon the death of the president? T. Roosevelt, 42. **The oldest?** Truman, 60.

What teams of president and vice president were reelected to a second term? Washington and J. Adams, Monroe and Tompkins, Wilson and Marshall, F. Roosevelt and Garner, Eisenhower and Nixon, Nixon and Agnew, Reagan and G.H.W. Bush, Clinton and Gore.

What vice presidents served under two different presidents? G. Clinton, Calhoun.

What vice president took the oath of office in another country? King, in Havana, Cuba.

ported the idea. But on Sept. 6, 1787, the convention approved his proposal. The Founding Fathers originally provided that the person who received the second highest electoral vote for president should become vice president. Electors had two votes, which they cast for the two people they considered best qualified for the presidency. Under this system, John Adams became the first vice president and Thomas Jefferson the second.

Adams and Jefferson developed different views of the vice presidency. Adams wrote his wife: "My country has in its wisdom contrived for me the most insignificant office that ever the invention of man contrived or his imagination conceived." Jefferson declared that "the second office in the government is honorable and easy; the first is but a splendid misery."

The rise of political parties caused the breakdown of this election system. In 1796, the Electoral College gave the greatest number of votes to Adams, a Federalist. Jefferson, a Democratic-Republican, received the next largest number of votes, and became vice president. The conflicting party loyalties of the two men created discord in the administration.

In 1800, Jefferson and Aaron Burr both ran as Democratic-Republicans. They tied with 73 electoral votes each, and the election was given to the House of Representatives, where each state has one vote in a presidential election. Burr hoped for Federalist support, and tried to be elected president instead of vice president. But he failed. After 36 ballots, Jefferson won a majority of the votes, and Burr became vice president. The system's weakness became apparent during this election. In 1804, Congress adopted Amendment 12 to the Constitution, which provided for separate ballots for president and vice president. This solved the immediate problem, but it also lessened the prestige of the vice presidency. The vice president was no longer elected as the second choice for the presidency.

In 1832, John C. Calhoun became the first vice president to resign. He resigned after being elected to fill a U.S. Senate seat from South Carolina.

Tyler takes over. The Constitution provides that in case of the death or disability of the president, "the powers and duties" of the office shall transfer to the vice president. How this would work remained uncertain until 1841, when William Henry Harrison died in office, the first president to do so. His vice president was John Tyler. Former President John Quincy Adams and other leaders believed Tyler should be called *acting president,* not president. They opposed Tyler's receiving the full presidential salary and even his occupying the White House. Tyler ignored them. He took the oath and title of *president,* occupied the White House, and asserted full presidential powers. His action was not challenged legally, and he thereby established the right of the vice president to full succession.

Vice presidents have responded in many ways when a president has become disabled. Vice President Chester A. Arthur did not see James A. Garfield from the day Garfield was shot until he died 80 days later. Arthur got reports of Garfield's condition from Secretary of State James G. Blaine. He refused to assume Garfield's duties for fear he would be doing wrong. Vice President Thomas R. Marshall also declined to take up the president's duties during Woodrow Wilson's six-month illness. During Dwight D. Eisenhower's illnesses in 1955 and 1956, Vice President Richard M. Nixon presided at Cabinet and National Security Council meetings. He kept in close touch with the president. These experiences, and the 1963 assassination of President John F. Kennedy, led to the 25th Amendment to the Constitution. This amendment, ratified in 1967, sets procedures for presidential and vice presidential succession.

Growth of the vice presidency. In 1791, Vice President John Adams attended a Cabinet meeting. No other vice president did so until 1918. That year, President Wilson asked Vice President Marshall to preside over the Cabinet while Wilson attended the Paris Peace Conference that followed World War I. After Wilson returned home, Marshall was again excluded.

President Warren G. Harding invited Vice President Calvin Coolidge to attend all Cabinet meetings. Coolidge did so until he became president after Harding's death. Vice President Charles G. Dawes declared that he would not attend Cabinet sessions, because if he did so "the precedent might prove injurious to the country." Therefore, Coolidge did not ask him to participate. Nor did President Herbert Hoover invite Vice President Charles Curtis to take part in Cabinet meetings.

Since the first term of President Franklin D. Roosevelt, all vice presidents have regularly attended Cabinet meetings. President Eisenhower strengthened the vice presidency further by directing that Vice President Nixon should preside at Cabinet meetings in the president's absence. Previously, the secretary of state had presided at such times. Congress made the vice president a member of the National Security Council in 1949. Eisenhower directed in 1954 that the vice president should preside over council meetings when the president was absent.

President John F. Kennedy further extended the duties of his vice president, Lyndon B. Johnson. Johnson was chairman of the National Aeronautics and Space Council and headed the President's Committee on Equal Employment Opportunity. After he became president, Johnson continued to upgrade the vice presidency. Vice President Hubert H. Humphrey helped unify the Johnson administration's antipoverty and civil rights programs.

President Richard M. Nixon also gave important duties to his vice president, Spiro T. Agnew. Agnew promoted the administration's domestic programs among state and local officials. His outspoken defense of Nixon's policies against criticism by liberals and the news media made Agnew a controversial figure.

In 1973, Agnew became the second vice president to resign. He left office when a federal grand jury began to investigate charges that he had participated in widespread graft as an officeholder in Maryland. Nixon nominated House Minority Leader Gerald R. Ford to succeed Agnew. Ford became the first vice president chosen under terms of the 25th Amendment. In 1974, Nixon resigned. Ford then became the first vice president to succeed to the presidency because of a president's resignation. Former New York Governor Nelson A. Rockefeller became vice president. For the first time, three vice presidents and two presidents had held office during one four-year term. Also for the first time, neither the president nor the vice president had been elected.

President Jimmy Carter continued the trend of giving

The White House

The vice president's official residence is a 33-room mansion located on the grounds of the United States Naval Observatory in Washington, D.C. Congress established this mansion as the official residence in 1974.

It's a fact

Richard B. Cheney earned about $1.3 million in 1999 as chief executive officer of Halliburton Company, an oil-field services and construction firm. The vice president's salary was $181,400 in 2001.

the vice president important assignments. His vice president, Walter F. Mondale, helped develop U.S. policy on southern Africa and helped draft a plan to reorganize U.S. intelligence agencies. He was one of Carter's most influential advisers.

Vice President George Bush headed a group of advisers that provided President Ronald Reagan with recommendations on how to respond to foreign crises. Bush became the first vice president to serve as acting president. He held the position for only about eight hours on July 13, 1985, when Reagan had cancer surgery.

During Bush's term as president, Vice President Dan Quayle traveled throughout the United States and to other countries to promote the policies of the Bush administration. Quayle also headed the National Space Council and a council to evaluate the effect of government regulations on the economic competitiveness of the United States.

Vice President Al Gore exercised considerable influence in the administration of President Bill Clinton. Gore played a leading role in foreign affairs, environmental protection, and efforts to improve U.S. communications technology. In 1993, he headed a federal panel called the National Performance Review, which recommended ways to increase the federal government's efficiency and reduce its costs. Marie D. Natoli

Outline

I. Choosing a vice president
  A. Nomination
  B. The campaign
  C. Election
  D. Inauguration
  E. The 25th Amendment
II. Roles of the vice president
  A. A typical day
  B. President of the Senate
  C. Administration and policymaking
  D. Social duties
III. History of the vice presidency

Questions

What is meant by "balancing a ticket"?
What are the legal qualifications for a vice presidential candidate?
What are the official duties of the vice president?
In what various ways have vice presidents responded when a president has become disabled?
What happened in 1800 to bring about a change in the method of electing the vice president?
How did the vice presidency change after 1804?
How has the vice presidency grown in importance since WWI?
How can a vice president be removed from office?
How is the vice president elected if the Electoral College fails to select one by majority vote?

Additional resources

Level I
Hoopes, Roy. *The Changing Vice-Presidency.* Crowell, 1981.
Lindop, Edmund. *Presidents by Accident.* Watts, 1991.

Level II
Feinberg, Barbara S. *Next in Line: The American Vice Presidency.* Watts, 1996.
Hatfield, Mark O., and others. *Vice Presidents of the United States.* U. S. Government Printing Office, 1997.
Purcell, L. Edward, ed. *The Vice Presidents.* Facts on File, 1998.
Walch, Timothy, ed. *At the President's Side: The Vice Presidency in the Twentieth Century.* Univ. of Mo. Pr., 1997.
Waldrup, Carole C. *The Vice Presidents.* McFarland, 1996.

Web sites

U.S. Presidents and the Presidency
http://www.worldbook.com/fun/presidents/html/intro.htm
An extensive report on the history of the presidency, including biographies of all the presidents, first ladies, and vice presidents, from *World Book.*

Office of the Vice President of the United States
http://www.whitehouse.gov/WH/EOP/OVP/index.html
The official White House site for the vice president of the United States.

Topic for study

Trace the growth of the vice presidency since the first term of President Franklin D. Roosevelt in the early 1930's. Describe some ways presidents gave new responsibilities to their vice presidents. Especially review the article **Gore, Al***, in this section.*

Section Six

Point of View

On November 8, the day after the 2000 presidential election in the United States, Americans awoke to the news that the election was "too close to call." The uncertain outcome led to a series of political maneuvers and legal challenges by the campaign teams of George W. Bush and Al Gore.

   As these tactics played out in the courts, Americans raised questions about almost every move by the candidates and about the American electoral system itself. In this section, five scholars who serve as *World Book* contributors or consultants present their points of view on the election.

These viewpoints are:

   The section ends with extended excerpts from speeches by the two principal candidates in the presidential election.

A Canadian Perspective
by David Jay Bercuson

On Monday, Nov. 27, 2000, while Americans were still trying to determine the result of their presidential election 20 days earlier, Canadians voted in their own general election. The last Canadian polls closed in the West Coast province of British Columbia at 7:00 p.m. Within an hour, Prime Minister Jean Chrétien was declared the victor, with a majority government.

The speed with which Canadians learned the result of their national election stood in stark contrast to the situation in the United States. But the quickness of the Canadian count was not due to a small population or a scarcity of ballots. More than 12 million Canadians voted on November 27, just over 62 percent of all who were eligible. That was a far higher rate of voter turnout than in the U.S. presidential contest. Moreover, Canada's ballots were individually counted by hand.

The chief reason for the quickness of the Canadian election result is that all Canadians vote by the same set of rules, on a ballot that is uniform in design, in an election managed by a single national election agency. That agency, Elections Canada, is a nonpartisan federal organization responsible to Parliament for the conduct of all national elections.

Led by the chief electoral officer for Canada, Elections Canada organizes and administers all aspects of Canadian federal elections in all provinces and territories. Duties range from registering official candidates to counting the ballots and reporting the results. Elections Canada is also responsible for recounts.

Thus, Canada holds a single national election, with a standard set of rules and procedures, under one national authority. The United States, in contrast, holds a national election with 50 sets of rules and procedures, under 50 state authorities. There is more local self-determination in the United States, but there is also less clarity and slower official reporting of results. Perhaps a more direct and unified approach to election management would reduce future delays and disputes.

David Jay Bercuson is Professor of History and Director of the Centre for Military and Strategic Studies at the University of Calgary.

A Constitutional Perspective
by Sanford Levinson

As a result of the 2000 presidential election, many constitutional experts have debated whether the current electoral institutions serve the will of the people. In particular, some have criticized the fact that the vote of the Electoral College decides an election's outcome, even if it runs contrary to the nationwide popular vote. What people should recognize, though, is that it may be nearly impossible to change these institutions.

Significantly altering the electoral process would require amending the Constitution of the United States. But the framers of the Constitution purposely made it extremely difficult to enact an amendment. Specifically, Article V of the Constitution requires that an amendment be proposed by a two-thirds vote of each house of Congress, and then approved by the legislatures of three-fourths of the nation's states. This requirement means that if even one house of the legislature in 13 states refused to *ratify* (approve) a proposed amendment, the amendment would fail.

Therefore, with regard to the Electoral College, any 13 states have, in effect, a power to veto any proposed changes. The current Electoral College system gives small states voting power out of proportion to their size by awarding them a minimum of three electoral votes. Therefore, the nation's 13 smallest states have a great incentive, as well as the power, to prevent any proposed changes to the system.

The procedure for settling Electoral College deadlocks is similarly weighted to the benefit of small states. The 12th Amendment to the Constitution states that, if the Electoral College vote does not determine a winner, the House of Representatives will decide the contest, with each state receiving one vote. Under this system, the single representative from Vermont has the same voting power as the 52 representatives from California. Changing this imbalance would also require a constitutional amendment, which, similarly, could be blocked by small states.

The 2000 election illustrated that the current electoral institutions can actually contradict the voice of the people on a national level. Many citizens favor changing the process, modifying the Electoral College and the role of the House in breaking deadlocks. However, the power to improve the weaknesses of the present system rests with those who benefit most from its flaws.

Sanford Levinson is Professor of Law at the University of Texas Law School in Austin.

A Teacher's Perspective
by Lee Thornton

Again and again during the 2000 election campaign, we heard that young voters were apathetic. "MTV News" reported apathy so deep that young citizens might qualify as the "most disconnected group of potential voters" ever. Indeed, an MTV survey showed that, unless they were prompted, 25 percent of young people ages 18 to 24 could not name the presidential candidates.

Imagine my surprise when my university students showed a lively, even passionate interest in the presidential election. My class often engaged in spirited political discussions. The students' interest was so great that, of a class of 24, 21 reported that they had voted. All of them said that they had stayed up most or all of election night, fascinated by the results.

The day after the voters went to the polls, a television news crew visited my class. Twenty-year-old Paul appeared on the news that night saying, "After seeing this, I mean, it was sort of like a live action history lesson. I thought it was more like a movie than real life because you'd never think that all of these things would happen in an election."

My students showed no sign of being disconnected from the process. True, Vice President Al Gore had visited our campus during the campaign, but was that single appearance enough to make the students as interested as they were? I think not. I think my students simply knew that if the issues did not yet affect them, they soon would.

Were my students more engaged than most young people because they are prospective journalists? I do not know. I do know that during campaign 2000, my students gave me hope that, like some exit polls, some polls of the nation's young people are far from accurate.

Lee Thornton is Professor of Journalism and Richard Eaton Chair at the College of Journalism, University of Maryland, College Park.

A Congressional Perspective
by Roger H. Davidson

In 2000, the congressional elections were just as closely fought as the presidential contest, and just as important. All 435 House seats and 34 of the 100 Senate seats were at stake, and the Democrats and Republicans were evenly matched and well financed. Like the presidential race, the congressional elections resulted in a nearly even split between parties. In the Senate, the Democrats gained 4 seats and fought the Republicans to a tie, with each party claiming 50 senators. In the House, the Democrats pared down the Republicans' already-slender majority by 2 seats. The House now has 221 Republicans and 212 Democrats, with 2 independents.

Who will control Congress? In the Senate, the answer could lie with the vice president of the United States, the chamber's presiding officer under the Constitution. The vice president can issue rulings about parliamentary procedure and cast tie-breaking votes. However, if the party ratio shifts during the session—if, for example, a Republican senator dies or resigns and is replaced by someone from the Democratic Party—the chamber would reorganize around the new majority. Democratic Senator Thomas A. Daschle would probably become the majority leader, and Republican Trent Lott would likely assume the post of minority leader.

The House faces a similar stand-off. The parties are so evenly matched that the Republicans may have difficulty rounding up enough votes to pass certain bills. As a result, neither party will have much opportunity to achieve its objectives. To pass bills, legislators must draft them to appeal to members from both sides. The evenly balanced situation will frustrate anyone who wants big policy changes. Perhaps a dramatic event, such as an economic collapse or a global threat, will spur voters to give one party a true working majority in a future election. Until then, we can expect small-scale tinkering with public problems, and plenty of complex compromises.

Roger H. Davidson is Visiting Professor of Political Science at the University of California, Santa Barbara.

An Anthropological Perspective
by Alan E. Mann

Anthropological research seldom focuses on an event like the United States presidential election. However, some insights from the anthropological study of human societies might prove useful as we consider the implications of the 2000 election for society.

Throughout human history, people have lived together in social groups. These societies have worked because the members have participated in a common culture with shared actions and behaviors. People learn these behaviors during childhood, as part of a process that anthropologists and other social scientists call *socialization.*

In the modern world, there are many complex, multicultural societies like our own. These societies consist of people with different cultural backgrounds and a variety of social behaviors and actions. In many multicultural societies, these differing behaviors have led to conflicts. On such occasions, people experience difficulties in successfully interacting because they do not fully understand the behaviors of others. Multicultural differences of this sort did not cause the 2000 election stalemate, but it did result from the American people holding different views on who should be president and on what the national priorities should be.

Anthropology has shown that many multicultural societies maintain a stable, integrated system, in spite of differing sets of beliefs and behaviors. The most successful of these societies are those in which the national government remains neutral in its institutions and policies, not supporting or promoting one group or another.

If there is a lesson from these observations, it involves the importance of impartiality. The United States has the best prospects for an effective presidency if federal and state agencies strive for absolute neutrality in determining the winner and if the public believes in their neutrality.

Alan E. Mann is Professor of Anthropology at University of Pennsylvania. He is the coauthor of Human Biology and Behavior *(1990).*

The end of the presidential election of 2000

The ruling in Bush v. Gore *by the Supreme Court of the United States on Dec. 12, 2000, in effect decided the 2000 presidential election. The next day, the long, hard-fought campaign ended when both Vice President Al Gore and Texas Governor George W. Bush addressed the nation on television. Following are excerpts from these speeches.*

Excerpts from Vice President Al Gore's concession speech on Dec. 13, 2000

The White House

Just moments ago, I spoke with George W. Bush and congratulated him on becoming the 43rd president of the United States.... I offered to meet with him as soon as possible, so that we can start to heal the divisions of the campaign and the contest through which we've just passed....

Now the U.S. Supreme Court has spoken. Let there be no doubt, while I strongly disagree with the court's decision, I accept it. I accept the finality of this outcome.... And tonight, for the sake of our unity as a people and the strength of our democracy, I offer my concession....

I know that many of my supporters are disappointed. I am too. But our disappointment must be overcome by our love of country.

And I say to our fellow members of the world community: Let no one see this contest as a sign of American weakness. The strength of American democracy is shown most clearly through the difficulties it can overcome....

I call on all Americans—I particularly urge all who stood with us—to unite behind our next president. This is America. Just as we fight hard when the stakes are high, we close ranks and come together when the contest is done.

And, while there will be time enough to debate our continuing differences, now is the time to recognize that that which unites us is greater than that which divides us.

While we yet hold and do not yield our opposing beliefs, there is a higher duty than the one we owe to political party. This is America and we put country before party. We will stand together behind our new president....

Some have asked whether I have any regrets. And I do have one regret: that I didn't get the chance to stay and fight for the American people over the next four years, especially for those who need burdens lifted and barriers removed, especially for those who feel their voices have not been heard. I heard you, and I will not forget.

I've seen America in this campaign and I like what I see. It's worth fighting for and that's a fight I'll never stop. As for the battle that ends tonight, I do believe, as my father once said, that no matter how hard the loss, defeat may serve as well as victory to shake the soul and let the glory out.

Excerpts from President-elect George W. Bush's victory speech on Dec. 13, 2000

© Bob Daemmrich, Corbis/Sygma

This evening I received a gracious call from the vice president. We agreed to meet early next week in Washington, and we agreed to do our best to heal our country after this hard-fought contest....

I have a lot to be thankful for tonight. I am thankful for America and thankful that we are able to resolve our electoral differences in a peaceful way. And I am thankful to the American people for the great privilege of being able to serve as your next president....

I am optimistic that we can change the tone of Washington, D.C. I believe things happen for a reason, and I hope the long wait of the last five weeks will heighten a desire to move beyond the bitterness and partisanship of the recent past.

Our nation must rise above a house divided. Americans share hopes and goals and values far more important than any political disagreements. Republicans want the best for our nation. So do Democrats. Our votes may differ, but not our hopes.

I know America wants reconciliation and unity. I know Americans want progress. And we must seize this moment and deliver. Together, guided by a spirit of common sense, common courtesy, and common goals, we can unite and inspire the American citizens.

We have discussed our differences. Now it is time to find common ground and build consensus to make America a beacon of opportunity in the 21st century....

I have faith that with God's help we as a nation will move forward together, as one nation, indivisible. And together we will create an America that is open, so every citizen has access to the American dream....

I was not elected to serve one party, but to serve one nation. The president of the United States is the president of every single American, of every race and every background. Whether you voted for me or not, I will do my best to serve your interests, and I will work to earn your respect.

I will be guided by President Jefferson's sense of purpose: to stand for principle, to be reasonable in manner, and, above all, to do great good for the cause of freedom and harmony. The presidency is more than an honor, it is more than an office. It is a charge to keep, and I will give it my all.

Elections Around the World

Although the election in the United States received much worldwide attention, it was only one of many held in 2000. Voters also went to the polls in about 50 other countries—including Mexico and Canada. A number of the elections brought the defeat of officeholders from parties that had long held power. This section reviews some notable elections outside the United States.

The democracies of the world have various forms of national government. The two most common arrangements are the *presidential* and the *parliamentary* systems. The kind of election a country holds depends on which system of government it uses. The United States and Mexico, for example, follow the presidential system, in which voters elect the president separately from members of the legislature. However, Canada and many other countries follow the parliamentary system. Under this system, the voters elect a legislature (parliament). The prime minister is then chosen from the party or *coalition* (group) of parties that holds a majority of seats in the parliament.

The Americas

Chile. In January 2000, voters in Chile elected Ricardo Lagos Escobar of the Socialist Party as president. Lagos was the country's first Socialist to be elected president since Salvador Allende Gossens, who died in a military coup in 1973.

Mexico. The presidential election in Mexico in July 2000 brought the end of a long era of dominance by one political party. In the election, Vicente Fox Quesada of the Partido de Acción Nacional (National Action Party, or PAN) defeated Francisco Labastida Ochoa of the ruling Partido Revolucionario Institucional (Institutional Revolutionary Party, or PRI). Fox, a strong supporter of free-market reforms, took office in December as the first non-PRI president of Mexico in 71 years.

Canada was not required to hold a new election until 2002. But in October 2000, with public opinion polls showing his Liberal Party well ahead of its opponents, Prime Minister Jean Chrétien called an early national election for the next month.

The two main parties in the contest were the Liberal Party, led by Chrétien, and the Canadian Alliance, headed by Stockwell Day. The Liberals and Chrétien had governed Canada since 1993. The Canadian Alliance was a new conservative party that had been established in January 2000. Its ranks swelled in March, when members of the Western-based Reform Party voted to join the new Alliance.

Several other main parties were involved in the election. They were the Bloc Québécois, led by Gilles Duceppe; the New Democratic Party, led by Alexa Mc-

AP/Wide World

Canadian Prime Minister Jean Chrétien led the Liberal Party to its third straight majority government in a national election in November 2000. This photo shows Chrétien, *left*, campaigning.

Donough; and the Progressive Conservative Party, led by former Prime Minister Joe Clark.

The election was held on November 27. In the vote, the Liberals increased their majority in the 301-member House of Commons to more than 170 seats. As a result, Chrétien became the first prime minister since 1945 to form three straight majority governments. The Liberal Party won nearly all the seats in Ontario, the most populous province, and at least one seat in every other province.

The Canadian Alliance came in second in the vote and remained the official opposition in the House. The Alliance's support came mainly from the Western provinces of Saskatchewan, Alberta, and British Columbia. Although the Alliance had hoped to reduce or end the Liberal dominance in Ontario, the new party won only two seats there. The Bloc Québécois, which favors independence for the French-speaking province of Quebec, came in third, with a reduced number of seats in Quebec. The NDP and the Progressive Conservatives finished a distant fourth and fifth, respectively.

The Dominican Republic held a presidential election in May 2000. Hipólito Mejía Dominguez of the center-left Dominican Revolutionary Party was elected president after his main rival withdrew from the race to avoid a runoff vote. Mejía became the first member of his party elected president since 1986.

Peru. In elections in April 2000, President Alberto Fujimori failed to receive a majority of the votes for the presidency, setting the stage for a runoff election between Fujimori and opposition candidate Alejandro Toledo Manrique. But Toledo, fearing that Fujimori would use fraud to win, withdrew shortly before the runoff in May. Many opposition supporters then boycotted the election. Fujimori was reelected to a third term.

In September 2000, Fujimori announced that he was calling for new general elections. The announcement came amid a bribery scandal involving Vladimiro Montesinos Torres, a top Fujimori aide and the head of Peru's National Intelligence Agency.

AP/Wide World

Vicente Fox Quesada of the National Action Party was elected president of Mexico in July 2000. His election brought to a close a long era of dominance by the Institutional Revolutionary Party.

Michael B. Schuldt, the contributor of this article, is Assistant Managing Editor, The World Book Encyclopedia.

In November, while on a diplomatic visit to Japan, Fujimori submitted his resignation as Peru's president. The Peruvian National Assembly refused to accept his resignation and instead declared him "morally unfit" for the presidency and removed him from office. Valentín Paniagua, the leader of the Assembly, then became president of an interim government. New elections were scheduled for April 2001.

Venezuela. In July 2000, Hugo Chávez Frías was reelected as Venezuela's president. Chávez had first been elected to that office in 1998 and had called for reform of the country's 1961 Constitution, which he claimed was a symbol of corrupt government. In December 1999, Venezuela's voters approved the new Constitution supported by Chávez. This approval led to the July 2000 elections for president and for a new National Assembly.

Haiti held a presidential election in November 2000. Few people voted in the election, which was boycotted by the main opposition parties. Former President Jean-Bertrand Aristide won the election.

Europe

Russia. Vladimir Putin won a landslide victory in national presidential elections held in March 2000. Putin had previously been named acting president by Boris Yeltsin, who unexpectedly resigned from the presidency on the last day of 1999. At the time, Putin was prime minister. As prime minister, Putin—a former head of FSB, the Soviet spy service—had focused most of his energies on the military campaign against separatist rebels in the republic of Chechnya.

Greece. The Socialist government of Prime Minister Costas Simitis won reelection in April 2000 in Greece, often called the "birthplace of democracy." As prime minister, Simitis had carried out moderate, market-oriented policies and other economic reforms.

Yugoslavia held a presidential election in September 2000. This vote saw the defeat of the fiercely nationalist President Slobodan Milošević, who had dominated Yugoslavia throughout the 1990's. Although some opposition groups boycotted the election, Vojislav Kostunica, leader of the Democratic Opposition party, won the majority of the votes. Milošević and his allies claimed that Kostunica had won by so narrow a majority that a runoff was necessary. The opposition claimed victory, and protesters demanding Milošević's resignation filled the streets of many of Serbia's major cities. Police forces were overwhelmed by the size of the protests, and Milošević agreed to give up power.

Poland. President Aleksander Kwasniewski easily won reelection in October 2000 with 54 percent of the vote. Kwasniewski, a former Communist leader, has been president of Poland since 1995, when he defeated then-President Lech Walesa.

Asia

Taiwan. Chen Shui-bian, the leader of the Democratic Progressive Party, was elected president of Taiwan in March 2000, ending 50 years of Nationalist Party rule. Chen had always advocated independence for Taiwan, but the Communist government of China claims that Taiwan belongs to China. During the election campaign, Chinese officials hinted that a victory by Chen might result in war. Chen tried to ease the Chinese government's fears. He said that he would not declare independence as long as China did not attempt to invade Taiwan.

Georgia. President Eduard Shevardnadze was elected to a second five-year term in April 2000 with 80 percent of the vote. Shevardnadze pledged to push for Georgia to become a member of the North Atlantic Treaty Organization (NATO). Georgia is a former Soviet republic.

Japan. Prime Minister Keizo Obuchi died in May 2000 and was succeeded by Yoshiro Mori, the secretary-general of his Liberal Democratic Party (LDP). Following an opposition motion of no confidence in the lower house of parliament, Mori called elections for a new lower house. The elections were held in late June. The LDP won the most seats, and Mori remained as prime minister at the head of a coalition government.

Sri Lanka elected a new parliament in October 2000. The ruling People's Alliance party of President Chandrika Kumaratunga won only 107 out of 225 seats. These results thwarted Kumaratunga's hopes of winning a sufficient majority for her party to enact a new constitution. A new constitution was intended to offer the nation's Tamil ethnic minority enough *autonomy* (self-rule) within Sri Lanka to end their 17-year war of independence.

Africa

Senegal held elections for president in February and March 2000. Abdoulaye Wade, leader of the Senegalese Democratic Party and the candidate of a coalition of opposition parties called the Alternance Front, defeated President Abdou Diouf of the Socialist Party. Diouf had been president of Senegal since 1981.

Mauritius. The resignation of two government ministers in August 2000 over a corruption inquiry led Prime Minister Navinchandra Ramgoolam to call an early general election. The September 11 election resulted in the defeat of the ruling alliance of Ramgoolam's Labor Party and the Parti Mauritian Xavier Duval.

An opposition alliance won 54 of the 62 directly elected National Assembly seats. Former Prime Minister Sir Anerood Jugnauth's Militant Socialist Movement and former Deputy Prime Minister Paul Berenger's Militant Mauritian Movement led the victorious alliance. Under the terms of a pre-election pact, Jugnauth and Berenger agreed to rule for three years and two years, respectively, if their coalition won the five-year premiership. Jugnauth, who had served as prime minister of Mauritius for 13 years before his electoral defeat by Ramgoolam in 1995, returned to office on Sept. 17, 2000.

Côte d'Ivoire. In July 2000, voters in Côte d'Ivoire, also known as the Ivory Coast, approved a new constitution designed to return the country to civilian rule. In December 1999, military officers led by General Robert Guéï had ousted President Henri Konan Bédié and set up a transitional government.

Côte d'Ivoire held a presidential election in October 2000. Before the vote, most opposition candidates were barred from running for the presidency. When it appeared during the counting of the vote that opposition candidate Laurent Gbagbo would defeat Guéï, Guéï shut down the election commission and declared himself the winner. In protest, tens of thousands of demonstrators then flooded the streets of Abidjan, Côte d'Ivoire's largest city. Guéï eventually fled the country, and Gbagbo was sworn in as president.

Index